UNDERSTANDING INTERNATIONAL CRIMINAL LAW SECOND EDITION

UNDERSTANDING INTERNATIONAL CRIMINAL LAW

SECOND EDITION

Ellen S. Podgor
Associate Dean of Faculty Development & Electronic Education
Professor of Law
Stetson University College of Law

Roger S. Clark
Board of Governors Professor, Rutgers School of Law at Camden

Library of Congress Cataloging-in-Publication Data
Understanding international criminal law / Ellen S. Podgor, Roger S.
Clark. -- 2nd ed.
p. cm.
Includes index.
ISBN 978-1-4224-2546-6 (softbound)
1. International offenses. 2. Criminal procedure (International law) 3.
International criminal courts. I. Title.
K5015.4.P63 2008
345--dc22
2008025650

NOTE TO USERS

To ensure that you are using the latest materials available in this area, please be sure to periodically check the LexisNexis Law School web site for downloadable updates and supplements at www.lexisnexis.com/lawschool.

Editorial Offices
744 Broad Street, Newark, NJ 07102 (973) 820-2000
201 Mission St., San Francisco, CA 94105-1831 (415) 908-3200
www.lexisnexis.com

MATTHEW◆BENDER

DEDICATION

To —
Cheryl L. Segal
and
Amelia H. Boss

PREFACE

International criminal law is a developing area of the law. Events throughout the world change the landscape on a daily basis. It is a new area because tribunals and the international criminal court are of recent vintage. But it is also an old area of law in that history provides many lessons.

This book is intended as an overview of this area of the law. It is divided into four parts. The first part provides a general overview, with definitions to key terms that will appear throughout the book. It covers the area of jurisdiction, as this is the starting point in determining the applicability of using international law. The second part covers selected areas of international criminal law. It is not exhaustive of all areas of international or transnational law. Choices of specific crimes to cover were made on the basis of showing a diversity of topics, new and developing areas such as computer crimes, and the older more traditional areas such as piracy. It provides materials on both violent and non-violent crimes. Areas of immediate importance, like terrorism and narcotics trafficking, are discussed. The third part covers procedural issues. It includes constitutional issues, immunities, obtaining evidence from abroad, obtaining people from abroad, and post conviction issues such as prisoner transfers. The final part of this book covers the international aspects of international criminal law. In addition to examining what constitutes an international crime, it looks at human rights issues, international tribunals, and the International Criminal Court.

Although the book includes an enormous amount of material, it also excludes an incredible amount of important material. As such, it is not intended as a definitive source to resolve a legal matter, but rather as a general overview to begin the study of international criminal law. Because of the continual changes in this area, it is important to realize that updating is necessary.

This book would not be without several very important people. Professor Roger S. Clark thanks David Batista, Hays Butler, Lucy Cox and Marshall Kizner for their research assistance and Professor Ellen S. Podgor thanks Stetson University College of Law and Dean Darby Dickerson and Associate Dean Terri Radwan for their support on this project. We both owe large debts of intellectual gratitude to the late Professors Edward Wise and Gerhard Mueller, whose pioneering 1965 book on International Criminal Law introduced the field to readers of English. Cherif Bassiouni's writings on the subject are always a source of considerable inspiration.

Ellen S. Podgor
Roger S. Clark
April 2008

Summary Table of Contents

Table of Contents

Table of Contents

Table of Contents

Table of Contents

Table of Contents

Table of Contents

PART ONE
GENERAL PRINCIPLES

Chapter 1

INTRODUCTION

§ 1.01 SCOPE OF INTERNATIONAL CRIMINAL LAW

It is difficult to provide a concrete definition of the term international criminal law because its boundaries are loosely constructed and expanding. Increased globalization through worldwide communication, transportation, and economic expansion has made international law a topic of enormous importance. Accompanying this globalization, however, comes a host of criminal activities that require punishment. These activities can be both a national and international concern. As such, criminal law issues that arise in the international setting, and international issues that arise in the context of national criminal law, provide the starting point for a discussion about international criminal law.

It could be argued that international criminal law is very limited, including only the law that arises in an international body. Approaching international law in a *stricto sensu* would include the law that comes from international courts such as Nuremberg, the *ad hoc* Tribunal in Yugoslavia, and most recently the International Criminal Court (ICC). Some important works on international criminal law restrict their discussion essentially to the roles of such tribunals and to the crimes with which they have been concerned, namely war crimes, crimes against peace (aggression), crimes against humanity, and genocide.[1] Although these tribunals and bodies of law clearly are encompassed within international criminal law, there are in fact many other instances where international law plays a role in the national criminal law of a state. This book therefore takes a more expansive view of the subject, as will be apparent in subsequent chapters.[2]

---

[1] *E.g.*, GERHARD WERLE, PRINCIPLES OF INTERNATIONAL CRIMINAL LAW (2005); ALEXANDER ZAHAR & GORAN SLUITER, INTERNATIONAL CRIMINAL LAW: A CRITICAL INTRODUCTION (2007).

[2] Among those taking a similarly broad view of the subject are: JORDAN J. PAUST ET AL, INTERNATIONAL

[A]   International Aspects of National Criminal Law

Although international criminal law initially focused especially on questions related to jurisdiction, today there are many issues of an international nature that surface in different nations' systems of criminal law. National legal systems cannot operate in a vacuum. Crimes routinely cross the borders of different nations. In addition to questions related to extraterritorial jurisdiction, procedural issues such as obtaining evidence from abroad, extradition of individuals, and questions of immunity become areas for consideration in national legal systems. National systems can also be faced with decisions of whether to proceed against conduct that violates international law.

Some authors designate any crimes that cross borders as "transnational crimes." Others use that term particularly to describe crimes like trafficking in drugs or persons, transnational organized crime, terrorism and foreign corrupt practices that are forbidden by treaty regimes but are not regarded (yet) as sufficiently egregious to be punished in an international tribunal. Like international criminal law, the term transnational crime is problematic. As noted by Professor Gerhard O.W. Mueller, the term "transnational crime" "did not have any juridical meaning" when initially used, and "does not have one now."[3] Crimes that could be seen as transnational would include those that might easily cross borders, such as computer criminality and money laundering and these are increasingly becoming the subject of treaty regimes. Issues, however, that might occur solely within one state also can be influenced by international law. Thus, there is a large body of human rights law and of norms and standards created by the United Nations and by regional organizations that have significant effects on the way modern domestic criminal justice systems operate.[4]

[B]   Criminal Aspects of International Law

At one level, international crimes can be seen as those crimes expressly prohibited by an international criminal law system. Crimes against humanity, genocide, and war crimes are examples of crimes that have been prosecuted by international tribunals. A broader definition, however, might include crimes that violate customary international law or treaties among countries. Narcotics trafficking and terrorism are examples of crimes that have emerged as issues requiring an international response. In addition to substantive questions of whether the conduct constitutes a crime under international law, there are also procedural questions that accompany these issues, such as extradition and mutual legal assistance. A crucial feature of the landscape is represented by "suppression conventions." These are treaties in which the parties undertake to make defined conduct criminal and to exercise their jurisdiction over it, sometimes even if the conduct takes place outside their territorial jurisdiction and does not even involve their nationals. Typical early examples of suppression treaties were those that the British entered into early in the nineteenth century with bilateral partners, such as Portugal and Spain banning the slave trade. Later slavery and other suppression treaties were multilateral in nature. A very large number of suppression treaties

---

CRIMINAL LAW: CASES AND MATERIALS 3rd ed. (2007); M. CHERIF BASSIOUNI, INTRODUCTION TO INTERNATIONAL CRIMINAL LAW (2003).

[3] Gerhard O.W. Mueller, *Transnational Crime: Definitions and Concepts, in* COMBATING TRANSNATIONAL CRIME 13 (Phil Williams & Dimitri Vlassis eds., 2001).

[4] *See generally* ROGER S. CLARK, THE UNITED NATIONS CRIME PREVENTION AND CRIMINAL JUSTICE PROGRAM: FORMULATION OF STANDARDS AND EFFORTS AT THEIR IMPLEMENTATION (1994).

have now been sponsored by the United Nations and by regional organizations such as the Council of Europe and the Organization of American States.

It should by now be apparent that the line between what will be considered international criminal law and what will not be included within this concept is extremely fuzzy and subject to change as international practice develops. The definition will in part be determined by the individual deciding the question. This book, to reiterate, uses a broad definition to cover crimes with international aspects in national law and also criminal aspects of what is considered to be international law.

§ 1.02   SOURCES OF INTERNATIONAL CRIMINAL LAW

[A]   Generally

International law is primarily consensual in nature. *The Restatement (Third) of the Foreign Relations Law of the United States* provides that "[a] rule of international law is one that has been accepted as such by the international community of states (a) in the form of customary law; (b) by international agreement; or (c) by derivation from general principles common to the major legal systems of the world."[5] One finds similar language in the Statute of the International Court of Justice which states that the sources for deciding international law questions are: "(a) international conventions, whether general or particular, establishing rules expressly recognized by the contesting states; (b) international custom, as evidence of a general practice accepted as law; (c) the general principles of law recognized by civilian nations; (d) . . . judicial decisions and the teachings of the most highly qualified publicists of the various nations, as subsidiary means for the determination of the rules of law."[6] As such, much of international law comes from generally accepted norms among nations and from agreements reached by countries. "General principles common to major legal systems, even if not incorporated or reflected in customary law or international agreement, may be invoked as supplementary rules of international law where appropriate."[7] The Rome Statute of the International Criminal Court has a statement of "applicable law" specific to its own circumstances. It says that the Court "shall apply: (a) In the first place, this Statute, Elements of Crimes and its Rules of Procedure and Evidence; (b) In the second place, where appropriate, applicable treaties and the principles and rules of international law, including the established principles of the international law of armed conflict; (c) Failing that, general principles of law derived by the Court from national laws of legal systems of the world including, as appropriate, the national laws of States that would normally exercise jurisdiction over the crime, provided that those principles are not inconsistent with this Statute and with international law and internationally recognized norms and standards."[8]

---

[5] The Restatement (Third) of the Foreign Relations Law of the United States § 102(1) (1987). The third of these sources, general principles, is mainly used to fill gaps in customary and treaty law.

[6] The Statute of the International Court of Justice, Art. 38 (1945). Art. 59 of the Statute adds that "[t]he decision of the Court has no binding force except between the parties and in respect of that particular case" but the Court generally follows its own prior decisions.

[7] The Restatement (Third) of the Foreign Relations Law of the United States at § 102(4).

[8] Rome Statute of the International Criminal Court (1998), Art. 21(1)(a). Para. 2 contains a permissive principle of *stare decisis*: "The Court may apply principles and rules of law as interpreted in its previous decisions."

[B]   The *Lotus* Case

Jurisdictional issues have always been central to international criminal law and the classic case that resolves a jurisdiction issue is *The Case of the S.S. Lotus (France v. Turkey)*.[9] It involved a collision between a French ship (*Lotus*) and a Turkish Ship (the collier *Boz-Kourt*). Eight Turkish nationals were killed as a result of this collision. The Turkish authorities investigating this case arrested the first officer of the *Lotus*, a French national, and the captain of the *Boz-Kourt*, who was Turkish. Lieutenant Demons, the first officer of the *Lotus*, and officer of the watch at the relevant time, objected to the jurisdiction of the Criminal Court in what was then called Constantinople. Both mariners were convicted and sentenced for manslaughter. The case arose in the Permanent Court of International Justice, the predecessor of the present International Court of Justice (ICJ), when the French government protested the decision of the Turkish court. The argument of France was that only the state under whose flag the vessel sails has authority to proceed with such a case. The issue was complicated by the fact that both France and Turkey were parties to the Convention of Lausanne of July 24, 1923, a companion to the peace treaty which concluded Turkey's involvement in the First World War. Under the old "capitulations" regime that had existed in the Ottoman Empire, Powers like France could exercise judicial jurisdiction in some cases on Ottoman soil, and even apply French law. Now the 1923 treaty provided that questions of jurisdiction between the parties would be decided "in accordance with the principles of international law." Both Turkey and France agreed to submit the question to the Permanent Court of International Justice.[10]

The international tribunal was left to wrestle with questions of how to interpret a treaty, what role the "law of the flag" (the flag under which the ship sails) would play in the decision, whether the Turkish Penal Law properly permitted this action, and if it did permit this action, should this law be trumped by international law. Arguments presented by the parties also raised issues of when a country could proceed beyond its territorial jurisdiction in a criminal matter, and when a country would be precluded from exercising jurisdiction outside its territory. Importantly, the court looked at the Convention of Lausanne, thus using a treaty upon which the parties had agreed. This sent the enquiry, in what one might think of as a conflict of laws analysis, out to "international law." As there was no overriding treaty law available to decide this specific issue, the court examined state practice, particularly municipal law, although it found the municipal jurisprudence divided on the subject.

The decision was evenly divided 6-6 with the judgment going to Turkey when the President of the Court (as he was entitled to do under the Court's Rules) cast a deciding vote. Turkey had argued that it was entitled to exercise what is called "passive personality" jurisdiction, (see Chapter 2), as it was Turkish citizens who were killed. The Court's majority was equivocal about this approach, but was more accepting of the alternative Turkish argument, territorial "effects" jurisdiction, as events on the French ship led to death on the Turkish collier, which as a Turkish boat could be considered a part of Turkey.

Perhaps the most significant aspect of this situation and case is that two countries saw it as proper to submit this question to an international tribunal. The specific ruling is less significant, as the holding has been replaced by several

---

[9] 1927 P.C.I.J. (ser. A) No. 10.

[10] A further question regarding reparations became irrelevant when France lost.

multilateral treaties.[11] *Lotus* is often thought of as a case that "epitomizes an 'extreme positivism' " in that it comes close to saying that Turkey is not bound by any restrictions on its freedom of action that it has not expressly or impliedly accepted.[12] A fundamental dispute between the parties, and also an issue on which the Court split, was whether Turkey had to show a permissive rule that empowered it to act or whether France had to prove that there was a rule prohibiting what Turkey did. The "majority's" assertion that the burden was on France remains highly controversial today and is a continuing source of debate about jurisdictional issues in modern international criminal law.

The judges did appear to agree that there could be *concurrent* jurisdiction. Turkey might prosecute at the least on its effects theory and, since it had M. Demons, the first officer of the Lotus, in its custody, it was calling the shots. But France, with its flag state theory and Demons's French nationality, could exercise jurisdiction too. It had only to persuade the Turks to hand him over, before or after they had finished with him. This, however, can present a host of issues. For example, as seen in § 1.03[F], international law on double jeopardy is a work in progress. Nor is there any clear hierarchy or priority of various jurisdictional bases. The concept of concurrent jurisdiction is, however, fundamental to what is going on in many modern suppression treaties where the aim is to avoid safe havens by having several concurrent possibilities.

[C]   Customary International Law

A key aspect to resolving international disputes is "customary international law." In the Supreme Court case of *The Paquete Habana*,[13] Justice Gray described customary international law as:

> International law is part of our law, and must be ascertained and administered by the courts of justice of appropriate jurisdiction as often as questions of right depending upon it are duly presented for their determination. For this purpose, where there is no treaty and no controlling executive or legislative act or judicial decision, resort must be had to the customs and usages of civilized nations, and, as evidence of these, to the works of jurists and commentators who by years of labor, research, and experience have made themselves peculiarly well-acquainted with the subjects of which they treat. Such works are resorted to by judicial tribunals, not for the speculations of their authors concerning what the law ought to be, but for trustworthy evidence of what the law really is.[14]

In the *Habana* decision, the Court referred to a variety of international law authors, from different countries,[15] in order to ascertain the appropriate principles for the

---

[11] *See* Convention on the High Seas, Art. 11(1) (Apr. 29, 1958), 13 U.S.T. 2312, 450 U.N.T.S. 82; United Nations Convention on the Law of the Sea, Art. 97 (1982), U.N. Doc. A/CONF. 62/122, *reprinted* in 21 I.L.M. 1261 (1982) (exclusive penal jurisdiction in matters of collision or any other incident of navigation in flag state or state of which accused is a national).

[12] Edward M. Wise, Ellen S. Podgor & Roger S. Clark, International Criminal Law: Cases and Materials 2d Ed. 18 (2004).

[13] 175 U.S. 677 (1900). (The Court held that international customary law forbade the seizure of Cuban fishing boats during the Spanish-American War.)

[14] *Id.* at 700.

[15] *E.g.*, Henry Wheaton, International Law (8th ed.); Joseph Ortolan, Regles Internationales et Diplomatie de la Mer (1864); T.J. Lawrence, Principles of International Law (1895).

Court to follow. The use of customary international law appears in treaties constituting international tribunals, such as The Statute of the International Court of Justice,[16] and also in case law.[17]

For example, in the civil case of *Filartiga v. Pena-Irala*,[18] the Second Circuit used customary international law to resolve a case that arose under the Alien Tort Statute. In the *Filartiga* case, the court held that there are certain basic human rights accepted by the international community. Specifically, the court held that "[a]mong the rights universally proclaimed by all nations, as we have noted, is the right to be free of physical torture." Of particular significance to the analysis was the prohibition of torture in a number of U.N. General Assembly resolutions and in global and multilateral human rights treaties, including some instruments to which the United States was not a party. Modern state practice has to take into account a multiplicity of sources.

Likewise, in the case of *Sosa v. Alvarez-Machain*,[19] the Court examined conduct to determine whether it was contrary to customary international law. The Court stated that "[i]t is enough to hold that a single illegal detention of less than a day, followed by the transfer of custody to lawful authorities and a prompt arraignment, violates no norm of customary international law so well defined as to support the creation of a federal remedy."[20]

Some questions that arise with respect to customary international law are whether it changes over time and whether it has roots in natural law.[21] There are instances where customary international law may become part of a later treaty or international agreement. For example, four years after the *Filartiga* case was decided, the U.N. General Assembly adopted the 1984 Convention Against Torture and Other Cruel, Inhuman or Degrading Treatment or Punishment.[22] Suppression treaties aimed at dealing further with evils that are already proscribed by customary law are typically focused on promoting explicit criminalization at the domestic level and often contain measures for international monitoring of state obligations to suppress.[23]

§ 1.03 KEY TERMS IN INTERNATIONAL CRIMINAL LAW

Often the language used in international criminal law is the same as that found in the criminal law systems of the United States. For example, the requirement of *mens rea* is a common principle in international criminal law just as it is in the law of the United States. Several terms that are commonly referenced in a discussion of international criminal law, however, may require definition. Some of these are listed below, but bear in mind that the usage is not always consistent.

---

[16] The Statute of the International Court of Justice, Art. 38 (1945).

[17] Filartiga v. Pena-Irala, 630 F.2d 876 (2d Cir. 1980).

[18] *Id.*

[19] 124 S. Ct. 2739 (2004).

[20] *Id.* at 2769.

[21] Jack L. Goldsmith & Eric A. Posner, *Understanding the Resemblance Between Modern and Traditional Customary International Law*, 40 Va. J. Int'l L. 639 (2000); *see also* Jordan Paust, *Customary International Law: Its Nature, Sources and Status as Law of the United States*, 12 Mich. J. Int'l L. 59 (1990).

[22] This convention was ratified by the U.S. in 1994. *See* Wise, Podgor & Clark, *supra* Note 12, at 30.

[23] Earlier examples include the Convention on the Prevention and Punishment of the Crime of Genocide, 78 U.N.T.S. 277 (1948) and the Counterfeit Currency Convention, 112 L.N.T.S. 371 (1929).

[A]   Comity

"Comity" has been interpreted to have many meanings and uses.[24] Sometimes it seems to be synonymous with "customary." Sometimes it is equated with reciprocity. At least courts have found it to "include a requirement of reciprocity."[25] It is important, however, to realize that the term "comity" can have different meanings and that the term should be examined within the context in which it appears. The Supreme Court, in *Hilton v. Guyot*,[26] dealing with the enforcement of foreign money judgments, offered a classic definition of the term, stating:

> Comity in the legal sense, is neither a matter of absolute obligation, on the one hand, nor a mere customary and good will, upon the other. But it is the recognition which one nation allows within its territory to the legislative, executive or judicial acts of another nation, having due regard both to international duty and convenience, and to the rights of its own citizens or of other persons who are under the protection of its laws.

In a later federal case, *United States v. Nippon Paper Industries Co., Ltd.*,[27] the First Circuit defined "comity" as follows:

> International comity is a doctrine that counsels voluntary forbearance when a sovereign which has a legitimate claim to jurisdiction concludes that a second sovereign also has a legitimate claim to jurisdiction under principles of international law. . . . Comity is more an aspiration than a fixed rule, more a matter of grace than a matter of obligation. . . .

[B]   Complementarity

In the case of the Tribunals for Former Yugoslavia and Rwanda, the international body has a general power to trump any jurisdiction that might be exercised by a domestic body and proceed with a prosecution itself. In the case of the International Criminal Court (ICC), the basic structure is that national courts are given primacy, but the international body can step in on a showing that the national approach has failed. This is described as the principle of "complementarity." The principle is enshrined in the Preamble and in Article 1 to the ICC's Rome Statute.[28] Basically it allows for the international court to punish international crimes when a State fails to do so or is unwilling to proceed. Although it does not specifically reference the term "complementarity," Article 17 of the Rome Statute for the International Criminal Court, headed "Issues of admissibility," gives practical effect to the principle. Article 17 provides that a case does not proceed in the ICC when (1) a State is investigating or prosecuting, unless that state is "unwilling or unable" to proceed, (2) a State decides not to proceed,

---

[24] *See* Joel R. Paul, *Comity in International Law*, 32 HARV. INT'L L.J. 1 (1991).

[25] Restatement (Third) of the Foreign Relations Law of the United States § 403, Comment (a). These remarks come in the context of a discussion by the Reporters of the Restatement of what they regard as a principle of reasonableness that has now gone beyond comity to become a rule of law. A state, they argue, may not exercise jurisdiction with respect to matters having connections with another state when the exercise of such jurisdiction is unreasonable.

[26] 159 U.S. 113, 164 (1895).

[27] 109 F.3d 1 (1st Cir. 1997).

[28] "Emphasizing that the International Criminal Court established under this Statute shall be complementary to national criminal jurisdictions." The Rome Statute of the International Criminal Court, Preamble, para. 10. It "shall be complementary to national criminal jurisdictions." *Id.*, Art. 1.

unless "the decision resulted from the unwillingness or inability of the State genuinely to prosecute," or (3) the person has already been tried and cannot be tried again because of *"ne bis in idem."*[29]

[C] *Erga Omnes*

The term *"erga omnes"* refers to a State's standing to enforce certain rights, usually rights that are *jus cogens*, rights that belong to the international community.[30] These rights may be provided either through treaty or by customary international law. It is not necessary for the specific State to be the victim of the breach of international law. The word "obligation" is often seen prior to the term *"erga omnes"* with some claiming that this term provides an obligation to enforce *jus cogens* violations.[31]

Many refer to the following two paragraphs from the dictum in the International Court of Justice in *Barcelona Traction* as the starting point for defining the term *erga omnes*:[32]

> 33. When a State admits into its territory foreign investments or foreign nationals, whether natural or juristic persons, it is bound to extend to them the protection of the law and assumes obligations concerning the treatment to be afforded them. These obligations, however, are neither absolute nor unqualified. In particular, an essential distinction should be drawn between the obligations of a State towards the international community as a whole, and those arising vis-à-vis another State in the field of diplomatic protection. By their very nature the former are the concern of all States. In view of the importance of the rights involved, all States can be held to have a legal interest in their protection; they are obligations *erga omnes*.

> 34. Such obligations derive, for example in contemporary international law, from the outlawing of acts of aggression, and of genocide, as also from the principles and rules concerning the basic rights of the human person, including protection from slavery and racial discrimination. Some of the corresponding rights of protection have entered into the body of general international law; others are conferred by international instruments of a universal or quasi-universal character.

A close relationship can be seen between paragraph 34 and international crimes *stricto sensu*.

[D] Extraterritoriality

Acts that occur outside the territory of a State are considered extraterritorial. This is an important term, as it raises issues of when there is appropriate jurisdiction for a country to proceed with a criminal case when the act occurs outside the State's territory.[33] Often, when one discusses extraterritoriality, it is necessary to consider issues of reasonableness and comity to determine whether

---

[29] *See* § 1.03[F]. Art. 17 of the Statute references the Preamble and Art. 1.

[30] *See* § 1.03[E].

[31] M. Cherif Bassiouni, Introduction to International Criminal Law 168 (2003).

[32] *Case Concerning the Barcelona Traction, Light & Power Co., Ltd. (Belgium v. Spain)*, Second Phase, 1970 I.C.J. 3, 32 (Feb. 5). *See also* Maurizio Ragazzi, The Concept of International Obligations *Erga Omnes* (1997).

[33] *See* § 2.04.

assertion of jurisdiction beyond the bounds of a country (including on its ships and aircraft) will implicate the jurisdiction of another State.

In the United States, Congress explicitly provides for extraterritorial jurisdiction within some statutes. Many statutes, however, do not specify whether they apply extraterritorially. These statutes require judicial interpretation to discern the intent of Congress. In addition to ascertaining the intent of Congress at the time the statute was written, jurisdiction principles of international law can also be used to decide whether an extraterritorial application is appropriate.

[E] *Jus Cogens*

Jus cogens is the "compelling law," the highest of obligations under law placed upon countries. It is usually said to include norms prohibiting crimes such as genocide and violations of human rights. It is a norm that a "large majority" of States accept, with only perhaps a "very small number of States" rejecting.[34] Under Article 53 of the Vienna Convention on the Law of Treaties, a *jus cogens* norm is "a norm accepted and recognized by the international community of States as a whole as a norm from which no derogation is permitted and which can be modified only by a subsequent norm of general international law having the same character."

[F] *Ne Bis in Idem*

The term *"ne bis in idem"* is the international version of the concept of double jeopardy that prohibits repeated trials for the same crime. This is an important concept in international criminal law, as more than one State may choose to proceed with a prosecution both in respect of "ordinary" crimes like transnational securities fraud, or in respect of crimes of international concern such as aircraft hijackings. Unfortunately, one cannot say with confidence that a previous conviction or acquittal in State A will preclude a subsequent prosecution in State B. State practice varies and many countries still follow some version of the dual sovereignty rule which is a prominent feature of United States federal/state practice. The main treaty provision dealing with rights in the criminal justice process, Article 17, paragraph 7 of the Covenant on Civil and Political Rights is applicable only in the domestic sphere. It provides that "[n]o one shall be liable to be tried or punished again for an offense for which he has already been finally convicted or acquitted in accordance with the law and penal procedure of each country."[35] Recent commentators remark that "although the principle applies internally in almost all domestic jurisdictions, its cross-border application remains controversial and is not recognized as a customary rule or a general principle of law."[36] The area is under development. Many extradition treaties contain various forms of *ne bis* provisions. Embodied within the Rome Statute for the International Criminal Court is a sophisticated provision describing the concept of

---

[34] The Restatement (Third) of the Foreign Relations Law § 102 (1987).

[35] International Covenant on Civil and Political Rights, Art. 14(7) (1966). Note also the U.S. "understanding" when ratifying the Covenant: "The United States understands the prohibition upon double jeopardy in paragraph 7 to apply only when the judgment of acquittal has been rendered by a court of the same governmental unit, whether the Federal Government or a constituent unit, as is seeking a new trial for the same cause." *See* Wise, Podgor & Clark, *supra* Note 12 at 593.

[36] Robert Cryer, Hakan Friman, Darryl Robinson & Elizabeth Wilmshurt, An Introduction to International Criminal Law and Procedure 68 (2007) (footnote omitted).

ne bis in idem in the context of potential international prosecutions[37] It essentially precludes a second trial in the ICC "with respect to conduct which formed the basis of crimes for which the person has been convicted or acquitted by the Court." (Paragraph 1.) Moreover, "No person shall be tried by another court for a crime referred to in article 5 [genocide, crimes against humanity, war crimes, crime of aggression] for which that person has already been convicted or acquitted by the Court." (Paragraph 2.) It adds, in respect of trials in domestic courts, that:

> No person who has been tried by another court for conduct also proscribed under article 6, 7 or 8 [genocide, crimes against humanity, war crimes] shall be tried by the Court with respect to the same conduct unless the proceedings in the other court:
>
> (a) Were for the purpose of shielding the persons concerned from criminal responsibility for crimes within the jurisdiction of the Court; or
>
> (b) Otherwise were not conducted independently or impartially in accordance with the norms of due process recognized by international law and were conducted in a manner which, in the circumstances, was inconsistent with an intent to bring the person concerned to justice.

It remains to be seen how these tentative steps will be worked out in national and international practice, as more states begin to exercise extraterritorial jurisdiction, especially on the basis of universal jurisdiction, and thus the opportunities for concurrent jurisdiction leading to issues of *ne bis in idem* become greater.

---

[37] The Rome Statute of the International Criminal Court, Art. 20.

Chapter 2
GENERAL PRINCIPLES OF JURISDICTION

§ 2.01 GENERALLY

Jurisdiction is an important issue in international criminal law because it determines who will have the ability to charge criminal conduct, what law will apply in the case, and what rights the accused will be entitled to assert in the criminal process. Substantive law issues, such as whether a crime has been committed, and procedural rights, such as whether the defendant can be extradited to the country that seeks to proceed with the criminal prosecution, often turn on whether a State has jurisdiction. Jurisdiction questions can also be important in determining whether States and individuals will be subject to actions of an international tribunal.

The law determining the appropriateness of a State's jurisdiction can be premised upon the law of that State or alternatively, upon international law. In some cases, treaties may resolve the issue. As seen in the *Lotus*,[1] countries may not agree on who has jurisdiction and an international tribunal will decide the question. In *Lotus*, the Court accepted that there was concurrent jurisdiction and that it was not inappropriate for Turkey to proceed. The principle of comity[2] will sometimes enable a state to concede graciously to another state also entitled to exercise jurisdiction.

---

[1] *See* § 1.02[B], *supra.*

[2] *See* § 1.03[A], *supra.*

From a national perspective, it is essential that the internal law of the United States concerning jurisdiction operate in conjunction with international law. The relationship is in fact complicated. In the United States, the Supremacy Clause of the Constitution, Article VI (2), declares the Constitution, laws of the United States and treaties "the supreme law of the land." Summarizing the Supreme Court's jurisprudence on this Article, *The Restatement (Third) of the Foreign Relations Law of the United States* provides that an act of Congress supersedes an earlier rule of international law or a provision of an international agreement as law of the United States if the purpose of the act is to supersede the earlier rule or provision is clear or if the act and the earlier rule or provision cannot be fairly reconciled.[3] Legislative disregard of a rule of international law, however, will not relieve the United States from its international obligation.[4] *The Restatement* also provides that treaties that become effective as law in the United States supersede any prior inconsistent law.[5] The last in time rule — that treaties and statutes are of equal weight and, in the event of conflict, whichever is last in time prevails, is not specifically stated in the Constitution but rests on the interpretations of the Supreme Court. Although the *Restatement* provides a strong emphasis on respect for international law and agreements, it also states that international law and agreements cannot, as a matter of domestic law, be inconsistent with the United States Constitution.[6] Other countries, such as France and the Netherlands, structure their constitutional arrangements in different ways. Treaties in some countries trump subsequent legislation and sometimes even constitutional provisions.

§ 2.02 EXTRATERRITORIAL APPLICATION OF UNITED STATES STATUTES

Extraterritorial application of a United States statute permits prosecution of criminal acts that occur outside the United States. There are two basic considerations in determining extraterritorial application of a United States statute. These are: 1) whether the statute permits extraterritoriality, and 2) whether international law allows the United States to apply its law to this particular conduct. The Courts generally try to interpret statutes consistently with international law.

[A] Explicit Statutory Authority for Extraterritorial Application

Deciding whether a statute permits extraterritoriality requires looking at whether Congress had the intent to give extraterritorial application to the statute. For example, in expanding the United States jurisdictional base over the crime of genocide in 2007, Congress made its intention very clear. It added these words in the relevant jurisdictional provisions: "(5) after the conduct required for the

---

[3] The Restatement (Third) of the Foreign Relations Law of the United States § 115 (1987). Note also the famous dictum by Marshall C.J. in *The Charming Betsy*, 6 U.S. (2 Cranch) 64, 118 (1804) that "an act of congress ought never to be construed to violate the law of nations, if any other possible construction remains. . . . "

[4] *Id.* at § 115(2).

[5] *Id.*

[6] *Id.* at § 115(3). The only occasion the Supreme Court struck down provisions in an international agreement on this ground is *Reid v. Covert*, 354 U.S. 1 (1957), (provisions for trial of military spouses by court martial held inconsistent with various requirements of the Bill of Rights).

offense occurs, the alleged offender is brought into, or found in, the United States, even if that conduct occurred outside the United States."[7]

In some cases, such as when the entire statute is focused on foreign conduct, the intent is easily discerned. Thus, in cases involving violations of the Foreign Corrupt Practices Act, it is very clear that Congress intended to cover bribery conduct occurring outside the United States.[8]

In some instances, the statute is not focused directly on foreign activities, but Congress places an explicit provision within it that authorizes extraterritorial application. For example, a key perjury statute provides that "[t]his section is applicable whether the statement or subscription is made within or without the United States."[9]

The definitions of terms within statutes may also provide for an extraterritorial application. For example, in passing the "Uniting and Strengthening America by Providing Appropriate Tools Required to Intercept and Obstruct Terrorism (USA Patriot Act) Act of 2001," Congress modified the computer fraud statute to include a new provision that states, "the term 'protected computer' means a computer — . . . (B) which is used in interstate or foreign commerce or communication, including a computer located outside the United States that is used in a manner that affects interstate or foreign commerce or communication of the United States."[10] This definition provides for prosecution of extraterritorial computer conduct when a "protected computer" is involved in the activity.

In some instances, an explicit provision may include restrictions on when extraterritorial application will be permitted. One finds this type of provision in a key money laundering statute that authorizes extraterritorial jurisdiction if the "conduct is by a United States citizen or in the case of a non-United States citizen, the conduct occurs in part in the United States; and the transaction or series of related transactions involves funds or monetary instruments of a value exceeding $10,000."[11]

[B] Judicial Interpretation Permitting Extraterritorial Application

Most statutes are not explicitly focused on foreign conduct, and do not contain explicit provisions authorizing extraterritorial application. Such statutes require that courts use judicial interpretation to decide whether Congress intended them to apply to extraterritorial acts. In looking at congressional intent, courts usually examine the statute as a whole in an attempt to discern whether extraterritorial application is in keeping with the purpose of the statute. In some cases, courts also examine international law in order to determine if the statute fits within the international principles that permit jurisdiction. "There is no constitutional bar to the extraterritorial application of penal laws."[12]

In 1922, the United States Supreme Court examined whether extraterritorial jurisdiction was proper in a case involving a conspiracy to defraud a corporation, of

---

[7] Genocide Accountability Act of 2007, amending 18 U.S.C. § 1091.

[8] *See* § 3.02, *infra.*

[9] 18 U.S.C. § 1621.

[10] 18 U.S.C. § 1030(e)(2)(B) (2002).

[11] 18 U.S.C. § 1956(f).

[12] United States v. King, 552 F.2d 833, 850 (9th Cir. 1976).

which the United States was the sole stockholder. In *United States v. Bowman*,[13] jurisdiction was challenged, claiming that the crime "was committed without the jurisdiction of the United States or any State thereof and on the high seas or within the jurisdiction of Brazil." The Court rejected this argument.

In finding extraterritorial jurisdiction proper, the Court stated that "[t]he necessary locus, when not specifically defined, depends upon the purpose of Congress as evidenced by the description and nature of the crime and upon the territorial limitations upon the power and jurisdiction of a government to punish crime under the law of nations." Crimes against individuals, such as "assaults, murder, burglary, larceny, robbery, arson, embezzlement and fraud of all kinds" were left for prosecution by the territorial jurisdiction where the act occurred. In contrast, crimes "not logically dependent on their locality for the Government's jurisdiction," would be subject to extraterritorial application. Thus, frauds against the government or acts requiring the government to "defend itself against obstruction" might be the subject of a United States prosecution, despite the fact that the conduct occurred outside this territory. It is common for lower courts to cite to the *Bowman* decision in support of a decision permitting extraterritoriality.[14]

A 2005 decision of the Supreme Court considered an issue that some would believe involved a question related to extraterritoriality. In *Pasquantino v. United States*[15] the Court took up a question that had divided circuit courts, that being whether it was appropriate to apply the federal wire fraud statute to actions in the United States aimed at defrauding a foreign government of taxes. The majority, in an opinion by Justice Thomas, emphasized that the legislation applied to conduct in the United States and as such this was merely a violation of the U.S. wire fraud statute. The Court considered whether to apply the so-called "common-law revenue rule," a canon of statutory construction amounting to a presumption against enforcing foreign revenue laws. The majority, however, found that the revenue rule did not preclude this prosecution, even if the effect was to assist the Canadian province of Ontario. Justice Thomas stated, "[i]t may seem an odd use of the Federal Government's resources to prosecute a U.S. citizen for smuggling cheap liquor into Canada. But the broad language of the wire fraud statute authorizes it to do so, and no canon of statutory construction permits us to read the statute more narrowly." In dissent, Justice Ginsburg came to a different conclusion on the revenue rule. She advocated that the "rule of lenity" should apply to an ambiguous statute and also applied a "presumption against extraterritoriality" which she believed cut against applying the statute here.[16]

Although at one point a general statute providing rules of extraterritoriality was considered by the National Commission on Reform of the Federal Criminal Laws,

---

[13]   260 U.S. 94 (1922).

[14]   *See, e.g.*, United States v. Cotton, 471 F.2d 744, 749–50 (9th Cir. 1973) (extraterritoriality permitted in case involving theft of government property that is outside the United States). *See also* Ellen S. Podgor & Daniel M. Filler, *International Criminal Jurisdiction in the 21st Century: Rediscovering United States v. Bowman*, 44 San Diego L. Rev. 585 (2007) (discussing how courts use the *Bowman* decision).

[15]   544 U.S. 349 (2005).

[16]   Justice Breyer joined her in seeing an extraterritoriality issue in the case; Justices Scalia and Souter saw only the foreign revenues and lenity issues and agreed with her on them.

the proposal was not adopted.[17] There has been no further attempt to provide a general extraterritoriality rule since this commission's proposal.

In addition to looking at the intent of Congress in interpreting a criminal statute to see if extraterritoriality applies, courts have also examined international law. Here the courts look at the international bases of jurisdiction to determine if an extraterritorial application is in keeping with international principles of jurisdiction.

§ 2.03 JURISDICTIONAL BASES

In international law, scholars, especially American ones, often find it useful for the purposes of analysis to speak of three categories of jurisdiction. These are: 1) jurisdiction to prescribe; 2) jurisdiction to adjudicate; and 3) jurisdiction to enforce.[18] Jurisdiction to prescribe concerns the power of a state "to make its law applicable to the activities, relations, or status of persons or the interests of persons in things" as determined by legislation, administrative rule, executive action, or judicial interpretation.[19] The crucial question in the present context is applying United States federal substantive law created by Congress to a particular situation, since the Supreme Court has held that there is no federal common law of crimes.[20]

Jurisdiction to adjudicate concerns jurisdiction of the person, and the ability to "subject persons or things to the process of its courts or administrative tribunals, whether in civil or in criminal proceedings, whether or not the state is a party to the proceedings."[21] Thus, if a nation is not able to secure the person for prosecution, jurisdiction to proceed with the matter may be lacking.

The final category, jurisdiction to enforce, concerns compliance with the procedures established and punishment for non-compliance. This can be attained through "courts or by use of executive, administrative, police, or other nonjudicial action."[22] Adjudicating punishment is worthless unless the State has the ability to impose and enforce the punishment. This requires a jurisdiction to enforce.

Enforcement jurisdiction is often an issue also when a government seeks, on the high seas or on the territory of another state, to capture a potential defendant for purposes of prosecution. In *Lotus*, the majority commented that "[n]ow the first and foremost restriction imposed by international law upon a State is that — failing the existence of a permissive rule to the contrary — it may not exercise its power in any form in the territory of another State."[23] Later the majority added "Thus, if a war vessel, happening to be at the spot where a collision occurs between a vessel flying its flag and a foreign vessel, were to send on board the latter an officer to make investigations or to take evidence, such an act would undoubtedly be contrary to

---

[17] Final Report of the National Commission on Reform of the Federal Criminal Laws § 208 (1971).

[18] The Restatement (Third) of the Foreign Relations Law of the United States, § 401(1987).

[19] *Id.* at § 401(a).

[20] United States v. Hudson & Goodwin, 11 U.S. (7 Cranch) 32 (1812). Occasionally, Congress incorporates international law as domestic substantive law. *See* United States v. Smith, 18 U.S. (5 Wheat) 153 (1820) ("piracy as defined by the law of nations").

[21] The Restatement (Third) of the Foreign Relations Law of the United States, at § 401(b) (1987).

[22] *Id.* at § 401(c).

[23] *The Lotus*, P.C.I.J. Ser. A, Pt. 2 at 18 (1927).

international law."[24] As M. Demons's vessel went into Constantinople, Turkey could exercise its enforcement jurisdiction.

International discourse commonly includes another classification of "jurisdiction." This classification is expressed by the following: jurisdiction *ratione materiae* (subject matter jurisdiction); jurisdiction *ratione personae* (personal jurisdiction); and jurisdiction *ratione temporis* (the time frame of the events in respect of which a court may act).

§ 2.04 JURISDICTION TO PRESCRIBE

There are five generally accepted principles in international law that form the categories of the jurisdiction to prescribe. Sometimes referred to as the Harvard Principles, these are 1) territorial jurisdiction, 2) the nationality principle, 3) the protective principle, 4) the passive personality principle, and 5) the universality principle.[25] It is important to note, however, that these categories do not operate as exclusive premises for jurisdiction.[26] It is common for courts to use more than one basis in justifying appropriate jurisdiction.

Courts in the United States tend to favor the territorial principle in finding sufficient jurisdiction to proceed with a criminal prosecution, although the *Restatement (Third) of the Foreign Relations Law of the United States* speaks in its black-letter to four categories: 1) territoriality, 2) nationality, 3) protective personality, and 4) universal jurisdiction. It includes an additional principle, the passive personality principle, in a Comment. The same principles used as a basis for finding jurisdiction for a substantive offense can also be used in instances of conspiratorial responsibility and liability such as accessory before the fact or aiding or abetting in the commission of the crime.[27]

[A] Territorial Principle

Territorial jurisdiction is the most common basis of criminal jurisdiction, as it is premised upon the place where the crime is committed. If the act occurs within the territory of the State, then there is a clear basis for asserting jurisdiction. Courts sometimes refer to this form of territoriality as the "subjective territorial principle" to contrast it with "objective territoriality" (see § 2.04[A][2]). Territory of a state is understood to include vessels or aircraft registered in that state.

Determining territorial jurisdiction is not as easy as it was pre-technology and travel. Today there can be questions with respect to territorial jurisdiction such as determining where the act actually occurred. This is particularly problematic with respect to crimes that transcend borders. For example, in the case of a computer crime, the question can arise as to whether the act occurs in the place of the keystroke or the place the harm is committed. Likewise, with illegal money laundering activity where the money may pass through various countries, there can be a question as to whether territorial jurisdiction is in the location of the bank or the place where the accused sets in motion the transfer of funds, or in both of these places.

---

[24] *Id.* at 25. *See also* § 12.06 (discussing abduction).

[25] Harvard Research in International Law, *Jurisdiction With Respect to Crime*, 29 AM. J.INT'L L. 437 (Supp. 1935).

[26] *See* United States v. Layton, 855 F.2d 1388 (9th Cir. 1988).

[27] *See* United States v. Hill, 279 F.3d 731 (9th Cir. 2002).

In inchoate crimes, such as conspiracy, issues can also arise as to whether the intent to commit an act or bring about a result within the territorial jurisdiction is a sufficient basis for jurisdiction in the United States. Under federal law, drug conspiracies do not require an overt act. In *United States v. Ricardo*,[28] the Fifth Circuit stated, "that when the statute itself does not require proof of an overt act, jurisdiction attaches upon a mere showing of intended territorial effects." Courts may hold the government to a strict showing of the accused having intent to bring about an effect on the United States in cases where the effect on the United States is not immediately seen.[29]

[1] Special Territorial Jurisdiction

Prosecutions for criminal acts occurring outside the United States borders can be achieved through "special territorial jurisdiction." Federal law provides for "special maritime and territorial jurisdiction," a term explicitly defined by statute.[30] For example, a United States court found special jurisdiction in a manslaughter case involving a United States citizen who killed another United States citizen, both of whom were employees of this country serving in the embassy of the Republic of Equatorial Guinea. Since the act took place outside the United States, but within its embassy in a foreign country,[31] there was appropriate jurisdiction for the prosecution.

Special maritime jurisdiction has also been found on a cruise ship in Mexican territorial waters.[32] Although the accused was not a citizen of the United States, in the case of *United States v. Neil*, the court found that he was "employed on a ship departing from and returning to an American port." Although the crime of sexual contact with a minor occurred in Mexican territorial waters, the Ninth Circuit found that "Congress has defined the 'special maritime and territorial jurisdiction of the United States' as including '[t]o the extent permitted by international law, any foreign vessel during a voyage having a scheduled departure from or arrival in the United States with respect to an offense committed by or against a national of the United States.' "[33] Because the victim was a United States national, the court found that "special maritime and territorial jurisdiction" was met.

In some cases, the "special maritime and territorial jurisdiction" is explicitly provided for within a criminal statute. For example, there are a host of criminal statutes that are earmarked for crimes committed in "special maritime and territorial jurisdiction." These include crimes such as assault,[34] maiming,[35] arson,[36] and embezzlement and theft.[37] Additionally, the Military Extraterritorial

---

[28] 619 F.2d 1124 (5th Cir. 1980).

[29] *See* United States v. James-Robinson, 515 F. Supp. 1343 (D.C. Fla. 1981).

[30] 18 U.S.C. § 7.

[31] *See* United States v. Erdos, 474 F.2d 157 (4th Cir. 1973).

[32] *See* United States v. Neil, 312 F.3d 419 (9th Cir. 2002).

[33] *Id.* at 422. This type of case can also be seen as an example of passive personality jurisdiction against an American victim. *See infra* § 2.04[C].

[34] 18 U.S.C. § 113.

[35] 18 U.S.C. § 114.

[36] 18 U.S.C. § 8.

[37] 18 U.S.C. § 661.

Jurisdiction Act of 2000 provides jurisdiction to U.S. District Courts over offenses committed by persons employed by or accompanying the Armed Forces outside the United States.[38]

The scope of whom and what are covered under "special maritime and territorial jurisdiction" was further extended as a result of the USA Patriot Act. It is now possible to indict individuals who are living in "residences in foreign States . . . irrespective of ownership" of the land if they are in the foreign country working for the government or military assigned to a mission or entity.[39]

Jurisdiction can also be a result of treaty. For example, "the special aircraft jurisdiction statute was originally created to comply with treaty obligations under the Tokyo Convention."[40]

[2] Objective Territoriality ("Effects Principle")

An outgrowth of the territorial principle is "objective territoriality," the most common basis upon which courts find extraterritorial jurisdiction in the United States. This was the strongest ground for upholding Turkish jurisdiction in *Lotus*. M. Demons's negligence had effects on the Turkish vessel, which was treated as Turkish soil. The concept of objective territoriality in United States law is attributed to Justice Holmes's decision in *Strassheim v. Daily*.[41] There, he stated that "[a]cts done outside a jurisdiction, but intended to produce and producing detrimental effects within it, justify a State in punishing the cause of the harm as if he had been present at the effect, if the State should succeed in getting him within its power." Although the *Strassheim* case involved conduct internally between two states within the United States, it has been applied to international cases. For example, in *Chua Han Mow v. United States*,[42] the appellant, who was in Malaysia at the relevant time, was convicted on charges of importing and distributing drugs within the United States. The Court commented that "Chua intended to create detrimental effect in the United States and committed acts which resulted in such an effect when the heroin unlawfully entered the country."[43]

Objective territoriality is often referred to as "effects jurisdiction," as it is jurisdiction premised upon "activity outside the state, but having or intending to have substantial effect within the state's territory." [44] Thus, if the defendant intends to sell drugs in the United States, the harmful effect of the drugs being sold or distributed in this country provides a basis for objective territorial jurisdiction. [45] Antitrust violations that can have an effect on prices in the United States can also be said to be within the realm of objective territoriality. [46] With

---

[38] 18 U.S.C. § 3261 (2000). This statute was found not to have a retroactive application and therefore only covers acts committed after the passage of this statute. *See* United States v. Morton, 314 F. Supp. 2d 509 (D. Md. 2004).

[39] 18 U.S.C. § 7(9).

[40] United States v. Georgescu, 723 F. Supp. 912 (E.D.N.Y. 1989).

[41] 221 U.S. 280 (1911) (fraudulent acts in Chicago; fraud consummated in Michigan).

[42] 730 F. 2d 1308 (9th Cir. 1984).

[43] *Id.* at. 1312. This is a case of concurrent jurisdiction in that Malaysia could prosecute for the conduct on its territory.

[44] The Restatement (Third) of the Foreign Relations Law of the United States, § 402 Comment d (1987).

[45] *See* Chua Han Mow v. United States, 730 F.2d 1308 (9th Cir. 1984).

[46] *See* United States v. Nippon, 109 F.3d 1 (1st Cir. 1997).

respect to an economic effect in the United States, the "Restatement takes the position that a state may exercise jurisdiction based upon effects in the state, when the effect or intended effect is substantial and the exercise of jurisdiction is reasonable" under section 403 of the Restatement.[47]

[B] Nationality Principle

Extraterritorial jurisdiction can be achieved when a national commits a crime outside the borders of the United States. [48] Unlike civil law countries such as France and Germany, the United States does not exercise jurisdiction on a nationality basis as a general rule. Whether a prosecution will actually occur in instances where the United States does claim jurisdiction may depend upon whether the defendant can be returned to the United States to stand trial. There can also be issues regarding obtaining the evidence from abroad. Finally, another country may wish to proceed with a prosecution, claiming their right to proceed as they have territorial jurisdiction.

One important example of nationality jurisdiction is the Prosecutorial Remedies and Other Tools to End the Exploitation of Children Today Act of 2003 ("Protect Act") [49] which deals with Americans who travel abroad to engage in the sexual exploitation of children. In *United States v. Clark*, [50] the majority of the Court upheld the statute against the argument that it violated principles of international law and that it was not within the federal government's Commerce Clause powers to regulate such activities. The dissent disagreed on the Commerce Clause point.[51]

The clearer cases of nationality jurisdiction appear in those instances where the national commits a crime specific to the United States. For example, in *United States v. Walczak*, [52] the accused was charged with violating the federal false statement statute [53] for an alleged false statement on a customs form. Walczak, a United States citizen, was about to board an airplane from Canada to the United States when the alleged act occurred. The Ninth Circuit affirmed the conviction, finding sufficient jurisdiction, in part because the defendant was a national, and from the law breached it was clear that it covered crimes outside the United States. Issues of comity would not arise in this situation, as no other country would likely wish to proceed against an individual who may have given a false statement on a United States customs form.

[C] Passive Personality Principle

Where the nationality principle extends jurisdiction to nationals accused of crimes, the passive personality principle extends jurisdiction when the victim of the crime is a national. It will be recalled that this was one of Turkey's theories in

---

[47] The Restatement (Third) of the Foreign Relations Law of the United States, § 402 Comment d (1987).

[48] *See* Geoffrey R. Watson, *Offenders Abroad: The Case for Nationality-Based Criminal Jurisdiction*, 17 Yale J. Int'l L 41 (1992).

[49] 18 U.S.C. § 2423.

[50] 435 F. 3d 1100 (9th Cir. 2006).

[51] As customary and treaty law expands to protect victims of sex tourism, one can expect such statutes to be justified on the basis of the treaty power or the "define and punish" clause of the Constitution.

[52] 783 F.2d 852 (9th Cir. 1986). This case may also be an example of the protective principle.

[53] 18 U.S.C. § 1001.

Lotus. This theory is gaining acceptance in the United States. As noted in the *Restatement (Third) of the Foreign Relations Law of the United States*, "[t]he principle has not been generally accepted for ordinary torts or crimes, but it is increasingly accepted as applied to terrorist and other organized attacks on a state's nationals by reason of their nationality, or to assassination of a state's diplomatic representatives or other officials."[54]

Although it is seen most often in the context of terrorist-type activity, this principle has been used for other criminal activity. For example, in *United States v. Roberts*,[55] the defendant was indicted for sexual conduct toward a minor while aboard a cruise ship. The ship, incorporated in Panama, was flying under a Liberian flag. The accused was a national of St. Vincent & the Grenadines employed by the cruise ship. The victim was a United States citizen. The defendant argued that both treaties and the "law of the flag" prevented the United States from having jurisdiction to proceed with this prosecution. The court, denying defendant's motion to dismiss, found jurisdiction in the United States proper under both passive personality and objective territorial principles. In its decision, the court noted how Congress was moving toward accepting passive personality jurisdiction in legislation outside the context of terrorism. The objective territorial argument here (effect on the victim) is perhaps a bit of a stretch. There is always an effect of some sort when there is a United States victim and "effects" here seems to be passive personality by another name.[56]

[D] Protective Principle

As described in the *Restatement (Third) of the Foreign Relations Law of the United States*, jurisdiction can be premised upon "certain conduct outside its territory by persons who are not its nationals that is directed against the security of the state or against a limited class of other state interests."[57] Its name aptly describes it as the *"protective* principle."[58] Examples are given in a *Restatement* Comment: "espionage, counterfeiting of the state's seal or currency, falsification of official documents, as well as perjury before consular officials, and conspiracy to violate the immigration or customs laws."[59]

This principle was invoked in *United States v. Gonzalez*,[60] a case involving drug activity within the "custom waters" of the United States. The coast guard boarded a Honduran vessel that was "approximately 125 miles due east of Fort Lauderdale, Florida," after receiving "no objection" from the Honduran government. On appeal of a denial of defendant's Motion to Dismiss, the Eleventh Circuit referenced the protective principle noting that Congress "adopted section 955a(c) and relied on the protective principle because it is often difficult to prove beyond a reasonable

---

[54] The Restatement (Third) of the Foreign Relations Law of the United States, § 402 Comment g (1987).

[55] 1 F. Supp. 2d 601 (E.D. La. 1998).

[56] *But see* United States v. Neil, 312 F.3d 419 (9th Cir. 2002) where, on similar facts, the Court emphasized that the victim, on her return to California, missed several days school and underwent counseling.

[57] The Restatement (Third) of the Foreign Relations Law of the United States, § 402(3) (1987).

[58] *See* IAIN CAMERON, THE PROTECTIVE PRINCIPLE OF INTERNATIONAL CRIMINAL JURISDICTION (1994).

[59] The Restatement (Third) of the Foreign Relations Law of the United States, § 402 Comment f (1987).

[60] 776 F.2d 931 (11th Cir. 1985).

doubt that a vessel seized on the high seas carrying contraband was headed for the United States." The court noted that using the protective principle meant that the government would not have to show an effect inside the United States. This is a very broad interpretation of "protective" since the drugs may well have been bound for Canada — or Greenland, for that matter.

[E] Universality Principle

Universal jurisdiction is jurisdiction by a nation to enforce international law. It is achieved irrespective of whether the offense took place in the nation enforcing the law, and irrespective of where the offender or victims are located.[61] Typically it entails jurisdiction to prescribe, to adjudicate, and to enforce "crimes against mankind."

Universal jurisdiction is achieved in two ways: 1) through customary international law, and 2) through international agreement. As stated in the *Restatement (Third) of the Foreign Relations Law of the United States*, "[u]niversal jurisdiction over the specified offenses is a result of universal condemnation of those activities and general interest in cooperating to suppress them, as reflected in widely-accepted international agreements and resolutions of international organizations."[62]

Historically, universal jurisdiction was used with crimes of piracy.[63] Because piracy took place on the high seas outside national jurisdiction and there was no international criminal court to oversee prosecutions, nations were, of necessity, left free to punish it. Universal jurisdiction was the basis for prosecuting atrocities committed during World War II. For example, Adolph Eichmann was prosecuted in Israel for committing universal crimes. Universal jurisdiction has also been used in the United States, in the *Demjanjuk* case, as a basis for granting extradition to a country that intended to prosecute an individual for allegedly committing war crimes and crimes against humanity during that period.[64] Some universal crimes are considered not to be subject to statutes of limitations.[65]

Today, universal jurisdiction has expanded to include many other offenses. Crimes considered as of "universal concern" include "piracy, slave trade, attacks on or hijacking of aircraft, genocide, war crimes, and perhaps certain acts of terrorism."[66] Thus, one often finds universal jurisdiction as the basis for

---

[61] The Restatement (Third) of the Foreign Relations Law of the United States, § 423 (1987) ("A state may exercise jurisdiction through its courts to enforce its criminal laws that punish universal crimes or other non-territorial offenses within the state's jurisdiction to prescribe.").

[62] *Id.* at § 404, Comment a.

[63] *Id.* at § 404, Rep. Notes 2 ("The previous Restatement cited only piracy as an offense subject to universal jurisdiction.").

[64] Demjanjuk v. Petrovsky, 776 F.2d 571, 582 (6th Cir. 1985), *vacated on other grounds*, 10 F.3d 338 (6th Cir. 1993), *cert. denied*, 513 U.S. 914 (1994). Demjanjuk was ultimately acquitted on appeal in Israel and returned to the United States which has been trying to deport him ever since.

[65] EDWARD M. WISE, ELLEN S. PODGOR & ROGER S. CLARK, INTERNATIONAL CRIMINAL LAW: CASES AND MATERIALS 644–46 (2d Ed., 2004) (war crimes and crimes against humanity); Rome Statute of the International Criminal Court, Art. 29 (genocide, crimes against humanity, war crimes, crime of aggression).

[66] The Restatement (Third) of the Foreign Relations Law of the United States at § 404 (1987). United States legislation does not in fact exercise universal jurisdiction over war crimes and only in 2007 asserted universal jurisdiction over genocide. *See also* THE PRINCETON PRINCIPLES ON UNIVERSAL JURISDICTION (2001) (endorsing an expanded use of universal jurisdiction).

jurisdiction when there is a human rights violation or what might generally be regarded as "terrorism." It is used as the jurisdictional base to prosecute violations of "universal moral values and humanitarian principles that lie hidden in the criminal law systems adopted by civilised nations."[67]

Since 1998, a number of countries have asserted universal jurisdiction over the core international crimes — genocide, crimes against humanity, and war crimes — in the course of enacting legislation to enable them to become parties to the Rome Statute of the International Criminal Court, adopted that year. State prosecution practice had been multiplying even before then. European states, in particular, have been prosecuting for atrocities committed in Rwanda and Former Yugoslavia and even Latin America. The extent to which this extended use of universal jurisdiction is acceptable is hotly debated. In the United States there have been legislative proposals, on the one hand, to assert strong opposition to universal jurisdiction on sovereignty grounds, and on the other hand, to assert it in such cases as human trafficking and the use of child soldiers. There were widespread protests at efforts to prosecute Israeli and United States leaders in Belgium and elsewhere in Europe.

In 2002, the International Court of Justice adjudicated a complaint from the Democratic Republic of Congo that Belgium had issued an arrest warrant for Congo's Minister of Foreign Affairs, charging him with war crimes and crimes against humanity.[68] Congo argued that Belgium had exceeded its jurisdiction and that the Minister was immune from prosecution. While the Court ultimately held that the Minister was entitled to immunity,[69] some of the judges rendered separate opinions on the jurisdictional question. In particular, Judges Higgins (United Kingdom), Kooijmans (the Netherlands) and Buergenthal (United States) expressed the view that "a State may choose to exercise a universal criminal jurisdiction *in absentia*."[70] By "in absentia" in the context, the trio was referring to the fact that the accused was outside Belgium at the relevant time and it would be necessary to obtain physical possession of him, probably by extradition. The stance of the case was thus essentially the same as that when Israel requested Demjanjuk's extradition from the United States. The three judges were of the view that certain safeguards were necessary (in addition to the immunity of some officials). In particular, they suggested that "[a] State contemplating bringing criminal charges based on universal jurisdiction must first offer to the national State of the prospective accused person the opportunity itself to act upon the charges concerned."[71] In addition, "such charges may only be laid by a prosecutor or *juge d'instruction* who acts in full independence, without links to or control by the government of that State. Moreover, the desired equilibrium between the battle against impunity and the promotion of inter-State relations will only be maintained if there are some special circumstances that do require the exercise of an international criminal jurisdiction and if this has been brought to the attention of the prosecutor or *juge d'instruction*. For example, persons related to the victims

---

[67] Israel v. Eichmann, 36 Int. L. Reps. 277, 291–93 (Isr. S. Ct. 1962).

[68] Case Concerning the Arrest Warrant of 11 April 2000 (D.R. Congo v. Belgium), 2002 I.C.J.

[69] *See* § 10.02[B][1].

[70] D.R. Congo v. Belgium, *supra* note 68. Joint Separate Opinion of Judges Higgins, Kooijmans and Buergenthal, ¶ 59.

[71] *Id.*

of the case will have requested the commencement of legal proceedings."[72] This is on the cutting edge of international criminal law.

Many modern suppression treaties contain a provision that requires states not only to exercise jurisdiction on such bases as territoriality and nationality but also to take such measures as may be necessary to establish jurisdiction over the treaty offences where the alleged offender is present in its territory and it does not extradite him to another state party. This is a "subsidiary" or "fallback" version of universal jurisdiction, the obligatory exercise of which may be triggered by presence.[73] The Joint Separate Opinion in the *Arrest Warrant* case makes reference to these treaties:

> The great treaties on aerial offences, hijacking, narcotics and torture are built on the concept of *aut dedere aut prosequi. Definitionally, this envisages presence on the territory.* There cannot be an obligation to extradite someone you choose not to try unless that person is within your reach. National legislation, enacted to give effect to these treaties, quite naturally, also may make mention of the presence of the accused. These sensible realities are critical for the obligatory exercise of *aut dedere aut prosequi* jurisdiction, but cannot be interpreted *a contrario so as to exclude* a voluntary exercise of universal jurisdiction.[74]

Some states in fact give effect to such treaties by treating their "presence" provisions as simple universal jurisdiction ones which could, for example, support an extradition request. This seems to have been the case with the British and Spanish legislation giving effect to the Convention against Torture and Other Cruel, Inhuman or Degrading Treatment or Punishment that was the subject of the extradition request in the *Pinochet* case.[75]

§ 2.05   EMERGING PRINCIPLES — "LANDING STATE" AND "TRANSFERRED" JURISDICTION

State practice never fitted precisely within the so-called five bases of jurisdiction. Modern treaty practice, both multilateral and bilateral, continues in creative directions, as does domestic legislation. Two examples merit attention.[76]

Thus the Hague Convention for the Suppression of Unlawful Seizure of Aircraft (Hijacking)[77] and the Montreal Convention for the Suppression of Unlawful Acts Against the Safety of Civil Aviation[78] require the exercise of jurisdiction for the offenses proscribed in those treaties in a range of situations including "when the aircraft on which the offence is committed lands in its territory with the alleged offender still on board." This jurisdiction can be referred to as "landing state

---

[72] *Id.*

[73] *See generally,* Roger S. Clark, *Offenses of International Concern: Multilateral State Treaty Practice in the Forty Years Since Nuremberg,* 57 Nordic J. Int'l L. 49, 58–63 (1988). This is sometimes referred to as "custodial state jurisdiction."

[74] Joint Separate Opinion, *supra* note 70, ¶ 57 (emphasis in original).

[75] Regina v. Bow Street Magistrate, Ex Parte Pinochet Ugarte (No. 3) [2001] 1 App. Cas. 147 (H.L.). *See* § 10.02.

[76] Another possible (re-)emerging theory is "connexity." *See* § 3.02[C].

[77] 860 U.N. T.S. 105 (1970).

[78] 974 U.N.T.S. 177 (1971).

jurisdiction." In *United States v. Georgescu*,[79] Judge Weinstein interpreted a statute permitting landing state jurisdiction over a much wider range of cases on aircraft. Over the Atlantic, on a Scandinavian Airlines flight from Copenhagen to New York, the defendant, a Romanian national, allegedly indecently assaulted a nine-year-old Norwegian girl. The judge held that there was jurisdiction in New York, although there might be concurrent jurisdiction elsewhere, at the least in Norway. Indeed, given evidentiary considerations and sensitivities concerning the child, it might be more appropriate to try the accused somewhere else.[80]

Another modern type of jurisdiction, especially among civil law countries, is "transferred jurisdiction" where a request to State A from State B to exercise jurisdiction provides the necessary competence for State A to do so. It is necessary that the conduct be criminal in both places ("double criminality"). There is even a Model United Nations Treaty on the Transfer of Proceedings in Criminal Matters.[81] Some treaties, such as Article 17 of the 1988 United Nations Convention against Illicit Traffic in Narcotic Drugs and Psychotropic Substances,[82] contemplate that a flag state may authorize another state to exercise enforcement and prescriptive jurisdiction over the persons on its ships who are alleged to be engaged in illicit trade. Such an agreement can be a general one or specific to a particular vessel. Similar transfer provisions are now appearing in some bilateral arrangements.[83] Article 8 of the 1988 Drug Convention exhorts the parties more generally to "give consideration to the possibility of transferring to one another proceedings for criminal prosecution" of the offenses delineated in the treaty. Such actions could be a useful way to consolidate prosecutions for those involved in illicit drug enterprises operating across several sovereignties. There is little doubt that novel state practice will continue to accumulate.

§ 2.06 LIMITATIONS TO JURISDICTION TO PRESCRIBE

Even though one or more of the jurisdiction bases may exist, jurisdiction may be denied when it would be considered "unreasonable." *The Restatement (Third) of the Foreign Relations Law of the United States* asserts that "all relevant factors" should be considered in deciding whether the jurisdiction is unreasonable, but also offers eight factors to assist in this evaluation. These are: (a) "the link of the activity to the territory of the regulating state . . . ," "(b) the connections, such as nationality, residence, or economic activity, between the regulating state and the

---

[79] 732 F. Supp. 912 (E.D. N.Y. 1989). As Judge Weinstein noted, the Tokyo Convention on Offences and Certain other Acts Committed on Board Aircraft, 704 U.N.T.S. 219 (1963), seeks to encourage states to take jurisdiction over conduct on aircraft registered in their jurisdiction. Art. 3 of the Convention requires measures to establish jurisdiction and adds: "This Convention does not exclude any criminal jurisdiction exercised in accordance with national law." Similar language occurs in most subsequent international criminal treaties and is an invitation to creativity.

[80] The "cruise ship" cases, such as *United States v. Roberts*, 1 F. Supp. 2d 601 (E.D.La. 1998) and *United States v. Neil*, 312 F.3d 419 (9th Cir.2002) suggest factual patterns that might support "landing state" jurisdiction, especially where the victim is not American. *See also* Michael Plachta, *Proposal for a Convention on Offenses on Board Ships*, 24 INT'L ENF. L. REP. 99 (2008) (discussing proposal by India to International Maritime Organization, *inter alia*, for coastal state jurisdiction, especially of enforcement nature, over offenses against the person committed aboard ships.).

[81] G.A. Res. 45/118, 45 U.N. GAOR, Supp. No. 49A, at 219 (1991).

[82] U.N. Doc. E/CONF. 15 (1988) (ratified by the United States in 1990).

[83] *See, e.g.*, Proliferation Security Initiative Ship Boarding Agreement, United States and Liberia, Art. 5 (weapons of mass destruction) (2004), *available at* http://www.state.gov/t/isn/trty/32403.htm.

person principally responsible for the activity to be regulated, or between that state and those whom the regulation is designed to protect; (c) the character of the activity to be regulated, the importance of regulation to the regulating state, the extent to which other states regulate such activities, and the degree to which the desirability of such regulation is generally accepted; (d) the existence of justified expectations that might be protected or hurt by the regulation; (e) the importance of the regulation to the international political, legal, or economic system; (f) the extent to which the regulation is consistent with the traditions of the international system; (g) the extent to which another state may have an interest in regulating the activity; and (h) the likelihood of conflict with regulation by another state."

In essence, courts are left to examine the appropriateness of the jurisdiction of the State that wishes to proceed, while also weighing issues of comity. Although comity may be relevant, it is not controlling.[84] When the United States has a strong interest in proceeding with the prosecution, this is likely to weigh heavily in finding the jurisdiction reasonable.[85]

§ 2.07 PROCEDURAL ISSUES RELATED TO JURISDICTION

[A] Detainees and Habeas Corpus

Historically, in Anglo-American law, the way for a person deprived of liberty to challenge jurisdiction for the deprivation was through the writ of habeas corpus. Recent years have seen challenges to the writ mounted both by the Executive and Congress. Many of the questions arising here have not as of yet been resolved. Post-September 11th, the United States detained foreign nationals who were captured abroad at Guantanamo Bay Naval Base, Cuba. The government claimed the right to hold these individuals, *inter alia*, pursuant to a joint resolution passed by Congress that authorized the President to use "all necessary and appropriate force against those nations, organizations, or persons he determines planned, authorized, committed, or aided the terrorist attacks . . . or harbored such organizations or persons." Other arguments relied on inherent powers of the President and on his role as Commander-in-Chief. In *Rasul v. United States*,[86] the Supreme Court accepted jurisdiction to determine whether challenges to this detention could be made in the courts.

Petitioners in this case, two Australian citizens and twelve Kuwaiti citizens, were captured abroad and housed at the Naval Base at Guantanamo Bay, along with approximately 640 other non-Americans who were captured abroad.[87] The United States occupies the land at Guantanamo Bay pursuant to a 1903 lease agreement with Cuba. The petitioners, through relatives, filed the action in *Rasul* in the U.S. District Court for the District of Columbia challenging the legality of this detention, claiming that they had not engaged in any terrorist acts against the United States.

---

[84] The Restatement (Third) of the Foreign Relations Law of the United States, § 403, Comment a (1987).

[85] *See, e.g.*, In re Grand Jury Proceedings (Marsoner), 40 F.3d 959 (9th Cir. 1994); United States v. MacAllister, 160 F.3d 1304 (11th Cir. 1998).

[86] 542 U.S. 466 (2004).

[87] *See also* § 7.03, *infra*, for a discussion of United States citizens captured abroad as "enemy combatants."

The District Court dismissed the Petition, finding no basis for jurisdiction. Relying on the decision of *Johnson v. Eisentrager*,[88] the lower court held that "aliens detained outside the sovereign territory of the United States [may not] invoke a petition for a writ of habeas corpus."[89] This decision was affirmed by the Court of Appeals.[90]

The Supreme Court, however, in a decision written by Justice Stevens, distinguished the *Eisentrager* case, finding that petitioners

> are not nationals of countries at war with the United States, and they deny that they have engaged in or plotted acts of aggression against the United States; they have never been afforded access to any tribunal, much less charged with and convicted of wrongdoing; and for more than two years they have been imprisoned in territory over which the United States exercises exclusive jurisdiction and control.[91]

Additionally the Court stated that, "[n]ot only are petitioners differently situated from the *Eisentrager* detainees, but the Court in *Eisentrager* made quite clear that all six of the facts critical to its disposition were relevant only to the question of the prisoners' *constitutional* entitlement to habeas corpus."[92] The Court referenced a later decision to distinguish the holding in *Eisentrager* when it came to a statutory entitlement, in this case under 28 U.S.C. § 2241, which allows district courts to hear habeas claims.[93]

The majority in *Rasul* reversed the lower court, stating that "[w]hat is presently at stake is only whether the federal courts have jurisdiction to determine the legality of the Executive's potentially indefinite detention of individuals who claim to be wholly innocent of wrongdoing." The Court did not, however, consider the merits, remanding it with a finding that jurisdiction exists to hear the matter.

Justice Kennedy, concurring in the decision, adhered to the *Eisentrager* decision, but noted two "critical" ways that the facts here could be distinguished. He stated that "[f]irst Guantanamo Bay is in every practical respect a United States territory, and it is one far removed from any hostilities," and "second" "that the detainees at Guantanamo Bay are being held indefinitely, and without benefit of any legal proceeding to determine their status."[94]

Justices Scalia, Thomas, and Rehnquist dissented, finding that *Eisentrager* controlled and was not negated by the later decision in *Braden v. 30th Judicial Circuit Court of Ky.*,[95] as claimed by the majority. The dissent stated that, "the Court springs a trap on the Executive, subjecting Guantanamo Bay to the oversight of the federal courts even though it has never before been thought to be within their

---

[88] 339 U.S. 763 (1950).

[89] 542 U.S. 466, 472–73 (2004).

[90] *Id.* at 473.

[91] Id. at 476.

[92] *Id.* at 476.

[93] The Court in Braden v. 30th Judicial Circuit Court of Ky., 410 U.S. 484 (1973), held that "that the prisoner's presence within the territorial jurisdiction of the district court is not 'an invariable prerequisite' to the exercise of district court jurisdiction under the federal habeas statute." *Id.* at 2695.

[94] 542 U.S. 466, 478 (2004) quoting from *Braden*, 410 U.S. at 495.

[95] 410 U.S. 484 (1973).

jurisdiction — and thus making it a foolish place to have housed alien wartime detainees."[96]

Following the decision in *Rasul*, Congress included in the Detainee Treatment Act of 2005 a statement that after December 30, 2005, "no court, justice, or judge" shall have jurisdiction to consider the habeas application of a Guantanamo detainee.[97] In *Hamdan v. Rumsfeld*,[98] discussed further in § 2.07[B], a majority of the Court[99] interpreted this legislation as applying only prospectively to habeas petitions filed after it became effective. A vigorous dissent[100] contended that the plain meaning of the amendment made by the 2005 Act to the jurisdictional rules pertaining to habeas corpus was to strip the Court of jurisdiction over all Guantanamo cases, including those already pending. In the Military Commissions Act of 2006, Congress legislated that "[n]o court, justice, or judge shall have jurisdiction to hear or consider an application for a writ of habeas corpus filed by or on behalf of an alien detained by the United States who has been determined by the United States to have been properly detained as an enemy combatant or is awaiting such determination."[101] Making perfectly clear its intentions, Congress added that this amendment "shall take effect on the date of the enactment of this Act, and shall apply to all cases, without exception, pending on or after the date of the enactment of this Act which relate to any aspect of the detention, transfer, treatment, trial, or conditions of detention of an alien detained by the United States since September 11, 2001."[102] This set up a constitutional showdown not just on interpretation, but on whether Congress could strip the Court of jurisdiction in this way. In *Boumediene v. Bush*, a majority decision of the D.C. Circuit Court of Appeals held that the Military Commissions Act had successfully removed common law and statutory rights to habeas corpus and that the legislation did not run foul of the Suspension Clause of the Constitution, Article 1, § 8: "The privilege of the Writ of Habeas Corpus shall not be suspended, unless when in Cases of Rebellion or Invasion the public Safety may require it." Does the legislation amount to a "suspension" of the writ, within the meaning of the Constitution? If it is, it is hard to see how the present situation meets the requirement for "rebellion or invasion." Or is this a situation that can be characterized as merely the legislature determining the jurisdiction of the federal courts?[103] The Supreme Court's decision is pending.

---

[96] 542 U.S. 466, 497–98 (2004).

[97] Detainee Treatment Act of 2005, § 1005.

[98] 126 S. Ct. 2749 (2006).

[99] Justice Stevens, joined by Justices Souter, Ginsburg, Breyer and, on this point, Kennedy. Roberts, C.J., did not participate.

[100] Justices Scalia, Thomas, and Alito.

[101] Military Commissions Act of 2006, § 7(a), amending 28 U.S.C. § 2241.

[102] *Id.* § 7(b).

[103] Art. III, § 1 of the Constitution says that "The judicial Power of the United States, shall be vested in one supreme Court, and such inferior Courts as the Congress may from time to time ordain and establish." Aside from cases where the Supreme Court has original jurisdiction, Art. III, § 2 cl. 2 of the Constitution says that it "shall have appellate Jurisdiction, both as to Law and fact, with such Exceptions, and under such Regulations as the Congress shall make." How much freedom these provisions give Congress over the jurisdiction of federal courts is debated.

[B] Military Commissions

It soon became apparent that the vast majority of those held at Guantanamo would not be subject to criminal prosecution. They would be interrogated and then either released or held indefinitely. With the expectation that some of them would be prosecuted, the President, in 2001, issued an Order concerning "Detention, Treatment and Trial of Certain Non-Citizens in the War Against Terrorism."[104] This Order raised two kinds of jurisdictional issues. In the first place, as to subject-matter, it contemplated trials by military commissions "for any and all offenses triable by military commission." Secondly, it contained the following on personal jurisdiction:

> The term "individual subject to this order" shall mean any individual who is not a United States citizen with respect to whom I [the President] determine from time to time in writing that:
>
> (1) there is reason to believe that such individual, at the relevant times,
>
> (i) is or was a member of the organization known as al Qaeda;
>
> (ii) has engaged in, aided or abetted, or conspired to commit, acts of international terrorism, or acts in preparation therefore, that have caused, threaten to cause, or have as their aim to cause, injury to or adverse effects on the United States, its citizens, national security, foreign policy, or economy, or
>
> (iii) has knowingly harbored one or more individuals described in subparagraphs (i) or (ii) of subsection 2(a)(1) of this order, and
>
> (2) it is in the interest of the United States that such individual be subject to this order.[105]

Membership in Al Qaeda as a jurisdictional hook must be either a universal jurisdiction theory (an "enemy of mankind") or one based loosely on the protection of the United States. The alternative[106] basis about acts "that have caused, threaten to cause, or have as their aim to cause" must be either an effects or a protective theory.[107]

Notable among the procedures that those subject to such trials would have to face was that the accused and his civilian counsel (although not military counsel) could be excluded from the trial and precluded from hearing the evidence against him. Except with prior authorization of the presiding officer, military defense

---

[104] 66 FED. REG. 57833 (Nov.16, 2001), amplified by various Orders of the Department of Defense. On military commissions, *see generally*, Roger S. Clark, *The Military Commissions Act of 2006: An Abject Abdication by Congress*, 5 RUTGERS J. L. & PUB. POL'Y (2008). The 2001 Order, § 7, made the sweeping assertion that with respect to any individual subject to it, "(1) military tribunals shall have exclusive jurisdiction with respect to the offenses by the individual; and (2) the individual shall not be privileged to seek any remedy or maintain any proceedings, directly or indirectly, or have any such remedy or proceedings sought on the individual's behalf, in (i) any court of the United States, or any State thereof, (ii) any court of any foreign nation, or (iii) any international tribunal."

[105] *Id.* § 2.

[106] There is no "and" between (i) and (ii) and they appear to be alternatives.

[107] There are possible constitutional issues in having the executive, rather than the courts, decide some basic jurisdictional issues. *See* § 6.01[C] (exploring the jurisprudential nature of determinations of jurisdiction). The Military Commissions Act of 2006 raises similar issues; it contemplates jurisdiction over "unlawful enemy combatants" who are found to be so by executive procedures of disputed constitutionality.

counsel could not disclose any information presented to a closed hearing. "Appeal" lay to a "Review Panel" of three Military Officers which could include civilians and one of whom was required to have experience as a judge, followed by review to the Secretary of Defense. Final review and decision would lie with the President (unless this function was delegated to the Secretary of Defense).

Salim Ahmed Hamdan, Osama Bin Laden's chauffeur and bodyguard, was charged with one count of conspiracy "to commit . . . offenses triable by military commission" based on his activities between 1996 and November 2001. Hamdan argued, *inter alia*, that the procedures violated basic tenets of military and international law, contained notably in the Uniform Code of Military Justice and the Geneva Conventions of 1949, and that conspiracy was not an offense triable by military commission. A 5-3 majority of the Court agreed with the basic thrust of the argument. It held that, while Congress had acknowledged the propriety of some uses of military commissions, their procedures had to conform to the standards of the laws of war, as contained particularly in Common Article 3 of the 1949 Conventions,[108] and that the procedures for military commissions had to be "uniform as far as possible" with those for courts-martial to which American servicemen are subject. They struck down the Order.[109]

A plurality of the Court (Justices Stevens, Souter, Ginsburg and Breyer with Justice Kennedy finding it unnecessary to decide the point) also addressed the subject-matter jurisdiction issue and concluded that conspiracy was not "among those offenses cognizable by a law-of-war military commission." They insisted that since "the charge does not support the commission's jurisdiction, the commission lacks authority to try Hamdan." The plurality commented that "none of the major treaties governing the law of war identifies conspiracy as a violation thereof. And the only 'conspiracy' crimes that have been recognized by international war crimes tribunals (whose jurisdiction often extends beyond war crimes proper to crimes against humanity and crimes against the peace) are conspiracy to commit genocide and common plan to wage aggressive war, which is a crime against the peace and requires for its commission actual participation in a 'concrete plan to wage war. . . . ' "[110]

Congress adopted the Military Commissions Act 2006 which gave a statutory basis for jurisdiction over essentially the same crimes as those contained in the President's original Order, but with procedures more favorable to the accused. In particular, it is much more difficult to exclude the accused and his civilian counsel from the proceedings. The Act asserts[111] that its provisions "codify offenses that have traditionally been triable by military commission" and because they are "declarative of existing law, they do not preclude trial for crimes [like Hamdan's] that occurred before the date of" enactment. This is debated. Some of the material does, indeed, codify existing military offenses, such as murder and rape of protected persons, attacking civilians, torture, and spying. These offenses are based on provisions in the Hague and Geneva Conventions, although the definitions in the

---

[108] Common Art. 3 requires trial by a "regularly constituted court affording all the judicial guarantees that are recognized as indispensable by civilized peoples."

[109] 126 S. Ct. 2749 (2006).

[110] *Id.* at 2784.

[111] § 950p of Pub. L. No. 109–366, 120 Stat. 2600 (2006) (enacting chapter 47A of title 10 of U.S.C. and amending 28 U.S. C. § 2241).

Act do not track precisely the organization or wording of those treaties.[112] One which is plainly not "traditionally triable by military commission," according to the plurality in *Hamdan*, is the offense of conspiracy which is carried forward into the statute. It is similarly hard to find anything "traditional" about the offenses of "hijacking or hazarding a vessel or aircraft," "terrorism" and "providing material support for terrorism."[113] Offenses against aircraft and vessels are proscribed by widely ratified suppression treaties and perhaps support universal jurisdiction in regular courts under customary law. But the effort to find a comprehensive definition of terrorism is still stalled.[114] Perhaps international law does not prohibit using universal jurisdiction here but whether it goes further and countenances trial by military commission is even more difficult.

This perhaps sets the stage, if the Courts get to the merits of the matter, for a challenge to the legislation based on whether Congress has properly exercised its power in Article I, § 8, cl. 10 of the Constitution to "define and punish . . . Offences against the Law of Nations." What if, as in the case of conspiracy and perhaps the terrorism offenses in the Statute, a judge would be hard-pressed to find those offenses to be "against the Law of Nations" as it currently stands? If *Hamdan* is any guide, the Courts are likely to look at the crimes tried in Nuremberg and Tokyo (war crimes, crimes against peace and crimes against humanity) as indicative of what is appropriate for a *military* trial. Is the legislation simply unconstitutional and *ultra vires* if, despite what Congress says, some crimes are not "traditionally" subject to trial by military commission, and are made retroactive for good measure? Past challenges to statutes based on the argument that Congress did not properly exercise the define and punish power have failed on the merits,[115] but on those occasions the Court was certainly prepared to enter into the discussion.

[C] Military Involvement in Civilian Criminal Matters

Military involvement in criminal matters can raise issues under the Posse Comitatus Act (PCA) which prohibits certain military involvement in civilian law enforcement activities. The statute originates from an 1878 Army Appropriations Act[116] that was intended to stop the military's involvement in aiding civilian law enforcement in matters such as "suppressing illegal whiskey production, quelling labor disturbances, and insuring the sanctity of the electoral process in the South."[117] The Posse Comitatus Act, 18 U.S.C. § 1385, provides for a fine and imprisonment for anyone who "willfully uses any part of the Army or the Air Force

---

[112] *See* George P. Fletcher, *On the Crimes Subject to Prosecution in Military Commissions*, 5 J. Int'l Crim. Just. 39, 40–6 (2007).

[113] The 2007 Manual For Military Commissions which fleshes out the Act adds an element to these crimes that they "took place in the context of and was associated with armed conflict." This narrows the literal breadth of the statute but still leaves it difficult to see how they are "traditionally" subject to trial by commission.

[114] *See* § 7.01[A].

[115] U.S. v. Arjona (customary law obligation to penalize those who counterfeit foreign currency); U.S. v. Smith, 18 U.S. (5 Wheat) 153 (1820) (piracy adequately defined by reference to law of nations); Ex Parte Quirin, 317 U.S. 1 (1942) (laws of armed conflict and military tribunal to try German saboteurs on United States soil).

[116] Army Appropriations Act, ch. 263, § 15, 20 Stat. 145, 152 (1878). *See* Matthew Carlton Hammond, Note, *The Posse Comitatus Act: A Principle in Need of Renewal*, 75 Wash. U. L. Quart. 953 (1997).

[117] *See* United States v. Thompson, 30 M.J. 570 (1990), aff'd, 33 M.J. 218 (1992).

as a posse comitatus or otherwise to execute the laws." There is an exception for those "cases and circumstances expressly authorized by the Constitution or Act of Congress."

Although the Navy and Marines are not specifically listed in the PCA, there is legislation (10 U.S.C. § 375) that precludes their involvement in civilian law enforcement activities. This statute provides for a prohibition against military involvement in law enforcement activities through an authorization to the Secretary of Defense to "prescribe such regulations as may be necessary to ensure that any activity . . . under this chapter does not include or permit direct participation by a member of the Army, Navy, Air Force, or Marine Corps in a search, seizure, arrest, or other similar activity. . . . " Again, it is permitted, however, when "authorized by law." An example of permission being given by Congress is seen in the Maritime Drug Law Enforcement Act that permits the use of Navy equipment and personnel.[118]

Omitted from the PCA and this legislation is the Coast Guard, who have become active players in drug enforcement activities.[119] Also, military personnel who may be performing activities in their private capacity are exempt from PCA mandates.[120] Indirect military assistance is not grounds for a violation of the PCA.[121] When the involvement is directly connected to the military, such as activities of the Naval Criminal Investigative Service (NCAS), it will be subject to PCA restrictions.[122]

More problematic are issues that arise when considering whether activities form an "independent military purpose" that exempts it from the PCA. For example, when military personnel are linked to the criminal activity and the military is conducting the investigation, the PCA has been held inapplicable.[123] If the "primary purpose" is to further "a military or foreign affairs function of the United States," the PCA does not preclude military involvement.[124] Thus, military involvement in the investigation of drug activity on a military base will not be precluded by the PCA as this goes to "maintenance of law and order on a military installation."[125] This has been held to allow for military involvement even when there is both a military and civilian objective, such as an accusation of theft of both civilian and military property.[126]

---

[118] *See* United States v. Rasheed, 802 F. Supp. 312 (D. Hawaii 1992) (citing to 46 U.S.C. App. § 1903).

[119] United States v. Chaparro-Almeida, 679 F.2d 423 (5th Cir. 1982).

[120] *See* United States v. Chon, 210 F.3d 990 (9th Cir. 2000).

[121] In United States v. Kahn, 35 F.3d 426 (9th Cir. 1994), the court used a three part test, as follows, for determining whether the military involvement constituted "indirect assistance." "[1] The involvement must not constitute the exercise of regulatory, proscriptive, or compulsory military power, [2] must not amount to direct active involvement in the execution of the law, and [3] must not pervade the activities of civilian authorities." (cited in United States v. Hitchcock, 286 F.3d 1064, *amended on other grounds*, 298 F.3d 1021 (9th Cir. 2002).

[122] *Id.*

[123] *Id. See also* Applewhite v. United States Air Force, 995 F.2d 997, 1001 (10th Cir. 1993).

[124] DoD Directive 5525.5(A)(2)(a)(5) cited in United States v. Chon, 210 F.3d 990 (9th Cir. 2000).

[125] United States v. Hitchcock, 286 F.3d 1064, *amended on other grounds*, 298 F.3d 1021 (9th Cir. 2002).

[126] United States v. Thompson, 33 M.J. 218 (1992).

PART TWO
SPECIFIC APPLICATIONS

Chapter 3

BUSINESS CRIMES

§ 3.01 GENERALLY

Although there is no recognized category called "business crimes," a host of business activities can become the subject of a criminal prosecution. As one might suspect, business conduct occurring outside the United States can have implications in this country. In many cases, such as those involving fraud, United States prosecutors will use generic statutes, such as mail or wire fraud,[1] as the basis for the prosecution. In other instances, Congress speaks directly to international implications within statutes (e.g., export and import controls).

The applicability of federal statutes to conduct occurring extraterritorially can be the subject of controversy. Two specific business crimes discussed in this chapter demonstrate how Congress can specifically write a statute to include extraterritorial conduct, as in the Foreign Corrupt Practices Act, or alternatively omit this consideration in the statute and leave it for the courts to decide this issue, as in the Sherman (Antitrust) Act.

Some federal statutes apply to both business and non-business types of conduct. For example, the Racketeer Influenced and Corrupt Organization Act (RICO) has been used in prosecutions against corporate officers and also for conduct that would typically be classified as street crime. Issues of extraterritoriality can be raised in these cases, as for example in *United States v. Parness*,[2] where the Second Circuit held that the "enterprise" element of the RICO statute included enterprises outside the United States.

§ 3.02 FOREIGN CORRUPT PRACTICES ACT

[A] History and Purpose

Enacted in 1977, the Foreign Corrupt Practices Act (FCPA) was designed to stop bribery by U.S. companies and individuals of foreign government officials.[3] Under a voluntary disclosure of the Securities and Exchange Commission, "more

---

[1] 18 U.S.C. §§ 1341, 1343.

[2] 503 F.2d 430 (2d Cir. 1974).

[3] 15 U.S.C. §§ 78a, 78dd-1–78dd-3, 78ff.

than 400 companies" admitted making "questionable or illegal payments in excess of $300 million to foreign government officials, politicians, and political parties."[4] The FCPA was intended to stop this type of payments and thus restore the reputation of U.S. companies conducting business abroad.

When initially passed, the FCPA was not welcomed in the business community, as the United States was the lone country with laws against foreign corruption. U.S. companies argued that they were being placed at a "competitive disadvantage" by these statutes.[5] This resulted in two key amendments to the FCPA, one in 1988 and another in 1998. The 1988 amendments "changed the focus of illegality from the status of the recipient to the purpose or nature of the payment."[6] The 1998 amendments came as a result of the 1997 Economic Cooperation and Development Convention on Combating Bribery of Foreign Public Officials in International Business Transactions (OECD Convention) which came into force in 1999.[7] The OECD Convention enlisted other countries to stop bribery of foreign officials. The 1998 amendments to the FCPA (The International Anti-Bribery and Fair Competition Act of 1998) were passed with the goal of having the FCPA conform to the goals of the OECD Convention. The Council of Europe's 1999 Criminal Law Convention on Corruption also contains provisions prohibiting foreign bribery.[8] United States corporations are no longer alone in finding themselves subjected to criminal sanctions when they engage in foreign corruption. There were further provisions on corruption of foreign officials in the 2000 United Nations Convention against Transnational Organized Crime[9] and even tougher ones in the United Nations Convention against Corruption, adopted in 2003.[10] The latter is a state-of-the-art suppression convention that includes sophisticated jurisdictional provisions, obligations concerning laundering of proceeds of crime, mutual legal assistance, extradition, and the liability of legal persons. This package of treaties is very much part of an American agenda.

[B]   Statutes

There are two basic parts to the FCPA. One part contains accounting standards that require record keeping and internal monitoring for companies subject to Securities and Exchange Commission jurisdiction. The second part of the FCPA

---

[4] H.R. 105-802.

[5] H. Lowell Brown, *Exterritorial Jurisdiction Under the 1998 Amendments to the Foreign Corrupt Practices Act: Does the Government's Reach Now Exceed its Grasp?*, 26 N.C. J. INT'L L. & COM. REG. 239 (2001).

[6] DONALD R. CRUVER, COMPLYING WITH THE FOREIGN CORRUPT PRACTICES ACT 20 (2d ed. 1999).

[7] The first international instrument prohibiting bribery of foreign officials was the Inter-American Convention against Corruption, 35 INT'L LEG. MAT. 724 (1996), but the OECD one was aimed at the major economic players. In addition to the United States and Europe, it has been ratified by major United States trading partners such as Korea, Australia, Canada, Chile and New Zealand. On the international developments, *See generally* STUART H. DEMING, THE FOREIGN CORRUPT PRACTICES ACT AND THE NEW INTERNATIONAL NORMS (2005) (discussing international developments). *See also* Peter J. Henning, *Public Corruption: A Comparative Analysis of International Corruption Conventions and United States Law*, 18 ARIZ. JRL. INT'L & COMP. L. 793 (2001).

[8] http://www.usdoj.gov/criminal/fraud/fcpa/intlagree/related/lawconvention.html. The United States signed this in 2000 but has not yet ratified it.

[9] G.A. Res. 55/25, 55 U.N. GAOR, Supp. No. 49, Vol. I at 43, U.N. Doc. A/55/49 (2001), ratified by United States in 2005.

[10] G.A. Res. 58/4, 58 U.N. GAOR, Supp. No. 49 (2004), ratified by the United States in 2006.

prohibits bribery of foreign officials by either an "issuer" or "domestic concern," terms defined in the FCPA.

To proceed on a FCPA prosecution for bribery of a foreign official, it is necessary that the prosecutor prove that the accused: (1) through use of the mails or instrumentality in interstate commerce, (2) corruptly, (3) "in furtherance of an offer, payment, promise to pay, or authorization of the payment of any money, or offer, gift, promise to give, or authorization of giving," (4) anything of value, (5) to a foreign official or political party, (6) in order to assist in securing or retaining business or directing business to any person.[11]

The statute contains an exception for "facilitating and expediting" payments made for "routine governmental action." These are often referred to as "grease payments." The statute defines "routine governmental action" as "only action which is ordinarily and commonly performed by a foreign official in" (1) obtaining permits, licenses or documents for doing business in the country, (2) processing papers such as visas and work orders, (3) "providing police protection, mail pick-up and delivery, or scheduling inspections associated with contract performance or inspections related to transit of goods across country," (4) "providing phone service, power and water supply, loading and unloading cargo, or protecting perishable products or commodities from deterioration," or (5) "actions of a similar nature."[12]

There are also two affirmative defenses in the FCPA. These are for payments that may be lawful "under the written laws and regulations of the foreign" country and for payments that are a "reasonable and bona fide expenditure." "Reasonable and bona fide expenditure(s)" can include travel and lodging expenses as long as they are "directly related to (A) the promotion, demonstration, or explanation of products or services; or (B) the execution or performance of a contract with a foreign government or agency thereof."

The statute provides for substantial fines for companies and the possibility of fines and jail time for individuals. There can also be severe collateral consequences as a conviction may bar a company from doing business with the United States. The collateral consequences to an investigation or conviction can be extremely detrimental to a company.[13] Additionally, the FCPA provides for the imposition of civil penalties. Fines against individuals may not be paid for by the company.[14] Courts have precluded civil litigants from bringing actions under the FCPA.[15]

Many of the FCPA cases[16] are resolved by the Department of Justice (DOJ) using deferred prosecution agreements.[17] These and non-prosecution agreements allow the company to agree to pay a fine and agree to implement certain measures to avoid future criminality in return for the DOJ not prosecuting or holding in abeyance a possible prosecution. After a set period of time, the company is freed of

---

[11] 15 U.S.C. §§ 78dd-1 to 78dd-3.

[12] 15 U.S.C. §§ 78dd-1(f)(3), 78dd-2(h)(4).

[13] Department of Justice, *Lay Person's Guide to the FCPA*, http://www.usdoj.gov/criminal/fraud/docs/dojdocb.html.

[14] 15 U.S.C. § 78dd-2(g), 15 U.S.C. § 78ff(c).

[15] Lamb v. Phillip Morris, Inc., 915 F.2d 1024 (6th Cir. 1990).

[16] *See* White Collar Crime Prof Blog, http://lawprofessors.typepad.com/whitecollarcrimeblog/fcpa/index.html.

[17] *Id.* at http://lawprofessors.typepad.com/whitecollarcrimeblog/deferred prosecution agreements/index.html (discussing deferred prosecution agreements).

the monitoring or restrictions placed upon it by a deferred prosecution agreement. The agreements have become controversial in part because of the selection of monitors, the terms of the agreement,[18] and the lack of judicial oversight in the process.

[C] Who is Liable

Individuals or companies who make payments to a "foreign official, political party, party official, or candidate" can be liable under the FCPA. The term "foreign official" is specifically defined in the statute, and includes officers or employees of a foreign government or their subdivisions. As a result of the 1998 amendments to the FCPA, "foreign official" also includes officers or employees of a public international organization or those acting on behalf of a public international organization. Prosecutions under the FCPA may not be brought against the foreign officials who may have accepted a bribe.

In the case of *United States v. Castle*,[19] federal prosecutors attempted to use the general conspiracy statute, 18 U.S.C. § 371, to charge foreign officials. Charging conspiracy to violate the FCPA, the government indicted two individuals from the United States and two individuals from Canada. The Fifth Circuit court in the *Castle* case adopted the position taken by the district court, and found that the general conspiracy statute could not be used to circumvent the language in the statute. The statute failed to include foreign officials from the list of people subject to prosecution under the FCPA. The court examined the legislative history of the FCPA and noted that there was "overwhelming evidence of a Congressional intent to exempt foreign officials from prosecution for receiving bribes."

Although this statute does not include foreign officials, it does not mean that all foreigners are exempt from prosecution. The 1998 amendments added a new statute, 15 U.S.C. § 78dd-3, which permits prosecution of "non-U.S. nationals" who commit acts within the United States. The amendments also expand the reach of the FCPA to include extraterritorial acts of U.S. nationals and businesses.[20]

Article 16 (3) of the United Nations Convention Against Corruption[21] provides that:

> Each State Party shall adopt such legislative and other measures as may be necessary to establish as a criminal offence, when committed intentionally, the solicitation or acceptance by a foreign public official or an official of a public international organization, directly or indirectly, of an undue advantage, for the official himself or herself or another person or entity, in order that the official act or refrain from acting in the exercise of his or her official duties.

---

[18] Candace Zierdt & Ellen S. Podgor, *Corporate Deferred Prosecutions: Through the Looking Glass of Contract Policing*, 96 KENTUCKY L.J. 1 (2007) (discussing problematic terms in deferred prosecution agreements).

[19] 925 F.2d 831 (1991).

[20] *See* H. Lowell Brown, *Exterritorial Jurisdiction Under the 1998 Amendments to the Foreign Corrupt Practices Act: Does the Government's Reach Now Exceed its Grasp?*, 26 N.C. J. INT'L L. & COM. REG. 239 (2001). In *United States v. Giffen*, 326 F. Supp. 2d 497 (S.D.N.Y. 2004), the Southern District of New York refused to dismiss a FCPA prosecution premised upon the "act of state doctrine" which requires that the U.S. not rule on the "legality or validity" of a foreign sovereign's acts.

[21] *See* § 3.02[A].

This provision is likely to spawn legislative efforts in various countries to take extraterritorial jurisdiction of a kind that is hard to characterize in traditional terms. In *Lotus*, Turkey put forward a theory called "connexity" that gained little traction at the time. The judges dismissed it as merely a principle of joinder in domestic cases, but not applicable as a general principle of international practice. The Turkish theory was that the negligent sailors on the two boats were bonded together in their incompetence, so jurisdiction over the Turkish captain meant jurisdiction over the French officer. Are, for example, a United States briber and a Canadian bribee linked by connexity and thus, given an appropriate statutory basis, capable of being tried together in either country? Subject, perhaps, to considerations of reasonableness, this may well be consistent with the 2003 Convention.

[D] Corruptly

The FCPA requires the government to prove that the defendant acted corruptly. Mere knowledge of a violation of a particular law is not the same as acting corruptly. "Corruptly" has been held to mean "an evil motive or purpose, an intent to wrongfully influence the recipient." Equating the way the term is used in the general bribery statute[22] to how it should be used in the FCPA, one court found that the government does not have to prove that "the defendant in fact knew that his or her conduct violated the FCPA to be guilty of such a violation."[23] That the individual acted with an "evil motive," however, was required.

Whether the accused acted "corruptly" is a question of fact. For example, a jury might find that payment of airline tickets for a foreign official's honeymoon might be considered an act performed "corruptly" if given for the purpose of influencing a government contract.[24]

[E] Nexus

Not all payments to foreign individuals violate the FCPA. It is necessary that there be a nexus between the payments and the action required. Thus, a *quid pro quo* is necessary; the payment needs to be for an intended result.

In the case of *United States v. Kay*,[25] the question arose as to whether payments with indirect benefits violate the FCPA. In *Kay*, the issue was whether alleged "payments made to foreign officials to obtain unlawfully reduced customs duties or sales tax liabilities can ever fall within the scope of the FCPA." The Fifth Circuit stated that the language in the FCPA statute was ambiguous on this issue. The statute failed to provide a clear indication of how closely related the bribe, and the results sought from the bribe, had to be in order for there to be a FCPA violation. The legislative history and intent, however, offered answers.

Looking to the legislative history, the court in *Kay* found that Congress intended a broad reading to include all aspects of foreign bribery. The specific exclusion of "routine government actions" and the inclusion of affirmative defenses

---

[22] 18 U.S.C. § 201.

[23] Stichting Ter Behartiging Van De Belangen Van Oudaandeelhouders In Het Kapitaal Van Saybolt International B.V. (Foundation of the Shareholders' Committee Representing the Former Sharholders of Saybolt International B.V.) v. Schreiber, 327 F.3d 173 (2d Cir. 2003).

[24] United States v. Liebo, 923 F.2d 1308 (8th Cir. 1991). The court in *Liebo*, however, reversed the conviction because of newly discovered evidence.

[25] 359 F.3d 738 (5th Cir. 2004), *appeal on remand*, 513 F.3d 432 (5th Cir. 2007), *denying reh. and reh. en banc*, 513 F.3d 461 (5th Cir. 2008).

for "bona fide expenditures" and payments legal in the host country, led the court to conclude that Congress intended "very limited exceptions to the kinds of bribes" allowed under the FCPA. Although the FCPA would include "payments intended to assist the payor, either directly or indirectly, in obtaining or retaining business for some person," it is still necessary for the prosecution to prove that "the bribery was intended to produce an effect." In the *Kay* case this would mean that the government had to show that the alleged payments to reduce customs and tax liability were intended to "assist in obtaining or retaining business."

§ 3.03 ANTITRUST

The U.S. has become a prominent player in international antitrust enforcement. In 1994, Congress passed the International Antitrust Enforcement Assistance Act that provides for increased mutual assistance in enforcing antitrust matters.[26] In April of 1995 the U.S. Department of Justice and the Federal Trade Commission issued updated "Antitrust Enforcement Guidelines for International Operations."[27] Although some of the antitrust matters pursued are civil matters, others proceed as criminal actions.

The basic criminal antitrust prosecutions are those brought by the Department of Justice under the Sherman Act. These prosecutions are brought despite the fact that the conduct occurs outside the United States. The key requirement to an extraterritorial prosecution is that there be an effect in this country.

In *United States v. Nippon*,[28] the First Circuit Court of Appeals faced the issue of whether it is proper to convict a foreign corporation under the Sherman Act, when the alleged price-fixing activities took place entirely in Japan. The case involved allegations of price-fixing of thermal fax paper. The district court in Nippon had dismissed this antitrust indictment. In reversing the lower court, the appellate tribunal cited to existing precedent that permitted extraterritorial actions in the civil arena. The court looked at issues such as the "difference in strength of presumption,"[29] the "rule of lenity"[30] and whether "international comity" offered a different result than provided in the civil context. The First Circuit concluded that the civil case rulings applied to criminal matters and as such Section One of the Sherman Act applied "to wholly foreign conduct which has an intended and substantial effect in the United States."

In *United States v. Anderson*[31] the Eleventh Circuit examined whether activity constituted a substantial effect on commerce in the United States. The defendant was convicted for his alleged involvement in a bid rigging scheme of Egyptian construction projects that was financed by USAID. In finding sufficient evidence of a substantial effect on domestic commerce, the court noted evidence such as that

---

[26] 15 U.S.C. §§ 6201–6212.

[27] http://www.usdoj.gov/atr/public/guidelines/internat.htm. (There are no later updates.)

[28] 109 F.3d 1 (1997).

[29] The court examined whether the case of United States v. Bowman, 260 U.S. 94 (1923), which placed tougher restrictions on extraterritoriality in the criminal arena, should operate to keep the civil cases from being extended in this criminal matter.

[30] The Rule of Lenity allows for a lenient interpretation toward the accused when the law is ambiguous. This rule, however, only operates when there is ambiguity in the law.

[31] 326 F.3d 1319 (11th Cir. 2003).

"[t]he big-rigging scheme took money from the federal treasury, depriving other projects and services of money," and that the equipment used in the construction projects was from the United States.[32]

§ 3.04 SECURITIES REGULATION

The Securities and Exchange Commission (SEC) enforces the Securities Act of 1933 and the Securities Exchange Act of 1934. The United States prosecution of extraterritorial securities violations is handled by the Department of Justice (DOJ). The International Securities Enforcement Cooperation Act of 1990 assists with these international prosecutions by providing mutual assistance among countries. The U.S. also reaches specific agreements with countries in order to facilitate the process of acquiring information for these prosecutions.

These extraterritorial actions can include questions of whether the U.S. has proper jurisdiction to proceed with the prosecution. Courts have not ruled consistently on the appropriate test to be used for determining exterritorial jurisdiction for securities matters. Some courts focus on the "effects" of the conduct,[33] while others use a "conduct test."[34]

The "effects analysis" looks at the conduct outside the United States to see if it has a "foreseeable and substantial harm to interests in the United States."[35] It can be met "[w]henever a predominately foreign transaction has substantial effects within the United States."[36]

In contrast, the "conduct test" looks at the conduct within the United States. "Under this test, if significant conduct related to a securities fraud occurred in the United States, then a federal court's jurisdiction is established regardless of the victim's nationality."[37] Courts have differed over the "degree to which the American-based conduct must be related causally to the fraud and the resultant harm to justify the application of American securities law."[38] Some courts require that the acts have to "directly cause" harm, where other circuits are less demanding in this nexus requirement.[39]

---

[32] The court in *Anderson* distinguished the conduct from conduct governed by the Foreign Trade Antitrust Improvements Act as this case involved domestic commerce as opposed to foreign commerce. *See also* F. Hoffman-La Roche Ltd. v. Empagran S.A., 542 U.S. 155 (2004). For some remarks supporting "effects" jurisdiction in this area, subject to principles of reasonableness, and even in respect of intended but unrealized effects, *see* The Restatement (Third) of the Foreign Relations Law of the United States, Vol. I, 239 (1987).

[33] Schoenbaum v. Firstbrook, 405 F.2d 200 (2d Cir. 1968).

[34] Kauthar Sdn Bhd v. Sternberg, 149 F.3d (7th Cir. 1998).

[35] *Id.*

[36] *Id.*

[37] Jonathan Shirley, Note, *International Law and the Ramifications of the Sarbanes-Oxley Act of 2002*, 27 B.C. Int'l & Comp. L. Rev. 501 (2004).

[38] Kauthar Sdn Bhd v. Sternberg, 149 F.3d (7th Cir. 1998).

[39] The effect of the extraterritoriality of securities cases in light of the passage of the Sarbanes-Oxley Act of 2002 remains to be seen. *See, e.g.*, Jonathan Shirley, Note, *International Law and the Ramifications of the Sarbanes-Oxley Act of 2002*, 27 B.C. Int'l & Comp. L. Rev. 501 (2004); Minodora D. Vancea, Note, *Exporting U.S. Corporate Governance Standards Through the Sarbanes-Oxley Act: Unilateralism or Cooperation?*, 53 Duke L.J. 833 (2003).

Chapter 4
EXPORT CONTROLS

§ 4.01   GENERALLY

In the United States, there are criminal laws that punish improper conduct related to both imports and exports. In some cases, the statutes are designed to regulate international trade. Other statutes are primarily focused on national security. The Export Administration Act and Arms Export Control Act are predominant players in this latter category. These statutes, as well as the Trading With the Enemy Act, are also tied to United States foreign policy initiatives. The legislation noted in this chapter may also be used to implement United States international obligations, such as economic measures required by the United Nations Security Council.[1]

Although this chapter will focus on statutes related to export controls, it is important to note that there are also a host of statutes on import controls that regulate the entry of commercial goods into the country. For example, the statute titled the "Entry of Goods Falsely Classified" provides criminal penalties to individuals who "knowingly" effect the improper entry of goods, allow goods to enter with improper weight designations, or falsely classify goods.[2] Since the entry of illegal goods can be accompanied by false statements, prosecutors may proceed with charges under specific importation statutes or the generic false statement statute.[3]

Importation statutes also address smuggling crimes.[4] For example, the crime of "smuggling goods into the United States" has been used to stop commercial products from illegally entering the country. Goods may be deemed illegal as a result of an executive order, and courts will determine the legality of the export or import based upon the existing executive order at the time of the offense. Individuals can be charged with the crime of smuggling goods into the U.S., if when the goods arrived in this country it was illegal pursuant to the executive order,

---

[1] *See, e.g.*, Text of the United States 30-day Report for the UN Security Council on Efforts Toward Implementing UNSCR 1718 (measures against North Korea for its nuclear program) (2006) at http://www.state.gov/t/isn/76138.htm.

[2] 18 U.S.C. § 541.

[3] 18 U.S.C. § 1001 (False Statement Statute). *See* United States v. Godinez, 922 F.2d 752 (11th Cir. 1991) (affirming convictions of importing goods in violation of both 18 U.S.C. § 541 and 18 U.S.C. § 1001 for not properly classifying plywood as "dutiable hardwood veneer."). There is also a statute titled, "Entry of Goods By Means of False Statements." 18 U.S.C. § 542.

[4] *See* 18 U.S.C. § 545 (Smuggling Goods into the United States); 18 U.S.C. § 546 (Smuggling Goods into Foreign Countries).

irrespective of the ban later being lifted.[5] There are also statutes that address the importation and exportation of narcotics into the United States.[6]

As with imports, exports are also extensively controlled by the federal government. Several government agencies are involved in export controls, including the Bureau of Industry and Security of the Department of Commerce and the Directorate of Defense Trade Controls of the U.S. State Department. The Department of Justice becomes involved when there is a criminal prosecution for a violation of an export control. In some cases the Department of Justice will bring charges under a host of different export related statutes. For example, a case could have charges for alleged violations of the International Emergency Economic Powers Act (IEEPA), conspiracy to export defense articles without a license, and violations of the Arms Export Control Act (AECA) and the International Traffic in Arms Regulation (ITAR).[7] Many of the export statutes are also included as specified unlawful activity under a key money laundering statute,[8] so money laundering may be an additional charge that the government may use with an export violation. In many cases there can be both civil and criminal penalties for violations of export regulation. For example, there are civil and criminal consequences for failure to adhere to export rules of the Department of Energy, Nuclear Regulatory Commission.[9] Criminal penalties can also attach for violation of antiboycott laws.[10]

§ 4.02 EXPORT ADMINISTRATION ACT

The Export Administration Act[11] provides the Commerce Department with authority over the export of goods and technology for commercial use, and also over items with a dual purpose use of both commercial or military. Although the Export Administration "has been in lapse since April 21, 2001, the system continues through the President's invocation of emergency powers under the International Enemy Economic Powers Act."[12]

The Bureau of Export Administration, renamed in April of 2003 the Bureau of Industry and Security, oversees Export Administration Regulations that provide the "departures, guidelines, and licensing requirements and restrictions."[13] The Act's congressional findings and policy emphasize the need to balance international commerce with national security.[14] They are intended to be used "after full consideration of the impact on the economy" and only to the extent necessary, in three circumstances: (a) when an export would "prove detrimental to national

---

[5] United States v. Hassanzadeh, 271 F.3d 574 (4th Cir. 2001).

[6] *E.g.*, 21 U.S.C. § 952 (Importation of Controlled Substances); 21 U.S.C. § 953 (Exportation of Controlled Substances). *See also* Chapter 6.

[7] White Collar Crime Prof Blog, http://lawprofessors.typepad.com/whitecollarcrime_blog/2008/02/export-controls.html.

[8] 18 U.S.C. § 1956.

[9] 10 C.F.R. § 110.67 (criminal penalties), 10 C.F.R. § 110.64 (civil penalties).

[10] http://www.bxa.doc.gov/ComplianceAndEnforcement/oacrequirements.html.

[11] 50 App. U.S.C. §§ 2401 et. seq.

[12] Bureau of Industry and Security, U.S. Department of Commerce, Export Administration Act, at http://www.bxa.doc.gov/eaa.html.

[13] United States v. Lachman, 278 F. Supp. 2d 68 (D. Mass. 2003), *vacated and remanded on other grounds*, 387 F.3d 42 (1st Cir. 2004).

[14] 50 App. U.S.C. § 2401.

security," (b) "when necessary to further significantly the foreign policy of the United States," and (c) "when necessary to protect the domestic economy from the excessive drain of scarce materials and to reduce the serious inflationary impact of foreign demand."[15]

The Export Administration Regulations provide a "Control List" listed by product category (e.g., telecommunications, navigation and avionics).[16] Export licenses are required for items on the Control List, while a general license is used for other commodities. In contrast to a general license, the export license requires exporters to file a specific license application. Criminal action can be taken against the exporter when he or she knowingly fails to file a license application.

Three elements are the basis for a prosecution under the Export Administration Act: (1) willfulness; (2) violation of the Act or a regulation; (3) "knowledge that the exports involved will be used for the benefit of, or that the destination or intended destination of the goods or technology involved is, any controlled country or any country to which exports are controlled for foreign policy purposes."[17]

Prosecutions brought for violations of the Export Act can involve the issue of whether an item requires a specific export license. This is particularly true in cases involving items that have a dual use of both commercial and military. For example, in *United States v. Shetterly*,[18] the defendant was convicted of attempting to export a controlled microwave amplifier, a device with national security implications. One issue on appeal was whether this item had a value in excess of $5,000 and therefore required an export license. The Seventh Circuit Court of Appeals found that the government presented sufficient evidence of the "net value" exceeding $7,000, and that therefore an export license was required.

Another issue common in these prosecutions is whether the defendant acted willfully and with knowledge. For example, in *United States v. Gregg*,[19] the Eighth Circuit Court of Appeals examined whether the defendant had acted with sufficient *mens rea* to meet the charges. The court found sufficient evidence from which the jury could infer that the defendant knew the destination of an item on the Control List. The inference was substantiated by evidence such as Gregg's having "two sets of paperwork in his possession for the shipment, stating different values."

This is an area where United States regulation runs the risk of coming into conflict with regulation (or non-regulation) of other countries. In a well-known incident in 1982, amendments to the Export Administration Regulations expanded United States controls on the export and re-export of goods and technical data relating to oil and gas exploration, exploitation, transmission, and refinement. The European Communities responded with some hard-hitting "Comments."[20] As well as arguing that the United States should have balanced off its interest against those of the Europeans, the Communities commented: "The European Community considers that the Amendments . . . are unlawful since they cannot be validly based on any of the generally accepted bases of jurisdiction in international law. Moreover, insofar as these Amendments tend to enlist companies whose main ties

---

[15] 50 App. U.S.C. § 2402.

[16] http://w3.access.gpo.gov/bis/ear/ear_data.html (Export Administration Regulations Database).

[17] United States v. Gregg, 829 F.2d 1430 (8th Cir. 1987); 50 App. U.S.C. § 2410.

[18] 971 F.2d 67 (1992).

[19] 829 F.2d 1430 (8th Cir. 1987).

[20] European Communities: *Comments on the U.S. Regulations concerning Trade with the U.S.S.R.*, 21 I.L.M. 891 (1982).

are to the E.C. Member States for the purposes of American trade policy vis-à-vis the U.S.S.R., they constitute an unacceptable interference in the independent commercial policy of the E.C. Comparable measures by third states have been rejected by the U.S. in the past."[21]

§ 4.03 ARMS EXPORT CONTROL ACT

The State Department has the authority to control the commercial export of "munitions." The Arms Export Control Act (AECA) serves as the governing legislation, and it is administrated with regulations of the Directorate Defense Trade Controls (DDTC).[22] The DDTC also controls arms via the International Traffic in Arms Regulations.[23] As with the Export Administration Act, the Arms Export Control Act has a list of controlled items. Here it is called the U.S. Munitions List,[24] and it is a list of "defense articles" that cannot be exported without a license from the State Department. Individuals in the export business are sometimes held to a higher standard of knowing what items are illegal for export under the list.[25] When the United States maintains an arms embargo with a country, a license to export an item on the munitions list may not be obtainable.[26]

Criminal convictions under the Arms Export Control Act require the prosecution to prove that the defendant "(1) willfully, (2) engaged in the business of exporting, (3) defense articles, (4) that are on the United States Munitions List, (5) without a license."[27] The regulations permit punishment for attempts.[28] The items placed on the Munitions List are not subject to judicial review.[29]

In some instances items on the "munitions list" will be exempt from needing a license, as when the export is part of the "Foreign Military Sales Program." These exemptions are outlined in the International Traffic in Arms Regulations.[30]

In the case of *United States v. Sun*,[31] the defense argued that the items in question were exempt under what is termed the "scrap exemption," an exemption contained in commerce department regulations.[32] When "an item which may have been on the Munitions List has been rendered useless beyond the possibility of restoration to its original identity by means of mangling, crushing, or cutting, the item is not subject to the export licensing requirements of the AECA and its implementing regulations." Although the court permitted the defendants to present a defense that the item was under the "scrap exemption," the Fourth Circuit

---

[21] *Id.*, at 904.

[22] 22 U.S.C. §§ 2778–2780.

[23] 22 C.F.R. §§ 120–130.

[24] 22 C.F.R. § 121.

[25] United States v. Sun, 278 F.3d 302 (4th Cir. 2002).

[26] *Id.*

[27] United States v. Murphy, 852 F.2d 1 (1st Cir. 1988) (citing United States v. Beck, 615 F.2d 441 (7th Cir. 1980)).

[28] United States v. Hsu, 364 F.3d 192 (4th Cir. 2004).

[29] 22 U.S.C. § 2778(h).

[30] 22 C.F.R. § 126.6.

[31] 278 F.3d 302 (4th Cir. 2002).

[32] 15 C.F.R. § 770.2(g)(3).

rejected defendant's argument that this was an element of the offense.[33] The court held this to be an affirmative defense.

Defendants have also argued that the Arms Export Control Act is unconstitutionally vague, an argument that courts have rejected as applied to that specific defendant. For example, in *United States v. Hsu*,[34] defendants presented a vagueness argument on appeal from their convictions for violations of the "Arms Export Control Act and related offenses." The Fourth Circuit court rejected defendants' arguments of vagueness, as defendant Hsu had been told by the undercover customs agent that the item in question, an encryption device, required an export license. The court found that there was sufficient notice given here, and thus no due process violation, because the defendants acted "knowingly and willfully." The fact that the notice was given by an undercover agent posing as a sales representative did not implicate vagueness, as the defendant was found to have engaged in conduct "knowing it was illegal."

Often the level of *mens rea* may be a key issue in the case. This is in part because of recent Supreme Court decisions that require knowledge of the illegality when confronted with complex statutes. This was an issue in the case of *United States v. Muthana*,[35] where a defendant was convicted for "knowingly and willfully using an export control document which contained a false statement and omitted a material fact." The evidence was an air waybill which stated that cargo was for "3,086 pounds of honey rather than approximately 56,000 rounds of ammunition."[36] The court required the element of willfulness to include proof of "knowledge of the law," but found the evidence sufficient in this case.[37]

§ 4.04   EXECUTIVE EXPORT RESTRICTIONS AND TRADE EMBARGOS

Restrictions also exist on trade with certain countries. The Trading with the Enemy Act is a key basis for criminal prosecution when an individual trades in violation of executive restrictions. The Treasury Department's Office of Financial Assets Control administers trade restrictions often based upon combating terrorists, narcotics trafficking, and foreign policy concerns.[38] For example, on September 23, 2001, President Bush issued an executive order, "Blocking Property and Prohibiting Transactions With Persons Who Commit, Threaten to Commit, or Support Terrorism."[39] The treasury department provides a list of those individuals that are "specially designated nationals and blocked persons."[40]

As with other export statutes, arguments that often arise in cases under this Act include issues of vagueness, whether the goods are in fact exports, and whether the

---

[33] *Id.*

[34] United States v. Hsu, 364 F.3d 192 (4th Cir. 2004).

[35] 60 F.3d 1217 (7th Cir. 1995).

[36] *Id.*

[37] This standard for willfulness comes from the Supreme Court decision in *Ratzlaf v. United States*, 510 U.S. 135 (1994), and *Cheek v. United States*, 498 U.S. 192 (1991).

[38] http://www.ustreas.gov/offices/eotffc/ofac/.

[39] Executive Order 13224 (Sept. 23, 2001).

[40] http://www.treas.gov/offices/eotffc/ofac/sdn/t11sdn.pdf (January 30, 2008).

accused acted with the required *mens rea*. The timing of the shipment can also be a point of contention when an embargo is later lifted.[41]

---

[41] United States v. Dien Duc Huynh, 246 F.3d 734 (5th Cir. 2001).

Chapter 5

COMPUTER CRIMES

§ 5.01   GENERALLY

Computers add a new dimension to the study of international criminal law. Computer viruses and worms have become prevalent throughout the world, often causing damage in the millions of dollars. Because one does not have to leave his or her home country to commit a computer crime, this form of crime involves significant obstacles for law enforcement. As stated by Former Attorney General Janet Reno, "a hacker needs no passport and passes no checkpoints."[1]

On the national level, the most common statute used for the prosecution of computer crimes is 18 U.S.C. § 1030. Internationally, the Council of Europe's Convention on Cybercrime has been at the forefront of the international initiatives aimed at curtailing cybercrime.

A host of problems arise when considering cybercrime from an international criminal law perspective. These include the questions: (1) what is cybercrime,[2] (2) is it a national, transnational, or international problem,[3] (3) should we examine cybercrime from the perspective of the underlying criminality, such as theft or pornography, or is it a crime that requires unique examination,[4] (4) should the crime determine whether the crime should be one in the national, transnational, or international realm,[5] (5) how does one deal with the procedural issues that accompany cybercrime (e.g. what are the constitutional rights afforded to individuals storing materials on computers), (6) who should prosecute the cybercrime, the country where the keystroke occurs, the country where the harm occurs, or the country through which the computer signal passes, (7) when more than one

---

[1] Keynote Address by U.S. Attorney General Janet Reno on High-Tech and Computer Crime, Delivered at the Meeting of the P-8 Senior Experts' Group on Transnational Organized Crime, Jan. 21, 1997, *available at* http://www.usdoj.gov/criminal/cybercrime/agfranc.htm. This same metaphor was also used in a report of one of the President's working groups. *See The Electronic Frontier: The Challenge of Unlawful Conduct Involving the Use of the Internet*, A Report of the President's Working Group on Unlawful Conduct on the Internet 22 (Mar. 2000) (http://www.usdoj.gov/criminal/cybercrime/unlawful.htm).

[2] Richard W. Aldrich, *Cyberterrorism and Computer Crimes: Issues Surrounding the Establishment of an International Regime*, INSS Ocasional Paper 32 (USAF Institute for National Security Studies, USAF Academy) 11–30 (April 2000) (discussing various international definitions of computer crimes).

[3] Ellen S. Podgor, *Cybercrime: National, Transnational, or International?*, 50 Wayne L. Rev. 97 (2004).

[4] Scott Charney & Kent Alexander, *Computer Crime*, 45 Emory L.J. 931, 934 (1996) (discussing how a computer can be "target of the offense," "tool of the offense," or "incidental to the offense."); Joe D. Whitley & William H. Jordan, *Computer Crime*, ABA White Collar Crime Institute E-1 (2000) (describing how a computer crime can be the "object, subject, or instrument of a crime").

[5] Ellen S. Podgor, *Cybercrime-Cyberterrorism*, 19 Nouvelles Études Pénales 283 (2004).

jurisdiction can prosecute a computer crime, who should have priority?[6] Professor Edward Wise noted the problems with countries becoming "computer crime havens" when he stated that "it seems futile to have laws restricting use of certain kinds of information if their provisions can be circumvented simply by moving the information to a jurisdiction with more lenient rules."[7]

§ 5.02 NATIONAL DIMENSION

18 U.S.C. § 1030 originates from the Counterfeit Access Device and Computer Fraud and Abuse Act of 1984, although there have been several amendments to the statute since its initial passage. The statute contains seven different types of computer criminality including espionage conduct, browsing in a computer, and interstate trafficking of passwords.[8]

Congress extended the reach of section 1030 as part of the "United and Strengthening America by Providing Appropriate Tools Required to Intercept and Obstruct Terrorism Act of 2001" (USA Patriot Act). This statute now allows for the prosecution of extraterritorial conduct. Although the Patriot Act is focused on terrorism, the extraterritorial provision is not limited to computer crimes involving terrorist activity. Rather, it includes all forms of conduct covered by the statute.

Prosecutions of computer criminality are not limited to this statute, and one sometimes finds prosecutions using a general criminal statute such as wire fraud.[9] Prosecutions can also proceed under the Economic Espionage Act of 1996,[10] enacted "against a backdrop of increasing threats to corporate security and a rising tide of international and domestic economic espionage."[11] This Act covers the knowing theft of trade secrets that "will benefit any foreign government, foreign instrumentality, or foreign agent,"[12] and also the conversion of a trade secret that "is produced for or placed in interstate or foreign commerce."[13] The term "trade secret" is defined by statute.[14]

§ 5.03 INTERNATIONAL DIMENSION

There have been cybercrime discussions and reports in both the G-8 and the United Nations. In 1999, the U.N. issued an extensive report titled, *International Review of Criminal Policy — United Nations Manual on the Prevention and Control of Computer-Related Crime*.[15] The topic was also the subject of an

---

[6] *See* Ellen S. Podgor, *International Computer Fraud: A Paradigm for Limiting National Jurisdiction* 35 U.C. — DAVIS L. REV. 267 (2002).

[7] Edward M. Wise, *Computer Crimes and Other Crimes Against Information Technology in the United States*, 64 INT'L REV. OF PENAL LAW 647, 668–69 (1993).

[8] ELLEN S. PODGOR & JEROLD H. ISRAEL, WHITE COLLAR CRIME IN A NUTSHELL 218 (3d ed. 2004).

[9] 18 U.S.C. § 1343.

[10] 18 U.S.C. § 1831 *et. seq.*

[11] United States v. Hsu, 155 F.3d 189 (3d Cir. 1998).

[12] 18 U.S.C. § 1831.

[13] 18 U.S.C. § 1832.

[14] 18 U.S.C. § 1839(3).

[15] UNCJIN, 8th U.N. Congress, Nos. 43 & 44, at 4 (1999), at http://www.uncjin.org/Documents/irpc4344.pdf.

extensive Workshop held at the Eleventh United Nations Congress on Crime Prevention and Criminal Justice held in Bangkok in 2005.[16]

At the forefront of combating cybercrime from an international perspective is the Council of Europe's Convention on Cybercrime. This Convention opened for signature on November 23, 2001, and entered into force on July 1, 2004. The United States (one of several non-European states that participated in the drafting of the Convention) deposited its instrument of ratification late in 2006 and the Convention became applicable to it on January 1, 2007. Given the existing federal statutory framework and several reservations, it was not necessary to adopt new United States legislation to give effect to it. The main objective of the Convention "is to pursue a common criminal policy aimed at the protection of society against cybercrime, especially by adopting appropriate legislation and fostering internal co-operation."[17]

The COE Convention on Cybercrime is a comprehensive document that covers a wide range of computer-related conduct. For example, Articles 2 through 10 contain provisions, typical of suppression conventions, that require the criminalization of the following: illegal access, illegal interception, data interference, system interference, misuse of devices, computer-related forgery, computer-related fraud, offenses related to child pornography and offenses related to infringements of copyright and related rights. Article 11 deals with attempts and aiding and abetting and Article 12 with corporate criminal responsibility (still a controversial issue in some civil law countries). Article 22 of the Convention pertains to jurisdiction. It requires the exercise of territorial jurisdiction (including on ships and aircraft) and nationality jurisdiction. It also requires that parties adopt such measures as are necessary to establish jurisdiction "in cases where the alleged offender is present in its territory and it does not extradite him to another Party, solely on the basis of his or her nationality, after a request for extradition." Finally, it addresses the *Lotus* problem of concurrent jurisdiction: "When more than one Party claims jurisdiction over an alleged offence established in accordance with this Convention, the Parties involved shall, where appropriate, consult with a view to determining the most appropriate jurisdiction for prosecution." No attempt is made, however, to list the criteria that states should take into account. The COE Convention on Cybercrime also covers procedural issues that can arise in combating computer criminality and contains what are often called "mini-treaties" on extradition and mutual legal assistance. An Additional Protocol that concerns the "criminalization of acts of a racist and xenophobic nature committed through computer systems" was opened for signature on January 28, 2003 and came into force in January 2006. Because some of its provisions on suppressing racist and xenophobic speech appear to create First Amendment issues, there is no present effort to proceed with United States signature and ratification.

Generally speaking, the discussion in multilateral forums has related to depredations by non-state actors. There is, however, the possibility that the criminals may be acting in the service of the state and this may become an area for increased concern.[18]

---

[16] *Workshop 6: Measures to Combat Computer-related Crime*, 11th U.N. Congress, U.N. Doc. A/CONF.203/14 (2005).

[17] Convention on Cybercrime, http://conventions.coe.int/Treaty/en/Summaries/html/185.htm.

[18] *See*, Christopher Rhoads, *Cyber Attack Vexes Estonia, Poses Debate*, WALL ST. J., May 18, 2007 (attacks on Estonian Government computers initially attributed to Russian Government); *cf.* Tim Stevens, *20-Year-Old Arrested for Estonian Cyber Attacks*, at http://switched.com/2008/01/25/estonian-

youngster (accused apparently disgruntled with government plan to move Russian statue); Hank
Schouten, *China denies role in NZ cyber attack*, DOMINION-POST, September 12, 2007 (accusations that
China was targeting sensitive computer material in New Zealand, Canada, Britain, Germany, France
and the United States).

Chapter 6
NARCOTICS AND MONEY LAUNDERING

§ 6.01 JURISDICTION FOR NARCOTICS PROSECUTIONS

[A] Jurisdiction Generally

It is not difficult for the United States to secure jurisdiction over extraterritorial narcotics activity, as the illegal conduct affects this country. The Department of Justice routinely prosecutes individuals who are outside the U.S. Individuals from many countries have been charged with various narcotics trafficking crimes.[1]

A variety of different criminal statutes are used for extraterritorial narcotics prosecutions. In some cases the statutes will explicitly provide for extraterritorial prosecutions, as in the statute criminalizing the "possession, manufacture, or distribution of controlled substances."[2] Congress explicitly provided that "[t]his section is intended to reach acts of manufacture or distribution committed outside the territorial jurisdiction of the United States."[3] The statute also sets the venue for these prosecutions as "the point of entry where such person enters the United States, or in the United States District Court for the District of Columbia."

---

[1] http://www.usdoj.gov/criminal/ndds.html (DOJ, Criminal Division, Narcotic and Dangerous Drug Section); http://www.dea.gov/agency/mission.htm (Drug Enforcement Agency, international cooperation).

[2] 21 U.S.C. § 959.

[3] 21 U.S.C. § 959(c).

[B] "Effects" Jurisdiction

Other statutes do not specifically authorize extraterritorial prosecutions, but courts interpret them to allow these prosecutions. For example, in *United States v. Larsen*,[4] the defendant was convicted "for his involvement in an international marijuana smuggling operation" that involved importing shipments of South East Asian marijuana into the United States and distributing it here. The defendant appealed the extraterritorial application of 21 U.S.C. § 841(a)(1), as the marijuana was seized by customs agents from a ship on the high seas outside of Singapore. Using "an intent of Congress/nature of the offense test" the Ninth Circuit joined other circuits that had previously found this statute to have extraterritorial application.[5] The court found this position in keeping with the Supreme Court's *Bowman* decision.[6] There the Court permitted extraterritoriality so as not to "open a large immunity for frauds" that are "as easily committed by citizens on the high seas and in foreign countries as at home."[7]

When a statute does not explicitly provide for extraterritorial jurisdiction, the courts must discern the intent of Congress. A major component in deciding whether there is sufficient jurisdiction is determining whether the connection to the United States produces a sufficient "effect" on this country. This question is the pivotal issue in cases that use an "objective territoriality" approach to satisfy the jurisdiction element.[8] Drug cases, however, are usually found to have a sufficient harm on society to warrant jurisdiction.

More problematic are those cases that do not directly involve drug trafficking, but are tangentially related to this type of conduct. For example, in the case of *United States v. Vasquez-Velasco*,[9] the defendant challenged jurisdiction in a case involving the alleged commission of a violent crime in aid of a racketeering enterprise.[10] He was found guilty of killing two "tourists" in Mexico, one of whom was an American citizen who seemed to have been living there, the other being a United States permanent resident who was visiting his friend south of the border. Even though the case did not involve the murder of a Drug Enforcement Agency (DEA) agent (where protective or passive personality jurisdiction might have been applicable), the case was prosecuted in the United States because the defendant's intent was to "adversely affect DEA activities." The court noted that if the "evidence at trial only suggested that two tourists were randomly murdered, extraterritorial application of § 1959 would be inappropriate." The Ninth Circuit, however, found that the murders in this case were "in retaliation for the DEA's activities in Mexico." As such, jurisdiction in the United States was warranted.

---

[4] 952 F.2d 1099 (9th Cir. 1991).

[5] *See, e.g.*, United States v. Wright-Barker, 784 F.2d 161 (3d Cir. 1986); United States v. Orozco-Prada, 732 F.2d 1076 (2d Cir. 1984); United States v. Arra, 630 F.2d 836 (1st Cir.1980); United States v. Baker, 609 F.2d 134 (5th Cir. 1980).

[6] *See* § 2.02[B].

[7] 952 F.2d 1099 (9th Cir. 1991).

[8] *See* § 2.04[A][2].

[9] 15 F.3d 833 (9th Cir. 1994).

[10] 18 U.S.C. § 1959.

[C] Questions of Law?

Are issues of jurisdiction primarily issues of law or fact? Who should decide jurisdiction questions? These questions arose under the Maritime Drug Law Enforcement Act until Congress amended the statute to add language that provided that "[a]ll jurisdictional issues arising under this chapter are preliminary questions of law to be determined solely by the trial judge."[11] It will be recalled that the Model Penal Code treats jurisdiction as one of the elements of a crime, and thus subject to proof beyond reasonable doubt.[12] The United States Supreme Court has required elements to be proved beyond a reasonable doubt,[13] so there may be some potential grounds for arguing for the right to a jury trial on at least some of the factual issues relating to whether extraterritorial jurisdiction should apply in particular instances.[14]

[D] Role of the Coast Guard

Some narcotics investigations occur off shore, with the assistance of the Coast Guard. Although the military is prohibited from participating in law enforcement activities under the Posse Comitatus Act,[15] this does not extend to the Coast Guard.[16] Therefore, the Coast Guard is an active player in narcotics enforcement activities that occur in the waters surrounding the United States.[17]

One issue that has proved controversial in cases alleging violations of the Maritime Drug Law Enforcement Act (MDLEA) is the Coast Guard's practice of boarding a "stateless vessel" in international waters. When a defendant, who is apprehended on the high seas, is flying under the flag of another country, courts have required a nexus between the defendant and the United States.[18] In contrast, however, courts have held that there is no need to prove this nexus when the vessel is stateless.[19] As stated by one court, "[b]ecause stateless vessels do not fall within the veil of another sovereign's territorial protection, all nations can treat them as their own territory and subject them to their laws."[20]

---

[11] 46 App. U.S.C. § 1903(f).

[12] Model Penal Code § 1.13 (1962) (including "attendant circumstance[]" that "establishes jurisdiction" in definition of elements of a crime); State v. Denofa, 187 N.J. 24 (2006) (same, interpreting New Jersey version of MPC). On the other hand, jurisdictional elements are not "material" elements within the MPC definition, so there is no need to prove *mens rea* in respect of them.

[13] *See* In re Winship, 397 U.S. 358 (1970), Apprendi v. New Jersey, 530 U.S. 466 (2000) and their progeny.

[14] Consider, for example, the situation in United States v. Gonzalez, 776 F.2d 931 (1985), discussed in § 2.04[D]. If there is a dispute about whether there was really an "arrangement" with Honduras, why is that not at least a mixed question of fact and law and open to a jury finding?

[15] 18 U.S.C. § 1385.

[16] *See* § 2.06[B].

[17] United States v. Chaparro-Almeida, 679 F.2d 423 (5th Cir. 1982); *see also* 14 U.S.C. §§ 2,141 (Coast Guard given authority to assist law enforcement).

[18] *See, e.g.*, United States v. Davis, 905 F.2d 245 (9th Cir. 1990). The nexus, however, may be quite attenuated in transferred jurisdiction cases, such as those discussed in § 2.05.

[19] *See* United States v. Moreno-Morillo, 334 F.3d 819, 828 n.6 (9th Cir. 2003).

[20] United States v. Caicedo, 47 F.3d 370, 373 (9th Cir. 1995).

§ 6.02 INTERNATIONAL NARCOTICS TRAFFICKING

There have been national and international efforts to curtail international narcotics trafficking. In the United States, in addition to the Drug Enforcement Agency (DEA) which is actively involved in efforts to stop international narcotics trafficking,[21] the State Department also plays a major role in "narcotics control and anti-crime assistance to foreign countries."[22]

[A] National Prosecutions

International narcotics trafficking is prosecuted in the United States through laws that explicitly allow for extraterritorial prosecutions[23] and through judicial approval of prosecutions of conduct occurring outside the United States. Additionally, Congress passed The Foreign Narcotics Kingpin Designation Act in 1999 which "provide[s] authority for the identification of, and application of, sanctions on a worldwide basis to significant foreign narcotics traffickers, their organizations, and the foreign persons who provide support to those significant foreign narcotics traffickers and their organizations, whose activities threaten the national security, foreign policy, and economy of the United States."[24] The first list of drug kingpins was issued on June 2, 2000, by President Clinton and subsequent lists have come from the White House in what now seems to be an annual June ritual.[25]

[B] International Cooperation

The cooperation of nations in combating drug activity can be traced to early conventions such as the International Opium Convention of 1912.[26] More recently, four international conventions have focused on international drug trafficking. These are the Single Convention on Narcotics Drugs, March 30, 1961;[27] the Convention on Psychotropic Substances, February 21, 1971;[28] the Protocol Amending the Single Convention on Narcotics Drugs, March 25, 1972;[29] and the United Nations [Vienna] Convention Against Illicit Traffic in Narcotic Drugs and Psychotropic Substances, December 20, 1988.[30] Andreas and Nadelmann comment

---

[21] DEA Dismantles International Drug Ring — Nine Month Investigation Brings Down Heroin and Cocaine Traffickers, DEA News Release, June 12, 2002, http://www.usdoj.gov/dea/pubs/pressrel/pr061202.html (discussing the arrest of twenty-five individuals after a nine month investigation by several DEA offices outside the United States).

[22] Annually, the State Department releases a report describing the "efforts of key countries to attack all aspects of the international drug trade." http://www.state.gov/g/inl/rls/nrcrpt/2003/ index.htm.

[23] 21 U.S.C. § 959(c).

[24] 18 U.S.C. § 1902.

[25] See, e.g., http://www.whitehouse.gov/news/releases/2007/06/20070601-23.html (2007 Presidential Designation).

[26] 8 L.N.T.S. 187. After its establishment, the League of Nations assumed functions under this treaty which were in turn taken over by the United Nations in 1946.

[27] 520 U.N.T.S. 151.

[28] 1019 U.N.T.S. 175.

[29] 976 U.N.T.S. 3.

[30] U.N. Doc. E/CONF.82/15, Corr.1 and Corr. 2. (1988). The 1988 Convention supplements, and in some cases supersedes, provisions of the earlier treaties. Art. 25 of the 1988 Convention states: "The

that "[t]he production, sale, and even possession of cannabis, cocaine, and most opiates, hallucinogens, barbiturates, amphetamine, and tranquillizers outside strictly regulated medical and scientific channels are now punished with criminal sanctions in virtually every nation."[31] They add that "[t]he processes by which this regime has evolved must be understood as a confluence of the perceptions, interests and moral notions among dominant sectors of the more powerful states, along with the exceptional influence of American protagonists in shaping the regime according to their preferred norms."[32] The "legislative" success of the program is stark: with 183 parties early in 2008, the 1988 Convention is more widely ratified than most major human rights treaties, including the Convention against Torture (145), the Genocide Convention (140), the Covenant on Economic, Social and Cultural Rights (157), and the Covenant on Civil and Political Rights (160), or, indeed most suppression treaties, including those in the area of terrorism.

The 1988 Convention contains comprehensive provisions on jurisdiction, including territorial (and flag state), effects and nationality theories. In addition, parties must take such measures as are necessary to establish jurisdiction when extradition is refused on the basis that the offense has been committed on its territory or one of its aircraft or vessels, or that the offense has been committed by one of its nationals.[33] There is also what can best be described as "optional fallback jurisdiction."[34] That is to say, a state *may* also take measures to establish its jurisdiction over the Convention offenses generally "when the alleged offender is present in its territory and it does not extradite him to another Party."[35] It also contains provisions designed to facilitate (optional) transfers of jurisdiction, either in respect to offenses on vessels[36] and more generally.[37] Given that drug trafficking activity typically passes through several countries, there is always the possibility of concurrent jurisdiction in various places. Transfer of parts of a complex case to a single jurisdiction may be a useful way to coordinate and consolidate. The Convention also includes "mini" extradition and mutual legal assistance provisions designed to encourage international cooperation. Article 11 of the Convention contains what, at the time, were seen in many countries as radical provisions on "controlled delivery." That is "the technique of allowing illicit or suspect consignments . . . to pass out of, through or into the territory of one or more countries, with the knowledge and under the supervision of their competent authorities, with a view to identifying persons involved in the commission of offences. . . . " As the official Commentary on the Convention[38] notes: "Article 11

---

provisions of this Convention shall not derogate from any rights enjoyed or obligations undertaken by Parties to this Convention under the 1961 Convention, the 1961 Convention as amended and the 1971 Convention." *See* United Nations, Commentary on the United Nations Convention against Illicit Traffic in Narcotic Drugs and Psychotropic Substances, 1988 at 393–96 (1998).

[31] Peter Andreas & Ethan Nadelmann, Policing the Globe: Criminalization and Crime Control in International Relations 38 (2006).

[32] *Id.*

[33] United Nations [Vienna] Convention Against Illicit Traffic in Narcotic Drugs and Psychotropic Substances, December 20, 1988, Art. 4(2)(a).

[34] *See* discussion of "fallback" or "subsidiary" jurisdiction in § 2.04[E].

[35] *Id.*, Art. 4(2)(b).

[36] *Id.*, Art. 17. *See also* § 2.05.

[37] *Id.*, Art. 8. *See also* § 2.05.

[38] United Nations, Commentary on the United Nations Convention against Illicit Traffic in Narcotic Drugs and Psychotropic Substances, 1988 at 235 (1998).

was the first international text to endorse the practice of controlled delivery. The earlier tradition, reflected, for example, in the 1961 Convention, was to emphasize the seizure of drugs, if not positively to require their seizure. . . . " A final notable feature of the Convention is a balanced provision that requires both measures to eradicate illicit cultivation of narcotic plants and measures to "eliminate" illicit demand for narcotic drugs and psychotropic substances. At a Special Session in 1998, the United Nations General Assembly followed up the demand reduction provisions of the 1988 Convention with a Declaration on the Guiding Principles of Drug Demand Reduction.[39]

The Commission on Narcotic Drugs, established by the Economic and Social Council in a 1946 resolution, serves as the "central policy-making body within the United Nations system dealing with drug-related matters." "[T]he Commission assists the Council in supervising the application of international conventions and agreements dealing with narcotic drugs."[40] The United Nations Office of Drugs and Crime, located in Vienna, provides the necessary secretariat for the program. It describes itself as "mandated to assist Member States in their struggle against illicit drugs, crime and terrorism." It notes that "In the Millenium Declaration, Member States . . . resolved to intensify efforts to fight transnational crime in all its dimensions, to redouble the efforts to implement the commitment to counter the world drug problem and to take concerted action against international terrorism."[41]

§ 6.03 MONEY LAUNDERING

[A] Generally

Money laundering crimes, when originally enacted, were designed to curtail the concealment of proceeds from drug activity.[42] These activities are not limited to the United States, and often involve individuals in other countries.[43]

The key money laundering statutes in the United States are 18 U.S.C. §§ 1956 and 1957. Both statutes permit extraterritorial prosecutions, but limit the circumstances when an extraterritorial prosecution will be allowed.[44] For example, in the case of a prosecution under 18 U.S.C. § 1956, extraterritorial jurisdiction exists if the conduct is by a United States citizen or if by other than a United States citizen, the "conduct occurs in part in the United States." Further, the "transaction or series of related transactions must involve funds or monetary instruments of a value exceeding $10,000."[45]

Additionally, the Department of Justice requires that prosecutors receive formal approval from the Criminal Division's Asset Forfeiture and Money

---

[39] *See* http://www.unodc.org/pdf/resolution_1998-09-08_1.pdf. "Reduction" is probably more realistic than "elimination."

[40] *See* http://www.unodc.org/unodc/en/cnd_mandate.html.

[41] *See* http:/ / www. unodc.org/unodc/en/about-unodc/index.html.

[42] Trujillo v. Banco Central Del Ecuador, 35 F. Supp. 2d 908, 913 (S.D. Fla. 1998).

[43] *See* United States v. Gurolla, 333 F.3d 944 (9th Cir. 2003) (Operation Casablanca was an international undercover drug investigation that lead to the indictment of international defendants for crimes such as money laundering).

[44] 18 U.S.C. § 1956(f); 18 U.S.C. § 1957(d).

[45] 18 U.S.C. § 1956(f).

Laundering Section prior to commencing an investigation into extraterritorial money laundering conduct. The rationale here is to allow higher authorities to consider the "potential international sensitivities, as well as proof problems" that emanate from these types of investigations and prosecutions.[46]

[B] White Collar Crime Cases

In recent years, prosecutions under these money laundering statutes have extended beyond drug activity with indictments being brought when the conduct involves white collar types of activity.[47] For example, in the case of *United States v. Tarkoff*,[48] the defendant, an attorney, was convicted of conspiring to violate and violating the money laundering statute[49] for his alleged involvement in "conceal[ing] or disguis[ing] the nature, the location, the source, the ownership, or the control of the proceeds of specified unlawful activity," namely funds related to fraudulent billing of Medicare by one of his clients.

In affirming the conviction against Attorney Tarkoff, the Eleventh Circuit rejected arguments that his conviction should not stand because it was premised on conduct that "occurred wholly outside the United States." The court distinguished this case from another money laundering case, *United States v. Kramer*,[50] where an extraterritorial prosecution was reversed because there was no showing of a transfer of funds to or from the United States.

The Eleventh Circuit in *Tarkoff* held that the Kramer decision was not controlling here "because Tarkoff was convicted under a different subsection of the money laundering statute (§ 1956(a)(1)(B)(i)) than the one at issue in *Kramer*." In *Kramer*, the subsection of the money laundering statute used for prosecution required "a transfer of funds to or from the United States." In contrast, in the *Tarkoff* case, the government need only prove that the defendant was involved in a "financial transaction" "that was engaged in, or the activities of which affected, interstate or foreign commerce *in any way or degree*."[51] Thus, because the government did not proceed under what is normally considered the international provisions of the money laundering statute,[52] there was no need to prove the elements provided for in that aspect of the statute.

[C] Money Laundering Prosecution to Combat Terrorism

Money laundering law has also been used as a means to defeat terrorist activity. The "Uniting and Strengthening America by Providing Appropriate Tools Required to Intercept and Obstruct Terrorism Act of 2001" (USA Patriot Act) provided additional provisions focused on money laundering. Title III of the Patriot Act is titled the *"International Money Laundering Abatement and Anti-Terrorist Financing Act of 2001."* In addition to having new reporting

---

[46] U.S. Attys. Manual 9-105.300.

[47] Teresa E. Adams, Note, *Tacking on Money Laundering Charges to White Collar Crimes: What Did Congress Intend and What Are the Courts Doing*, 17 GA. ST. U. L. REV. 531 (2000).

[48] 242 F.3d 991 (11th Cir. 2001).

[49] 18 U.S.C. § 1956(h) and (a)(1)(B)(i).

[50] 73 F.3d 1067 (11th Cir. 1996).

[51] 242 F.3d 991, 995.

[52] 18 U.S.C. § 1956(a)(2).

requirements, this portion of the Patriot Act calls for cooperation to deter money laundering.[53]

[D] International Cooperation

In recent years there has been significant international cooperation in combating money laundering and, in particular, encouraging search, seizure and confiscation of illicit funds.[54] For example, the Financial Action Task Force (FATF),[55] an inter-governmental body, issued forty recommendations on how to strengthen international cooperation in money laundering. Over 130 countries endorsed these recommendations. These recommendations were reviewed and revised in 2003.[56] The new recommendations include nine "Special Recommendations" regarding financing of terrorist activities.

One also finds money laundering provisions in the 1988 United Nations Convention Against Illicit Traffic in Narcotic Drugs and Psychotropic Substances, in the 2000 United Nations Convention Against Transnational Organized Crime and in the United Nations Convention against Corruption of 2003. The first recommendation of the FATF is that countries "should criminalize money laundering on the basis of the . . . " United Nations Conventions of 1988 and 2000.[57] As was the case at the domestic level, drug crimes were initially the only predicate offenses that brought the ancillary laundering offenses into play at the international level. With the later conventions, transnational organized crime in general and official corruption provide additional possibilities for the source of illicit funds that may lead to laundering prohibitions. In Vienna, the Anti-Money Laundering Unit of the United Nations Office of Drugs and Crime endeavors to implement the Global Program against Money Laundering which was established in 1997 as a followup to the 1988 Drug Convention. The Unit's mandate was strengthened the next year by the Political Declaration and Action Plan against Money Laundering adopted by a Special Session of the General Assembly. The program seeks to strengthen the capacity of states to implement measures in anti-money laundering and countering the financing of terrorism.

At the regional level, the Council of Europe's 1990 Convention on Laundering, Search, Seizure and Confiscation of the Proceeds from Crime[58] offers a broad basis for criminalization and cooperation in respect of a broad range of offenses. All Members of the Council of Europe and Australia are parties to it, but not the United States. On May 16, 2005, the Council opened for signature and ratification its Convention on Laundering, Search, Seizure and Confiscation of the Proceeds from Crime and the Financing of Terrorism.[59] It extends the predicate acts on

---

[53] "Uniting and Strengthening America by Providing Appropriate Tools Required to Intercept and Obstruct Terrorism Act of 2001" (USA Patriot Act) §§ 314, 318.

[54] *See* William M. Hannay & John A. Hedges, *International Trends in the Criminalization of Money Laundering*, INTERNATIONAL TRADE: AVOIDING RISKS 5-12 to 5-22 (W.M. Hannay ed. 1991).

[55] The FATF states as its purpose "the development and promotion of policies to combat money laundering." http://www.oecd.org/fatf/recommendations.htm.

[56] http://www1.oecd.org/fatf/pdf/40Recs-2003_en.pdf.

[57] http://www1.oecd.org/fatf/40Recs_en.htm.

[58] http://conventions.coe.int/Treaty/Commun/QueVoulezVous.asp?NT=141&CM=7&DF=2/5/2008&CL=ENG.

[59] http://conventions.coe.int/Treaty/Commun/QueVoulezVous.asp?NT=198&CM=7&DF=2/5/2008&CL=ENG.

which the laundering provisions are based to the financing of terrorism.[60] It had the necessary six ratifications to bring it into force by January 2008. Over time, it will replace the 1990 Convention.

§ 6.04 CURRENCY TRANSACTION REPORTS

Currency Transaction Reports (CTRs) have also been used as a means of combating drug trafficking. By requiring banks[61] and other entities[62] to file reports when cash funds are received, the government can trace funds that might be laundered as a result of drug activity. Title III of the Patriot Act, *The International Money Laundering Abatement and Anti-Terrorist Financing Act of 2001*, extended the reach of the currency reporting statutes.

For example, the Patriot Act created a new crime for bulk cash smuggling into and outside the United States. It is likely that this new crime will defeat the Supreme Court's decision in *United States v. Bajakajian*,[63] where the Court refused to permit a forfeiture of $357,144 that the accused failed to declare when leaving the United States. Although federal law required that he report transporting more than $10,000 in cash, the Court held that the forfeiture of the entire undeclared amount was a violation of the Excessive Fines Clause of the Eighth Amendment as "grossly disproportional to the gravity of his offense." The new bulk cash smuggling crime in the Patriot Act states as its purposes "to make the act of smuggling bulk cash itself a criminal offense," and "to emphasize the seriousness of the act of bulk cash smuggling."[64]

---

[60] In this respect it also enhances compliance with S. C. Res. 1373 (2001) on terrorist financing and the 1999 International Convention for the Suppression of the Financing of Terrorism, G.A. Res. 54/109 (1999).

[61] The Bank Secrecy Act was "designed to obtain financial information having 'a high degree of usefulness in criminal, tax, or regulatory investigations or proceedings.' " California Bankers Association v. Shultz, 416 U.S. 21 (1974).

[62] 26 U.S.C. § 6050I requires reporting of certain money transactions by "trades or businesses."

[63] 524 U.S. 321 (1998).

[64] "Uniting and Strengthening America by Providing Appropriate Tools Required to Intercept and Obstruct Terrorism Act of 2001" (USA Patriot Act) § 371.

Chapter 7
PIRACY AND TERRORISM

SYNOPSIS

§ 7.01 TERRORISM GENERALLY

[A] Definition

Terrorism is not an easily defined term, although what is considered terrorist activity is often evident.[1] In the United States, terrorism is defined broadly to include a wide array of activity.[2] 18 U.S.C. § 2332(b)(5) provides the contours for the "federal crime of terrorism" by providing first that it "means an offense that" "is calculated to influence or affect the conduct of government by intimidation or coercion, or to retaliate against government conduct."[3] The second prong of the definition requires that it be in violation of one of the many statutes specifically listed in section 2332(b)(5)(B). One finds a host of statutes that can be a predicate for a terrorism charge, including "relating to violence at international airports,"[4] "relating to chemical weapons,"[5] and "relating to wrecking trains."[6]

Although there are many multilateral anti-terrorism agreements dealing with specific manifestations of the phenomenon,[7] there is no established comprehensive

---

[1] *See generally* Nicholas J. Perry, *The Numerous Federal Legal Definitions of Terrorism: The Problem of Too Many Grails*, 30 J. Legis. 249 (2004).

[2] *See* 18 U.S.C. § 2332b (2002) (Acts of Terrorism Transcending National Boundaries).

[3] Terrorism is also defined or used in other parts of the criminal code. Many of the definitions have been modeled after the definition provided in the Foreign Intelligence Surveillance Act (FISA). Nicholas J. Perry, *The Numerous Federal Legal Definitions of Terrorism: The Problem of Too Many Grails*, 30 J. Legis. 249, 256 (2004). For example, "terrorist activities" is defined in immigration laws in discussing "inadmissible aliens." (8 U.S.C. § 1182(a)(3)(B)(iii)). *Id.* at 261.

[4] 18 U.S.C. § 37.

[5] 18 U.S.C. § 229.

[6] 18 U.S.C. § 1992.

[7] *See, e.g.*, Hague Convention for the Suppression of Unlawful Seizure of Aircraft, Dec. 16, 1970, 22 U.S.T. 1641, T.I.A.S. No. 7192, 860 U.N.T.S. 105; Montreal Convention for the Suppression of Unlawful Acts Against the Safety of Civil Aviation, Sept. 23, 1971, 24 U.S.T. 564, T.I.A.S. No. 7570, 974 U.N.T.S. 177; International Convention Against the Taking of Hostages, Dec. 17, 1979, T.I.A.S. No. 11081, 18 I.L.M. 1456 (1979); International Convention for the Suppression of Terrorist Bombings, Jan. 9, 1998, 37 I.L.M. 249 (1998); International Convention for the Suppression of Financing of Terrorism, December

international definition of terrorism.[8] For example, there are agreements regarding the seizure of aircraft[9] and the protection of nuclear materials.[10] Such specialized agreements underscore the understanding that, no matter how worthy the cause, there are some violent ways of achieving it that simply cannot be justified. Thus, the international community, through the United Nations and its associated organizations dealing with activities such as air and sea transport and regulation of nuclear materials, is entitled to work cooperatively to suppress such conduct. The United Nations family of organizations, however, has not been successful in providing a definition acceptable to all countries.

The main reason for trying to find an acceptable definition is so that it might be incorporated in a suppression convention describing what it is that must be dealt with through the criminal processes. A draft Comprehensive Convention on International Terrorism has been on the table at the United Nations since 2002.[11] The basic definition of the draft says that a person:

> commits an offence within the meaning of this Convention if that person, by any means, unlawfully and intentionally, causes: (a) death or serious bodily injury to any person; or (b) serious damage to public or private property, including a place of public use, a State or government facility, a public transportation system, an infrastructure facility or the environment; or (c) damage to property, places, facilities, or systems referred to in [(b)], resulting or likely to result in major economic loss, when the purposes of the conduct, by its nature or context, is to intimidate a population, or to compel a Government or an international organization to do or abstain from doing any act.

As a generic definition to fill in the cracks in existing terrorism suppression treaties, this seems to catch the essence of the problem. The twin sticking points on the way to successful conclusion of the negotiations involve the inclusion or exclusion, as the case may be, of violent acts committed by Governments (whether in armed conflict or in "law enforcement") and those committed by Liberation Movements as part of an armed struggle. Notwithstanding the failure to agree upon what exactly the concept is, the General Assembly has come out unequivocally against it and has devised strategies for the organization and capacity building for Member States in efforts to eliminate it.[12] At the same time, the Assembly has insisted on "protecting human rights and fundamental freedoms while countering terrorism."[13]

9, 1999, 39 I.L.M. 270 (2000); International Convention for the Suppression of Acts of Nuclear Terrorism, April 13, 2005, G.A. Res. 59/290 (2005).

[8] *See generally* CHRISTOPHER L. BLAKESLEY, TERRORISM, DRUGS, INTERNATIONAL LAW, AND THE PROTECTION OF HUMAN LIBERTY (1992); TAL BECKER, TERRORISM AND THE STATE: RETHINKING THE RULES OF STATE RESPONSIBILITY (2006); WAYNE MCCORMACK, UNDERSTANDING THE LAW OF TERRORISM 19–24 (2007).

[9] Hague Convention for the Suppression of Unlawful Seizure of Aircraft, Dec. 16, 1970, 22 U.S.T. 1641, T.I.A.S. No. 7192, 860 U.N.T.S. 105.

[10] Convention on the Physical Protection of Nuclear Materials, Mar. 3, 1980, I.A.EA. Legal Series No. 12 (1982), 18 I.L.M. 1419 (1979).

[11] *See* Report of the Ad Hoc Committee established by General Assembly resolution 51/210 of 17 December 1996, Sixth Session (28 January–1 February 2002), GAOR, 57th Sess., Supp. No. 37, U.N.Doc. A/57/37 (2002) (contains draft text).

[12] *See, e.g.*, United Nations Global Counter-Terrorism Strategy, G.A. Res. 60/288 (2006).

[13] G.A. Res. 60/158 (2005). In 2005, the United Nations created the post of "Special Rapporteur on the promotion and protection of human rights and fundamental freedoms while countering terrorism" in order to dramatize the need to protect human rights at the same time as opposing terrorism.

Meanwhile, the Security Council has entered the area and required states to take action to criminalize provision or collection of funds for terrorist entities,[14] to prohibit activities with weapons of mass destruction[15] and to adopt measures to prohibit by law incitement to terrorist acts and to deny safe haven to those believed to be guilty of such conduct.[16] Monitoring Committees have been set up to enforce the Council's mandates. The power of the Security Council to engage in such general "legislative" work, as opposed to dealing with particular situations under its powers over international peace and security conferred by Chapter VII of the Charter, is being debated.[17]

It has been suggested, moreover, that there is a "dark side" to the Council's efforts. Professor Alvarez writes:

> At the same time, the human rights problems posed by the Council's own listing of alleged terrorists and their supporters are beginning to get attention. Consider what happens in practice. The Security Council announces to the world that "Mohamed Z" is on its 1267 list. At a minimum, Mohamed cannot draw on his bank account, he loses government benefits, and is barred from interstate travel. In the normal case, he and sometimes his spouse also lose their jobs. Mohamed's children, now the sons and daughters of someone who the "international community" has identified as at least "associated with terrorism" may be hounded from school. The entire Mohamed family may be ostracized from the community. All of this occurs, in the usual case, without anyone in the Mohamed family being charged with a crime, at either the national or the international level.[18]

In agreeing to assist the Security Council in its endeavors, the International Criminal Police Organization (Interpol) has insisted in response to problems such as these that there be procedures to protect the human rights of those in respect of whom information is processed by Interpol at the request of the Security Council.[19]

[B] Terrorism Laws in the U.S.

Post September 11, terrorism has been a priority in the United States. This can be seen in the passage of the "Uniting and Strengthening America by Providing Appropriate Tools Required to Intercept and Obstruct Terrorism Act of 2001" (USA Patriot Act)[20] and creation of a Homeland Security Office.[21] Terrorism laws, however, are not all of recent vintage. For example, a modern prosecution made use of "sedition conspiracy,"[22] under a statute dating back to the Civil War.[23]

---

[14] S.C. Res. 1373 (2001).

[15] S.C. Res. 1540 (2004).

[16] S.C. Res. 1624 (2005).

[17] *See* Axel Marschik, *Legislative Powers of the Security Council*, in Towards World Constitutionalism 457 (Ronald St. John Macdonald & Douglas M. Johnston eds, 2005).

[18] Jose Alvarez, *The "Dark Side" of the UN's War on Terrorism*, in Abuse: The Dark Side of Fundamental Rights 163,172–3 (A. Sajo ed. 2006). (S.C. Res. 1267 (1999) deals with sanctions against the Taliban.)

[19] *See* Bruce Zagaris, *Interpol to Introduce New International Notice on Terrorist Financing and Travel*, 21 Int'l Enf. L. Rep. 479 (2005).

[20] USA Patriot Act, Pub. L. No. 107-56, 115 Stat. 272 (codified as amended in scattered sections of 18 U.S.C.) (2001).

[21] Homeland Security Act of 2002, Pub. L. No. 107-296, 116 Stat. 2135 (2002).

[22] 18 U.S.C. § 2384.

Specific legislation consistent with multilateral treaty obligations on terrorism has been a feature of the United States laws beginning with the ratification and implementation of the Hague Hijacking Convention of 1970. The United States is party to all the major subsequent terrorism suppression treaties and normally gives effect to them by discrete criminal legislation.

In addition to legislation tied to particular treaties, the United States has a number of other criminal provisions that address various aspects of terrorism. In these instances it is often either "going it alone" or hoping to bring others around to its position.

Title 18 U.S.C. § 2332, for example, makes it a crime to kill a national of the United States while that national is outside the United States. It also includes attempts and conspiracies with respect to homicide and intentionally causing serious bodily injury to a United States national abroad. It is not, however, a general passive personality protection of traveling Americans. The section goes on to provide that "[n]o prosecution for any offense described in this section shall be undertaken by the United States except on written certification of the Attorney General or the highest ranking subordinate of the Attorney General with responsibility for criminal prosecutions that, in the judgment of the certifying official, such offense was intended to coerce, intimidate, or retaliate against a government or a civilian population."[24] This latter requirement, an apparent surrender by Congress to the difficulty of defining terrorism, may be open to a due process attack on the basis that it is an improper allocation of the determination of one of the elements of the offense to the Executive.[25]

Using weapons of mass destruction against a national of the United States[26] or within the United States, or by a national outside the United States, can be prosecuted under 18 U.S.C. § 2332a. This statute was used in the prosecution of Timothy McVeigh for his role in the Oklahoma bombing.[27]

The key statute used in the United States in the fight against international terrorism is 18 U.S.C. § 2332b. This statute prohibits "conduct transcending national boundaries"[28] that "kills, kidnaps, maims," or constitutes a serious assaultive type of offense or "creates a substantial risk of serious bodily injury to any other person by destroying or damaging" certain property by violating the laws of a state or of the United States.[29] In addition to criminalizing attempts and conspiracies of this form of conduct, the statute also criminalizes conduct by one who "threatens to commit an offense."[30]

Jurisdiction under 18 U.S.C. § 2332b is found in a multitude of different ways, such as the use of the mails, the structure being United States government

---

[23] *See* United States v. Rahman, 189 F.3d 88 (2d Cir. 1999).

[24] 18 U.S.C. § 2332(d).

[25] *See* discussion of similar issues in § 6.01[C] *supra*. If it is contrary to due process to leave jurisdictional issues to a judge rather than a jury, it must be so *a fortiori* to leave them to the Executive. Similar questions are raised by § 948d(c) of the Military Commissions Act of 2006 under which decisions of a tribunal appointed by the Executive are "dispositive for purposes of jurisdiction for trial by military commission."

[26] A rare example of the United States asserting passive personality jurisdiction.

[27] *See* United States v. McVeigh, 153 F.3d 1166 (10th Cir. 1998).

[28] This phrase is defined in 18 U.S.C. § 2332b(g)(1).

[29] 18 U.S.C. § 2332b(a)(1).

[30] 18 U.S.C. § 2332b(a)(2).

property, or when "committed within the special maritime and territorial jurisdiction of the United States."[31] The legislation specifically provides that it is not necessary for the government to prove that the defendant had knowledge of the jurisdictional base.[32] There is extraterritorial jurisdiction for the offenses outlined in the statute, including threats, conspiracies, attempts and also certain forms of conduct by an accessory after the fact.[33]

The penalties for the crimes committed under 18 U.S.C. § 2332b vary, based upon the specific conduct involved. For example, threatening to commit an offense under this statute carries a penalty of up to ten years, while killing can result in a death sentence.[34]

There are at least five other important general criminal statutes dealing with terrorism. 18 U.S.C. § 2339 provides a criminal penalty of up to ten years for harboring or concealing terrorists. The statute applies to whoever harbors or conceals "any person who he knows, or has reasonable grounds to believe, has committed, or is about to commit" one of ten different terrorism crimes listed in this statute.[35] The crimes include 18 U.S.C. §§ 2332a and 2332b, as well as crimes "relating to violence against maritime navigation."[36] A second statute is 18 U.S.C. § 2339A which makes it a crime to provide material support to terrorists. Carrying a penalty of fifteen years, the punishment can be increased to life imprisonment if a death results from the actions of the defendant. A third is 18 U.S.C. § 2339B which proscribes "providing material support or resources to designated foreign terrorist organizations." A fourth is § 2339C which prohibits the financing of terrorism and a fifth is § 2339D on "receiving military-type training from a foreign terrorist organization." Both 2339 and 2339A allow a prosecution for a violation "in any Federal judicial district in which the underlying offense was committed, or in any other Federal judicial district as provided by law."[37] This could be interpreted either as a generous venue provision or as supporting extraterritorial jurisdiction.

Each of these five provisions is in fact capable of being interpreted to include jurisdiction over events that occurred extraterritorially, or contains specific language to that effect. § 2339 is silent beyond the language just mentioned, but the "whoever" is capable of broad interpretation, given the fundamental objective of the section. The original version of § 2339A spoke to "acts within the United States." This phrase was deleted by the USA Patriot Act of 2001, § 805, suggesting that Congress intended that it should now apply extraterritorially, although the section does not say so in as many words. On the other hand, § 2339B, in language added in 2004, says expressly that "there is extraterritorial Federal jurisdiction over an offense under this section" and contains a series of jurisdictional bases, including "after the conduct required for the offense occurs an offender is brought into or found in the United States, even if the conduct required for the offense

---

[31] 18 U.S.C. § 2332b(b).

[32] 18 U.S.C. § 2332b(d)(1). In accordance with the normal rules for proving elements of crimes, it would appear that the prosecution must nevertheless prove the existence of the circumstances giving rise to jurisdiction beyond reasonable doubt, See § 6.01[C] *supra*.

[33] 18 U.S.C. § 2332b(e).

[34] 18 U.S.C. § 2332b(c).

[35] 18 U.S.C. § 2339.

[36] 18 U.S.C. § 2280.

[37] 18 U.S.C. §§ 2339(b), 2339A(a).

occurs outside the United States." Similar language appears in § 2339D, but not § 2339C which has a complex mix of territorial, effects, passive personality and protective theories.[38]

"Extraterritorial" in the present context need not necessarily mean "based on universal jurisdiction." A prosecution for many of these offenses could be based solidly on an effects or a protective basis. It is, however, not clear whether some of the prosecutions, in the absence of a nexus to the United States, *could* be anchored on universal jurisdiction in the current state of international law. The breadth of the notion of terrorism in parts of the legislation, or of what the Government might think amounts to "material support,"[39] may well go beyond the scope of what is currently agreed as customary law, and not all of it is supported by the terrorism treaties and other instruments. For example, while some aspects of the material support provisions are consistent with the financing of terrorism proscriptions in Security Council Resolution 1373 or with the provisions of the Convention for the Suppression of Financing of Terrorism, others go beyond them and encompass acts unrelated to financing. Bear in mind the absence of a general terrorism convention.

[C] Foreign Intelligence Surveillance Act

The Foreign Intelligence Surveillance Act (FISA), was enacted in 1978, following revelations of what Congress regarded as decades of abuse of executive power through warrantless domestic surveillance. It provides relaxed rules for electronic surveillance and warrants for investigators seeking certain foreign intelligence information. The Act "authorizes a judge on the FISA court to grant an application for an order approving electronic surveillance to 'obtain foreign intelligence information' if 'there is probable cause to believe that . . . the target of the electronic surveillance is a foreign power or an agent of a foreign power,' and that 'each of the facilities or places at which the surveillance is directed is being used, or is about to be used, by a foreign power or an agent of a foreign power.' "[40] Absent the Foreign Intelligence Surveillance Act, the government would have to proceed under restricted rules of electronic surveillance that require probable cause "for belief that an individual is committing, has committed, or is about to

---

[38] Sections 2339B and 2339D also contain this jurisdictional base: "an offender aids and abets any person over whom jurisdiction exists under this paragraph in committing an offense under [the section] or conspires with any person over whom jurisdiction exists under this paragraph to commit an offense under [the section]." This may be a case of "connexity" jurisdiction. *See* § 3.02[C] *supra*.

[39] Section 2339A(b)(1) defines the term "material support" as "any property, tangible or intangible, or service, including currency or monetary instruments or financial securities, financial services, lodging, training, expert advice or assistance, safehouses, false documentation or identification, communications equipment, facilities, weapons, lethal substances, explosives, personnel (one or more individuals who may be or include oneself), and transportation, except medicine or religious materials." This casts a very wide net!

[40] In re Sealed Case, 310 F.3d 717, 722 (U.S. FISA Ct. 2002) (citing 50 U.S.C. § 1805(a)(3)).

commit a particular offense"[41] set forth by statute.[42] The FISA also provides less restrictive rules than "normal" surveillance in other instances.[43]

The first appeal ever from a United States Foreign Intelligence Surveillance Court to the United States Foreign Intelligence Surveillance Court of Review was issued in 2002 in a case titled In re Sealed Case.[44] The government appealed a FISA court surveillance order that imposed restrictions upon the government. Since the court does not operate on an adversarial basis, the only official party in the case was the government. The FISA appellate court, however, permitted amici curiae briefs from two outside groups, the American Civil Liberties Union (ACLU) and the National Association of Criminal Defense Lawyers (NACDL).

The Court of Review did not agree with the lower court's view that it could "approve applications for electronic surveillance only if the government's objective is not primarily directed toward criminal prosecution of the foreign agents for their foreign intelligence activity."[45] The government argued that the Patriot Act changed this position "to make clear that an application could be obtained even if criminal prosecution is the primary counter mechanism."[46]

After considering the effect of Patriot Act amendments to the Foreign Intelligence Surveillance Act, the Review Court held in favor of the government. The court concluded "that the FISA as passed by Congress in 1978 clearly did not preclude or limit the government's use or proposed use of foreign intelligence information, which included evidence of certain kinds of criminal activity, in a criminal prosecution."[47] It also did not find that the Fourth Amendment barred this interpretation. The court stated that even if the "procedures and government showings required under FISA" did "not meet the minimum Fourth Amendment warrant standards," they came "close" and thus were constitutional as reasonable under existing case law.[48]

Apparently, soon after September 11, 2001, the Executive began a warrantless electronic surveillance program ("Terrorist Surveillance Program" or "TSP") outside the confines of FISA. It permitted surveillance of communications between an overseas person and someone in the United States where one person was suspected of being associated with Al Qaeda. The Government argued that FISA's prohibitions on warrantless domestic surveillance were superseded by Congress's Authorization for the Use of Military Force Act (AUMF). Alternatively it argued that FISA's restrictions were contrary to Article II of the Constitution and the separation of powers, as an incursion on the inherent powers of the President.

---

[41] 18 U.S.C. § 2518.

[42] 18 U.S.C. § 2516. The judge must also find that "there is probable cause for belief that particular communications concerning that offense will be obtained through such interception," 18 U.S.C. § 2518(3)(b), and "normal investigative procedures have been tried and have failed or reasonably appear to be unlikely to succeed if tried or to be too dangerous." 18 U.S.C, § 2518(3)(c). There is, however, an exception to the specificity requirements that can apply here. 18 U.S.C. § 2518(3)(d) and § 2518(11).

[43] NORMAN ABRAMS, ANTI-TERRORISM AND CRIMINAL ENFORCEMENT 528 (2d ed. 2005).

[44] 310 F.3d 717 (U.S. FISA Ct. 2002).

[45] Id. at 721.

[46] Id.

[47] Id. at 727.

[48] Id. at 746. The court used the balancing test of United States v. United States District Court (Keith), 407 U.S. 297 (1972).

Critics insisted that Congress had spoken clearly in FISA and nothing in the generalities of the AUMF could be interpreted as an implied repeal of FISA.[49] Suits against the program emphasized the chilling effect that the program had on defense counsel representing foreign citizens such as those confined in Guantanamo, whose communications with clients and witnesses could be intercepted, and on scholars and journalists communicating with people outside the United States. They pointed out that FISA, unlike TSP, has "minimization" procedures "that are reasonably designed . . . to minimize the acquisition and retention, and prohibit the dissemination, of nonpublicly available information concerning unconsenting United States persons,"[50] and that privileged communications remain such under FISA.[51] In *ACLU v. NSA*, the trial judge held that the programs violated "the APA; the Separation of Powers doctrine; the First and Fourth Amendments of the United States Constitution; and the statutory law."[52] This result was reversed on appeal in a 2-1 decision by the Court of Appeals for the Sixth Circuit on July 6, 2007.[53] The majority held that the plaintiffs lacked standing, applying different reasoning, but essentially on the basis that the plaintiffs could not show they had been personally affected by the program. The dissent believed that the attorney-plaintiffs had shown standing because of the chilling effects on their practice and would have reached the merits, holding that the program ran counter to the clear language of FISA. He also addressed the Government's argument of mootness, based on its announcement in January of 2007 that it had reached a secret agreement with the Foreign Intelligence Surveillance Court whereby the TSP would comply with FISA. Nevertheless, the Government continued to assert that the TSP did not violate the Constitution or any statute and that the President maintains that he has authority to "opt out" of the FISA framework at any time. In these circumstances, the dissent did not regard the issues as moot. The Supreme Court denied a petition for certiorari without comment in February 2008.[54]

In August 2007, shortly after the Court of Appeals decision, Congress adopted the Protect America Act[55] which re-defined electronic surveillance under FISA so that it does not include "surveillance directed at a person reasonably believed to be located outside the United States."[56] The Attorney General or the Director of National Intelligence was empowered to authorize the acquisition of foreign intelligence information with the assistance of a communications service provider (such as phone companies, AOL, Gmail, Skype, internet services). The only role for the FISA court is to ensure that the procedures used by the Government are reasonably designed to ensure that the acquisitions do not constitute electronic

---

[49] This side of the separation of powers argument relies in part on Hamdan v. Rumsfeld, 126 S. Ct. 2749 (2006), in which the Court both held the Executive within statutory limits and refused to give a broad interpretation to the AUMF as over-riding prior statutes. *See also* Little v. Barreme, 6 U.S. (2 Cranch) 170 (1804); Youngstown Sheet and Tube Co. v. Sawyer, 343 U.S. 579 (1952).

[50] 50 U.S.C. § 1801(h)(1)–(4).

[51] *Id.* § 1806(h).

[52] 438 F. Supp. 2d 754, 782 (E.D. Mich. 2006).

[53] ACLU v. Nat'l Sec. Agency, 493 F.3d 644 (6th Cir. 2007).

[54] 2008 WL 423556 (U.S.).

[55] Public Law No: 110-55.

[56] *Id.*, inserting § 105B(a) of FISA.

surveillance (as re-defined).[57] The legislation was subject to a sunset clause expiring in February 2008. The President and the House tussled over renewing, with the House refusing to accept a bill approved by the Senate containing immunity for providers who had cooperated with the Government in the past.[58]

§ 7.02   PROSECUTING TERRORISM

In recent years there have been indictments, plea agreements,[59] trials, and convictions[60] for terrorism-related conduct. Jurisdiction to prosecute has not proved problematic, although defendants have questioned the government's ability to proceed with some actions. For example, in the case of *United States v. Yousef*,[61] the defendants were charged with a twenty-one count Indictment for conduct related to the bombing of the World Trade Center in 1993 and conspiracy to bomb United States airlines in Southeast Asia in 1994 and 1995. Yousef alone was also charged in Count Nineteen of the indictment with placing a bomb aboard a Philippine Airlines flight traveling from the Philippines to Japan. One of the issues raised on appeal was whether it was proper to prosecute Yousef for his alleged extraterritorial conduct. The arguments related to jurisdiction were different for many of the counts in the Indictment.

In *Yousef*, the Second Circuit easily found that the intent of Congress with respect to 18 U.S.C. § 32(a), involving United States registered aircraft, was to provide extraterritorial jurisdiction with respect to crimes alleging the placing of a "destructive device on board any such aircraft if it would be likely to endanger the aircraft's safety."[62] Finding jurisdiction for the substantive crimes and for the crime of "attempted destruction of aircraft in the special aircraft jurisdiction of the United States," the court had no difficulty also finding jurisdiction for the conspiracy charge.

Finally, Yousef claimed an insufficient basis for jurisdiction because "customary international law does not provide a basis for jurisdiction over these counts and that United States law is subordinate to customary international law and therefore cannot provide a basis for jurisdiction."[63] This argument was pressed most strongly in relation to the Philippine Airlines bombing where there was no nexus with the United States. The court rejected these arguments, finding a sufficient basis in United States law for this prosecution. Although the lower court rested its analysis on the "universality" principle, the Second Circuit did not agree. Instead, the court, in finding jurisdiction for Count Nineteen in the Indictment, stated that jurisdiction was proper "under domestic law, 18 U.S.C. § 32; second, under the *aut dedere aut punire* ('extradite or prosecute') jurisdiction created by the Montreal Convention . . . ; and third, under the *protective* principle of the customary international

---

[57] *Id.*, inserting § 105C(b) of FISA. "The Court's review is limited to whether the Government's determination is clearly erroneous." *Id.*

[58] *See President Bush Discusses FISA*, March 13, 2008, available at http://www.whitehouse.gov/news/releases/2008/03/20080313.html.

[59] *E.g.*, United States v. John Lindh — Plea Agreement at http://news.findlaw.com/ hdocs/docs/lindh/uslindh71502pleaag.pdf.

[60] *E.g.*, United States v. Salameh, 152 F.3d 88 (2d Cir. 1998).

[61] 327 F.3d 56 (2d Cir. 2003).

[62] *Id.* at 86.

[63] *Id.* at 90–91.

law of criminal jurisdiction . . . ."[64] The court stated "that terrorism — unlike piracy, war crimes, and crimes against humanity — does not provide a basis for universal jurisdiction."[65] Nevertheless, there was sufficient warrant for United States jurisdiction in the Montreal Convention. The court also rejected defendant's argument that he was not "found" in the United States for purposes of 18 U.S.C. § 32b, because he was brought into the country against his will from Pakistan to answer for the World Trade Center bombing, and then charged, once he was here, with the Philippines Airline count. The Court interpreted "found" as not meaning "discovered by chance" but the equivalent of the Montreal Convention's "present" in the United States.[66]

§ 7.03 ENEMY COMBATANTS

In some terrorism-related cases, the United States has proceeded outside the judicial process. Most recently, the government has held individuals as detainees or enemy combatants.[67] Many have voiced disagreement with this method of proceeding.[68]

In *Hamdi v. Rumsfeld*,[69] the United States Supreme Court examined the propriety of the government's designating an individual an enemy combatant, and also the rights that should be accorded to such an individual if the status is permitted. Hamdi, an American citizen born in Louisiana and later residing in Afghanistan, was captured by "members of the Northern Alliance, a coalition of military groups opposed to the Taliban government" and turned over to the United States military in Afghanistan.[70] Initially taken to the naval base in Guatanamo, he was eventually moved to a naval brig in South Carolina.[71]

The case to the Supreme Court resulted from a petition for habeas corpus filed by Hamdi's father. The petition requested that Hamdi be provided with constitutional rights such as the right to counsel, that the government cease interrogating him, and that he be "released from his 'unlawful custody.' "[72] During the proceedings the government filed what has been called the "Mobbs Declaration," a declaration of Special Advisor to the Under Secretary of Defense for Policy, Michael Mobbs, providing the basis for detaining Hamdi. Mobbs found that Hamdi was an "enemy combatant." The Supreme Court vacated a decision of the Fourth Circuit, that had found "that the District Court had failed to extend appropriate

---

[64] *Id.* at 91–92.

[65] *Id.* at 108.

[66] *Id.* at 88–90. Yousef had an argument, based on the extradition doctrine of "speciality," that his extradition from Pakistan did not extend to the Philippines offense, but he was deemed to have made this argument too late. *Id.* at 171.

[67] *See* § 2.07[A],*supra.*

[68] *E.g.*, William Glaberson, *Critics' Attack on Tribunals Turn to Law Among Nations*, N.Y. TIMES, Dec. 26, 2001, at B1; American Bar Association Report on the Use of Military Commissions, available at http://www.abanet.org/leadership/military.pdf; JORDAN J. PAUST, BEYOND THE LAW: THE BUSH ADMINISTRATION'S UNLAWFUL RESPONSES IN THE "WAR" ON TERROR 100–31 (2007).

[69] 124 S. Ct. 2633 (2004).

[70] *Id.* at 2635–36.

[71] *Id.* at 2636.

[72] *Id.* at 2636.

deference to the Government's security and intelligence interest," and remanded the case for proceedings consistent with its decision.[73]

The Court first examined the question of whether the executive "has authority to detain citizens who qualify as 'enemy combatants.' "[74] In a plurality opinion authored by Justice O'Connor, the Court noted the historical basis for permitting "the capture, detention, and trial of unlawful combatants."[75] The Court found that the Authorization for Use of Military Force ("AUMF") permitted, under its exercise of "necessary and appropriate force" the detention of "individuals who fought against the United States in Afghanistan as part of the Taliban." These facts are distinguishable from the case of *Ex Parte Milligan*,[76] where the defendant was "not a prisoner of war but a resident of Indiana arrested while at home." The government failed to convince the Court that all rights could be bypassed for those designated as "enemy combatants." The Court stated "that a citizen-detainee seeking to challenge his classification as an enemy combatant must receive notice of the factual basis for his classification, and a fair opportunity to rebut the Government's factual assertions before a neutral decisionmaker."[77]

The Court did not provide a definitive structure for hearings, but noted that once the government set forth the basis for holding someone as an enemy combatant, the burden "could shift to the petitioner to rebut that evidence with more persuasive evidence that he falls outside the criteria."[78] The Court did, however, uphold the due process rights of the defendant, finding that "while the full protections that accompany challenges to detentions in other settings may prove unworkable and inappropriate in the enemy combatant setting, the threats to military operations posed by a basic system of independent review are not so weighty as to trump a citizen's core rights to challenge meaningfully the Government's case and to be heard by an impartial adjudicator."[79]

Justices Souter and Ginsburg joined with an opinion that concurred and dissented in part, although they concurred in the judgment of the Court. These two justices rejected the plurality view that the AUMF allowed this detention. They noted how the Patriot Act, amended shortly after the AUMF, only authorized aliens who were not being deported or criminally charged to be detained for seven days. Justices Souter and Ginsburg stated, "[i]t is very difficult to believe that the same Congress that carefully circumscribed Executive power over alien terrorists on home soil would not have meant to require the Government to justify clearly its detention of an American citizen held on home soil incommunicado." Since the plurality's judgment vacated the Fourth Circuit's judgment and remanded the case, they joined in the judgment of the plurality.

A dissent presented by Justices Scalia and Stevens, also called for a reversal of the Fourth Circuit decision. They took a stronger position than the other five

---

[73] *Id.* at 2634, 2636.

[74] *Id.* at 2639.

[75] *Id.* at 2640. The Court referenced the case of Ex Parte Quirin, 317 U.S. 1 (1942).

[76] 71 U.S. 2 (1866).

[77] 124 S. Ct. 2633, 2648 (2004).

[78] *Id.* at 2649. The Court used as an example, allowing hearsay, as something that might be used to lessen the requirements on the government in these hearings. *Id.*

[79] *Id.* at 2650.

justices by saying that Hamdi should be released "unless (1) criminal proceedings are promptly brought, or (2) Congress has suspended the writ of habeas corpus."[80]

Justice Thomas, the one justice who accepted the government's position, stated that he did "not think that the Federal Government's war powers can be balanced away by this Court."[81] Justice Thomas presented the view that Hamdi's habeas claim should not be allowed and that the case should not be remanded because "[t]he Executive Branch, acting pursuant to the powers vested in the President by the Constitution and with explicit congressional approval, has determined that Yaser Hamdi is an enemy combatant and should be detained."[82]

In a settlement agreement dated September 15, 2004, the United States agreed to release Hamdi to Saudi Arabia. Hamdi maintained his position that he was never part of nor supported forces hostile to the United States. He agreed, *inter alia*, to renounce any continuing claims to United States nationality and not to engage in activities supportive of the Taliban, al Qaeda or terrorism in general.[83]

Jose Padilla, also an American citizen, was likewise held as an enemy combatant by the government. Captured at Chicago's O'Hare International Airport, he was held initially on a material witness warrant issued in New York after the 9-11 attacks. Like Hamdi he was eventually sent to a Naval Brig in South Carolina, accused at this point of plotting to detonate a "dirty bomb" in the United States. He sought habeas corpus through his attorney. The Court in *Rumsfeld v. Padilla*,[84] however, refused to consider the merits of his case, ruling instead that there was improper jurisdiction because "the District of South Carolina, not the Southern District of New York, was the district court in which Padilla should have brought his habeas petition."[85]

A four person dissent authored by Justice Stevens argued that "this is an exceptional case" and as such the Court should have reached the merits of the case. The dissent was opposed to the "incommunicado detention" under which Padilla was being held.[86]

Padilla tried again in what seemed to be the right court, the District of South Carolina. He was successful at the District Court level,[87] but the Fourth Circuit Court of Appeals reversed.[88] The Government frustrated his attempt to reach the merits of his detention without charge in the Supreme Court by changing tack and charging him with crimes in federal district court. He was eventually convicted on counts totally unrelated to the dirty bomb, namely conspiracy to murder, kidnap and maim people in a foreign country, and two lesser counts involving material support to terrorists. He was sentenced to 17 years in prison.[89]

---

[80] *Id.* at 2671.

[81] *Id.* at 2674.

[82] *Id.* at 2674.

[83] Text of Agreement at http://news.findlaw.com/hdocs/hamdi/91704stlagrmnt.html.

[84] 124 S. Ct. 2711 (2004).

[85] *Id.* at 2727.

[86] *Id.* at 2735.

[87] Padilla v. Hanft, 389 F. Supp. 2d 678 (D.S.C. 2005).

[88] Padilla v. Hanft, 432 F.3d 582 (4th Cir. 2005).

[89] N.Y. TIMES, Jan. 22, 2008.

The Military Commissions Act of 2006[90] gives rise to complex issues of international and constitutional law in its reliance on the concept now called "alien unlawful enemy combatants." These are the people over whom the Commissions have personal jurisdiction. The concept has no exact equivalent in international law, but the obvious intention is that it refers to people who are not entitled to be treated as prisoners of war. The determination of who fits the category would normally be made by what are called Combat Status Review Tribunals (CSRTs). Those bodies were originally a creation solely of the Executive, but their procedures and status gain some direction from provisions in the Detainee Treatment Act of 2005 and the Military Commissions Act. Whether the procedures pass muster under the Geneva Conventions and the Constitution are fundamental issues at the back of the litigation about the right to habeas corpus of those detained at Guantanamo.[91] If they have no remedy in habeas, even those charged with crime may find it difficult to get to the substantive issues of the legality of the CSRT (and Commission) process. Those held indefinitely based on a determination (or pending determination) by a CSRT may never succeed in obtaining any kind of hearing on the deeper issues.

So far as substance is concerned, the offenses set out in the Military Commissions Act as being subject to trial by commission include several that can be categorized as "terrorism" offenses. These include "Hijacking or Hazarding a vessel or Aircraft,"[92] "Terrorism,"[93] and "Material Support for Terrorism."[94] These offenses are each an amalgam of international and United States domestic material, put together in a unique way. Whether they represent, as the Military Commissions Act asserts, "offenses that have traditionally been triable by military commission,"[95] is a question that will no doubt be litigated should any of the cases come to trial. The concept of terrorism has been finding its way into the laws of armed conflict, although in a narrower way than seems to be contemplated in the 2006 Act. Thus, both Article 51(1) of Additional Protocol I to the Geneva Conventions (dealing with international armed conflicts)[96] and Article 13(2) of Additional Protocol II (on non-international armed conflicts)[97] provide that: "The civilian population as such, as well as individual civilians, shall not be the object of attack. Acts or threats of violence the primary purpose of which is to spread terror among the civilian population are prohibited." Neither of these is subject to the "grave breach" regime of the Geneva Conventions which requires universal efforts at punishment. Nevertheless, in *Prosecutor v. Galic*,[98] a majority of the Appeals Chamber of the International Criminal Tribunal for Former Yugoslavia held, in a case arising from

---

[90] *See* § 2.07[B] *supra.*

[91] *See* § 2.07 *supra.*

[92] Military Commissions Act of 2006, § 950v(b)(23).

[93] *Id.* § 950v(b)(24).

[94] *Id.* § 950v(b)(25).

[95] *Id.* § 950p.

[96] Art. 51(1), Protocol Additional to the Geneva Conventions of 12 August 1949, and relating to the Protection of Victims of International Armed Conflicts (Protocol I) of 8 June 1977. *See also* Geneva Convention relative to the Protection of Civilian Persons in Time of War of 12 August 1949, Art. 33 ("Collective penalties and likewise all measures of intimidation or of terrorism are prohibited").

[97] Art. 13(2), Protocol Additional to the Geneva Conventions of 12 August 1949, and relating to the Protection of Victims of Non-international Armed Conflicts (Protocol II) of 8 June 1977.

[98] IT-98-29-A (Appeals Chamber, International Criminal Tribunal for Former Yugoslavia, decision of Nov. 30, 2006).

the siege of Sarajevo, that these provisions were a part of customary law. It went further and held that "a breach of the prohibition of terror against the civilian population gave rise to individual criminal responsibility pursuant to customary law at the time of the commission of the offenses for which Galic was convicted."[99]

§ 7.04 PIRACY

The pirates of the eighteenth century were the terrorists of their time. Piracy is a crime in both national and international law. In the United States one finds a criminal statute, going back to the First Congress, which provides that "[w]hoever on the high seas, commits the crime of piracy as defined by the law of nations, and is afterwards brought into or found in the United States shall be imprisoned for life."[100] The United States provides for jurisdiction under the "special maritime and territorial jurisdiction of the United States."[101] Piracy has also been found to be a crime permitting universal jurisdiction under international law and the United States legislation proceeds on this basis.[102]

Internationally, several Conventions define what acts may constitute piracy, most recently the United Nations Convention on the Law of the Sea (Montego Bay Convention).[103] Article 100 of the Montego Bay Convention states that piracy can be "any illegal acts of violence, detention, or any act of depredation, committed for private ends by the passengers of a private ship or a private aircraft." It requires that the act be directed "(a) on the high seas, against another ship or aircraft, or against persons or property on board such ship or aircraft; (b) against a ship, aircraft, persons or property in a place outside the jurisdiction of any State." It can also be "any act of voluntary participation in the operation of a ship or of an aircraft with knowledge of facts making it a pirate ship or aircraft." Acts that incite or "intentionally facilitat[e] an act described" above are also included as piracy.[104] Piracy covers acts by private parties, and as such is not intended to include acts by a government.[105] A key part of the definition is the requirement that the acts be against "another" ship. Other acts of violence on a ship cruising the high seas may be offenses under the domestic law of the flag state, or under other treaties,[106] but they are not piracy. There is international cooperation to suppress piracy.[107] The Law of the Sea Convention is explicit in contemplating universal jurisdiction:

> On the high seas or in any other place outside the jurisdiction of any State, every State may seize a pirate ship or aircraft, or a ship or aircraft taken by piracy and under the control of pirates, and arrest the persons and seize

---

[99] *Id.* ¶ 86.

[100] 18 U.S.C. § 1651.

[101] 18 U.S.C. § 7(1).

[102] *See generally* ALFRED P. RUBIN, THE LAW OF PIRACY (2d ed. 1998).

[103] United Nations Convention on the Law of the Sea, Dec. 10, 1982, 21 I.L.M. 1261 (1982), reproducing U.N. Doc. A/CONF.62/122 (1982), carried forward from Art. 15, Geneva Convention on the High Seas, Apr. 28, 1958, 13 U.S.T. 2312, T.I.A.S. No. 5200, 450 U.N.T.S. 82.

[104] *Id.* at Art. 101.

[105] Restatement (Third) of Foreign Relations Law of the United States § 522, Comment c (1987).

[106] Notably the International Maritime Organization's Convention for the Suppression of Unlawful Acts against the Safety of Maritime Navigation, March 10, 1988, which does essentially for ships what the Hague and Montreal Conventions do for aircraft, prohibiting hijacking and other violent acts involving navigation.

[107] Law of the Sea Convention, Arts. 100 and 110.

the property on board. The courts of the State which carried out the seizure may decide upon the penalties to be imposed, and may also determine the action to be taken with regard to the ships, aircraft or property, subject to the rights of third parties acting in good faith.[108]

The United States is not yet a party to the United Nations Convention on the Law of the Sea, largely because of objections to the regime it includes for exploitation of the deep seabed. It tends to regard this, and other parts of the treaty to which it is favorably disposed, as reflecting customary international law.

Piracy is far from a problem of the past. A number of Asian states have found it necessary this century to enter into a regional cooperation agreement;[109] ten crew members of a vessel chartered by the United Nations were seized while on a humanitarian mission to Somalia and held until the organization paid a ransom;[110] and there have been recent attacks on cruise ships and other merchant vessels, especially off the coast of Somalia.[111]

§ 7.05   AIRCRAFT HIJACKING AND SABOTAGE

Aircraft hijacking is prohibited by both national and international law. In the United States, it is called the crime of aircraft piracy and is now codified at 49 U.S.C. § 46502.[112] That section defines "aircraft piracy" as "seizing or exercising control of an aircraft in the special aircraft jurisdiction of the United States by force, violence, threat of force or violence, or any form of intimidation, and with wrongful intent."[113] It includes crimes of attempted aircraft piracy and conspiracy to commit it.[114]

Whether aircraft piracy and attempted aircraft piracy require proof of specific intent, that is to say proof that the defendant had the conscious purpose to effect the hijacking, is a question examined by several courts. Some have concluded that only a general intent is required, even when the crime involves attempted aircraft piracy.[115] A "general intent" will be satisfied by a showing that the defendant knew his actions would produce the prohibited result or recklessly disregarded a known

---

[108] *Id.*, Art. 105. *Cf.* Art. 99 on the slave trade which appears to contemplate only flag state jurisdiction. Some nineteenth century treaties and legislation tended to assimilate the slave trade to piracy but generally stopped at flag or nationality criminal jurisdiction over the offenders, even though any ship might free the slaves.

[109] Regional Cooperation Agreement on Combating Piracy and Armed Robbery against Ships in Asia, April 28, 2005, 44 I.L.M. 829 (2005).

[110] *Attack Shows Boldness of Somali Pirates*, Associated Press Report, Nov. 7, 2005.

[111] Ethan McNern, *Big rise in pirate attacks on shipping*, THE SCOTSMAN, Jan. 10, 2008 (quoting figures from International Maritime Bureau of 269 acts of piracy in 2007, including 18 successful hijackings).

[112] Prior to this codification, the statute that prohibited aircraft piracy was found in 49 U.S.C. § 1472(I). The legislation gives effect to the Hague Convention for the Suppression of Unlawful Seizure of Aircraft, Dec. 16, 1970, 22 U.S.T. 1641, T.I.A.S. No. 7192, 860 U.N.T.S. 105.

[113] 49 U.S.C. § 46502(a)(A).

[114] 49 U.S.C. § 46502(a)(B). The Hague Convention does not mention conspiracy. It is common for United States legislation giving effect to suppression conventions to add a conspiracy count over and above what the treaty requires. *See also* similar examples in notes 127 and 132, *infra*.

[115] *E.g.*, United States v. Compton, 5 F.3d 358, 360 (9th Cir. 1993); United States v. Castaneda-Reyes, 703 F.2d 522, 525 (11th Cir. 1983).

risk that they would do so. In *United States v. Calloway*,[116] a case involving an attempted aircraft piracy, the Sixth Circuit held that although aircraft piracy might be a general intent crime, when the crime was inchoate it required proof of a specific intent in accordance with the normal rules on inchoate crimes.[117]

In *United States v. Rezaq*,[118] the defendant was convicted of aircraft piracy for hijacking "an Air Egypt flight shortly after takeoff from Athens." He ordered the plane to "fly to Malta" where he "shot a number of passengers, killing two of them."[119] Rezaq served seven years in prison in Malta, after pleading guilty there to murder. "[H]e was later taken into custody in Nigeria by United States authorities and brought to the United States for trial" (apparently without any formal extradition). In the United States he was convicted of the hijacking, ordered to pay restitution, and sentenced to life in prison.

Several issues were raised by Rezaq on appeal, including whether his conviction in Malta was a bar to his conviction in the United States under the principle of double jeopardy. The court held that there was no impediment to his United States conviction, because dual sovereigns may both proceed against an individual without violating the Double Jeopardy Clause of the United States Constitution. The court also found that Rezaq's prosecution in Malta was for "murder, attempted murder, and hostage-taking" while the prosecution in the United States was for aircraft piracy, so that "under the usual double jeopardy analysis, . . . the first prosecution does not bar the second."[120]

The court also considered whether the Double Jeopardy Clause was the exclusive consideration for determining whether the United States could proceed with this prosecution. Rezaq argued that "both the Hague Convention and section 1472(n) incorporate a special ban on sequential prosecution."[121] Here again, the court rejected the defendant's arguments, finding that "[n]either the Hague Convention nor section 1472(n) appears to have been intended to establish a firm allocation of prosecutorial authority between nations."[122] Although a treaty can provide a more restrictive basis for prosecutions, the court did not find this element to exist here. "[T]he Hague Convention's requirement that a state either prosecute offenders or extradite them does not imply a bar on (at different times) doing both."[123]

Other statutes also relate to conduct associated with aircraft piracy. For example, in 2001 Congress added a statute on "interference with security screening personnel," that provides a ten year sentence to "[a]n individual in an area within a commercial service airport in the United States who, by assaulting a Federal, airport, or air carrier employee who has security duties within the airport, interferes with the performance of the duties of the employee or lessens the ability of the employee to perform those duties." The sentence can be increased to life if

---

[116] 116 F.3d 1129 (6th Cir. 1997).

[117] *Id.* at 1135–36.

[118] 134 F.3d 1121 (D.C. Cir. 1998).

[119] *Id.* at 1125.

[120] *Id.* at 1128.

[121] *Id.* at 1128.

[122] *Id.* at 1131.

[123] *Id.* at 1129.

the individual uses "[a] dangerous weapon in committing the assault or interference."[124]

The Montreal Convention for the Suppression of Unlawful Acts against the Safety of Civil Aviation[125] obligates states to ensure that any person commits an offense who:

(a)   performs an act of violence against a person on board an aircraft in flight if that act is likely to endanger the safety of that aircraft; or

(b)   destroys an aircraft in service or causes damage to such aircraft which renders it incapable of flight or which is likely to endanger its safety in flight; or

(c)   places or causes to be placed on an aircraft in service, by any means whatsoever, a device or substance which is likely to destroy that aircraft, or to cause damage to it which renders it incapable of flight, or to cause damage to it which is likely to endanger its safety in flight; or

(d)   destroys or damages air navigation facilities or interferes with their operation, if any such acts is likely to endanger the safety of aircraft in flight; or

(e)   communicates information which he knows to be false, thereby endangering the safety of an aircraft in flight.[126]

Attempts and accomplice liability are also covered. The Montreal Convention is given effect in United States law by 18 U.S.C. § 32.[127]

§ 7.06   HOSTAGE TAKING

Here again we find both national and international law prohibiting this conduct. Under United States law, the crime of hostage taking is prohibited by 18 U.S.C. § 1203, commonly referred to as the Hostage Taking Act. It was passed in 1984 to implement the 1979 International Convention Against the Taking of Hostages.[128] The act covers "whoever, . . . seizes or detains and threatens to kill, to injure, or to continue to detain another person in order to compel a third person or a governmental organization to do or abstain from doing any act as an explicit or implicit condition for the release of the person detained . . . ."[129] The location of the crime can be either inside or outside the United States, but there are jurisdictional restrictions depending upon where it occurs. If outside the United States, "the offender or the person seized or detained [must be] a national of the United States," be found in the United States, or the "governmental organization sought to be compelled is the Government of the United States."[130] Likewise, it is not an offense if it occurs "within the United States, each alleged offender and each person seized or detained are nationals of the United States, and each alleged

---

[124]   49 U.S.C. § 46503.

[125]   Sept. 23, 1971, 24 U.S.T. 564.

[126]   *Id.* Art. 1.

[127]   Like the hijacking legislation, *supra* note 114, this section adds a conspiracy count beyond what the treaty requires.

[128]   International Convention Against the Taking of Hostages, Dec. 17, 1979, 18 I.L.M. 1456 (1979).

[129]   18 U.S.C. § 1203.

[130]   18 U.S.C. § 1203(b)(1).

offender is found in the United States, unless the governmental organization sought to be compelled is the Government of the United States."[131]

Both attempts and conspiracies are included by statute. The crime carries a penalty of up to life, but if a death results the penalty must be death or life imprisonment.[132]

The ratification and legislative implementation of the International Convention Against the Taking of Hostages was the subject of controversy in *United States v. Lue*.[133] One of the defendants (Mr. Chen) argued that the Executive had exceeded its authority in entering into the Convention because the "Hostage Taking Convention regulates matters of purely domestic concern not touching on relations with other nations."[134] Thus, he argued, if the Executive could not validly enter into the treaty, Congress could not validly give effect to it under the treaty power and the necessary and proper power in the Constitution. The court rejected this argument, noting that the *Restatement (Third) of the Foreign Relations Law of the United States* does not limit international agreements to "matters of international concern."[135] The Restatement comments provide that "the United States may make an agreement on any subject suggested by its national interests in relations with other nations."

The court in *Lue* also rejected a Tenth Amendment argument that it was improper to have an Act that "criminalizes 'domestic, nonpolitical abductions.' "[136] The court found it unnecessary "to decide the question," of whether this was in keeping with case law, "because in this case there is a sufficient national (indeed, international) interest supporting Congress's passage of the Hostage Taking Act."[137] The *Lue* case and other cases have also examined whether the Hostage Taking Act violates equal protection, and have found no violation.[138]

The facts in *Lue* are interesting, but not entirely clear from the report. The 1979 Convention was drafted with the hostage taking (and eventual assassination) of the Israeli athletes at the Munich Olympics in mind. Nevertheless, the literal language of both the Convention and the United States legislation includes, but goes beyond, political kidnappings. In *Lue*, the defendant whose appeal was before the Court (Mr. Chen) seems to have been a foreign citizen, the victim (Mr. Chan) an American, and the situation a simple one of kidnapping for ransom.

---

[131] 18 U.S.C. § 1203(b)(2).

[132] 18 U.S.C. § 1203(a). The conspiracy provision is not required by the Convention. *See* note 114.

[133] 134 F.3d 79 (2d Cir. 1998).

[134] *Id.* at 83.

[135] Restatement (Third) of the Foreign Relations Law of the United States § 302, Comment c (1987).

[136] 134 F.3d at 84.

[137] *Id.* at 85. The Court relied heavily on the Birds Case, Missouri v. Holland, 252 U.S. 416 (1920).

[138] 134 F.3d at 85–87. *See also* United States v. Ferreira, 275 F.3d 1929 (11th Cir. 2001); United States v. Montenegro, 231 F.3d 389 (7th Cir. 2000).

Chapter 8
TRANSNATIONAL ORGANIZED CRIME

§ 8.01 INTRODUCTION

The United Nations Convention against Transnational Organized Crime,[1] adopted by the General Assembly in 2000, came into force in September 2003. By early 2008 it had 147 parties, including the United States. It was inspired in part by the federal Racketeer Influenced and Corrupt Organizations Act (RICO).[2] To a considerable extent this was a United States initiative, as the policy to invest more resources on transnational crime had been spelled out by President Clinton in 1995 in Presidential Decision Directive 42.[3] That Directive described transnational crime as a threat to national security. This was followed by the United States formally taking an initiative at the United Nations that led to the adoption by the General Assembly, the following year, of the United Nations Declaration on Crime and Public Security.[4] Article 1 of the Declaration included the following agenda which focused on transnational crime:

> Member States shall seek to protect the security and well-being of their citizens and all persons within their jurisdiction by taking effective national measures to combat serious transnational crime, including organized crime, illicit drug and arms trafficking, smuggling of other illicit articles, organized trafficking in persons, terrorist crimes and the laundering of proceeds from serious crimes, and shall pledge their mutual cooperation in those efforts.

---

[1] G.A. Res. 55/25 (2000), *available at* http://www.unodc.org/pdf/crime/a_res_55/res5525e.pdf.

[2] *See generally* Edward Wise, *RICO and its Analogues: A Comparative Perspective*, 27 Syracuse J. Int'l L. & Com. 303 (2000).

[3] *See* Peter Andreas & Ethan Nadelmann, Policing the Globe 158 (2006); *See also* John Wagley for Congressional Research Service, Transnational Organized Crime: Principal Threats and U.S. Responses (2006) (discussing the history).

[4] G.A. Res. 51/60 (1996), *available at* http://www.un.org/documents/ga/res/51/ares51-60.htm.

The Convention[5] and its accompanying Protocols on "Trafficking in Persons, especially Women and Children,"[6] the "Smuggling of Migrants by Land, Sea and Air,"[7] and on "Illicit Manufacturing and Trafficking in Firearms"[8] flesh out the transnational crime aspects of these policy proscriptions in treaty form. Samuel M. Witten, Deputy Legal Adviser to the State Department, testifying in favor of ratification, said the following:

> Since the relevant U.S. criminal laws already provide for broad and effective application in these areas, we can comply with the Convention's criminalization obligations without need for new legislation. The value of these Convention provisions for the United States is that they oblige other counties that have been slower to react legislatively to the threat of transnational organized crime to adopt new criminal laws in harmony with ours.[9]

The stated aim of the Convention against Transnational Organized Crime is to "promote cooperation to prevent and combat transnational organized crime more effectively."[10] The basic obligation is to make it an offense to participate in an organized criminal group.[11] There are subsidiary obligations to criminalize some particular activities — money laundering, corruption and obstruction of justice — typically associated with organized crime. For those who become parties to the Protocols, criminalization is required of the proscribed activities therein.[12] The details represent the increasing complexity of treaty techniques, and, in particular, build on models developed in relation to drugs[13] and to terrorism.[14]

The Convention[15] applies to certain offences which are "transnational in nature" and involve an organized criminal group.[16] An offense is said to be "transnational in nature" when "[i]t is committed in more than one State," when "a substantial part

---

[5] See note 1, *supra.*

[6] Adopted by the same resolution. The effort to arrive at a definition of trafficking revealed deep fault lines, including whether prostitution in itself should be illegal. *See* Anne Gallagher, *Human Rights and the New UN Protocols on Trafficking and Migrant Smuggling: A Preliminary Analysis,* 23 HUM. RTS. Q. 975 (2001).

[7] Also adopted by the same resolution.

[8] Adopted by G.A. Res. 55/255 (2001), *available at* http://www.un.org/Depts/dhl/resguide/r55.htm.

[9] Testimony of Samuel M. Witten, on Law Enforcement Treaties, before the Committee on Foreign Relations, United States Senate, June 17, 2004, *available at* http://foreign.senate.gov/hearings/2004/hrg040617a.html.

[10] Convention against Transnational Organized Crime, Art. 1.

[11] *Id.* at Art. 5.

[12] The United States is party to the Trafficking and Migrants Protocols, but not the Protocol on Firearms.

[13] *See* §§ 6.01–6.03, *supra.*

[14] *See* §§ 7.01, 7.02, 7.05 and 7.06. *See* Emmanouela Amylonaki, *The Manipulations of Organised Crime by Terrorists: Legal and Factual Perspectives,* 2 INT'L CRIM. L. REV. 213 (2002) (discussing assertions about connections between drugs and terrorism).

[15] *See* ORGANIZED CRIME: A COMPILATION OF U.N. DOCUMENTS 1975–1998 (M. Cherif Bassiouni & Eduardo Vetere, with Dimitri Vlassis, comp. & ed., 1998) (providing previous work by the United Nations in the area). *See also* THE UNITED NATIONS AND TRANSNATIONAL ORGANIZED CRIME (Phil Williams & Ernesto U. Savona eds., 1996); TRANSNATIONAL CRIME (Nikos Passas ed., 1999); COMBATING TRANSNATIONAL CRIME (P. Williams & D. Vlassis, eds., 2001).

[16] § 8.02, *infra.*

of its preparation, planning, direction or control takes place in another State," when it "involves an organized criminal group that engages in criminal activities in more than one State," or when it "has substantial effects in another State."[17]

§ 8.02   THE CORE OBLIGATION TO CRIMINALIZE GROUP ACTIVITIES

Article 5, paragraph 1 of the Convention requires State Parties to "adopt such legislative and other measures as may be necessary" to establish certain activities "as criminal offences when committed intentionally."[18]

The opening words of this portion of the Convention are crucial as a new substantive offense is to be created, involving participation in a criminal group; it is to be additional to ("distinct from")[19] any other specific offense (or attempted offense) committed by one or more of the participants. States have a choice about how the criminal offense is to be structured.

The first option is to make it an offense to agree with one or more others "to commit a serious crime for a purpose relating directly or indirectly to the obtaining of financial or other material benefit."[20] A Party may limit the generality of this somewhat, "where required by domestic law," by including a requirement that "an act [be] undertaken by one of the participants in furtherance" of the agreement, or that the activities involve "an organized criminal group."[21]

The second option is to make criminal "[c]onduct by a person who, with knowledge of either the aim and general criminal activity of an organized criminal group or its intention to commit the crimes in question, takes an active part" in the group.[22] That role may involve engagement in the "[c]riminal activities of the organized group," or "[o]ther activities of the organized criminal group in the knowledge that his or her participation will contribute to the achievement" of the criminal aim.[23]

Article 2 defines "organized criminal group," for the purposes of the Convention, as "a structured group or three or more persons, existing for a period of time and acting in concert with the aim of committing one or more serious crimes or offences established in accordance with this Convention, in order to obtain, directly or indirectly, a financial or other material benefit."[24] "Structured group" means "a group that is not randomly formed for the immediate commission of an offence and that does not need to have formally defined roles for its members, continuity of membership or a developed structure."[25] "Serious crime", in turn, means "conduct constituting an offence punishable by a maximum deprivation of liberty of at least four years or a more serious penalty."[26]

---

[17] Convention against Transnational Organized Crime, Art. 3, ¶ 2.

[18] *Id.* at Art. 5, ¶ 1.

[19] There are possibilities of cumulative punishment here that not all legal systems will necessarily accept.

[20] Convention against Transnational Organized Crime, Art. 5(1)(a)(i).

[21] *Id.*

[22] *Id.* at Art. 5(1)(a)(ii).

[23] *Id.*

[24] *Id.* at Art. 2(a).

[25] *Id.* at Art. 2(c).

[26] *Id.* at Art. 2(b).

This specific-content-free definition of serious crime is fundamental to the way the Convention itself operates. The scope of the Convention's application turns ultimately on the seriousness of the particular activities rather than on substantive content. This is determined by the length of the penalty. It is left to its Protocols to spell out some particular substantive areas to which the basic obligations of the Convention are to be applied. Obviously, not all potential applications are included therein.

The late-Professor Edward Wise, in writing on the subject of RICO, made the point that:

> diverse systems of criminal law have greater unity than is commonly realized, not necessarily on the surface, but in their underlying principles; not necessarily in their results, but in the perennial problems they generate. The universal debate about the desirability and contours of crimes involving membership in criminal associations is one example.[27]

Article 5 is very much the result of a negotiation incorporating group criminality as it is approached in different legal systems. It is not a question of choosing one system over the others, but of attaining a functional synthesis. Thus, the first option, subparagraph (a)(i) of Article 5, paragraph 1, while it avoids the word "conspiracy," is speaking essentially of that institution as understood in the Anglo-American common law.[28] It is clearly an inchoate, preparation-type, offense which could catch participants in the criminal net before a substantive crime, or even an attempt, has occurred.

In both English and American law, conspiracy is well-established as an inchoate offense. One does not, generally, find conspiracy as an inchoate offense in international criminal law treaties.[29] In the present Convention, "conspiracy to commit," as an inchoate offense, appears only (and it would seem randomly) in respect of the crime of money laundering, the criminalization of which is required by Article 6.[30]

In many American jurisdictions, conspiracy is also used as an alternative to complicity theories such as aiding and abetting. Typically it imposes liability for substantive offenses, including attempts, on people at the periphery of criminality who could not be convicted on standard complicity theories. This is often achieved by basing liability on a showing of what amounts to a negligent connection with the criminal activity, rather than an intentional or knowing one.[31]

This version of conspiracy as a theory of secondary responsibility is not found in the Convention. Nor is it found in international criminal law treaties in general. Something close to it, under the guise of contributing to crime by a group of persons acting with a "common purpose" has, however, been appearing in international case-law[32] and in some recent treaties.[33] In addition, the Convention appears to

---

[27] Wise, *supra* note 2, at 323.

[28] *See* Richard P. Barrett & Laura E. Little, *Lessons of the Yugoslav Rape Trials: A Role for Conspiracy Law in International Tribunals,* 88 Minn. L. Rev. 30 (2003) (discussing American conspiracy doctrine and potential international implications).

[29] An exception is the Genocide Convention, Art. III, G.A. Res. 260A (III), 3(1) U.N. GAOR (Resolutions) at 174, U.N. Doc. A/810 (1948). *See* § 14.03[B] *infra.*

[30] *See* § 8.03, *infra.*

[31] *See* Pinkerton v. United States, 328 U.S. 640 (1946).

[32] *See* Appeals Chamber of the Inernational Tribunal for Former Yugoslavia in Prosecutor v. Tadic, IT-94-1-A, 15 July 1999, at 80–105.

follow the American common law position that punishment for the agreement and any completed offenses may be cumulative.[34]

The Convention includes the words "where required by domestic law." This injects some flexibility into the requirement to criminalize the activity. A State may add a requirement that there be "an act undertaken by one of the participants in furtherance of the agreement." This is similar to the common law "overt act" requirement that is required by some federal and state statutes. Like its common law counterpart, it appears to be a minimal requirement as there is no suggestion that the "act" needs to be criminal in itself or that it amount to an attempt. A State can also be in compliance with its obligations under the Convention if it limits conspiracy liability to situations where the conspiracy involves an "organized criminal group." This phrase is explicitly defined in the Convention.[35]

Both the requirement of an aim to commit "serious crime" (with potential of at least four years deprivation of liberty) and the requirement that the group be "organized," and thus "structured," narrow the types of conspiracy that will be the basis of a criminal charge. States requiring involvement of an organized group for the purposes of subparagraph (a)(i) must "ensure that their domestic law covers all serious crimes [as defined] involving organized criminal groups."[36] Thus, although deference is given to the individual States, it is necessary that the activity be criminal.

The second option, subparagraph (a)(ii) of Article 5, paragraph 1, on the other hand, is designed to be more congenial to civil law systems with which conspiracy has not found favor. It penalizes those who knowingly associate themselves with and take an "active part" in an organized criminal group.[37] To come within the ambit of this subparagraph the perpetrator must either be active in the *criminal* activities of the group, or active in its *other* activities with the appropriate knowledge, namely that the participation will contribute to the achievement of the criminal aim. It is fairly clear that a perpetrator may contravene this standard without doing acts that make him or her complicit under traditional principles for a serious crime as defined in the Convention. The conduct may, in itself, be a "non-serious" crime or even lawful. One who goes as far as complicity in a serious crime involving an organized criminal group, is, however, covered under subpara-

---

[33] *See generally* Mahnoush Arsanjani, *The Rome Statute of the International Criminal Court*, 93 Am. J. Int'l L. 774, 776 (1998) (discussing Rome Statute, Art. 25(2)(d), U.N. Doc. A/CONF.183/9 (1998) (as corrected), and International Convention for the Suppression of Terrorist Bombings, Art. 2(3)(c), G.A. Res. 52/164, U.N. GAOR, 52d Sess., Supp. No. 49, at 389, U.N. Doc. A/52/49 (1998)).

[34] This seems to be a viable interpretation of the opening words in subparagraph (a): "distinct from those involving the attempt or completion of the criminal activity." *See* Callanan v. United States, 364 U.S. 587 (1961) (presenting the cumulative rule). This does not appear to be the English rule and is rejected in the Model Penal Code. *See* Model Penal Code § 5.03 (1962).

[35] Parties limiting their legislation either by the "act" requirement or that of an "organized criminal group" must notify the United Nations Secretary-General, the depositary of the Convention; Convention against Transnational Organized Crime, Art. 5, ¶ 3. The United States informed the Secretary-General that "the commission of an overt act in furtherance of the agreement is generally required."

[36] Convention against Transnational Organized Crime, Art. 5(3).

[37] Civil law countries do not use a uniform system. Wise, *supra* note 2, at 313–19. For example, French law has a concept of "association of wrongdoers" that is similar to the Anglo-American conspiracy. But "[t]he French reworking of the idea of a criminal association is exceptional. Elsewhere, a criminal association still is required to have more or less durable character, and thereby differs from the sort of ad hoc agreement that suffices to make out a conspiracy." *Id.* at 316.

graph (b) for organizing, directing, aiding, abetting, facilitating or counseling the commission of serious crime. In some cases the conduct may fall under both (a)(i) and (a)(ii).

§ 8.03 THE OBLIGATION TO CRIMINALIZE LAUNDERING

Article 6 of the Convention deals with criminalization of the laundering of the proceeds of a crime. Parties are to seek to apply this principle to "the widest range of predicate offences."[38] At the least, it must include all "serious" crimes as defined by Articles 5,[39] 8, [40] and 23 (which deals with laundering). This covers crimes such as corruption and obstruction of justice.

Subject to a double criminality requirement, predicate offences must include "offences committed both within and outside the jurisdiction of the State Party in question."[41] In what appears to be a recognition of potential double jeopardy or merger problems under some legal systems, the Convention provides that: "[i]f required by fundamental principles of the domestic law of a State Party, it may be provided that the [laundering offences] do not apply to the persons who committed the predicate offence."[42]

In a striking example of the way in which modern suppression treaties often require extensive enforcement regimes at the domestic level, the criminalization obligations for money laundering are backed up by a requirement in Article 7 of the Convention that States Parties institute a comprehensive domestic regulatory and supervisory regime for banks and non-bank financial institutions, and where appropriate, other bodies particularly susceptible to money laundering.[43]

§ 8.04 THE CRIMINALIZATION OF CORRUPTION

Article 8 focuses on corruption.[44] Parties are required to establish as criminal, both the promise, offering or giving to a public official[45] and the solicitation or acceptance by such an official "of an undue advantage, for the official himself or

---

[38] The definition of "predicate offence" is a little circular: " . . . any offence as a result of which proceeds have been generated that may become the subject of an offence as defined in article 6 of this Convention." Convention against Transnational Organized Crime, Art. 2(h). The term "predicate" is a term that is used in the U.S. RICO statute. See 18 U.S.C. § 1961.

[39] See § 8.02, supra.

[40] See § 8.04, infra.

[41] Convention against Transnational Organized Crime, Art. 6(2)(c). See also § 13.02 infra on the significance of crime committed in another country.

[42] Id. at Art. 6(2)(e).

[43] Id. at Art. 7(1)(b). The article also encourages exchanges of information at the national and international levels (subparagraph (1)(b)); consideration of measures to monitor movement of cash and negotiable instruments across borders (paragraph 2); calls upon states to "use as a guideline the relevant initiatives of regional, interregional and multilateral organizations against money laundering (paragraph 3)" and encourages them to "develop and promote global, regional, subregional and bilateral cooperation among judicial, law enforcement and financial regulatory authorities in order to combat money laundering (paragraph 4)."

[44] The United Nations subsequently developed a broader based Convention against Corruption. See § 3.02, supra.

[45] "Public official," for these purposes, means a public official or a person who provides a public service as defined in the domestic law and as applied in the criminal law of the State Party in which the

herself or another person or entity, in order that the official act or refrain from acting in the exercise of his or her official duties."[46] "Participation as an accomplice" in corruption is also to be made criminal.[47] States Parties must take legislative, administrative and prosecutorial measures to promote integrity and to prevent, detect and punish the corruption of public officials.[48]

§ 8.05 CRIMINAL RESPONSIBILITY OF LEGAL PERSONS

Some legal systems still find it difficult to conceptualize criminal responsibility of entities, referred to in international usage as legal persons. Since a corporation cannot be placed in jail and cannot form the intent to commit a crime, the concept of holding an entity liable is not universally accepted Article 10 of the Convention deals with this area.[49] It provides for entity liability, but allows States options in handling this form of liability. For example, it can be through a choice of criminal, civil, or administrative control. The Convention also provides that this "liability shall be without prejudice" to a finding of criminal liability of the individuals associated with or a part of the entity.

Corporate criminal responsibility was controversial during the drafting of the Rome Statute of the International Criminal Court. France and Solomon Islands led an unsuccessful effort to include such responsibility in the Statute.[50] A more modest effort succeeded in this Convention. The proposed I.C.C. provision would have been obligatory on all parties, whereas the Convention on Transnational Organized Crime defers to the "legal principles" of individual States Parties.

§ 8.06 GRAVITY OF PENALTIES

As is now typical in international criminal law treaties, the Parties are required to make the offences established in accordance with the treaty "liable to sanctions that take into account the gravity of that offence."[51] They are similarly required to establish a long statute of limitations period.[52] Nonetheless, there are some constraints on how far homogenization of domestic systems will go. A matter implied in previous international criminal law treaties is spelled out in this one:

> Nothing contained in this Convention shall affect the principle that the description of the offences established in accordance with this Convention and of the applicable legal defences or other legal principles controlling the lawfulness of conduct is reserved to the domestic law of a State Party and

---

person in question performs that function. Convention against Transnational Organized Crime, Art. 8, ¶ 4.

[46] *Id.* at Art. 8(1). Parties are also required to consider criminalizing corruption involving a foreign public official or international civil servant. *Id.* at ¶ 2.

[47] *Id.* at Art. 8(3).

[48] *Id.* at Art. 9(1). Those doing the prevention, detection and punishment must be provided with adequate independence, *id.* at ¶ 2.

[49] *Id.* at Art. 10.

[50] *See* Andrew Clapham, *The Question of Jurisdiction Under International Criminal Law Over Legal Persons: Lessons from the Rome Conference on the International Criminal Court*, in LIABILITY OF MULTINATIONAL CORPORATIONS UNDER INTERNATIONAL LAW 139 (M.T. Kamminga & S. Zia-Zarifi, eds, 2000).

[51] Convention against Transnational Organized Crime, Art. 11, ¶ 1.

[52] *Id.* at Art. 11, ¶ 5.

that such offences shall be prosecuted and punished in accordance with that law.[53]

§ 8.07 FORFEITURE

Forfeiture, sometimes referred to as confiscation, has been a significant part of the United States strategy against organized crime. One finds forfeiture statutes in both the U.S. money laundering statute and in the RICO statutes. Forfeiture is the subject of two articles in the Convention against Transnational Organized Crime, Article 12, headed "Confiscation and seizure" and Article 13 on "International cooperation for purposes of confiscation."

Article 12 requires that State Parties adopt, to the greatest extent possible within their domestic legal systems, measures to enable confiscation of proceeds derived from the Convention offences, property, equipment or other instrumentalities used in or destined for use in offences covered by the Convention, property into which proceeds have been transferred, proceeds intermingled with property derived from legitimate sources, and income or other benefits derived from the proceeds.[54] Moreover, the confiscation provision encourages the stripping of bank secrecy. It provides that for the purposes of Article 12 and of Article 13 (on international cooperation), "each State Party shall empower its courts or other competent authorities to order that bank, financial or commercial records be made available." States may not decline to act under this obligation on the ground of bank secrecy.[55]

Article 13, on international cooperation for purposes of confiscation, is a kind of mini-Mutual Legal Assistance Treaty.[56] Parties are to assist one another to the greatest extent possible within their legal systems, especially to identify, trace and freeze or seize assets subject to the regime of the Organized Crime Convention. They are encouraged to enter into further bilateral and multilateral arrangements to enhance the effectiveness of this provision.[57]

Article 14 of the Convention, which deals with the disposal of proceeds of crime or confiscated property, has some similarities with earlier provisions in international criminal law. When a request to confiscate has been made by another State Party, for example, States are required, to the extent permitted by domestic law and if so requested, to give careful consideration to returning the property to the state of origin so that there may be compensation to victims or a return of property to their legitimate owners.[58] States are encouraged to enter into arrangements to make some of the proceeds available for technical assistance or to assist intergovernmental bodies engaged in the fight against organized crime.[59] They are also to consider "[s]haring with other States Parties, on a regular or case-by-case basis, such proceeds of crime or property, or funds derived from the sale of such proceeds of crime or property, in accordance with its domestic law or administrative

---

[53] *Id.* at Art. 11, ¶ 6.

[54] *Id.* at Art. 12, ¶¶ 1–5.

[55] *Id.* at Art. 12, ¶ 6.

[56] There are also more detailed mutual legal assistance provisions in Art. 18.

[57] Convention against Transnational Organized Crime, Art. 13.

[58] *Id.* at Art. 14, ¶ 2.

[59] *Id.* at Art. 14, ¶ 3(a).

procedures."[60] Such arrangements, a type of contingency fee deal, are a feature of drug conventions[61] and Mutual Legal Assistance Treaties.[62]

§ 8.08 JURISDICTION

Article 15 is the fundamental jurisdictional provision that goes with the suppression obligation.[63] It requires that each State Party adopt such measures as may be necessary to establish its jurisdiction over the Convention offenses when, (a) the offense is committed in the territory of that Party, or (b) when it is committed on board a vessel that is flying the flag of that Party or an aircraft that is registered under the laws of the Party at the time that the offense is committed.[64] The United States made an interesting reservation to this provision. It states that

> [t]he United States of America reserves the right not to apply in part the obligation set forth in Article 15, paragraph 1(b) with respect to the offenses established in the Convention. The United States does not provide plenary jurisdiction over offenses that are committed on board ships flying its flag or aircraft registered under its law. However, in a number of circumstances, U.S. law provides for jurisdiction over such offenses committed on board U.S.-flagged ships or aircraft registered under U.S. law. Accordingly, the U.S. will implement paragraph 1(b) to the extent provided for under its federal law.[65]

In addition,[66] there is also permissive jurisdiction where the offense is committed against a national of the party (passive personality jurisdiction)[67] and where it is committed by a national of the Party or a stateless person who has his or her habitual residence there.[68] There is also permissive jurisdiction in respect of certain of the organized criminal group situations[69] and laundering[70] that might not literally fit within a territorial theory. In what has now become a boilerplate

---

[60] *Id.* at Art. 14, ¶ 3(b).

[61] *See* United Nations Convention against Illicit Traffic in Narcotic Drugs and Psychotropic Substances, Art. 5(5)(b)(ii), U.N. Doc. E/CONF.82/15, Corr.1 and Corr. 2 (1988).

[62] *See, e.g.,* Optional Protocol to the United Nations Model Treaty on Mutual Assistance in Criminal Matters, G.A. Res. 45/117, U.N. GAOR, 45th Sess., Supp. No. 49A at 211, U.N. Doc. A/45/49 (1991).

[63] Art. 15 underscores the complexity of state practice in respect of "extraterritorial" jurisdiction and the difficulty of fitting some of this practice within categories such as territorial, protective, passive personality and universal. *See generally* § 2.04[F].

[64] Convention against Transnational Organized Crime, Art. 15, ¶ 1.

[65] Reservation made on ratification, *available at* United Nations treaty register, http://untreaty.un.org.proxy.law.rutgers.edu/ENGLISH/bible/englishinternetbible/partI/chapterXVIII/treaty13.asp.

[66] And subject to Art. 4 which protects the principle of non-intervention in the domestic affairs of other states.

[67] Convention against Transnational Organized Crime, Art. 15, ¶ 2(a). This is another example in state practice of the increasing acceptability of passive personality jurisdiction, although it is notable that its exercise is permissive not obligatory in the Convention.

[68] *Id.* at Art. 15, ¶ 2(b).

[69] *Id.* at Art. 15, ¶ 2(c)(i). (Where the offense is one of those established in accordance with article 5, ¶ 1 "and is committed outside its territory with a view to the commission of a serious crime within its territory.") This is an expanded "effects" theory of jurisdiction, or perhaps a "protective" one.

[70] *Id.* at Art. 15, ¶ 2(c)(ii). (Where the offense is established in accordance with art. 6, ¶ 1(b)(ii) "and is committed outside its territory with a view to the commission of an offense established in accordance

provision in multilateral practice, States that do not extradite their nationals must adopt the measures necessary to establish their jurisdiction over offences covered by the Convention when they do not extradite on this basis.[71]

Article 15 also includes an interesting coordination provision to the effect that if a State Party exercising jurisdiction under either the mandatory or the permissive theories of the Convention has been notified, or has otherwise learned, that one or more other States Parties are conducting an investigation, prosecution or judicial proceeding in respect of the same conduct, the competent authorities of those States Parties shall, as appropriate, consult with one another with a view to coordinating their actions.[72] As is the case with the various terrorism treaties, one of the objects of the Convention against Transnational Organized Crime is to make sure that there are no safe havens. Potential costs of this cause lie in the possibility of clashes of jurisdiction where two or more States may act concurrently and the chance of double jeopardy.

International law in both these areas is a work in progress. Since general international law has not established a priority system among various jurisdictional theories, the solution is negotiation, especially on the basis of where the strongest case may be mounted. The danger of the "risks of concurrent jurisdiction" was downplayed at an early stage of the drafting, when it was "pointed out, however that concurrent jurisdiction might not be a negative development, as it would indicate the interest of numerous States to deal with specific problems. In addition, conflicts of jurisdiction were rather rare and were invariably resolved at the practical level by an eventual determination of which jurisdiction would be ultimately exercised on the basis of the chances for successful prosecution and adjudication of the particular case."[73]

§ 8.09   PROCEDURAL MATTERS

The Convention has a number of machinery provisions that are in some instances based on work done earlier with terrorism[74] and drug treaties.[75] Article 16 deals with extradition, Article 17 with the transfer of sentenced persons, Article 18 with mutual legal assistance, Article 19 with joint investigations, and Article 20 with

---

with article 6, paragraph 1(a)(i) or (ii) or (b)(i) of this Convention within its territory.") This is another expansive "effects" or "protective" theory.

[71] There is an even broader permissive provision in the Convention empowering a State Party to "adopt such measures as may be necessary to establish its jurisdiction over the offences covered by the Convention when the alleged offender is present in its territory and it does not extradite him or her." Convention against Transnational Organized Crime, Art. 15, ¶ 4. This appears to be a universal jurisdiction provision, or at least the modest (permissive) version of it, "custodial" or subsidiary jurisdiction.

[72] *Id.* at Art. 15, ¶ 5. The paragraph presumably contemplates that the parties may be able to consolidate the case by authorizing one State to exercise jurisdiction transferred from one or more other States. *See also* Art. 21 (encouraging transfer of criminal proceedings in such cases); § 2.05[F] *supra* (discussing transfer of proceedings).

[73] Report of the Meeting of the Inter-Sessional Open-Ended Intergovernmental Group of Experts on the Elaboration of a Possible Comprehensive International Convention against Organized Transnational Crime (Warsaw, 2–6 February 1998) at 10, U.N. Doc. E/CN.15/1998/5 (1998).

[74] The initial model for many of these provisions was the Convention for the Suppression of Unlawful Seizure of Aircraft, signed at the Hague, 16 December 1970, 10 I.L.M. 133 (1971).

[75] Notably the 1988 United Nations Convention on Narcotic Drugs and Psychotropic Substances, § 6.02[B], *supra.*

special investigative techniques, such as controlled delivery and electronic or other forms of surveillance. Article 21 invites States to explore the possibility of transferring proceedings to one another, in particular in cases where several jurisdictions are involved. Article 24 deals with the protection of witnesses and Article 25 with assistance to and protection of victims.[76] Article 26 is aimed at enhancing cooperation with law enforcement authorities on the part of those who participate or have participated in organized criminal groups. In particular, it contemplates the possibility of mitigating punishment and even granting immunity for an accused who provides substantial cooperation in the investigation or prosecution of an offence. Article 27 deals with law enforcement cooperation and Article 28 with collection, exchange and analysis of information on the nature of organized crime. Articles 29 and 30 speak quite comprehensively to training and bilateral and multilateral technical assistance, particularly to developing countries and countries in transition. Finally, at the national level, Article 31 requires States to endeavor to develop and evaluate projects and to establish and promote best practices and policies aimed at the prevention of transnational organized crime. A particular feature of this involves strategies for dealing with governmental corruption.

All in all, these machinery provisions represent a good example of the detailed ways in which multilateral treaties are used to encourage States to move in particular directions under their domestic law in order to approach a problem that has been perceived and conceptualized on the global level.

§ 8.10   REVIEW BY THE CONFERENCE OF THE PARTIES

Article 32 of the Convention provides for the establishment of a Conference of the Parties to the Convention to "improve the capacity of States Parties to combat transnational organized crime and to promote and review the implementation of this Convention."[77] The Conference is to agree upon mechanisms for achieving these objectives, including: facilitating activities under Articles 29 (training and technical assistance), 30 (economic development and technical assistance) and 31 (prevention), including encouraging the mobilization of voluntary contributions; facilitating the exchange of information on patterns and trends in transnational organized crime and successful practices for combating it; cooperating with relevant international and regional organizations and non-governmental organizations; reviewing periodically the implementation of the Convention; making recommendations to improve it.[78] Parties are to supply information as required by the Conference and to such supplemental review mechanisms as the Conference may create.[79]

Early responses to requests to supply information have been limited, and emphasis is, of necessity, being given to technical assistance (including assistance in

---

[76] Convention against Transnational Organized Crime, Art. 25 speaks of assistance and protection of victims (¶ 1) and compensation and restitution (¶ 2). Paragraph 3 says that "[e]ach State Party shall, subject to its domestic law, enable views and concerns of victims to be presented and considered at appropriate stages of criminal proceedings against offenders in a manner not prejudicial to the rights of the defence." Paragraph 3 echoes language in the General Assembly's 1985 Declaration of Basic Principles of Justice for Victims of Crime and Abuse of Power, G.A. Res. 40/34 (1985) and Art. 68(3) of the Rome Statute of the International Criminal Court.

[77] Convention against Transnational Organized Crime, Art. 32, ¶ 1.

[78] *Id.* at Art. 32, ¶ 3.

[79] *Id.* at Art. 32, ¶¶ 4 and 5.

providing information).[80] Nevertheless, the United Nations Office on Drugs and Crime, located in Vienna, regards the implementation of this "framework" Convention as a major part of its task[81] and one is certain to see strong continuing efforts to that effect.

---

[80] See Report on the meeting of the Open-ended Interim Working Group of Government Experts on Technical Assistance held in Vienna from 3 to 5 October 2007, U.N. Doc. CTOC/COP/2008/7 (Oct. 16. 2007).

[81] *See* UNODC and Organized Crime, *available at* http://www.unodc.org/unodc/en/organized-crime/index.htm.

PART THREE
PROCEDURE

Chapter 9
EXTRATERRITORIAL APPLICATION OF U.S. CONSTITUTION

SYNOPSIS

§ 9.01 CONSTITUTIONAL RIGHTS ABROAD

Initially, the United States had consular courts to oversee the prosecution of United States citizens abroad. These courts did not afford these citizens the panoply of rights provided to citizens at home, and were considered to operate below the norms required by the U.S. judicial system.[1] The host countries, moreover, tended to regard them as violative of local sovereignty and imposed by unequal treaties. It is not surprising, therefore, that consular courts do not exist today.[2]

Some of the issues that arise in cases involving crimes committed abroad by United States citizens, involve individuals with a relationship to the military. In the case of *Reid v. Covert*,[3] the Court considered whether it was appropriate for military tribunals to try the wife of a United States Air Force sergeant stationed in England and the wife of an Army officer in Japan. Both of these women were accused of killing their husbands. Although the Supreme Court initially approved of a trial for these women under the Uniform Code of Military Justice, on rehearing the Court decided otherwise. The Court held that the court-martial procedure used in these cases did not conform to the requirements of Article III of the Constitution and did not provide adequate Fifth and Sixth Amendment rights to the accused. The Court held that "under our Constitution courts of law alone are given power to try civilians for their offenses against the United States."[4]

Although consular courts have been discarded, and federal criminal cases must be brought within Article III courts, the conduct covered by these courts has been greatly expanded. Today, the impediments to a prosecution for crimes such as those presented in the case of *Reid v. Covert* no longer exist, as the United States can

---

[1] *See* Geoffrey R. Watson, *Offenders Abroad: The Case for Nationality-Based Criminal Jurisdiction,* 17 YALE J. INT'L L. 41, 49–52 (1992).

[2] 22 U.S.C. § 141 et seq. (repealed Aug. 1, 1956).

[3] 354 U.S. 1 (1957).

[4] *Id.* at 40–41.

proceed through 18 U.S.C. § 1119 which provides U.S. jurisdiction for the killing of a national by a national of the United States. Additionally, Congress passed The Military Extraterritorial Jurisdiction Act of 2000 to alleviate the problems created when civilians who accompany the military overseas commit crimes.[5] This Act extends federal criminal jurisdiction over crimes "punishable by imprisonment for more than 1 year if the conduct had been engaged in within the special maritime and territorial jurisdiction of the United States while employed by or accompanying the Armed Forces."[6]

The U.S. has also worked with other countries to assure that U.S. citizens outside the country receive appropriate procedural rights. Today, Status of Force Agreements (SOFAs) negotiated with NATO and other countries provide procedural rights to members of the military, civilians working for the military, and their dependents.[7] These agreements include the right to a speedy trial, due process notice of the charges, the right to confront witnesses, the right to have compulsory process, as well as rights to an interpreter, lawyer, and communication with a representative of the United States.[8] Since the situation is typically one of concurrent jurisdiction, the agreements allocate jurisdiction between the sending and host states. Local courts normally have priority in matters affecting their citizenry; the United States has priority when its interests are primarily affected.

§ 9.02 FOURTH AMENDMENT

[A] *Verdugo-Urquidez*

United States v. Verdugo-Urquidez[9] was a landmark Supreme Court decision that provided some guidance on extraterritorial Fourth Amendment rights. It did not, however, provide answers to all of the questions that can arise when a search and seizure occurs outside the United States and prosecutors later seek to use that evidence in a trial within this country.

Verdugo-Urquidez, a citizen and resident of Mexico, was subjected to a search in his home country for evidence related to narcotics trafficking and the defendant's possible "involvement in the kidnapping and torture-murder of a DEA (Drug Enforcement Agency)" agent.[10] The search was conducted by DEA agents in conjunction and with approval of the Mexican Federal Judicial Police. The district court which initially heard this matter suppressed the evidence seized

---

[5] *See* United States v. Gatlin, 216 F.3d 207, 209 (2d Cir. 2000) (reversing a conviction for lack of jurisdiction, the court directed the "Clerk of the Court to forward a copy" of the "opinion to the Chairmen of the House and Senate Armed Service and Judiciary Committees.").

[6] 18 U.S.C. § 3261(a)(1) (2000). The Act also provides for jurisdiction in some instances over military personnel. It also includes in the category entitled "employed," a Department of Defense contractor or subcontractor whose contract "relates to supporting the mission of the Department of Defense overseas." Some private contractors in Iraq, especially those providing security, are contracted to the State Department and may not come within the jurisdiction of the statute. They may be immune from local prosecution also. *See* § 9.02[D], *infra*.

[7] *See* Joseph M. Snee & A. Kenneth Pye, Status of Forces Agreements: Criminal Jurisdiction (1957).

[8] NATO, Agreement Between the Parties to the North Atlantic Treaty Regarding the Status of their Forces (June 19, 1951), *available at* http://www.nato.int/docu/basictxt/ b510619a.htm.

[9] 494 U.S. 259 (1990).

[10] *Id.* at 262.

during the search. This decision was affirmed by a divided panel of the Ninth Circuit Court of Appeals.

In an opinion authored by Chief Justice Rehnquist, the lower courts were reversed. Distinguishing the Fourth Amendment from the Fifth and Sixth Amendments, the Court noted that "the people" as used in the Fourth Amendment refers to "a class of persons who are part of a national community or who have otherwise developed sufficient connection with this country to be considered part of that community."[11] The Court found that the Fourth Amendment did not apply because "[a]t the time of the search, he was a citizen and resident of Mexico with no voluntary attachment to the United States, and the place searched was located in Mexico."[12] The Court did leave open the possibility for there to be restrictions on searches and seizures conducted outside the United States but stated that this "must be imposed by the political branches through diplomatic understanding, treaty, or legislation."[13]

Justices Kennedy and Stevens authored concurring opinions. A dissent by Justices Brennan and Marshall stressed the need for "[m]utuality" "to ensure the fundamental fairness that underlies our Bill of Rights." This dissent states that "[w]hen we tell the world that we expect all people, wherever they may be, to abide by our laws, we cannot in the same breath tell the world that our law enforcement officers need not do the same." A dissent was also written by Justice Blackmun, who wanted the case remanded to consider whether there was sufficient probable cause to render the search "reasonable."

[B] Beyond *Verdugo-Urquidez*

Verdugo-Urquidez did not address several issues that have since been raised in lower courts. For example, should aliens within the United States be afforded Fourth Amendment rights; do United States citizens outside the country have Fourth Amendment rights; and when do individuals have "substantial connections" with this country to permit the application of the Fourth Amendment to them? Although the Fourth Amendment may not apply, this does not preclude a court from refusing to admit evidence that might be a violation of due process rights under the Fifth Amendment.[14]

[1] Aliens Within the United States

In *Theck v. Warden, Immigration and Naturalization Service*,[15] a district court held that *Verdugo-Urquidez* does not apply to situations that occur within the United States. In holding that *Verdugo-Urquidez* is limited to "the extraterritorial application of the Fourth Amendment," the California District Court found an unreasonable seizure in prohibiting the petitioner from marrying someone where his marriage to this individual would allow him to be deported. Absent this marriage, the petitioner would remain incarcerated indefinitely. Finding no "legitimate penological interest" for prohibiting this marriage, the court stated that "[d]enying petitioner the right to marry, in these circumstances, results in an

---

[11] *Id.* at 265.

[12] *Id.* at 274–75.

[13] *Id.* at 275.

[14] *See* Wang v. Reno, 81 F.3d 808 (9th Cir. 1996). *See also* § 9.03, *infra*.

[15] 22 F. Supp. 2d 1117 (C.D. Cal. 1998).

unreasonable seizure under the Fourth Amendment."[16] Because this was occurring within the United States, *Verdugo-Urquidez* was found to be inapplicable.

[2] U.S. Citizens Outside the United States

United States citizens are protected against unreasonable searches and seizures conducted against them while they are abroad when the search or seizure is by an official of the United States. The United States, however, cannot preclude a foreign government from conducting a search or seizure abroad. As such, United States citizens who are outside this country can be subject to violations of the Fourth Amendment in countries that do not adhere to a similar constitutional provision. This issue takes on a new posture, however, when the evidence obtained by the other country is provided to United States law enforcement officers for the purpose of a prosecution in the U.S.

Although normally, evidence obtained by foreign police can be used against individuals in United States courts,[17] there are exceptions to this general statement. U.S. courts have found there to be Fourth Amendment violations if the search producing the evidence is a joint venture of the U.S. police and the foreign country.[18] To be a joint venture it is necessary that "the conduct of foreign law enforcement officials rendered them agents, or virtual agents, of United States law enforcement officials."[19] There can also be a Fourth Amendment violation when "the cooperation between the United States and foreign law enforcement agencies is designed to evade constitutional requirements applicable to American officials."[20] In situations of a joint venture or deliberate evasion of constitutional rights, courts can find that the evidence was improperly obtained and exclude the evidence from trial.

Further, courts may find it improper if the search is "shock[ing] to the [judicial] conscience."[21] This latter exception is not premised upon the Fourth Amendment, but rather on the use of the court's "supervisory powers."[22]

[3] Substantial Connections

Justice Rehnquist's opinion in *Verdugo-Urquidez* stated "that aliens receive constitutional protections when they have come within the territory of the United States and developed substantial connections with this country."[23] This decision did not provide a definition of "substantial connections." It left open the question of whether a "minimum-contacts" type of approach should be employed.[24]

---

[16] *Id.* at 1122.

[17] *See* Joshua Dressler, Understanding Criminal Procedure § 4.04(E) (4th ed. 1996).

[18] *See* United States v. Maturo, 982 F.2d 57 (2d Cir. 1992).

[19] *Id.* at 61.

[20] *Id.*

[21] *See* United States v. Barona, 56 F.3d 1087, 1091 (9th Cir. 1995).

[22] *Id.*

[23] 494 U.S. at 270.

[24] *See* David Haug, *Recent Developments, United States: Extraterritorial Application of the Fourth Amendment* — United States v. Verdugo-Urquidez, *110 S. Ct. 1056 (1990)*, 32 Harv. Int'l L.J. 295, 301 n.39 (1991).

In *United States v. Esparza-Mendoza*,[25] the court looked at whether the accused was " 'part of a national community' or otherwise had 'developed sufficient connection with this country to be considered part of that community.' "[26] The court concluded that a "previously deported felon" lacked sufficient connection to assert Fourth Amendment rights. The court in *Esparza-Mendoza* left open the question of whether the Fourth Amendment might apply to illegal aliens who had never been deported.

[C]   Planes, Boats, and Borders

Border searches of individuals entering the United States are a recognized exception within Fourth Amendment jurisprudence.[27] The exception provides that "routine searches of the persons and effects of entrants are not subject to any requirement of reasonable suspicion, probable cause, or warrant."[28] Several lower courts have extended this Supreme Court jurisprudence to border searches of outgoing travelers.[29]

The Fourth Amendment may also be inapplicable when a search emanates from air travel. Border searches have been found to apply to air travel, as the search is considered to be occurring at the "functional equivalent" of the border.[30] In some cases treaties or executive agreements may facilitate searches occurring at borders.[31]

Entry of boats may also allow for a relaxed Fourth Amendment application. For example, in *United States v. Hilton*,[32] the First Circuit held that "the limited intrusion represented by a document and safety inspection on the high seas, even in the absence of a warrant or suspicion of wrongdoing, is reasonable under the Fourth Amendment."[33] These searches are often conducted by the coast guard, as there is statutory authority for them to search, seize, and arrest on the high seas.[34] Customs officers also have the ability to board vessels and vehicles in a variety of places including "within the customs waters or, as he may be authorized, within a customs-enforcement area established under the Anti-Smuggling Act."[35]

[D]   Foreign Intelligence

Extraterritorial searches of U.S. citizens, when conducted as part of foreign intelligence by U.S. agents, may also be allowed as an exception to the Fourth Amendment. This exception was emphasized in the case of *United States v. Bin*

---

[25] 265 F. Supp. 2d 1254 (D. Utah 2003).

[26] *Id.* at 1260 (noting that some courts consider the "sufficient connection" language to be merely a part of a plurality decision and therefore not binding precedent).

[27] *See* United States v. Montoya de Hernandez, 473 U.S. 531 (1985).

[28] *Id.* at 538.

[29] *See* United States v. Beras, 183 F.3d 22 (1st Cir. 1999).

[30] *See* Almeida-Sanchez v. United States, 413 U.S. 266, 272–73 (1973).

[31] *See* United States v. Walczak, 783 F.2d 852 (9th Cir. 1986).

[32] 619 F.2d 127 (1st Cir. 1980).

[33] *Id.* at 131.

[34] *See* 14 U.S.C. § 89(a).

[35] *See* 19 U.S.C. § 1581.

Laden,[36] a case where defendant El-Hage, a United States citizen, moved to suppress evidence seized from his home in Kenya. The government argued that this search and seizure was proper because it was necessary for foreign intelligence and also because the defendant was "an agent of a foreign power." In accepting a "foreign intelligence" exception to the Fourth Amendment, the Southern District of New York noted that the government "would be significantly frustrated by the imposition of a warrant requirement in this context."[37]

The court in *Bin Laden* provided a three part test to ascertain whether the "foreign intelligence" exception to the Fourth Amendment could apply. First it is necessary to show that the accused "was an agent of a foreign power." Second the government must demonstrate that the "searches in question were conducted 'primarily' for foreign intelligence purposes." The final prong of this test requires the government to show that the search was "authorized by the President or Attorney General." In the *Bin Laden* case the court found that the government had met the three prong test articulated by the court and denied the defendant's motion to suppress the evidence.[38]

§ 9.03 FIFTH AMENDMENT

Where the Fourth Amendment has been held to protect "the People of the United States," the Fifth Amendment protects "all 'persons.' "[39] Several arguments have been raised with respect to the Fifth Amendment;[40] most common are claims of a violation of the Privilege Against Self-Incrimination.[41]

The Self-Incrimination Clause of the Fifth Amendment poses concerns when testimony given in the United States poses extraterritorial ramifications. For example, in the case of *United States v. Balsys*,[42] the question presented was whether a fear of criminal prosecution by a foreign country was sufficient for asserting a Fifth Amendment privilege in the United States.

Balsys, a resident alien living in New York, was subpoenaed to testify at a deposition. The testimony sought was for a civil deportation hearing concerning whether "contrary to his representations" on an application for an immigrant visa and alien registration, he had "participated in Nazi persecution during World War II."[43] After he refused to provide answers to questions, and asserted his Fifth Amendment privilege, the Office of Special Investigations of the Criminal Division of the United States Department of Justice (OSI) proceeded to federal district court to secure an enforcement order. The district court granted the Order, and the Second Circuit Court of Appeals responded by vacating the Order. In accepting

---

[36] 126 F. Supp. 2d 264 (S.D.N.Y. 2000).

[37] *Id.* at 277.

[38] The Court in Bin Laden also discussed issues beyond the foreign intelligence exception. *Id.* at 270.

[39] *See* United States v. Barona, 56 F.3d 1087, 1093 (9th Cir. 1995).

[40] *E.g.*, Lea Brilmayer & Charles Norchi, *Federal Extraterritoriality and Fifth Amendment Due Process*, 105 Harv. L. Rev. 1217 (1992).

[41] Double jeopardy presents less of a concern. The dual sovereignty rule allows for different states or countries to proceed against someone for the same conduct, as it is considered different offenses when conduct breaks the law of more than one jurisdiction. *E.g.*, Heath v. Alabama, 474 U.S. 82, 88 (1985); United States v. Lanza, 260 U.S. 377, 382 (1922).

[42] 524 U.S. 666 (1998).

[43] *Id.* at 670.

certiorari, the Supreme Court was positioned to decide whether "a real and substantial fear of prosecution by a foreign country" was a proper basis for assertion of Fifth Amendment rights.[44]

Balsys did not assert that he might be incriminating himself under United States law. Rather, his claim was that his responses might "subject him to criminal prosecution by Lithuania, Israel, and Germany."[45] The Supreme Court rejected his arguments and reversed the decision of the Court of Appeals. In an opinion authored by Justice Souter, the Court held that "[s]ince the likely gain to the witness fearing foreign prosecution is thus uncertain, the countervailing uncertainty about the loss of testimony to the United States cannot be dismissed as comparatively unimportant."[46] The Fifth Amendment privilege against self-incrimination would not apply when the privilege was being asserted because of fear of foreign prosecution. One exception was noted by Justice Souter in his opinion. This applies when the United States is working in a "cooperative prosecution" with another country. The Court stated that,

> [i]f it could be said that the United States and its allies had enacted substantially similar criminal codes aimed at prosecuting offenses of international character, and if it could be shown that the United States was granting immunity from domestic prosecution for the purpose of obtaining evidence to be delivered to other nations as prosecutors of a crime common to both countries, then an argument could be made that the Fifth Amendment should apply based on fear of foreign prosecution simply because that prosecution was not fairly characterized as distinctly "foreign."[47]

The Court held that a treaty between two countries to provide evidence, as existed in this case, would not be sufficient to "rise to the level of cooperative prosecution."[48]

When it is not testimony being sought, but rather records pursuant to a grand jury subpoena *duces tecum*, and the production of the records may result in a violation of another country's criminal laws, courts have been asked to resolve whether the Fifth Amendment privilege applies. In some instances courts have ordered that the documents be produced, saying that they cannot "acquiesce in the proposition that United States criminal investigations must be thwarted whenever there is conflict with the interest of other states."[49] The courts have applied United States law rather than the foreign law.[50] Other courts, however, have used a balancing test, balancing the interests of the two jurisdictions.[51]

---

[44] *Id.* at 670–71.

[45] *Id.* at 670.

[46] *Id.* at 697.

[47] *Id.* at 698.

[48] *Id.* at 699. There was a concurring opinion by Justice Stevens, and a dissent by Justice Ginsburg, and another dissent by Justice Breyer that Justice Ginsburg joined.

[49] 49 In re Grand Jury Proceedings (United States v. Bank of Nova Scotia), 691 F.2d 1384, 1391 (11th Cir. 1982) (*citing* In re Grand Jury Proceedings (United States v. Field), 532 F.2d 404, 410 (5th Cir. 1976)).

[50] *See* In re Grand Jury Subpoena dated Aug. 9, 2000, 218 F. Supp. 2d 544 (S.D.N.Y. 2002).

[51] *E.g.*, United States v. First Nat'l Bank of Chicago, 699 F.2d 341 (7th Cir. 1983); United States v. Chase Manhattan Bank, 584 F. Supp. 1080 (S.D.N.Y. 1984).

Courts have also been faced with questions regarding requests for court orders to require individuals to sign a directive authorizing the release of documents from a foreign financial institution. Some courts have found that this does not involve a "testimonial communication," and therefore is not a violation of the Fifth Amendment Privilege Against Self-Incrimination.[52] Where the directive, however, "did 'admit and assert consent' " a court found it could be considered incriminating and thus violate the Fifth Amendment.[53] But, the Supreme Court in *Doe v. United States*,[54] held that where a consent directive is "carefully drafted not to make reference to a specific account, but only to speak in the hypothetical,"[55] the consent directive is not testimonial in nature and a court order "compelling petitioner to sign the directive does not violate his Fifth Amendment Privilege Against Self Incrimination."[56]

§ 9.04   SIXTH AMENDMENT

Issues of extraterritoriality can also arise during a defendant's trial or sentencing. Specifically with regard to the Sixth Amendment, there can be issues regarding the right to compulsory process, to confront witnesses, and even the right to a jury trial.

An issue of compulsory process arose in the case of *United States v. Valenzuela-Bernal*,[57] where the government was deporting a witness that the defendant wished to call at his trial. Justice Rehnquist's majority opinion found that this was not a violation of the Sixth Amendment, as the defendant in this case had not demonstrated how the "testimony would have been favorable and material."[58] A dissenting opinion of Justices Brennan and Marshall accused the court of "mak[ing] a mockery" of the right to compel witnesses, because the defendant was being deprived of an opportunity to interview the witnesses, "the surest and most obvious means by which he could establish the materiality and relevance of such witnesses testimony."[59]

The Confrontation Clause of the Sixth Amendment also presents new considerations when faced with problems of admitting evidence obtained from abroad. Prior to the Supreme Court decision in *Crawford v. Washington*,[60] courts sometimes allowed into evidence foreign depositions[61] that met the test of reliability. These were admitted despite arguments that claimed a violation of the Confrontation Clause. The *Crawford* decision may change the resolution of this issue, as unavailability and opportunity to cross-examine now take a prominent place in resolving Confrontation Clause questions.

---

[52] *E.g.*, In re Grand Jury Subpoena (Two Grand Jury Contemnors v. United States), 826 F.2d 1166 (2d Cir. 1987); United States v. Ghidoni, 732 F.2d 814 (11th Cir. 1984).

[53] *E.g.*, In re Grand Jury Proceedings (Ranauro), 814 F.2d 791 (1st Cir. 1987).

[54] 487 U.S. 201 (1988).

[55] *Id.* at 215.

[56] *Id.* at 219.

[57] 458 U.S. 858 (1982).

[58] *Id.* at 872.

[59] *Id.* at 880.

[60] 124 S. Ct. 1354 (2004).

[61] *E.g.*, United States v. McKeeve, 131 F.3d 1 (1st Cir. 1997); United States v. Siddiqui, 235 F.3d 1318 (11th Cir. 2000).

A prominent argument of recent vintage questions the status which should be afforded to convictions from abroad. Sentences in the United States are often increased when there is a showing of a prior criminal conviction. The question becomes, however, what if the prior conviction was not from a United States court and the rights accorded to the accused at the prior disposition were not equivalent to the process provided in United States courts.

In *United States v. Kole*,[62] the defendant argued that the court should not be allowed to use a prior conviction from the Philippines because it was obtained without a jury trial and with an attorney who had a conflict of interest. The Third Circuit held that all that was required was "fundamental fairness." Because the case involved an increased sentence for a repeat drug offender, and the statute was clearly aimed at international drug trafficking, it would be improper to limit the sentence only to repeat offenders who had prior convictions in the United States. The court also rejected the conflict argument raised by the defendant, in that there was no showing of prejudice resulting from the joint representation.[63]

---

[62] 164 F.3d 164 (3d Cir. 1998). On the propriety of using foreign criminal judgments for various purposes, see § 13.02, *infra*.

[63] *Id.* at 176.

Chapter 10
IMMUNITIES FROM JURISDICTION

§ 10.01 DIPLOMATIC, CONSULAR, AND ORGANIZATIONAL IMMUNITY

[A] Generally

Certain privileges and immunities are provided "to members of foreign diplomatic missions and consular posts."[1] The immunities provided to a diplomat and to a consular officer are not exactly the same. According to the *Restatement (Third) of Foreign Relations Law*, "[t]he principal difference is that, in the absence of special agreement, a consular officer's immunity from arrest, detention, and criminal or civil process is not general, but applies only to acts or omissions in the performance of his official functions."[2] Comparable immunities apply to persons accredited to international organizations, to officials of those bodies, and to substantial numbers of personnel, including military, on mission for international organizations, especially the United Nations.

In the United States, specific privileges and immunities are outlined in a document that tells law enforcement what they can and cannot do with respect to a diplomat and consular officer.[3] For example, law enforcement may issue a diplomat or consular officer a traffic ticket, but they may not enter the residence of a diplomat using ordinary procedures.[4] They may, however, enter the residence of a career consular officer using ordinary procedures, except that if the consular office is "located within the official consular premises" then the "official office space

---

[1] U.S. Department of State, Diplomatic and Consular Immunities, *available at* http:www.state.gov/m/ds/immunities/c9118.htm.

[2] The Restatement (Third) of Foreign Relations Law § 465, Comment a (1987).

[3] Diplomatic and Consular Privileges and Immunities From Criminal Jurisdiction, Summary of Law Enforcement Aspects, *available at* http://www.state.gov/documents/organization/20047.pdf.

[4] *Id.*

is protected from police entry."[5] Other countries also have procedures to implement the privileges and immunities provided to diplomats and consular officers.[6]

[B] Diplomatic Immunity

Diplomatic immunity can be traced back "to antiquity."[7] Ambassador Selwa Roosevelt, in a statement before the Senate Foreign Relations Committee in 1987, described its purpose as follows:

> Diplomatic immunity is a fundamental principle of international law under which certain foreign officials are not subject to the jurisdiction of local courts or other authorities for official or personal activities. The reason for immunity is simple and basic: it is to assure that diplomatic representatives are able to carry out the official business of their governments without undue influence or interference from the host country. It enables them to work in an environment of freedom, independence, and security.[8]

The document that provides the basic foundation for these diplomatic rights is the Vienna Convention on Diplomatic Relations, which was adopted in 1961, and went into force in 1964,[9] with the United States becoming a party to the Convention in 1972.[10] It is mostly self-executing. The United States passed the Diplomatic Relations Act of 1978,[11] replacing an Act of 1790 that had provided diplomatic immunity.[12] It deals with some issues that were not totally resolved in the 1961 Convention, like insurance for traffic accidents, and delineates some of the procedural aspects of invoking immunity in United States courts.

According to the Vienna Convention on Diplomatic Relations, "the purpose of such privileges and immunities is not to benefit individuals but to ensure the efficient performance of the functions of diplomatic missions as representing States."[13] According to the *Restatement (Third) of Foreign Relations Law*, diplomatic agents are immune:

> (1) from the exercise by the receiving state of jurisdiction to prescribe in respect of acts or omissions in the exercise of the agent's official functions, as well as from other regulation that would be incompatible with

---

[5] *Id.* at n.4.

[6] *See, e.g.*, Australian Protocol, Department of Foreign Affairs and Trade, *available at* http://www.info.dfat.gov.au/protocol_Guidelines/05.html.

[7] Diplomatic Immunity and U.S. Interest, Selwa Roosevelt's Statement Before the Senate Foreign Relations Committee, Aug. 5, 1987, *available at* http://www.findarticles.com/p/articles/mi_m1079/is_n2127_v87/ai_6101599.

[8] *Id.*

[9] Vienna Convention on Diplomatic Relations, April 18, 1961, 23 U.S.T. 3227, T.I.A.S. No. 7502, 500 U.N.T.S. 95, *available at* http://www.un.org/law/ilc/texts/diplomat.htm.

[10] Vienna Convention on Diplomatic Relations and Optional Protocols, n.6, *available at* http://www.un.int/usa/host_dip.htm#TWO.

[11] *See* 22 U.S.C. § 254a et seq.

[12] 3B C.J.S. Ambassadors and Consuls § 12.

[13] Vienna Convention on Diplomatic Relations, *available at* http://www.un.org/law/ilc/texts/ diplomat.htm. Accordingly, a diplomat is not exempt from the criminal jurisdiction of his home state. *Id.*, Art. 31(4). There is an expectation of Sending State prosecution in egregious cases.

the agent's diplomatic status; and (2) from arrest, detention, criminal process, and, in general civil process in the receiving state.[14]

Because the diplomatic immunity is a benefit to the Sending State, it can be waived by the Sending State,[15] and the receiving State can always declare an offender *persona non grata* and insist on that person's recall. It is not unusual to see requests for waiver or recall in cases of drunken driving.[16] The Department of State maintains the list of individuals eligible for diplomatic immunity.[17]

[C]   Consular Immunity

Consular officials have some of the same immunities as diplomats.[18] The Vienna Convention on Consular Relations of 1963 describes the immunities provided. According to the *Restatement (Third) of Foreign Relations Law*, consuls are immune from certain acts that "interfere with the officer's official functions," and that are contrary to their status as a consul. Additionally they are immune "from arrest, detention, and criminal or civil process in respect of acts or omissions in the exercise of the officer's official functions."[19] Although the *Restatement* limits consular immunity with respect to certain acts within their "official functions," "a consular officer is subject to arrest or detention pending trial only in case of a grave crime[20] and pursuant to a decision of a competent judicial authority, in which case criminal proceedings must be instituted with a minimum of delay."[21]

As noted, there are limitations to the immunity provided to consuls. For example, it has been found proper to have a vice consul made to appear pursuant to a subpoena, but he could not thereafter be forced to testify.[22] It has also been found proper to handcuff for an hour and a half someone entitled to consular immunity, where an officer believes that the individual is a threat to public safety.[23]

[D]   Persons Associated with International Organizations

In modern diplomatic practice, immunities of various kinds are extended to a wide array of persons who are accredited not to a country or its government but as temporary or permanent representatives to an international organization located on its territory. Officials in the employ of the organization also typically receive

---

[14] The Restatement (Third) of the Foreign Relations Law of the United States § 464 (1987).

[15] *See* LaFontant v. Aristide, 844 F. Supp. 128, 134 (E.D.N.Y. 1994); *see also* Vienna Convention on Diplomatic Relations, Art. 32(1). The Convention states that the "[w]aiver must always be express." *Id.* at Art. 32(2); *available at* http://www.un.org/law/ilc/texts/diplomat.htm.

[16] *See, e.g.*, Sean Murphy, *Waiver of Georgian Diplomat's Immunity from Criminal Prosecution*, 93 Am. J. Int'l L. 485 (1999) (diplomat enters plea in District of Columbia and sentenced to 7–21 years in federal prison for manslaughter).

[17] Department of State, Diplomatic List, *available at* http://www.state.gov/s/cpr/rls/dpl/.

[18] *See generally* Jame E. Hickey Jr. & Annette Fisch, *The Case to Preserve Criminal Jurisdiction Immunity Accorded Foreign Diplomatic and Consular Personnel in the United States*, 41 Hastings L.J. 351 (1990).

[19] The Restatement (Third) of the Foreign Relations Law of the United States § 465 (1987).

[20] Courts have interpreted a "grave crime" to be a felony. *See, e.g.*, Salazar v. Burresch, 47 F. Supp. 2d 1105, 1111 (C.D. Cal. 1999) (citing United States v. Cole, 717 F. Supp. 309, 323 n.5 (E.D. Pa. 1989)).

[21] The Restatement (Third) of the Foreign Relations Law of the United States at § 465(2) (1987).

[22] *See* United States v. Wilburn, 497 F.2d 946, 948 (5th Cr. 1974).

[23] Salazar v. Burresch, 47 F. Supp. 2d 1105, 1112–13 (C.D. Cal. 1999).

immunities. In the United States, for example, a large number of diplomats are stationed for a term of years in New York at the United Nations and in Washington D.C. at the World Bank family of organizations and at the Organization of American States. Others come in for particular meetings like the United Nations General Assembly from September to December. Permanent members of the missions and senior officials (such as the United Nations Secretary-General) have absolute immunity; others have immunity similar to consular officials and are protected for what they do in the course of official business. Some of these immunities are found in instruments unique to a particular organization;[24] others in more general treaties[25] or legislation.[26]

Then there are peace makers, peace keepers, and peace enforcers. Unlike typical United States Status of Forces Agreements with its allies which proceed on the basis that there is concurrent jurisdiction between Sending State and Host State,[27] the usual United Nations arrangements contemplate total immunity for the military personnel of a Sending State from the Host State's jurisdiction. A widely-used arrangement in particular cases is some variant of the 1990 United Nations Model Status-of-Forces Agreement for Peacekeeping Operations.[28] Under the model, various players have the equivalent of diplomatic immunity; others have functional immunity; the Secretary-General must obtain assurances from participating States that they will be prepared to exercise jurisdiction in respect of crimes committed by members of national contingents; and members of the military component are subject to the "exclusive jurisdiction" of their home State. Participating States have often been unable or unwilling to deliver on their promises, either in respect of war crimes or more mundane breaches of the law. There have been particular difficulties with sexual exploitation of women in Host States and with sex trafficking.[29] Members of the United Nations Secretariat involved in peace keeping enterprises will typically have functional immunity under the General Convention on the Privileges and Immunities of the United Nations.[30]

---

[24] In the case of the United Nations, the General Convention on the Privileges and Immunities of the United Nations, Feb.13, 1946, 21 U.S.T. 1418, T.I.A.S. 6900, 1 U.N.T.S. 16, ratified by the United States in 1972, and the United Nations Headquarters Agreement, signed June 26, 1947, in force Nov. 21, 1947, 61 Stat. 3416 (Joint Resolution of Congress approving), 11 U.N.T.S. 11.

[25] There is a separate Convention on the Privileges and Immunities of the Specialized Agencies, Nov. 21, 1947, 33 U.N.T.S. 261 which governs the situation in a majority of countries. The United States is not a party and deals with most of them (substantially along the lines of the Convention) under the statute mentioned in the next footnote.

[26] Particularly the International Organizations Immunities Act of 1945, 22 U.S.C.A. § 288 et seq.

[27] See § 8.01. Note, however, that the United States sometimes negotiates with host countries to treat its military as members of the "administrative and technical staff" of the Embassy and thus entitled to diplomatic immunity. See EDWARD M. WISE, ELLEN S. PODGOR & ROGER S. CLARK, INTERNATIONAL CRIMINAL LAW: CASES AND MATERIALS 400–01 (2d ed. 2004).

[28] U.N. Doc. A/45/94, of Oct. 9, 1990, reproduced as Annex F to THE HANDBOOK OF THE LAW OF VISITING FORCES (Dieter Fleck ed. 2001).

[29] See generally A Comprehensive Strategy to Eliminate Future Sexual Exploitation and Abuse in United Nations Peacekeeping Operations (Report of Prince Zeid to the Secretary-General), U.N. Doc. A/59/710 (2004); Jennifer Murray, Who Will Police the Peace-Builders? The Failure to Establish Accountability for the Participation of United Nations Civilian Police in the Trafficking of Women in Post-Conflict Bosnia and Herzegovina, 34 COLUM. HUM. RTS. L. REV. 475 (2003).

[30] Supra notes 24–28 and accompanying text.

The Secretary-General is sometimes called upon to waive the immunity of those subject to his control.[31]

In order to deal more adequately with such immunity problems and with gaps in jurisdiction over crime, especially crimes against the person, and to implement the organization's "zero tolerance" approach to sexual exploitation, the General Assembly is engaged in a project entitled "Criminal accountability of United Nations officials and experts on mission."[32] At present under consideration is a draft convention that would try to close jurisdictional gaps. Discussions continue on whether such a treaty should be concluded and, if so, what its scope should be. Some would stop short of including military personnel in such a regime.[33] The United Nations, while it can take contractual disciplinary action over those in its employ, has no powers of criminal enforcement. Criminal jurisdiction would have to be allocated between the Host State, the Sending State (or perhaps the State of nationality or residence in the case of employees of international organizations) and any universal jurisdiction regime that might be negotiated.

Similar issues arise also in relation to military operations that are not mounted under United Nations auspices. Despite some prodding from Members of Congress,[34] the United States has no Status of Forces Agreement with Iraq. The Coalition Provisional Authority, however, in an Order that was continued in effect after the re-establishment of Iraqi sovereignty,[35] prescribed immunity for all the relevant actors as follows:

1) Unless provided otherwise herein, the [Multinational Force], the [Coalition Provisional Authority], Foreign Liaison Missions, their personnel, property, funds and assets, and all International Consultants shall be immune from Iraqi legal process.

2) All MNF, CPA and Foreign Liaison Mission Personnel and International Consultants shall respect the Iraqi laws relevant to those personnel and Consultants in Iraq including the Regulations, Orders, Memoranda and Public Notices issued by the Administrator of the CPA.

3) All MNF, CPA and Foreign Liaison Mission Personnel, and International Consultants shall be subject to the exclusive jurisdiction of their Sending States. They shall be immune from any form of arrest or detention other than by persons acting on behalf of their Sending States, except that nothing in this provision shall prohibit MNF personnel from preventing acts of serious misconduct by the above-mentioned personnel or Consultants, or otherwise temporarily detaining any such Personnel or Consultants who pose a risk of injury to themselves or others, pending expeditions turnover to the appropriate authorities of the Sending State. In all such circumstances, the appropriate senior representative of the detained person's Sending State in Iraq shall be notified immediately.

---

[31] Since they are international civil servants, the immunity is for the benefit of the Organization, and it is for the Organization, not the State of origin of the international civil servant, to waive.

[32] *See* U.N. Doc. A/60/980 (Report of Group of Legal Experts), U.N. Doc. A/62/54 (Report of Ad Hoc Committee).

[33] *See generally* GEERT-JAN ALEXANDER KNOOPS, THE PROSECUTION AND DEFENSE OF PEACEKEEPERS UNDER INTERNATIONAL CRIMINAL LAW (2004) (discussing the military aspects that are relevant here).

[34] *See* H. Con. Res. 231, submitted Oct. 10, 2007.

[35] Coalition Provisional Authority Order No. 17 (revised), June 27 2004, *available at* http://www.cpa-iraq.org/regulations/20040627_CPAORD_17_Status_of_Coalition__Rev__with_Annex_A.pdf.

4) The Sending States of MNF personnel shall have the right to exercise within Iraq any criminal and disciplinary jurisdiction conferred on them by the law of that Sending State over all persons subject to the military law of that Sending State.[36]

In addition to the broad exemptions from Iraq's jurisdiction to prescribe, to adjudicate and to enforce,[37] the Sending State (as is commonly the case with visiting forces) is empowered to exercise its own jurisdiction along these lines (with enforcement help from its friends), within the territorial sovereignty of Iraq.

§ 10.02   HEAD OF STATE AND ACT OF STATE IMMUNITIES

[A]   Generally

Customary international law recognizes what has been called "head of state immunity."[38] It prohibits the prosecution in domestic courts of foreign leaders for criminal acts. Technically, the "Head of State" is an individual such as the Queen or the President who personifies the international personality of the state, but the customary law immunity extends to a Head of Government, a Foreign Minister and perhaps other high officials. The rationale is said to be "that one sovereign state does not adjudicate on the conduct of another."[39] Lord Hope of Craighead in the *Pinochet* case stated that "[a] head of state needs to be free to promote his own state's interests during the entire period when he is in office without being subjected to the prospect of detention, arrest or embarrassment in the foreign legal system of the receiving state."[40] The ability of a head of state to travel among countries is an important component of allowing "head of state immunity." Comity[41] has also been noted as a motivating factor for allowing this form of immunity.[42] It is without doubt that "head of state immunity" is grounded in the belief that "[h]eads of state must be able to freely perform their duties at home and abroad without the threat of civil and criminal liability in a foreign legal system."[43]

Early in its history, the Supreme Court of the United States accepted the doctrine of head of state immunity and of other immunities. *The Schooner Exchange v. McFaddon*[44] involved a question of title to a warship commissioned by Napoleon and docked in Philadelphia. An American plaintiff claimed it had been confiscated from him. In dismissing the suit, Chief Justice Marshall recognized "a class of cases in which every sovereign is understood to waive the exercise of a part of the exclusive territorial jurisdiction, which has been stated to be the attribute of

---

[36] *Id.* at § 2.

[37] *See* § 2.03, *supra*.

[38] *See* In re Grand Jury Proceedings, John Doe # 700 Under Seal, 817 F.2d 1108, 1110 (4th Cir. 1987).

[39] Regina v. Bow Street Metropolitan Stipendiary Magistrate and Others, Ex Parte Pinochet Ugarte (No.3), [2000] 1 App. Cas. 147, 210 [1999] 2 All E.R. 97, 119 (House of Lords) (Opinion of Lord Goff of Chieveley).

[40] *Id.* at 242, [1999] 2 All E.R. at 147 (Opinion of Lord Hope of Craighead).

[41] *See* § 1.03[A], *supra*.

[42] *See* LaFontant v. Aristide, 844 F. Supp. 128 (E.D.N.Y. 1994).

[43] *Id.* at 132.

[44] 11 U.S. (7 Cranch) 116 (1812).

every nation."[45] "One of these," he said, "is admitted to be the exemption of the person of the sovereign from arrest or detention within a foreign territory."[46] "A second case," he added, "standing on the same principles with the first, is the immunity which all civilized nations allow to foreign ministers."[47] (It is clear from the context, that his reference to a Minister residing at the Court of another sovereign, is used to speak of a Minister in the sense of permanent diplomatic representative, not a Cabinet Minister. "Minister" was the typical level at which the resident head of a diplomatic mission was accredited at the time.) Finally, for Marshall, "[a] third case in which a sovereign is understood to cede a portion of his territorial jurisdiction is, where he allows the troops of a foreign prince to pass through his dominions."[48]

[B] Limitations of Head of State Immunity

[1] Who Is Entitled to Head of State Immunity?

Several aspects of "head of state immunity" limit the doctrine's blanket immunity. First is the determination of "who" should be allowed immunity as a head of state. There are two parts to this question. First is whether the individual is in fact a head of state. Second is whether the State is a recognized State allowing its leaders to benefit from this immunity.

In the United States, the decision of who is entitled to immunity is within the province of the executive, as opposed to the judiciary. Thus, Manuel Noriega was not entitled to "head of state immunity" because the executive branch had "manifested a clear sentiment that Noriega should be denied head-of-state immunity."[49] Additionally, the Eleventh Circuit found that Noriega was not a "head of state," because he "never served as the constitutional leader of Panama," Panama was not seeking immunity for Noriega, and the "charged acts relate to Noriega's private pursuit of personal enrichment."[50]

The executive also determines whether a State is a recognized State, allowing its head of state to have immunity.[51] Unrecognized states may be deprived of the benefits of head of state immunity to its leaders. As one district court noted, "[r]ecognition of a foreign entity as a sovereign state, or of a regime as the government of a state, may be effectuated by express declaration of the executive branch, by bilateral agreement with the foreign state, by the presentation of credentials by the United States to the authorities of the state and by the United States receiving the credentials of the diplomatic representatives of the foreign state."[52] Irrespective of whether a State is recognized or not, the executive decision

---

[45] *Id.* at 137.

[46] *Id.*

[47] *Id.* at 138.

[48] *Id.*, at 139. For some further thoughts on immunity of troops, see George P. Barton, *Foreign Armed Forces: Immunity from Criminal Jurisdiction* [1950] Brit. Y.B. Int'l L. 186.

[49] United States v. Noriega, 117 F.3d 1206, 1212 (11th Cir. 1997).

[50] *Id.* at 1212.

[51] Knox v. The Palestine Liberation Organization, 306 F. Supp. 2d 424, 440 (S.D.N.Y. 2004).

[52] *Id.*

to allow head of state immunity is considered "an expression of United States international relations policy," and as such to be respected by the courts.[53]

[2] Crimes Covered Under Head of State Immunity

Not all crimes may be covered under head of state immunity in domestic courts. What crimes might be entitled to head of state immunity was an issue at the forefront in the *Pinochet* case. Augusto Pinochet Ugarte, the former president of Chile, was the subject of an extradition request of Spain. Pinochet was in England for medical treatment when a provisional warrant was issued for his "alleged [] participation in torture, conspiracy to torture, detention of hostages, conspiracy to detain hostages, and in a conspiracy to commit murder which extended to Spain and other European countries."[54] One of the issues considered in this case was whether these particular crimes were subject to immunity. The decision of the House of Lords suggests that a distinction has to be drawn between sitting and former heads of state. In relation to a sitting head of state there may well be absolute immunity, even for international crimes. The immunity is in respect to the person, *ratione personae*, and is not dependent on any relationship of the office to the conduct in question. After the person leaves office, immunity is *ratione materiae* and relates to official acts.[55] The hard question will be what is "official"? Is it, for example, official to torture people (or have them tortured)?

Pinochet made several arguments contesting the extradition. Using the double criminality rule, he alleged that certain crimes charged, namely torture and conspiracy to torture, committed before September 1988 (the date on which the relevant legislation came into effect) were not crimes in the United Kingdom at the time the acts were done.[56] The question here was whether the rule looked at when the acts occurred or when the extradition would be occurring. Lord Browne-Wilkinson, one of several judges authoring opinions, found that looking at the history of an "extradition crime," "the conduct must be criminal under the law of the United Kingdom at the conduct date and not [only] at the request date."[57] Torture became a crime in England in 1988 under the legislation giving effect to the Torture Convention. Lord Browne-Wilkinson held that "Senator Pinochet as former head of state enjoys immunity *ratione materiae* in relation to acts done by him as head of state as part of his official functions as head of state."[58] But did that include torture?

A key issue throughout many of the judicial opinions in the *Pinochet* case is whether "crimes against humanity," particularly torture, are subject to immunity. Consideration was given as to whether Chile, the United Kingdom, Spain and the other parties, by agreeing to the Torture Convention, accepted that there was no

---

[53] *Id.* at 443–44.

[54] Regina v. Bow Street Metropolitan Stipendiary Magistrate and Others, Ex Parte Pinochet Ugarte (No.3), [2000] 1 App. Cas. 147, [1999] 2 All E.R. 97 (House of Lords).

[55] " 'Personal immunities' refers to immunities inuring from acts closely related to an official state function." Paul J. Toner, Comment, *Competing Concepts of Immunity: The (R)evolution of the Head of State Immunity Defense*, 108 PENN ST. L. REV. 899, 902 (2004). "*Ratione materiae* or functional immunity refers to immunities inuring to state officials with respect to acts they perform in their official capacity." *Id.*

[56] [2000] 1 App. Cas. at 196 [1999] 2 All E.R. at 107 (Opinion of Lord Browne-Wilkinson).

[57] *Id.*

[58] *Id.* [2000] 1 App. Cas. at 202; [1999] 2 All E.R. at 112.

immunity *ratione materiae* for those who engaged in torture.[59] Consideration was also given as to whether the crimes were *jus cogens*.[60] As stated by one judge, "[i]nternational law cannot be supposed to have established a crime having the character of a *jus cogens* and at the same time to have provided an immunity which is coextensive with the obligation it seeks to impose."[61] Although the majority of the court allowed for Pinochet's extradition, they limited it to "crimes of torture and conspiracy to torture" after the date on which all three countries were parties to the Convention and torture had been made a statutory crime in England.[62] Any immunity there might have been before that date was no longer available and there was also double criminality. Pinochet returned to Chile after he was found "medically unfit to stand trial."[63]

Not all decisions will balance in favor of the gravity of the offense as opposed to allowing for head of state immunity. The importance of head of state immunity is seen in the International Court of Justice decision in *Congo v. Belgium*.[64] A Belgian Magistrate had issued an arrest warrant for the Minister of Foreign Affairs of Congo, charging him with war crimes and crimes against humanity for speeches inciting racial hatred before he was the Minister. Congo objected to the issue of the warrant. The Court stated that "the functions of a Minister for Foreign Affairs are such that, throughout the duration of his or her office, he or she when abroad enjoys full immunity from criminal jurisdiction and inviolability."[65] The Court did not distinguish "between acts performed by a Minister for Foreign Affairs in an 'official' capacity, and those claimed to have been performed in a 'private capacity.' "[66] The Court also distinguished this case from cases such as the Nuremberg and Tokyo Tribunals, as these tribunals did not pertain to "immunities of incumbent Ministers of Foreign Affairs before national courts."[67]

In a vote of thirteen to three, the Court in the *Congo v. Belgium* case found that the arrest warrant was improper, as it failed "to respect the immunity from criminal jurisdiction and the inviolability which the incumbent Minister for Foreign Affairs of the Democratic Republic of the Congo enjoyed under international law."[68] The court did not, however, preclude actions to be brought against former heads of state. The Court specifically stated that, "the immunities enjoyed under international law by an incumbent or former Minister for Foreign Affairs do not

---

[59] Regina v. Bow Street Metropolitan Stipendiary Magistrate and Others, Ex Parte Pinochet Ugarte, (No.3) [2000] 1 App. Cas. 147, 205 [1999] 2 All E.R. 97, 114–5 (House of Lords) (Opinion of Lord Browne-Wilkinson).

[60] *See* § 1.03[E], *supra*.

[61] Regina v. Bow Street Metropolitan Stipendiary Magistrate and Others, Ex Parte Pinochet Ugarte (No.3), [2000] 1 App. Cas. 147, 278 [1999] 2 All E.R. 97, 179 (House of Lords) (Opinion of Lord Millett).

[62] THE PINOCHET PAPERS: THE CASE OF AUGUSTO PINOCHET IN SPAIN AND BRITAIN 251, 253 (Reed Brody & Michael Ratner ed. 2000) (providing a summary of the holding, made by Lord Browne-Wilkinson to the House of Lords on March 24, 1999).

[63] *See* EDWARD M. WISE, ELLEN S. PODGOR & ROGER S. CLARK, INTERNATIONAL CRIMINAL LAW: CASES AND MATERIALS 387–88 (2d ed. 2004).

[64] Case Concerning the Arrest Warrant of 11 April 2000 (D.R. Congo v. Belgium), I.C.J. Rep. 2002.

[65] *Id.* at ¶ 54.

[66] *Id.* at ¶ 55.

[67] *Id.* at ¶ 58.

[68] *Id.* at ¶ 78.

represent a bar to criminal prosecution in certain circumstances."[69] One of the circumstances is where a State decides to waive the immunity.[70] Another is that "[p]rovided it has jurisdiction under international law, a court of one State may try a former Minister of Foreign Affairs of another State in respect of acts committed prior or subsequent to his or her period of office, as well as in respect of acts committed during that period of office in a private capacity."[71]

The International Court is likely to re-visit some of these issues when it renders its decision in a case involving the other Congo, the former French colony of Congo-Brazzaville.[72] Although the case was filed in 2002, the parties were still exchanging their written memorials early in 2008. The dispute arises over proceedings for crimes against humanity and torture commenced, *inter alia*, against the Congolese Minister of the Interior, and in connection with which a warrant was issued for the witness hearing of the President of the Republic. Issues are raised, once again, concerning Head of State immunity and the propriety of universal jurisdiction.

[3]   Waiver of Head of State Immunity

A State may waive "head of state immunity" for a head or state (or more likely a former head of state) just as it may waive the immunity of its diplomats. For example, the Aquino government in the Philippines waived any immunity that Ferdinand and Imelda Marcos might have been able to assert as the former leaders of the Philippines.[73] Noting that "head of state immunity" serves a purpose of promoting comity, the court found that the Marcoses would not have the benefit of "head of state immunity" if the existing government of the Philippines chose to waive that immunity. They were not permitted to use "head of state immunity" to quash grand jury subpoenas requesting their testimony and production of documents. The court found that "head-of-state immunity is primarily an attribute of state sovereignty, not an individual right."[74]

[C]   The International Criminal Court and Head of State Immunity

Customary law is now well established that "head of state immunity" is impermissible when the crime is an international crime prosecuted in an international court or tribunal. Article 27(1) of the International Criminal Court Statute specifically states that the official capacity of the accused is irrelevant.[75] The Statute states that it:

---

[69] *Id.* at ¶ 61.

[70] *Id.*

[71] *Id.*

[72] Certain Criminal Proceedings in France (Congo v. France) International Court of Justice (2002).

[73] In re Grand Jury Proceedings, John Doe # 700 v. Under Seal, 817 F.2d 1108 (4th Cir. 1987).

[74] *Id.* at 1111.

[75] Although the language of the Rome Statute is clear in Article 27, Article 98(1) may present problems in obtaining custody in that it provides that,

> [t]he Court may not proceed with a request for surrender or assistance which would require the requested State to act inconsistently with its obligations under international law with respect to the State or diplomatic immunity of a person or property of a third State, unless the Court can first obtain the cooperation of that third State for the waiver of the immunity.

shall apply equally to all persons without any distinction based on official capacity. In particular, official capacity as a Head of State or Government, a member of a Government or parliament, an elected representative or a government official shall in no case exempt a person from criminal responsibility under this Statute, nor shall it, in and of itself, constitute a ground for reduction of sentence.[76]

This provision is in the tradition of the Nuremberg[77] and Tokyo[78] Charters and of the Statutes of the tribunals for Former Yugoslavia[79] and Rwanda,[80] all of which contain provisions to the same effect. The Special Court for Sierra Leone, which was established as an international criminal court by agreement between the United Nations Security Council and the Government of Sierra Leone,[81] issued a very thoughtful opinion on the subject in holding that former Liberian President Charles Taylor was not entitled to immunity even though he was an incumbent head of state at the time when he was indicted.[82]

The United States, which has not ratified the Rome Statute, has expressed concern over the ability of the ICC to prosecute United States individuals and adopted the American Service-members' Protection Act of 2002 as a protection against this possibility.[83] It has also entered into a number of bilateral agreements whereby the parties promise not to hand Americans and American government personnel over to the Court. The validity of these agreements, purportedly made in reliance on Article 98(2) of the Rome Statute,[84] is hotly debated.[85]

The United States has also sought in the Security Council to ensure that military and other personnel participating in missions established or authorized by the United Nations will be subject to the exclusive jurisdiction of the contributing State, where that State is not a party to the Rome Statute.[86] For a time, the Security Council requested the ICC more generally that "if a case arises involving current

---

See also EDWARD M. WISE, ELLEN S. PODGOR & ROGER S. CLARK, INTERNATIONAL CRIMINAL LAW: CASES AND MATERIALS 400–01 (2d ed. 2004).

[76] The Rome Statute of the International Criminal Court, Art. 27(1). This Article also states "[i]mmunities or special procedural rules which may attach to the official capacity of a person, whether under national or international law, shall not bar the Court from exercising its jurisdiction over such a person." *Id.* at Art. 27(2); *see also* § 17.02[C], *infra.*

[77] Agreement for the Prosecution and Punishment of the Major War Criminals of the European Axis and Charter of the International Military Tribunal, August 8, 1945, Art. 7, 82 U.N.T.S. 279.

[78] Charter of the International Military Tribunal for the Far East, established at Tokyo, Jan. 19, 1946, U.S. Dep't of State Pub. No. 2675.

[79] Adopted by S.C. Res. 827 (1993).

[80] Adopted by S.C. Res. 955 (1994).

[81] S.C. Res. 1315 (2000). *See* § 16.06 *infra.*

[82] Prosecutor v. Taylor, Special Court for Sierra Leone, Appeals Chamber, Case No. SCSL-2003-01-I, May 31, 2004.

[83] See § 17.03, *infra*, where the United States attitude to the ICC is discussed more fully.

[84] "The Court may not proceed with a request for surrender which would require the requested State to act inconsistently with its obligations under international agreements pursuant to which the consent of a Sending State is required to surrender a person of that State to the Court, unless the Court can first obtain the cooperation of the Sending State for the giving of consent for the surrender."

[85] *See* EDWARD M. WISE, ELLEN S. PODGOR & ROGER S. CLARK, INTERNATIONAL CRIMINAL LAW: CASES AND MATERIALS 401–02 (2d ed. 2004).

[86] *See, e.g.*, S.C. Res. 1497 (2003), ¶ 7 (Multinational Force for Liberia).

or former officials or personnel from a contributing State not a Party to the Rome Statute over acts or omissions relating to a United Nations established or authorized operation, shall for a twelve-month period . . . not commence or proceed with investigation or prosecution of any such cases, unless the Security Council decides otherwise."[87] Such request was made in 2002 and renewed in 2003, but an effort to renew again was withdrawn in 2004 in the shadow of the reports of mistreatment at Abu Ghraib.[88]

---

[87] S.C. Res. 1422 (2002), renewed for a further twelve months in S.C. Res. 1487 (2003).

[88] *See* Frederic L. Kirgis, *US Drops Plan to Exempt G.I.s from UN Court*, ASIL INSIGHT, July 2004, *available at* http://www.asil.org/insights.htm. For an argument that the Security Council's action was *ultra vires* Art. 16 of the Rome Statute and Art. 39 of the United Nations Charter, see GEERT-JAN ALEXANDER KNOOPS, THE PROSECUTION AND DEFENSE OF PEACEKEEPERS UNDER INTERNATIONAL CRIMINAL LAW 256–98 (2004).

Chapter 11
OBTAINING EVIDENCE FROM ABROAD

§ 11.01 LETTERS ROGATORY

[A] Generally

Letters rogatory are a formal way for one country to assist another in obtaining evidence for an investigation or trial. The court in *The Signe*,[1] stated:

> Letters rogatory are the medium, in effect, whereby one country, speaking through one of its courts, requests another country, acting through its own courts and by methods of court procedure peculiar thereto and entirely within the latter's control, to assist the administration of justice in the former country; such request being made, and being usually granted, by reason of the comity existing between nations in ordinary peaceful times.[2]

Because the request occurs through a court, it is considered a formal method for obtaining evidence and testimony. Informal methods also exist to assist prosecutors in the United States and abroad in obtaining evidence from other countries.[3] Prosecutors for the federal government are advised to be sensitive to sovereignty concerns in obtaining evidence from abroad and to consult the Office of International Affairs of the Department of Justice in selecting "an appropriate method for requesting assistance from abroad."[4]

Historically, while it has been held that federal courts have inherent power to issue and respond to letters rogatory,[5] the field has largely been occupied by statute. There have in fact been several acts that have given courts the power to assist foreign tribunals. In some instances the acts offered extensive cooperation, such as the Act of March 2, 1855 which "granted broad powers to the United States

---

[1] 37 F. Supp. 819 (E.D. La. 1941).

[2] *Id.* at 820.

[3] U.S. Attys. Manual, Criminal Resource Manual § 278 (2006), *available at* http://www.usdoj.gov.usao/eousa/foia_reading_room/usam/title9/crm00278.htm.

[4] U.S. Attys. Manual, Criminal Resource Manual § 267 (2006), *available at* http://www.usdoj.gov.usao/eousa/foia_reading_room/usam/title9/crm00267.htm.

[5] *See* United States v. Reagan, 453 F.2d 165, 173 (6th Cir. 1971).

courts to compel the testimony of witnesses to assist foreign courts."[6] In other instances the laws restricted assistance to foreign tribunals, such as a 1948 amendment that spoke in terms of *"any civil action* pending in any court in a foreign Country."[7] International assistance was greatly expanded in 1964 when Congress amended existing statutes with a purpose of "prod[ding] other nations into following the lead of the United States in expanding procedures for the assistance of foreign litigants."[8]

[B]   The Letters Rogatory Process

Today, letters rogatory can be used in criminal matters. Prior to a 1996 amendment, a question sometimes arose as to whether letters rogatory could be issued pre-indictment. An amendment to 28 U.S.C. § 1782 resolved this issue when Congress explicitly provided that assistance to foreign and international tribunals includes assistance in "criminal investigations conducted before formal accusation." Because letters rogatory operate by statute in the United States, parties who are the subject of the investigation have standing to intervene and raise this question of "the validity of such a subpoena on the ground that it is in excess of the terms of the applicable statute."[9]

Letters rogatory can work through the State Department or directly between parties in the two countries. 28 U.S.C. § 1781 provides that the State Department can serve as the United States intermediary to process a letter rogatory. In this capacity, the State Department would request a foreign country to produce evidence desired by a tribunal in the United States, and likewise obtain for a foreign country evidence from a tribunal in the United States. Although the State Department can serve as the intermediary, tribunals inside the United States also have the ability to negotiate on their own with foreign and international courts to effectuate a letter rogatory. Likewise, foreign countries have the option to directly approach individual United States tribunals, bypassing the State Department.

Federal district courts in the United States have the authority, pursuant to 28 U.S.C. § 1782, to assist foreign and international tribunals by issuing orders for the taking of statements or production of documents in the United States. The order may be premised upon a letter rogatory or a request by an interested party. Individuals ordered to provide a statement or produce evidence are allowed to assert applicable privileges.

[C]   Deficiencies of the Letters Rogatory Process

Letters rogatory can be a slow process, often taking a year or more.[10] Because it can take time to procure the necessary approvals and to obtain the evidence from abroad, the statute of limitations can raise concerns for the prosecution. To

---

[6] 5 In re: Letter Rogatory From the Justice Court, District of Montreal, Canada — John Fecarotta, 523 F.2d 562, 564 (6th Cir. 1975).

[7] *Id.* at 564–65.

[8] *Id.* at 565.

[9] *See* In re: Letter Rogatory From the Justice Court, District of Montreal, Canada — John Fecarotta, 523 F.2d 562, 564 (6th Cir. 1975).

[10] U.S. Attys. Manual, Criminal Resource Manual § 275 (2006), *available at* http:// www.usdoj.gov/ usao/eousa/foia_reading_room/usam/title9/crm00275.htm.

alleviate this problem, prosecutors can request a suspension of the action until there is "final action" on the request for information from the foreign country.[11]

What constitutes "final action," for ending a suspension of the statute of limitations, has been the subject of court interpretation, as the statute does not explicitly provide a definition. This issue has been addressed by several courts. For example, in *Bischel v. United States*,[12] the Ninth Circuit Court of Appeals held that "final action" should be construed "to include a dispositive response to each item set out in the official request, including a request for certification."[13] Although courts have granted a suspension of a statute of limitations, the time of suspension is not indefinite as the statute does express some outer limits.[14]

[D] Defense Use of Letters Rogatory

The prosecution is not the sole user of the letters rogatory process, as defense counsel may also need to obtain evidence from abroad. There is, however, no automatic right to have a court issue letters rogatory, and a court may deny a defense request absent a showing that the witness the defense wished to obtain "would have been both material and favorable to his [or her] defense."[15]

The defense can seek from the court a subpoena to compel a witness to testify, but if the witness is a foreign national then the defense may find this avenue unproductive. The government does have to act in "good faith." It, therefore, would be improper to deny a visa for a needed defense witness.[16]

§ 11.02 MUTUAL LEGAL ASSISTANCE TREATIES AND EXECUTIVE AGREEMENTS

To ease the ability to exchange evidence necessary for a judicial process, countries often reach agreements that promote legal assistance. These agreements often take the form of Mutual Legal Assistance Treaties (MLATs).[17] Unlike letters rogatory, MLATs do not require court approval. Although the defense may be able to secure letters rogatory, using an MLAT to obtain information may be more difficult for the defense, as standing to pursue rights under a treaty is usually left to States.[18] Defense counsel may be able to claim a basis when there is a possible deprivation of constitutional rights.[19]

---

[11] 18 U.S.C. § 3292.

[12] 61 F.3d 1429 (9th Cir. 1995).

[13] *Id.* at 1433. *See also* United States v. Meador, 138 F.3d 986 (5th Cir. 1998).

[14] It cannot "exceed three years; and shall not extend a period within which a criminal case must be initiated for more than six months if all foreign authorities take final action before such period would expire without regard to this section." *Id.*

[15] United States v. Korogodsky, 4 F. Supp. 2d 262, 268 (S.D.N.Y. 1998).

[16] *See* Daniel R. Alonso, *Obtaining Testimony and Evidence from Overseas Witnesses*, 15 Bus. Crimes Bull. (March 2008).

[17] For a discussion on early United States practice, in particular efforts in the 1970s to deal with Swiss bank secrecy issues, see Ethan Nadelmann, Cops Across Borders: The Internationalization of U.S. Criminal law, Chapter 6 (1993).

[18] *See* Michael Abbell, *DOJ Renews Assault on Defendants' Right to Use Treaties to Obtain Evidence from Abroad*, 21 Champion 21 (1997). *See also* United States v. Davis, 767 F.2d 1025 (2d Cir. 1985).

[19] *See* United States v. Sturman, 951 F.2d 1466, 1485 (6th Cir. 1992).

In an effort to promote mutual assistance among nations, the United Nations developed a Model Treaty on Mutual Assistance in Criminal Matters.[20] The resolution adopting it states that it serves "as a useful framework that could be of assistance to States interested in negotiating and concluding bilateral agreements aimed at improving co-operation in matters of crime prevention and criminal justice."[21] Mutual assistance to be afforded in accordance with the Model Treaty may include:

(a) Taking evidence or statements from persons;

(b) Assisting in the availability of detained persons or others to give evidence or assist in investigations;

(c) Effecting service of judicial documents;

(d) Examining objects and sites;

(f) Providing information and evidentiary items;

(g) Providing originals or certified copies of relevant documents and records, including bank, financial, corporate or business records.[22]

Many modern Mutual Assistance treaties contain essentially this list of modalities. In addition, assistance in forfeiting the proceeds of crime has also emerged as a significant issue in legal assistance practice. Accordingly, the Model contains procedures whereby a State must, upon request, endeavor to ascertain whether any proceeds of an alleged crime are located within its jurisdiction and notify the requesting State of the results of its inquiries. In pursuance of a request the requested State shall endeavor to trace assets, investigate financial dealings, and obtain other information or evidence that may help to secure the recovery of proceeds of crime.[23] Two specialized United Nations models suggest some directions in which state practice is going in respect of illegally acquired items. They are the Model treaty for the prevention of crimes that infringe on the cultural heritage of peoples in the form of movable property,[24] and the Model bilateral treaty for the return of stolen or embezzled vehicles.[25]

In order to encourage States to enter into a kind of contingent fee arrangement to share the spoils from confiscated proceeds, the United Nations has drafted a Model Bilateral Agreement on the Sharing of Confiscated Proceeds of Crime or Property.[26] Such sharing agreements are fairly common in the drug area.

---

[20] See U.N. Model Treaty on Mutual Assistance in Criminal Matters, U.N. GAOR, 68th Plen. Mtg., U.N.Doc.A/RES/45/117 (1990), available at http://www.un.org/documents/ga/res/45/a45r117.htm, discussed in ROGER S. CLARK, THE UNITED NATIONS CRIME PREVENTION AND CRIMINAL JUSTICE PROGRAM: FORMULATION OF STANDARDS AND EFFORTS AT THEIR IMPLEMENTATION 216–19 (1994).

[21] U.N.Doc.A/RES/45/117 at operative para. 1.

[22] United Nations Model Treaty on Mutual Assistance in Criminal Matters, Art. 1 (1990) modified in 1998, modified text in UNITED NATIONS OFFICE ON DRUGS AND CRIME, COMPENDIUM OF UNITED NATIONS STANDARDS AND NORMS IN CRIME PREVENTION AND CRIMINAL JUSTICE (2006).

[23] Id. at Art. 18, as modified by G.A. Res. 53/112 (1998).

[24] See UNITED NATIONS OFFICE ON DRUGS AND CRIME, COMPENDIUM OF UNITED NATIONS STANDARDS AND NORMS IN CRIME PREVENTION AND CRIMINAL JUSTICE 202 (2006).

[25] See UNITED NATIONS OFFICE ON DRUGS AND CRIME, COMPENDIUM OF UNITED NATIONS STANDARDS AND NORMS IN CRIME PREVENTION AND CRIMINAL JUSTICE 207 (2006).

[26] See UNITED NATIONS OFFICE ON DRUGS AND CRIME, COMPENDIUM OF UNITED NATIONS STANDARDS AND NORMS IN CRIME PREVENTION AND CRIMINAL JUSTICE 215 (2006).

As a reminder of the antiquity of some international criminal principles, it is worth recording that provisions on sharing confiscated proceeds are at least as old as the British nineteenth century treaties on the salve trade, both those with European States and those with what the Consolidated Treaty Series coyly calls "African Potentates."[27]

The United Nations has also encouraged the growth of mutual legal assistance relationships by including "mini-MLATs" in a number of its multilateral conventions dealing with drugs, transnational organized crime and corruption.[28] In some instances an executive agreement or a bilateral mini-MLAT may provide the basis for the prosecution to secure needed evidence. These agreements are limited, such as an agreement to exchange evidence with respect to a specific form of crime such as drug crimes, or in the case of mini-MLATs, agreements that "have specialized issues relating to the specific substantive areas concerned."[29]

Although MLATs and executive agreements can assist in the process of securing mutual legal assistance, they are not without controversy. In a case of first impression, *In re Commissioner's Subpoenas*,[30] subpoenaed witnesses filed a motion to quash their subpoenas that compelled testimony prior to charges being filed against them. The district court granted the motion, finding that the "information sought in the United States" did not meet the "foreign discoverability requirement" of 28 U.S.C. § 1782. The court found that because Canada did not permit authorities "to compel witness testimony in domestic criminal investigations at the pre-charge stage, such testimony cannot be compelled in this case . . . ."[31]

In reversing this opinion, the Eleventh Circuit held that where there is a treaty, as in this case, the treaty is the controlling document. The court stated that "the Treaty utilizes § 1782 as a procedure for executing requests, but not as a means for deciding whether or not to grant or deny a request so made." As such there was no need to decide whether the subpoenaed parties had a privilege under Canadian law. Had the request proceeded using the statutory authority under section 1782, a different result might have been warranted.[32] The court said the subpoenas should be enforced because "subpoena-compelled testimony pursuant to a Canadian criminal investigation occurring prior to the filing of formal charges, was within the scope of the two countries' obligations under the MLAT."[33] Although the Canadian court would have the right to reject the compelled testimony because it was procured beyond the bounds of Canadian law, the court did not find this an impediment to enforcement of the treaty.

---

[27] Roger S. Clark, *Steven Spielberg's "Amistad" and Other Things I Have Thought About in the Past Forty Years: International (Criminal) Law, Conflict of Laws, Insurance and Slavery*, 30 RUTGERS L.J. 371, 431 n. 195 (1999).

[28] *See, e.g.*, Art. 7, United Nations Convention on Illicit Traffic in Narcotic Drugs and Psychotropic Substances, U.N. Doc. E/CONF.82/15 (1988); Art. 18, United Nations Convention against Transnational Organized Crime, G.A. Res. 55/25, U.N. GAOR, 55th Sess., Supp. No. 49, Vol. I at 43, U.N. Doc. A/55/49 (2001); Art. 46, United Nations Convention against Corruption, G.A. Res. 58/4 (2003), *available at* http://www.unodc.org/pdf/crime/convention_corruption/signing/Convention-e.pdf.

[29] Bruce Zagaris, *Uncle Sam Extends Reach for Evidence Worldwide*, 15 CRIM. JUST. 5, 54 (Winter 2001).

[30] 325 F.3d 1287 (11th Cir. 2003).

[31] *Id.* at 1291–92.

[32] *Id.* at 1297–98.

[33] *Id.* at 1306.

In January 2006, the Republic of Djibouti presented the International Court of Justice with a dispute between it and France concerning the latter's investigations into the mysterious death of a French judge who was acting as an adviser to the Djibouti Ministry of Justice.[34] Djibouti is seeking an order from the Court that France turn over the investigation dossiers and withdraw summonses against government officials, including President Ismael Omar Guelleh, to testify as witnesses in the proceedings [35] A judgment is expected later in 2008.

§ 11.03 GRAND JURY SUBPOENAS AND DEPOSITIONS

[A] Grand Jury Subpoenas

There is no requirement that the government use letters rogatory or that a MLAT exist to obtain information.[36] On occasion, federal prosecutors will issue grand jury subpoenas to obtain testimony from individuals who are abroad or to obtain documents located outside the United States. These subpoenas can be issued to nationals or residents of the United States who are in a foreign country. 28 U.S.C. § 1783 provides the statutory authority for a court to issue these subpoenas when it "finds that particular testimony or the production of the document" "is necessary in the interest of justice." Courts have contempt powers when there is noncompliance with these subpoenas.[37] Courts do not, however, have the ability to compel aliens to respond to these subpoenas.[38]

A court may compel documents, located outside the United States, to be produced before a grand jury when it can be shown that the court has personal jurisdiction. For example, when prosecutors seek bank records outside the United States, they may be able to compel the production if there is a branch of the bank located within the United States.

In the case of *Marc Rich & Co. v. United States*,[39] the Second Circuit affirmed a district court order holding Marc Rich & Co., A.G. in civil contempt "for failing to comply with the court's order directing it to produce certain records pursuant to a grand jury subpoena duces tecum." Marc Rich & Co., A.G. was a Swiss commodities trading corporation that had a wholly-owned subsidiary in New York. The court, in finding sufficient jurisdiction premised upon the territorial principle, noted that the investigation in this case involved a tax scheme. Although it expressed concern for possible international ramifications caused by issuing subpoenas abroad, it stated that the United States can be "injuriously affected by the wrongful evasion of its revenue laws." The court found that "[t]he test for the production of documents is control, not location."[40] Although there might be no

---

[34] Certain Questions of Mutual Assistance in Criminal Matters (Djibouti v. France), International Court of Justice, filed Jan. 9, 2006.

[35] *Certain Questions of Mutual Assistance in Criminal Matters (Djibouti v. France). Conclusion of public hearing. Court begins its deliberation.* International Court of Justice, Press Release No. 2008/3 (Jan. 30, 2008).

[36] *See* In re Grand Jury Proceedings (United States v. The Bank of Nova Scotia), 691 F.2d 1384, 1387 (11th Cir. 1982).

[37] 28 U.S.C. § 1784.

[38] *E.g.*, United States v. Korolkov, 870 F. Supp. 60, 65 (S.D.N.Y. 1994).

[39] 707 F.2d 663 (2d Cir. 1983).

[40] *Id.* at 667.

violation of the tax laws by the company, the government was entitled to production for purposes of its investigation.

Some courts have permitted the production of documents despite the possibility that the production may violate the secrecy laws of the country where they are located.[41] Other courts, however, have been reluctant to require the entity to produce records requested by a grand jury subpoena *duces tecum* where the production would result in the violation of the laws of another country.[42] Some courts in resolving these issues have considered the *Restatement (Second) of Foreign Relations Law of the United States*, which provides that when resolving inconsistent positions taken by States, each State should consider five factors: "(a) vital national interests of each of the states, (b) the extent and the nature of the hardship that inconsistent enforcement actions would impose upon the person, (c) the extent to which the required conduct is to take place in the territory of the other state, (d) the nationality of the person and (e) the extent to which enforcement by action of either state can reasonably be expected to achieve compliance with the rule prescribed by that state."[43] The *Restatement (Third)* lists the factors this way:

> In deciding whether to issue an order directing production of information located abroad, and in framing such an order, a court or agency in the United States should take into account the importance to the investigation or litigation of the documents or other information requested; the degree of specificity of the request; whether the information originated in the United States; the availability of alternative means of securing the information; and the extent to which noncompliance with the request would undermine important interests of the United States, or compliance with the request would undermine important interests of the state where the information is located.[44]

To protect international relations, federal prosecutors are required to obtain the permission of the Office of International Affairs prior to "issuing any subpoenas to persons or entities in the United States for records located abroad."[45]

[B]   Depositions

Prosecutors may seek to obtain testimony of witnesses via depositions. It may depend upon the foreign countries' laws and practices as to whether they will accommodate such a request from the United States.[46] United States Attorneys and their assistants need to consult the Office of International Affairs of the Criminal Division when foreign courts request the taking of depositions in the United States.[47]

---

[41] *E.g.*, In re Grand Jury Proceedings v. The Bank of Nova Scotia, 740 F.2d 817 (11th Cir. 1984). *See also* § 9.03, *supra*.

[42] *See* In re Sealed Case, 825 F.2d 494, 497–98 (D.C. Cir. 1987) (citing cases both for and against this position).

[43] Restatement (Second) of Foreign Relations Law of the United States § 40 (1965).

[44] Restatement (Third) of the Foreign Relations Law of the United States § 442(1)(c) (1987).

[45] U.S. Attys. Manual, Criminal Resource Manual § 279 (2006), *available at* http://www.usdoj.gov/usao/eousa/foia_reading_room/usam/title9/crm00279.htm.

[46] U.S. Attys. Manual, Criminal Resource Manual § 285 (2006), *available at* http:// www.usdoj.gov/usao/eousa/foia_reading_room/usam/title9/crm00285.htm.

[47] U.S. Attys. Manual § 3-19.812.

In the case of *United States v. Drogoul*,[48] the Eleventh Circuit reversed a district court denial of a government motion to take depositions of witnesses located in Italy. The Eleventh Circuit court held that when the government demonstrates unavailability and materiality, the motion should be granted despite concerns about the accuracy of the forthcoming translation. Likewise, the Eleventh Circuit found that concerns with respect to cross-examination were premature. The court in *Drogoul* held that there is a "crucial distinction that exists between the propriety of taking depositions versus the propriety of using the depositions at trial."[49] Although the court may later find the depositions inadmissible at trial, this does not foreclose the government from taking them.

---

[48] 1 F.3d 1546 (11th Cir. 1993).

[49] *Id.* at 1555. The use of this testimony at trial may also be problematic as a result of Crawford v. Washington, 541 U.S. 36 (2004) which evidently strengthens an accused's right to confront witnesses.

Chapter 12
OBTAINING PERSONS FROM ABROAD

§ 12.01 GENERALLY

The most common and accepted way to obtain persons from abroad, whether for the United States or another country, is to use the extradition process.[1] Extradition is not a new concept, as it traces back to early world history.[2] Members of the Commonwealth (Great Britain and many of its former colonies) transfer accused persons among themselves based on parallel legislation adapted from the colonial period. The "Scheme"[3] that provides the basis for this is not formally a treaty, but it incorporates many of the aspects of modern extradition treaties. In most cases,

---

[1] For discussion of alternatives to extradition, see § 12.05 (Luring); § 12.06 (Abduction), *infra*.

[2] EDWARD M. WISE, ELLEN S. PODGOR & ROGER S. CLARK, INTERNATIONAL CRIMINAL LAW: CASES AND MATERIALS 445–46 (2d ed. 2004); John T. Parry, *The Lost History of International Extradition Litigation*, 43 VA. J. INT'L L. 93 (2002); Quinn v. Robinson, 783 F.2d 776, 792 (9th Cir. 1986) ("The first-known extradition treaty was negotiated between an Egyptian Pharoah and a Hittite King in the Thirteenth Century B.C.").

[3] The London Scheme for Extradition within the Commonwealth, *available at* http://www.thecommonwealth.org/shared_asp_files/uploadedfiles/%7B56F55E5D-1882-4421-9CC1-71634DF17331%7D_London_Scheme.pdf. Note also the European Union's "European Arrest Warrant," a simplified procedure that is replacing extradition between the members of the Union. *See* http://

however, treaties form the legal basis for extraditions of people between countries.[4] These treaties can be multilateral[5] or bilateral. The United Nations provides a Model Treaty on Extradition that serves as a guide for countries formulating treaty alliances for the purposes of extradition.[6] There is an accompanying manual to assist in the process.[7] Older treaties contained a list of "extradition" (or "extraditable") offenses, such as homicide, theft and forgery. Modern ones (and the United Nations Model) usually provide that crimes punishable in both countries with a certain level of severity (typically one year in prison) come within the scope of the treaty. Some countries, like Canada, have legislation permitting a "one-off" extradition to a country with which they do not have a general extradition treaty. In such cases, the normal judicial and executive procedures are followed, as in the case where there is a general extradition treaty.

A number of multilateral treaties concerned primarily with suppressing a particular type of criminal behavior contain provisions that can be regarded either as mini-extradition-treaties or as extradition treaty modifiers. A typical example, which provided the model for many subsequent provisions, is the 1970 Hague Convention on the Suppression of Unlawful Seizure of Aircraft.[8] It, of course, deals with aircraft hijacking. Article 8 of the treaty provides that "If a Contracting State which makes extradition conditional on the existence of a treaty receives a request for extradition from another Contracting State with which it has no extradition treaty, it may at its option consider this Convention as the legal basis for extradition in respect of the offence."[9] The Convention also addresses the situation of "list" style treaties when it requires that "[hijacking] shall be deemed to be included as an extraditable offense in any extradition treaty existing between Contracting States. Contracting States undertake to include the offense as an extraditable offense in every extradition treaty to be concluded between them."[10] In short, existing "list" treaties are modified by an addition to the list and a promise is made to add hijacking to any subsequent lists.

Some of the key issues that surround extradition are double criminality,[11] the rule of speciality,[12] and the political offense exception.[13] Modern extradition treaties typically contain a list of both "optional" and "mandatory" grounds for declining extradition. In some instances these principles will rise to a level of customary international law. Countries may also reject extradition or place certain

---

ec.europa.eu/justice_home/fsj/criminal/extradition/fsj_criminal_extradition_en.htm.

[4] M. Cherif Bassiouni, International Extradition: United States Law and Practice (4th ed. 2002); Extradition Laws and Treaties, United States (loose-leaf, I.I. Kavass comp. 1980).

[5] See generally Isidoro Zanotti, Extradition in Multilateral Treaties and Conventions (2006).

[6] See United Nations, G.A. Res. 45/116 (1990 as amended in 1998), Model Treaty on Extradition, available at http://www.un.org/documents/ga/res/45/a45r116.htm and in United Nations Office on Drugs and Crime, Compendium of United Nations Standards and Norms in Crime Prevention and Criminal Justice 163 (2006).

[7] U.N. Manual on the Model Treaty on Extradition, in 45 and 46 Int'l Rev. Crim. Pol'y 1 (1995).

[8] 860 U.N.T.S. 105, 22 U.S.T. 1641, T.I.A.S. 7192.

[9] Id. Art. 8(2).

[10] Id. at Art. 8(1). Note that in modern treaties defining extraditability in terms of severity of punishment, hijacking will inevitably be of a sufficient level of severity in the domestic law of all treaty partners.

[11] See § 12.02[C], infra.

[12] See § 12.02[B], infra.

[13] See § 12.04, infra.

requirements upon the extradition premised on their fundamental policy or constitutional principles, even in the absence of treaty provisions. For example, some countries will not extradite to the United States unless there is an agreement that the death penalty will not be pursued as part of the prosecution.

Extradition is not the sole method used by countries to secure a person from abroad. Sometimes a country will turn the accused over to the United States without using the extradition process.[14] In some instances countries will lure suspects onto the high seas, into their country, or into a country with which they have an extradition treaty.[15] The United States, and other countries have, on occasion, also abducted individuals in order to bring them here for trial.[16]

Deportation has also been used as an alternative to extradition.[17] According to Department of Justice Policy, "[i]f the fugitive is not a national or lawful resident of the country in which he or she is located, the Office of International Affairs (OIA), through the Department of State or other channels, may ask that country to deport or expel the fugitive."[18] Using deportation as a way to bypass the extradition process can raise concern as it precludes political offense exception claims.[19] It may also short-circuit human rights protections to which the accused may be entitled, including the right not to be tortured.[20]

§ 12.02 EXTRADITION TO THE UNITED STATES

[A] Extradition Procedure

In order to obtain a person from abroad using the extradition process, it is necessary that certain documents be submitted requesting a formal extradition to the United States. The statutory authority for extraditing people to the United States is found in 18 U.S.C. § 3184 and it allows extradition in cases where there is "a treaty or convention for extradition between the United States and any foreign government," or in cases arising under 18 U.S.C. § 3181(b).[21] The Department of Justice requires that individuals requesting extradition first contact and receive approval from the Office of International Affairs, that there be a "preliminary determination of extraditability," and that a decision be made "whether to ask for provisional arrest."[22]

Several factors come into play in making a determination of extraditability. First and foremost is the location of the individual sought to be extradited to the United States. If the individual is in a country without an extradition treaty with

---

[14] *See, e.g.,* United States v. Herbert, 313 F. Supp. 2d 324 (S.D.N.Y. 2004).

[15] *See* § 12.05, *infra.*

[16] *See* § 12.06, *infra.*

[17] *See* Ruiz Massieu v. Reno, 915 F. Supp. 681 (D.N.J. 1996), *rev'd on other grounds,* 91 F.3d 416 (3d Cir. 1996).

[18] 13 U.S. Attys. Manual § 9-15.610 (last visited on Feb. 15, 2008) *available at* http://www.usdoj.gov/usao/eousa/foia_reading_room/usam/title9/15mcrm.htm.

[19] *See* § 12.04, *infra.*

[20] *See* § 15.02, *infra.*

[21] Section 3181(b) addresses the surrender of individuals in the United States to foreign governments.

[22] U.S. Attys. Manual, Criminal Resource Manual § 602 (2006), *available at* http://www.usdoj.gov/usao/eousa/foia_reading_room/usam/title9/crm00000.htm.

the United States, consideration needs to be given as to whether there is statutory authority for this particular extradition. Another consideration is whether the individual holds dual citizenship. In some cases it may also be important to determine whether the country from which extradition is sought extradites nationals. Considering the dual criminality of the charge (*see* § 12.02[C], *infra*) is also important, as this may resolve future obstacles.[23]

In addition to considering the above factors and others outlined in the *Criminal Resource Manual* of the Department of Justice, it is also necessary to decide whether there should be a request for provisional arrest. The Office of International Affairs decides if a provisional arrest is warranted. If not, the prosecutor proceeds with a formal request.[24] As noted in the *Manual*, "[i]n a provisional arrest situation, a treaty deadline may make it impossible to prepare the necessary documentation and have it translated in time."[25]

The paperwork for preparation of an extradition request can require expertise as it will likely require a prosecutor's affidavit,[26] copies of the warrant or indictment,[27] and affidavits establishing the crime and the identity of the individual sought in the extradition order.[28] In some cases, in addition to certified copies of items such as the indictment, evidence may need to be submitted to assure extradition.[29] The Office of International Affairs provides guidance in preparing the necessary paperwork as minor errors can stall the extradition process.[30]

Most often, the U.S. Department of State serves as the link between the United States Attorneys' Office and the country where the individual is located. The State Department sends the paperwork to the American Embassy in the country for presentation to the appropriate agency in that government.[31] In many Embassies, the Justice Department has a representative who serves as part of the staff of the Mission. These representatives keep in close touch with local authorities and ensure that the two-way extradition traffic and other cooperative efforts work smoothly.

Prosecutors need to be cognizant of timing issues in processing an extradition. This is because some courts have held that speedy trial rules can come into play once the person sought by the United States is located. When there is no showing that an extradition would be denied, and the accused requests to be extradited, the failure of the United States government to proceed with the extradition may be grounds for dismissal of the action by the court.[32] In contrast, when someone deliberately flees the country to avoid prosecution, and also attempts to avoid extradition, it is unlikely that a speedy trial argument will bar the prosecution.

---

[23] U.S. Attys. Manual, Criminal Resource Manual § 603 (2006), *available at* http://www.usdoj.gov/usao/eousa/foia_reading_room/usam/title9/crm00000.htm.

[24] U.S. Attys. Manual § 9-15.230 (last visited Feb.15, 2008).

[25] *Id.*

[26] U.S. Attys. Manual, Criminal Resource Manual § 605 (2006), *available at* http://www.usdoj.gov/usao/eousa/foia_reading_room/usam/title9/crm00000.htm.

[27] *Id.* at § 606.

[28] *Id.* at § 608.

[29] U.S. Attys. Manual § 9-15.240 (last visited Feb. 15, 2008).

[30] *Id.*

[31] *Id.* at § 9-15.300.

[32] *See* United States v. Pomeroy, 822 F.2d 718 (8th Cir. 1987).

[B]　Rule of Speciality

Most treaties contain a clause reflecting the rule of speciality.[33] The essence of the rule of speciality is that a defendant may be tried only for the crimes for which he or she is extradited.[34] Thus, in requesting extradition, countries need to include all charges that they plan to use in the prosecution. Adding new charges after the extradition can present problems.

Although the rule of speciality appears to bar new charges being added, in reality some courts place limitations on the enforcement of this principle.[35] An underlying rationale for having the rule of speciality is international comity.[36] As such, some courts only allow objections to violations of the rule of speciality when the objections are from surrendering countries. This position was taken in *United States v. Van Cauwenberghe*,[37] where the court stated that an extradited individual "may be tried for a crime other than that for which he was surrendered *if the asylum country consents*."[38]

Other circuit courts, however, take an opposite posture. For example, in *United States v. Puentes*,[39] the court held "that an individual extradited pursuant to an extradition treaty has standing under the doctrine of specialty to raise any objections which the requested nation might have asserted."[40]

In addition to determining who has standing to assert a violation of the rule of speciality, questions can also arise as to what is considered a violation of the rule. As stated in *United States v. Saccoccioa*,[41] the determination as to whether the rule of speciality has been violated, boils down to whether, under the totality of the circumstances, the court in the requesting state reasonably believes that prosecuting the defendant on particular charges contradicts the surrendering state's manifested intentions, or, phrased another way, whether the surrendering state would deem the conduct for which the requesting state actually prosecutes the defendant as interconnected with (as opposed to independent from) the acts for which he was extradited.[42]

Several court decisions provide precedent for what is considered acceptable under the rule of speciality. For example, added forfeiture charges have been found not to violate the rule of speciality.[43] Likewise, it has been held proper to add additional counts if it is for the same crime for which the accused was extradited.[44]

---

[33] United Nations, G.A. Res. 45/116, Model Treaty on Extradition, Art. 14, *available at* http://www.un.org/documents/ga/res/45/a45r116.htm, and in UNITED NATIONS OFFICE ON DRUGS AND CRIME, COMPENDIUM OF UNITED NATIONS STANDARDS AND NORMS IN CRIME PREVENTION AND CRIMINAL JUSTICE 163 (2006).

[34] *See* U.S. Attys. Manual § 9-15.500 (last visited Feb. 15, 2008).

[35] *See* United States v. Herbert, 313 F. Supp. 2d 324 (S.D.N.Y. 2004) (discussing the circuit split on whether an accused has standing to raise a rule of speciality argument to an extradition).

[36] *See* § 1.03[A], *supra*.

[37] 827 F.2d 424 (9th Cir. 1987).

[38] *Id.* at 428 (quoting Berenguer v. Vance, 473 F. Supp. 1195, 1197 (D.D.C. 1979)).

[39] 50 F.3d 1567 (11th Cir. 1995).

[40] *Id.* at 1575.

[41] 58 F.3d 754 (1st Cir. 1995).

[42] *Id.* at 767.

[43] *Id.* at 784.

[44] *See, e.g.*, United States v. LeBaron, 156 F.3d 621 (5th Cir. 1998).

In one case, the court held it proper to use a *Pinkerton* instruction, an instruction that allows for conviction of substantive offenses that are in furtherance of a conspiracy, even though the originating country might not allow this form of criminal liability. The court found it sufficient that the prosecution was "based on the same facts as those set forth in the request for extradition."[45]

[C] Dual Criminality Principle

Typically, in order for extradition to be proper, the crime must be a crime in both countries (the country requesting the individual and the country upon which the request is made). Normally the extradition treaty between countries will incorporate this requirement. A rationale for having a dual criminality rule is to make certain that extraditable crimes are serious offenses. Having the conduct as criminal in both countries helps to assure that it is a crime that both countries consider sufficiently wrongful.

Requiring dual criminality does not, however, require that the two countries call the law the same crime. As several cases have stated:

> the law does not require that the name by which the crime is described in the two countries shall be the same; nor that the scope of liability shall be coextensive, or, in other respects, the same in the two countries. It is enough if the particular act charged is criminal in both jurisdictions.[46]

Courts defer to the surrendering country in its "reasonable determination that the offense in question is extraditable."[47]

[D] Refusal to Extradite to the United States

Extradition is not automatic even when the mechanical and procedural requirements are met. Some countries will refuse extradition on grounds that go beyond rules of dual criminality and the doctrine of speciality. For example, countries may refuse to extradite due to the poor health of the accused and a right to so refuse is sometimes written into extradition treaties.

Countries may also assert nationality in refusing to extradite. For example, in the case of Samuel Sheinbein, Israel refused to return the accused to the United States because of Israeli nationality law. Israel did, however, proceed with the criminal action, and Samuel Sheinbein was convicted and sentenced to prison in Israel.[48] While the treaty between the United States and Israel was silent on the matter, some treaties, such as that with Mexico,[49] obligate the parties to prosecute if they decline to extradite on the basis of nationality.

---

[45] Gallo-Chamorro v. United States, 233 F.3d 1298, 1305 (11th Cir. 2000) (quoting United States v. Sensi, 879 F.2d 888, 895–96 (D.C. Cir. 1989)).

[46] United States v. Van Cauwenberghe, 827 F.2d 424, 428 (9th Cir. 1987) (citing In re Extradition of Russell, 789 F.2d 801, 803 (9th Cir. 1986) (quoting Collins v. Loisel, 259 U.S. 309, 312 (1922)). *See also* United Nations Model Treaty on Extradition, *supra*, Art. 2(2).

[47] United States v. Saccoccia, 58 F.3d 754, 766 (1st Cir. 1995).

[48] *See also* Abraham Abramovsky & Jonathan I. Edelstein, *The Sheinbein Case and the Israeli-American Extradition Experience: A Need for Compromise*, 32 Vand. J. Transnat'l L. 305 (1999).

[49] *See, e.g.*, Extradition Treaty Between the United States of America and the United Mexican States, May 4, 1978, in Extradition Law and Treaties of the United States 590.19 (I.I. Kavass comp., looseleaf). Art. 9 provides that if extradition is not granted on the grounds of nationality, "the requested Party shall submit the case to its competent authorities for the purpose of prosecution, provided that Party has jurisdiction over the offense."

Extradition may also be refused by a country with concurrent jurisdiction over the offenses that prefers to conduct the prosecution itself. This happened in the case of Ahmad Omar Saeed Sheikh, who was accused of killing *Wall Street* journalist Daniel Pearl. Despite a two count indictment in the United States, Pakistan's president chose to proceed with the prosecution in Pakistan where the killing occurred.[50] The prosecution resulted in Sheikh receiving a sentence of death.[51] This result is consistent with the United Nations Model Treaty on Extradition which provides the following as an optional ground for the refusal of extradition, effectively giving priority to the state of territoriality, if it wishes to exercise its jurisdiction:

> If the offense for which extradition is requested is regarded under the law of the requested State as having been committed in whole or in part within that State. Where extradition is refused on this ground, the requested State shall, if the other State so requests, submit the case to its competent authorities with a view to taking appropriate action against the person for the offense for which extradition is requested.[52]

In an obvious nod in the direction of *The Lotus,*[53] a footnote to Article 4(f) adds: "[s]ome countries may wish to make specific reference to a vessel under its flag or an aircraft registered under its laws at the time of the commission of the offense."

In some cases a treaty will employ the principle of *"Aut Dedere Aut Judicare."* The parties agree to either prosecute the individuals themselves or extradite them to the requesting country. For example, the International Convention for the Taking of Hostages of 1979 is a treaty that operates from this principle.[54]

Extradition may also be refused by a country that disapproves of a procedure in the United States. For example, in the Ira Einhorn case, France originally refused to extradite the accused as he had been convicted *in absentia*, sentenced to life in prison, and the State of Pennsylvania did not have a provision for retrial with Einhorn present. To obtain the extradition, Pennsylvania passed a law that would permit retrial. France then agreed to extradite Einhorn, and he was convicted at the second trial, at which he was present.[55]

The United Nations Model Treaty on Extradition contains the following as an optional ground for refusing extradition: "[i]f the person whose extradition is requested has been sentenced, or would be liable to be tried or sentenced in the requesting State by an extraordinary or ad hoc court or tribunal." There are indications that some treaty partners may decline to extradite anyone to the United States who appears likely to face trial before a Military Commission, unless appropriate assurances are received.[56]

---

[50] *Pakistan Resists U.S. Extradition*, WALL ST. J., May 6, 2002, at A18.

[51] *Sheikh Omar Gets Death Penalty for Daniel Pearl Murder*, PAKISTAN NEWS SERVICE, July 15, 2002, *available at* http://www.paknews.com/top.php?id=1&date1=2002-07-15. (The killer was also known as "Sheikh Omar" and "Omar Sheikh.")

[52] Model Treaty on Extradition, Art. 4(f), UNITED NATIONS OFFICE ON DRUGS AND CRIME, COMPENDIUM OF UNITED NATIONS STANDARDS AND NORMS IN CRIME PREVENTION AND CRIMINAL JUSTICE 163 (2006).

[53] *See* § 1.02[B], *supra.*

[54] International Convention Against the Taking of Hostages, Dec. 17, 1979, Art. 8, T.I.A.S No. 11,081, 1316 U.N.T.S. 205.

[55] *See* Martha Moore & Vivian Walt, *France Sends Fugitive Back to USA*, USA TODAY, July 20, 2001, at 3A.

[56] *See e.g.*, Ahmad v. Gov't of U.S., [2006] EWHC 2927 (Queen's Bench Divisional Court, 2006) (the

Perhaps the most controversial block in extradition proceedings today is the fact that some countries refuse to extradite to the United States if the accused will face the possibility of the death penalty. European countries, Canada and the Latin American countries typically insist on including a capital punishment clause in their extradition treaties. These countries argue that the death penalty is a human rights violation. In fact, even in the absence of a capital punishment provision in a bilateral extradition treaty, their multilateral obligations under human right treaties may get the same result.[57] To proceed with the extradition, agreements may be reached between the United States and these countries to extradite on condition that a sentence of death not be included as one of the possible sentences.[58] Some European and Latin American countries are also reluctant to extradite where there is an issue of life imprisonment without the possibility of parole, which they also regard as a human rights issue.[59]

§ 12.03   EXTRADITION FROM THE UNITED STATES

[A]   Authorization to Extradite

As with extraditions to the United States, extraditions from the United States also occur most often pursuant to an extradition treaty. In *Ntakirutimana v. Reno*,[60] the issue was raised whether it was constitutional to extradite Ntakirutimana to the International Criminal Tribunal of Rwanda (ICTR) when the extradition was pursuant to a Surrender Agreement between the Executive and the Tribunal affirmed by a statute as opposed to a treaty. In *Valentine v. United States*,[61] the Supreme Court accepted that authority for extradition could come from either a treaty or a statute. As such, the court in *Ntakirutimana* found that "although some authorization by law is necessary for the Executive to extradite, neither the Constitution's text nor *Valentine* require that the authorization come in the form of a treaty."[62]

[B]   Treaty Interpretation

[1]   Guiding Principles

Several principles have developed over time that guide courts in interpreting extradition treaties. These rules instruct courts to give deference to the executive in treaty interpretation.[63] Thus courts will usually give weight to the executive

---

British Government sought and received assurances that an accused terrorist suspect would not be designated as an enemy combatant or tried by a military commission) (promises against capital punishment were also sought and given). *See also id.* at ¶ 77 (Germany sought similar assurance before extraditing from Frankfurt to New York).

[57] *See* § 15.03, *infra.*

[58] *See* § 15.03, *infra*, for detailed discussion.

[59] *See generally* DIRK VAN ZYL SMIT, TAKING LIFE IMPRISONMENT SERIOUSLY IN NATIONAL AND INTERNATIONAL LAW (2002); Rodrigo Lambardini, *Mexico's Supreme Court Clarifies When to Submit Assurances that Life Imprisonment Will Not Be Imposed When Requesting Extradition from Mexico*, 20 INT'L ENF. L. REP. 295 (2004).

[60] 184 F.3d 419 (5th Cir. 1999), *cert. denied*, 120 S.Ct. 977 (2000).

[61] 299 U.S. 5 (1936).

[62] 184 F.2d at 425.

[63] *See, e.g.*, In re Extradition of Howard, 996 F.2d 1320 (1st Cir. 1993).

interpretation when interpreting a treaty. For example, if the Attorney General makes the decision not to extradite, instead prosecuting that individual within this country, the defendant does not have a basis to contest this decision. Despite the existence of an extradition treaty, the government retains the discretion to proceed with a prosecution in the United States when the individual has violated U.S. law.[64]

Courts also construe treaties liberally, a difference from how courts normally interpret criminal statutes.[65] In construing treaties liberally, courts can examine executive material created when the treaty was drafted. As stated in the Supreme Court decision in *Factor v. Laubenheimer*,[66] courts will "look beyond its written words to the negotiations and diplomatic correspondence of the contracting parties relating to the subject-matter, and to their own practical construction of it."[67]

Additionally, a "rule of non-inquiry" applies in extradition matters. The "rule of non-inquiry" restricts the judiciary in its interpretation of treaties by holding that courts should not scrutinize the requesting state's judicial system. Under a strict reading of this rule, defendants would not be able to claim that they might be subject to torture if extradited to the requesting country.[68] Human rights advocates, however, call for exceptions to the "rule of non-inquiry,"[69] and the future of the rule remains uncertain.[70] The "rule of non-inquiry" does not preclude the Secretary of State from denying extradition on human rights grounds. As stated by one court, "[i]t is not that questions about what awaits the relator in the requesting country are irrelevant to extradition; it is that there is another branch of government, which has both final say and greater discretion in these proceedings, to whom these questions are more properly addressed."[71] The United Nations Model Treaty on Extradition contains, as a mandatory ground of refusing rendition:

> If the requested State has substantial grounds for believing that the request for extradition has been made for the purposes of prosecuting or punishing a person on account of that person's race, religion, nationality,

---

[64] *See, e.g.*, United States v. Wharton, 320 F.3d 526, 532–34 (5th Cir. 2003); United States v. White, 51 F. Supp. 2d 1008, 1012 (E.D. Cal. 1997).

[65] United States v. Lui Kin-Hong, 110 F.3d 103, 110 (1st Cir. 1997). Normally, in criminal cases, the rule of lenity applies which interprets statutes that may have two possible meanings in favor of the accused if both positions are constitutional. *See* Liparota v. United States, 471 U.S. 419, 427 (1985).

[66] 290 U.S. 276 (1933).

[67] *Id.* at 294–95.

[68] *See* In re Extradition of Singh, 123 F.R.D. 127 (D.N.J. 1987).

[69] *See, e.g.*, Valerie Epps, *The Development of the Conceptual Framework Supporting International Extradition*, 25 Loy. L.A. Int'l & Comp. L. Rev. 369 (2003); John Dugard & Christine Van Den Wyngaert, *Reconciling Extradition with Human Rights*, 92 Am. J. Int'l L. 187 (1998).

[70] See In re Extradition of Cheung, 968 F. Supp. 791, 798 (D. Conn. 1997), quoting dicta from Gallina v. Fraser, 278 F.2d 77, 79 (2d Cir. 1960) (the court "left open the possibility of judicial inquiry in cases where 'the relator, upon extradition, would be subject to procedures or punishment so antipathetic to a federal court's sense of decency as to require reexamination of the principle [of non-inquiry]' "). *See also* Corejo-Barreto v. Siefert, 379 F.3d 1075 (9th Cir.), vacated, 386 F.3d 938 (9th Cir. 2004).

[71] United States v. Lui Kin-Hong, 110 F.3d 103, 111 (1st Cir. 1997). *See also* 22 C.F.R. § 94 (2004) empowering Secretary of State to refuse extradition to a country in which torture is likely. The Regulation seeks to implement the non-extradition/non expulsion provision in Art. 3 of the 1984 United Nations Convention against Torture and Other Cruel, Inhuman or Degrading Treatment or Punishment.

ethnic origin, political opinions, sex or status, or that that person's position may be prejudiced for any of these reasons.[72]

The Model Treaty is silent on whether the task of making this determination lies with the Executive or the Courts, and indeed that is left to particular countries to determine for themselves. As this paragraph finds its way into more treaties, however, the rule of non-inquiry is losing much of its force.

Finally, as with extraditions to the U.S., extraditions from the U.S. also require adherence to the doctrine of speciality[73] and dual criminality.[74] In some cases the treaty (especially an older one) will provide an appendix that lists the offenses upon which an extradition can occur. For example, Mexico sought extradition of an individual from the U.S. where the charges in Mexico were aggravated homicide. Since the appendix to the treaty specified murder as an extraditable offense and murder was a crime in the U.S. under both state and federal law, the extradition met the dual criminality requirement.

[2] Parties to the Treaty

What happens when a country changes government and the predecessor country had a treaty with the United States? In *United States v. Lui Kin-Hong*,[75] a district court granted a writ of habeas corpus finding that Lui Kin-Hong's extradition should not be allowed, as the extradition treaty between the United States and Hong Kong would expire before he could be tried and punished in Hong Kong. This was because of the reversion of Hong Kong to the People's Republic of China.

Despite Lui Kin-Hong's arguments that treaties should not be interpreted to cover a different government, the First Circuit reversed the lower court and found that the reversion of Hong Kong to the People's Republic of China would not be an impediment to the extradition. In part this decision was premised upon principles of "reciprocity and liberal construction." As stated by the court, "[i]f the executive chooses to modify or abrogate the terms of the Treaties that it negotiated, it has ample discretion to do so."[76]

[C] Extradition Procedure

[1] 18 U.S.C. § 3184

The procedure for extradition from the United States to another country is outlined in 18 U.S.C. § 3184. Despite attacks on the constitutionality of this statute, it has been upheld by courts.[77] The procedure for extradition, as provided by the statute, was summarized in the case of *United States v. Lui Kin-Hong* where the First Circuit stated:

---

[72] United Nations Model Treaty on Extradition, Art. 3(b), UNITED NATIONS OFFICE ON DRUGS AND CRIME, COMPENDIUM OF UNITED NATIONS STANDARDS AND NORMS IN CRIME PREVENTION AND CRIMINAL JUSTICE 163 (2006). See also *infra* note 122 for two variations on this paragraph in United States practice.

[73] *See* § 12.02[B], *supra.*

[74] *See* § 12.02[C], *supra.*

[75] 110 F.3d 103 (1st Cir. 1997).

[76] *Id.* at 112.

[77] Lobue v. Christopher, 82 F.3d 1081 (D.C. Cir. 1996).

The statute establishes a two-step procedure which divides responsibility for extradition between a judicial officer and the Secretary of State. The judicial officer's duties are set out in 18 U.S.C. § 3184. In brief, the judicial officer, upon complaint, issues an arrest warrant for an individual sought for extradition, provided that there is an extradition treaty between the United States and the relevant foreign government and that the crime charged is covered by the treaty. . . . If a warrant issues, the judicial officer then conducts a hearing to determine if "he deems the evidence sufficient to sustain the charge under the provisions of the proper treaty." . . . If the judicial officer makes such a determination, he "shall certify" to the Secretary of State that a warrant for the surrender of the relator "may issue." . . . The judicial officer is also directed to provide the Secretary of State with a copy of the testimony and evidence from the extradition hearing. . . .[78]

The extradition decision is ultimately "within the Secretary of State's sole discretion."[79] In this capacity the Secretary can negotiate for conditions upon which the extradition will be premised, but can also refuse the extradition request. As stated in the *Kin-Hong* case, "[t]his bifurcated procedure reflects the fact that extradition proceedings contain legal issues peculiarly suited for judicial resolution, such as questions of the standard of proof, competence of evidence, and treaty construction, yet simultaneously implicate questions of foreign policy, which are better answered by the executive branch."[80]

[2]   Necessary Proof for an Extradition

When extradition is sought by another country, a federal magistrate reviews the evidence to determine if the extradition should be granted. In *Ross v. United States Marshall for the Eastern District of Oklahoma*,[81] the court stated that

[t]he scope of review of a magistrate judge's extradition order under a treaty with a foreign country is limited to "determining whether the magistrate had jurisdiction, whether the offense charged is within the treaty and, by a somewhat liberal construction, whether there was any evidence warranting the finding that there was reasonable ground to believe the accused guilty."[82]

In *Ross*, the accused argued that the charges in his case were beyond the statute of limitations and therefore not within the treaty. Although the charges had been "brought approximately twelve years after" the commission of the alleged offense, the question was whether the statute would be tolled because Ross fled the jurisdiction and moved to the United States.

In deciding what constitutes "fleeing from justice," the court noted that jurisdictions had reached different resolutions. Some held "mere absence from the jurisdiction" sufficient to toll the statute, while others required "the prosecution to prove the accused had an intent to avoid arrest or prosecution." In *Ross*, the Tenth Circuit held that "'fleeing from justice' requires the government to prove, by a preponderance of the evidence, the accused acted with the intent to avoid arrest or

---

[78]   110 F.3d at 109 (citations omitted).

[79]   *Id.* at 109.

[80]   *Id.* at 110.

[81]   168 F.3d 1190 (10th Cir. 1999).

[82]   *Id.* at 1193 (quoting Peters v. Egnor, 888 F.2d 713, 716 (10th Cir. 1989)).

prosecution."[83] The court further found that the evidence did not demonstrate the district court's conclusion that Ross had the "intent to flee arrest or prosecution" was error.

Fleeing the jurisdiction can also serve to restrict the defendant's rights in the United States. For example, in *Parretti v. United States*,[84] Giancarlo Parretti, who was initially being held in the United States in order to be extradited to France, fled while his appeal was pending. His appeal alleged that his Fourth and Fifth Amendments rights were being violated. The court dismissed his appeal saying that because he "is a fugitive from justice," the "disentitlement doctrine" applied.[85] This doctrine provides that one who flees the jurisdiction while an appeal is pending loses his or her rights to proceed with the appeal. A strong dissent in *Parretti*, however, stressed that disentitlement should not apply in the context of an extradition where the defendant receives no benefit from the judicial process.

For the purposes of an extradition, it is necessary for the government to demonstrate that the individual being held for extradition is the same individual charged with the crime in the other country. In the case of *Joseph v. Hoover*,[86] the court noted that the standard here is probable cause to believe that the defendant committed the crime. It is not necessary to have proof that the individual will be convicted of the charged crime.[87]

This "probable cause" requirement of United States law, or the need to show a "prima facie case" as it is usually referred to in other common law countries, was always a bone of contention between common law and civil law countries. Civil law countries, such as France, Spain and Germany, tended not to have such a requirement in their relations with one another and they claimed that it was very difficult to meet the evidentiary requirements that common law countries imposed on their applications. In its Extradition Act of 1989,[88] the United Kingdom moved away from the requirement of a prima facie case and it then ratified the European Extradition Convention.[89] Article 12 of that treaty "requires only that the request is accompanied by a certificate of conviction or the warrant for arrest, a statement of the offence and a copy of the necessary laws."[90] Since the United States still retains the requirement of probable cause in applications to it, the most recent Extradition Treaty between the United States and the United Kingdom[91] has something of an imbalance. No prima facie case need be made in applications by the United States to the United Kingdom, but the reverse is not so. An application to the United Kingdom has to be supported by "(a) a copy of the warrant or order of arrest issued by a judge or other competent authority; (b) a copy of the charging

---

[83] *Id.* at 1193.

[84] 143 F.3d 508 (9th Cir. 1998).

[85] *Id.* at 509.

[86] 254 F. Supp. 2d 595 (D.V.I. 2003).

[87] *Id.* at 601.

[88] Now contained in Extradition Act 2003 (U.K.).

[89] Council of Europe, European Convention on Extradition, Dec. 13, 1957, EUROP. T.S. No. 24 (1957).

[90] GEOFF GILBERT, TRANSNATIONAL FUGITIVE OFFENDERS IN INTERNATIONAL LAW: EXTRADITION AND OTHER MECHANISMS 123 (1998). Gilbert adds: "It is a major change of policy for the United Kingdom and should guarantee a freer flow of fugitives because of the simpler requirements."

[91] Extradition Treaty Between the Government of the United States of America and the Government of the United Kingdom of Great Britain and Northern Ireland, Mar. 31, 2003, S. Treaty Doc. No. 108-23 (2003); *see also* http://www.state.gov/p/eur/rls/fs/34885.htm.

document, if any."[92] There is an additional requirement for obtaining a fugitive from the United States: "(c) *for requests to the United States*, such information as would provide a reasonable basis to believe that the person sought committed the offence for which extradition is requested."[93] This change, which typically affects the ease with which the United States can extradite its own citizens abroad, is regarded with suspicion by human rights organizations.[94]

§ 12.04 POLITICAL OFFENSE EXCEPTION

[A] Rationale for Political Offense Exception

The political offense exception, commonly included in extradition treaties, provides that an extradition should not be allowed when the offense being charged is of a political character. "Political motivation," however, "does not convert every crime into a political offense."[95]

Although extradition dates back in history, the political offense exception is of more recent vintage, dating from the nineteenth century.[96] Three justifications have been expressed as support for having a political offense exception. These are: "a belief that individuals have a 'right to resort to political activism to foster political change,' " that "unsuccessful rebels should not be returned to countries where they may be subjected to unfair trials and punishments because of their political opinions," and "governments — and certainly their nonpolitical branches — should not intervene in the internal political struggles of other nations."[97]

[B] What Is a Political Offense?

The Ninth Circuit, in the landmark case of *Quinn v. Robinson* examined the political offense exception and whether the exception covers violent crimes.[98] William Joseph Quinn, an Irish Republican Army (IRA) member was found extraditable by a U.S. magistrate. Quinn then filed a writ of habeas corpus alleging that the political offense exception precluded him from being extradited to the United Kingdom.

The treaty between the United States and the United Kingdom provided for the political offense exception,[99] but political offense was not defined. The government argued that this determination is a political question, and therefore one that should be resolved by the executive.[100] Circuit Judge Reinhardt's opinion rejected this

---

[92] *Id.* at Art. 8(3)(c).

[93] *Id.* (emphasis added).

[94] *See generally* Richard Goldberger, *It's Just Not Cricket: Is the Principle of Reciprocity Being Honored in the U.S.-U.K. Extradition Treaty?* 29 Cardozo L. Rev. 819 (2007).

[95] Ahmed v. Wigen, 910 F.2d 1063, 1066 (2d Cir. 1990).

[96] *See* Quinn v. Robinson, 783 F.2d 776 (9th Cir. 1986).

[97] *Id.* at 793 (citations omitted).

[98] *Id.*

[99] The treaty specified that "extradition shall not be granted if . . . the offense for which extradition is requested is regarded by the requested party as one of a political character." *Id.* at 783.

[100] The government argued that Baker v. Carr, 369 U.S. 186 (1962), requires the court to abstain from determining this issue as this falls under the "political question doctrine." 783 F.2d at 787–88.

argument, stating that the judiciary makes the initial determination of the applicability of the political offense exception.[101]

Setting the contours of what will be a political offense, Circuit Judge Reinhardt categorized political offenses into two groups: "pure political offenses" and "relative political offenses."[102] As stated in the *Quinn* case, "pure political offenses are, 'acts aimed directly at the government.' " They "have none of the elements of ordinary crimes." Crimes that typically fit this category are "treason, sedition, and espionage."[103] Pure political offenses are usually considered to be non-extraditable.[104]

In contrast, "relative political offenses," "include 'otherwise common crimes committed in connection with a political act.' "[105] Courts throughout the world do not always agree on when crimes that fit this category should be extraditable. The majority in the *Quinn* case discussed the three tests that have been used to ascertain whether the "nexus between the crime and the political act is sufficiently close . . . [for the crime to be deemed] not extraditable." The tests described in this case are the "(1) the French 'objective' test; (2) the Swiss 'proportionality' or 'predominance' test; and (3) the Anglo-American 'incidence' test."[106] This last test is further explained by later cases in the United States.

The French "objective" test seldom protected normal criminal acts. It offered protection only to those acts that "directly injured the rights of the state."[107] It is an extremely narrow test that seldom offered an accused the benefit of the political offense exception.

In contrast, the Swiss posture, as described in *Quinn*, "protects both pure and relative political offenses." "The Swiss test examines the political motivation of the offender . . . but also requires (a) a consideration of the circumstances surrounding the commission of the crimes, . . . and (b) either a proportionality between the means and the political ends, . . . or a predominance of the political elements over the common crime elements . . . ."[108] There is some disagreement as to whether a "political movement" is necessary and the degree to which the role of the defendant's motivation suffices as a basis for meeting this test.[109]

Finally, the Anglo-American "incidence test" emanates from a case that held "that common crimes committed 'in the course of' and 'in furtherance' of a political disturbance would be treated as political offenses."[110] This test has developed in various directions throughout the years with a recent judicial "split almost evenly over whether the traditional American incidence test should be applied to new methods of political violence in two categories — domestic revolutionary violence and international terrorism — or whether fundamental new restrictions should be

---

[101] *See* In re Doherty, 599 F. Supp. 270, 277 n.6 (S.D.N.Y. 1984).

[102] *See* Quinn v. Robinson, 783 F.2d 776, 793 (9th Cir. 1986).

[103] *Id.*

[104] *Id.* at 794.

[105] *Id.*

[106] *Id.*

[107] *See* Quinn v. Robinson, 783 F.2d 776, 794 (9th Cir. 1986).

[108] *Id.* (citations omitted).

[109] *Id.* at 794–95.

[110] *Id.* at 795 (citing In re Castioni, [1891] 1 Q.B. 149 (1890)).

imposed on the use of the political offense exception."[111] As one might suspect, there is a strong desire to make certain that international terrorism prosecutions are not hamstrung by this doctrine. As noted in *Quinn* "[w]hen we extradite an individual accused of international terrorism, we are not interfering with any internal struggle; rather, it is the international terrorist who has interfered with the rights of others to exist peacefully under their chosen form of government."[112]

In the *Quinn* case, the court found that Quinn could be extradited on the murder charge.[113] Circuit Judge Reinhardt emphasized that the political offense exception would not cover "acts of international terrorism" or "crimes against humanity."[114] The "two components" of the "incidence test" that need to be met are: (1) "there must be an uprising — a political disturbance related to the struggle of individuals to alter or abolish the existing government in their country" and (2) "the charged offense must have been committed in furtherance of the uprising; it must be related to the political struggle or be consequent to the uprising activity."[115]

The "incidence test" has been the subject of criticism, with some claiming it is "underinclusive"[116] and others claiming it to be "overly broad."[117] Despite this criticism, *Quinn* and other cases have held that "the American test in its present form remains not only workable, but desirable."[118]

Circuit Judge Duniway concurred with Circuit Judge Reinhardt's decision, but did not agree with all aspects of that opinion.[119] Circuit Judge Fletcher dissented with respect to Quinn's extraditability on the murder charge, finding that "the acts of Irish nationalists against the British in London are not international terrorism or other criminal conduct exported to other locations."[120] Because Quinn was a United States citizen who resided in San Francisco, Circuit Judge Fletcher believed that the case should be remanded to determine if Quinn had "demonstrate[d] tangible and substantial connections with the country in which an uprising occurs." He stated that this initial determination by the district court should be necessary in deciding "whether Quinn should be treated as an Irish national and afforded the protection of the political offense exception."[121]

Some modern bilateral[122] and multilateral[123] treaties create exceptions to the political offense exception in the cases of violent offenses, especially those that can be characterized as terrorist offenses.

---

[111] *Id.* at 801.

[112] *Id.* at 806.

[113] The court did remand the case on the conspiracy charge to determine if it was "time barred." *Id.* at 818.

[114] *Id.* at 817.

[115] *Id.* at 817.

[116] Claims are made that it fails to include "all offenses that are not contemporaneous with an uprising even though the acts may represent legitimate political resistance." *Quinn*, 783 F.2d at 797–78.

[117] It makes non-extraditable "some offenses that are not of a political character merely because the crimes took place contemporaneously with an uprising." *Id.* at 798.

[118] *Id.* at 801; *see also* United States v. Pitawanakwat, 120 F. Supp. 2d 921, 930 (D. Ore. 2000).

[119] *Quinn*, 783 F.2d at 818–19.

[120] *Id.* at 820.

[121] *Id.* at 820–22.

[122] *E.g.*, Art. 1, Supplementary Extradition Treaty between the Government of the United States and

[C]   Proving a Political Offense

The defendant has the burden of establishing the elements of the political offense exception. The burden then shifts, however, "to the demanding government 'to prove that the crime charged in the Complaint was not of a political character.' "[124]

Even were the accused to assert the political offense exception with Canada as the requesting country, the court would not discard the assertion merely because of the close ties between the United States and Canada and the democratic nature of that country.[125] There must be a full examination of whether the "incidence test" applies. "The uprising must be 'both temporally and spatially limited' and involve 'a certain level of violence' by those 'seeking to accomplish a particular objective.' "[126]

Denying an extradition request in *United States v. Pitawahakwat*,[127] a district court in Oregon found that the political offense exception was met when the incident in question "was not an isolated violent incident by a mere handful of insurgents," but rather "was part of a broader protest in 1995 aimed at the Canadian government in support of sovereignty by the native people over their land."[128] Even though Canada's request for extradition was for a parole violation, occasioned by his move to the United States, the defendant was permitted to assert the political offense exception. The court concluded that the "defendant's crimes for which he was convicted and later paroled were 'of a political character' and therefore may not provide the basis for extradition of defendant to Canada."[129]

§ 12.05   LURING

The United States Attorneys' Manual states that "[a] lure involves using a subterfuge to entice a criminal defendant to leave a foreign country so that he or she can be arrested in the United States, in international waters or airspace, or in a third country for subsequent extradition, expulsion, or deportation to the United States."[130] Although the United States permits lures, other countries may not

---

the Government of the United Kingdom of Great Britain and Northern Ireland, June 25, 1985, in EXTRADITION LAW AND TREATIES OF THE UNITED STATES 920.20f (I.I. Kavass comp., loose-leaf). This treaty was controversial among the United States Irish community and ultimately contained an "exception to the exception to the exception," where the accused proves to the court on the preponderance of the evidence that "the request for extradition has in fact been made with a view to try to punish him on account of his race, religion, nationality, or political opinions, or that he would, if surrendered, be prejudiced at his trial or punished, detained or restricted in his personal liberty by reason of his race, religion, nationality or political opinions." *Id.*, Art. 3. Similar "human rights" provisions appear in many modern extradition treaties. *See* note 72, *supra*. The most recent US/UK Extradition Treaty, in force April 26, 2007, Art. 4, leaves the ultimate decision on political motivation to the Executive. The treaty is at S. Treaty Doc. No. 108-23 (2003) and also at http://www.state.gov/p/eur/rls/fs/34885.htm.

[123] *E.g.*, Art. 15, Convention against Nuclear Terrorism, April 13, 2005, G.A. Res. 59/290, *available at* http://daccessdds.un.org/doc/UNDOC/GEN/N04/494/53/PDF/N0449453.pdf?OpenElement.

[124] United States v. Pitawanakwat, 120 F. Supp. 2d 921 (D. Ore. 2000) (citing Ramos v. Diaz, 121 F.3d 1322, 1326 (9th Cir. 1997)).

[125] United States v. Pitawanakwat, 120 F. Supp. 2d 921 (D. Ore. 2000).

[126] *Id.* at 934 (citing Quinn v. Robinson, 783 F.3d 776, 807, 817 (9th Cir. 1986)).

[127] *Id.* at 921.

[128] *Id.* at 938.

[129] *Id.* at 938.

[130] U.S. Attys. Manual § 9-15.630 (last visited Feb.15, 2008), *available at* http://www.usdoj.gov/usao/

accept this practice. Some countries consider this to be kidnapping through use of fraud and a violation of human rights.[131] Because of concerns of sovereignty, in the United States a federal prosecutor is required to consult the Office of International Legal Affairs prior to participating in a lure.[132]

In some cases individuals are lured to countries that have extradition treaties with the United States in order to then proceed with the extradition process. In other instances, the individual may be lured directly to the United States. For example, one reported incident involved a Dominican policewoman who convinced a man to meet her in a bar for a date. He was then lured to the United States to face criminal charges.[133] Another case involved a man invited to the United States by individuals who operated a computer security firm. Once he was in the United States, he was arrested.[134]

In the case of *United States v. Yunis*,[135] the FBI employed an undercover operation to lure Yunis onto a "yacht in the eastern Mediterranean Sea with promises of a drug deal." Once aboard the ship they traveled into international waters.[136] Yunis was then transferred to a U.S. Navy ship and eventually flown to the United States. Yunis argued that his being lured to the United States was improper. The court found that although the "government's conduct was neither 'picture perfect' nor 'a model for law enforcement behavior,' " it did not rise to the level of being so shocking to the conscience as to warrant a reversal.[137]

§ 12.06   ABDUCTION

[A]   United States v. Alvarez-Machain

Perhaps the most controversial method of obtaining people from abroad is through abduction. Despite the controversy surrounding the practice of abduction, it has been used by the United States and approved of by the United States Supreme Court in the case of *United States v. Alvarez-Machain*.[138]

Alvarez-Machain, a citizen and resident of Mexico, was indicted by the United States "for participating in the kidnap and murder of a United States Drug Enforcement Administration (DEA) 'special agent.' " He was "forcibly kidnapped from his medical office in Guadalajara, Mexico" by individuals associated with the DEA, although the DEA did not themselves abduct him. Alvarez-Machain, a physician, was taken to Texas.

---

eousa/foia_ reading_room/usam/title9/15mcrm.htm#9-15.630.

[131] *See* JORDAN J. PAUST, ET AL., INTERNATIONAL CRIMINAL LAW 443–48 (2d ed. 2000).

[132] U.S. Attys. Manual § 9-15.630 (last visited Feb. 15, 2008), *available at* http://www.usdoj.gov/usao/eousa/foia_ reading_room/usam/title9/15mcrm.htm#9-15.630.

[133] Bruce Zagaris, *U.S. and Dominican Policewoman Lure Narcotics Fugitive*, 16 INT'L ENF. L. REP. 825 (2000).

[134] *Russian Hacker Sentenced to 3 Years in Prison*, AP, Oct. 5, 2002, *available at* http://www.modbee.com/24hour/technology/story/562860p-4430289c.html.

[135] 924 F.2d 1086 (D.C. Cir. 1991).

[136] *Id.* at 1089.

[137] *Id.* at 1093.

[138] 504 U.S. 655 (1992). The case of Julius and Ethel Rosenberg's co-defendant provides an earlier, and equally notorious abduction, this time with the aid of Mexican officials. *See* United States v. Sobell, 142 F. Supp. 515 (1956), *aff'd* United States v. Sobell, 244 F.2d 520 (1957).

Pre-trial, Alvarez-Machain contested the method used to secure his presence in the United States. The district court dismissed the indictment, and the appellate court affirmed. The Supreme Court reversed, holding that Dr. Alvarez-Machain could be tried in the United States. That trial resulted in a verdict of not guilty and was followed by an Alien Torts Claim action contesting the conduct by the United States.[139]

In allowing the prosecution to proceed with the case of Alvarez-Machain, Chief Justice Rehnquist, the author of the Court's majority opinion, rejected the argument that the respondent had been abducted in violation of a treaty between the United States and Mexico. The Court found that although there was an extradition treaty between the United States and Mexico, the explicit terms of that treaty did not address abductions and the Court was unwilling to imply such a term in the treaty. The majority, in rejecting the position of the respondent, stated that although the abduction may be "shocking" and a "violation of general international law principles," the executive branch would have the decision-making authority to determine if Dr. Alvarez-Machain should be returned to Mexico.[140]

To address these issues, the Court looked at precedent such as *United States v. Rauscher*,[141] *Ker v. Illinois*,[142] and *Frisbee v. Collins*.[143] In *Rauscher*, the Court faced an issue regarding the rule of speciality and whether the defendant could be prosecuted for a crime that had not been included in his initial indictment. Rauscher was controlled by the Webster-Ashburton Treaty of 1842 and by statutes that "imposed the doctrine of speciality upon extradition treaties to which the United States was a party."[144] *Rauscher*, however, did not involve a forcible abduction.

Unlike *Rauscher*, *Ker*, a case decided the same day and also with an opinion authored by Justice Miller, involved a forcible abduction. In *Ker*, the Court found that due process did not preclude proceeding against the defendant despite his being brought to the United States by forcible abduction. *Frisbee* also rejected due process arguments to an abduction in Chicago, Illinois, by Michigan police officers who then brought the defendant to Michigan for trial.

The defense distinguished the Ker case from that presented in *Alvarez-Machain*, as *Ker's* abduction did not include government participation and there was no objection to proceeding with the case by Peru, the country from which Ker had been abducted. The Court, however, noted that Mexico was well aware of the *Ker* doctrine and failed to include a specific provision in the treaty that would preclude abductions. The Court in *Alvarez-Machain* found that "the language of the Treaty, in the context of its history, does not support the proposition that the Treaty prohibits abduction outside of its terms."[145]

---

[139] *See* § 1.02[C], *supra*.

[140] United States v. Alvarez-Machain, 504 U.S. 655, 669 (1992).

[141] 119 U.S. 407 (1886).

[142] 119 U.S. 436 (1886).

[143] 342 U.S. 519 (1952).

[144] United States v. Alvarez-Machain, 504 U.S. 655, 660 (1992).

[145] *Id.* at 666. Alvarez-Machain was the subject of another leading case in the Supreme Court when he sued those responsible for abducting him. The United States was held to be immune from suit in respect of the tort matter in Mexico. The kidnapper against whom he had obtained a judgment in the lower court was held not to be amenable to suit under the Alien Tort Claims Act on the basis that a

A strong dissent voiced by Justices Stevens, Blackmun, and O'Connor, stressed that the majority was not distinguishing between private versus government abductions. The dissent stated that the Court's opinion "fails to differentiate between the conduct of private citizens, which does not violate any treaty obligation, and conduct expressly authorized by the Executive Branch of the Government, which unquestionably constitutes a flagrant violation of international law" and "also constitutes a breach of our treaty obligations."[146]

The Court's opinion in the *Alvarez-Machain* case was not well received in international circles. The Department of Justice's reaction to this criticism was to include a statement in the United States Attorneys' Manual that "[d]ue to the sensitivity of abducting defendants from a foreign country, prosecutors may not take steps to secure custody over persons outside the United States (by government agents or the use of private persons, like bounty hunters or private investigators) by means of *Alvarez-Machain* type renditions without advance approval by the Department of Justice."[147] The United States and Mexico in fact negotiated a treaty banning abductions in 1994, but it was never ratified by the United States.[148] Prior to that, President Clinton had written to his Mexican counterpart on March 30, 1993, that: "I want to assure you that my administration will not conduct, encourage or condone illegal transborder abductions in Mexico."[149] Whether this was merely a political statement and binding only on the Clinton administration, or a more general undertaking for future Governments, is unclear.

Practice in other common law countries has been running against the Supreme Court's approach. In *R. v. Horseferry Road Magistrates' Court, ex parte Bennett*,[150] the House of Lords specifically rejected *Alvarez-Machain*. On the other hand, at the international level, the ad hoc Tribunals for Former Yugoslavia and Rwanda have been able to tolerate a degree of coercion (to say nothing of trickery) when it comes to acquiring their defendants.[151]

Some multilateral treaties contain promises apparently aimed at such actions as abductions, but they are not necessarily honored. Thus Article 2 of the United Nations Convention against Illicit Traffic in Narcotic Drugs and Psychotropic Substances (in force for Mexico and the United States at the time of the Alvarez-Machain abduction) provides that:

---

simple abduction is not a tort in international law — prolonged arbitrary detention is required. Sosa v. Alvarez-Machain, 542 U.S. 692 (2004).

[146] 504 U.S. at 682.

[147] U.S. Attys. Manual § 9-15.610 (last visited Feb. 15, 2008).

[148] Treaty to Prohibit Transborder Abductions, Nov. 23, 1994, U.S.-Mex., *reprinted in* MICHAEL ABBELL, EXTRADITION TO AND FROM THE UNITED STATES, at A-303 (2002).

[149] "Transcript" of letter supplied by Embassy of Mexico to Rutgers Law Library.

[150] [1993] All E.R. 138 (H.L.). *See also* R. v. Hartley, [1978] 2 N.Z.L.R. 199 (C.A. New Zealand) (same); R. v. Jewitt, [1985] 2 S.C.R. 128 (Sup. Ct. Canada). One extensive review of recent state practice concludes that there is now a rule of customary international law opposed to the decision in Alvarez-Machain: Stephen Wilske & Teresa Schiller, *Jurisdiction Over Persons Abducted in Violation of International Law in the Aftermath of United States v. Alvarez-Machain*, 5 U. CHI. L. SCH. ROUNDTABLE 205 (1998).

[151] Robert J. Currie, *Abducted Fugitives before the International Criminal Court: Problems and Prospects*, 18 CRIM. L. F. 349 (2007); WILLIAM A. SCHABAS, THE UN INTERNATIONAL CRIMINAL TRIBUNALS: THE FORMER YUGOSLAVIA, RWANDA AND SIERRA LEONE 381-2 (2006).

2. The parties shall carry out their obligations under this Convention in a manner consistent with the principles of sovereign equality and territorial integrity of States and that of non-intervention in the domestic affairs of other States.

3. A Party shall not undertake on the territory of another Party the exercise of jurisdiction and performance of functions which are exclusively reserved for the authorities of that other Party by its domestic law.[152]

Speaking of these paragraphs, the Official Commentary on the Convention explains that the Convention contemplates quite broad jurisdiction to prescribe, but that this does not mean open-ended enforcement jurisdiction:

> The conditions governing the establishment by parties of prescriptive jurisdiction are regulated in detail in article 4, which envisages the establishment of such jurisdiction on either a territorial or an extraterritorial basis. The establishment of prescriptive extraterritorial jurisdiction, widely accepted under international law, must be distinguished from the power to exercise jurisdiction and take enforcement action abroad, which, as emphasized by article 2, paragraph 3 is prohibited under international law, save when undertaken with the consent of the State concerned.[153]

[B] Other Abduction Cases

Courts have interpreted the *Alvarez-Machain* case in several later decisions involving abduction type conduct. For example, in *United States v. Matta-Ballesteros*,[154] the defendant was abducted in Honduras and brought to the United States for trial. The Ninth Circuit used the case of *Alvarez-Machain* as the basis for holding that when a treaty does not exclude other methods of securing individuals from abroad, abduction can be used.

In *Matta-Ballesteros* the court refused to dismiss the case because the government conduct did not rise to the level of "outrageous governmental conduct," as seen in the case of *United States v. Toscanino*.[155] The court in *Matta-Ballesteros* found no basis for the court to use its supervisory powers, because the defense had failed to "make 'a strong showing of grossly cruel and unusual barbarities inflicted upon him by persons who can be characterized as paid agents of the United States.' "[156]

Another case of abduction was seen in the capture and eventual prosecution of Manuel Antonio Noriega, who "served as commander of the Panamanian Defense Forces in the Republic of Panama."[157] In *United States v. Noriega*, the Eleventh Circuit affirmed the conviction of Noriega, finding that his abduction did not violate the provisions of the treaty. The court also held that there was no basis for the court's use of supervisory powers. The court stated that "we are aware of no

---

[152] United Nations Convention against Illicit Traffic in Narcotic Drugs and Psychotropic Substances, December 20, 1988, U.N. Doc. E/CONF. 82/15, Art. 2.

[153] UNITED NATIONS, COMMENTARY ON THE UNITED NATIONS CONVENTION AGAINST ILLICIT TRAFFIC IN NARCOTIC DRUGS AND PSYCHOTROPIC SUBSTANCES, 1988, ¶ 2.22, at 47 (1998). *See* § 2.03, *supra* (discussing the difference between prescriptive and enforcement jurisdiction).

[154] 71 F.3d 754 (9th Cir. 1995), *amended*, 98 F.3d 1100 (9th Cir. 1996).

[155] 500 F.2d 267 (2d Cir. 1974).

[156] 71 F.3d at 764.

[157] United States v. Noriega, 117 F.3d 1206 (11th Cir. 1997).

authority that would allow a court to exercise its supervisory power to dismiss an indictment based on harm done by the government to third parties."[158]

Internationally, the best-known abduction was probably that of Adolph Eichmann from Argentina, carried out without the consent of Argentina, by Israeli Mossad agents. Argentina sought an urgent meeting of the United Nations Security Council over this breach of its sovereignty.[159] After debating the issue, the Council voted by 8 votes to 0, with two abstentions and one (Argentina) not participating in the vote, to adopt a resolution critical of the kidnapping.

Its condemnation of Israel was, however, nuanced. The Council noted both that "the repetition of acts such as that giving rise to this situation would involve a breach of the principles upon which international order is founded creating an atmosphere of insecurity and distrust incompatible with the preservation of peace," and that it was "mindful of the universal condemnation of the persecution of the Jews under the Nazis, and of the concern of people in all countries that Eichmann should be brought to appropriate justice for the crimes of which he is accused." It accordingly requested Israel to "make appropriate reparation in accordance with the Charter of the United Nations and the rules of international law."[160] Argentina sought reparation in the form of the return of Eichmann and the punishment of those guilty of violating its territory.[161]

The dispute was ultimately resolved through a joint statement that "the Governments of Israel and the Republic of the Argentine, imbued with the wish to give effect to the resolution of the Security Council of June 23, 1960, in which the hope was expressed that the traditionally friendly relations between the two countries will be advanced, have decided to regard as closed the incident that arose out of the action taken by Israeli nationals which infringed the fundamental rights of the State of Argentina."[162] Thus were vindicated both the principle of territorial integrity and the principle against impunity for those guilty of the greatest of crimes. Argentina had more success in vindicating its interests in territorial integrity than Eichmann did in enforcing his right not to be kidnapped. The Supreme Court of Israel relied heavily on the United States abduction decisions in upholding the conviction and hanging of Eichmann.[163]

"Rendition," or what is sometimes called "extraordinary rendition," has been a subject of concern in the United States. It is a process of removing people from a country without judicial authorization, and taking them to a secret prison in another country for holding or interrogation. In some cases, the transfer is done deliberately to take them to a country that will allow them to be tortured. In contrast to the more usual abductions, the person is not being brought to the United States to face charges.[164] There are some historical antecedents. In

---

[158] *Id.* at 1214.

[159] [1960] U.N. Y.B. 196 ("Question relating to the case of Adolph Eichmann").

[160] *Id.* at 198.

[161] Return of the abducted person is widely regarded as at least part of an appropriate remedy in such cases. The Inter-American Juridical Committee later expressed the opinion that the United States exercise of jurisdiction over Alvarez-Machain, "ignore[d] the obligation of the United States to return Alvarez to the country from whose jurisdiction he was kidnapped." Legal Opinion on the Decision of the Supreme Court of the United States of America, in 4 CRIM. L. F. 119, 125.

[162] Quoted in L.C. Green, *Legal Issues of the Eichmann Trial*, 37 TUL. L. REV. 641, 647 (1962–3).

[163] Attorney-General of Israel v. Eichmann, 36 Int'l L. Rep. 5 (Sup.Ct. Israel).

[164] On this practice, see JORDAN J. PAUST, BEYOND THE LAW: THE BUSH ADMINISTRATION'S UNLAWFUL

December 2007, a judge in Rome issued warrants for 140 former officials from Argentina, Bolivia, Brazil, Chile, Paraguay, Peru and Uruguay in respect of the disappearance of 25 Italian citizens in the course of actions in the 1970s and 1980s, known as Operation Condor.[165] According to a press report, the Condor countries (with the United States playing a "complicit role") "helped one another locate, transport, torture and ultimately make disappear dissidents across their borders, and even collaborated on assassination operations in Europe and the United States."[166] President Garcia of Peru described the judge's efforts as an attempt to depict Peru as "a little banana republic."[167]

The disappearance variety of abduction, transnational and national, was the subject of a recent suppression treaty adopted by the United Nations General Assembly, the International Convention for the Protection of all Persons from Enforced Disappearance.[168] The Convention, which had been co-sponsored by more than 100 Member States and adopted by the newly-established Human Rights Council the previous June, recognizes the right of persons not to be subjected to enforced disappearance, regardless of circumstances, and the right of victims to justice and reparation. It commits States party to it to criminalize enforced disappearance, to bring those responsible to justice and to take preventive measures.

RESPONSES IN THE "WAR" ON TERROR 34–36 (2007); Leila Nadya Sadat, *Ghost Prisoners and Black Sites: Extraordinary Rendition under International Law*, 37 CASE WEST. RES. J. INT'L L. 309 (2006).

[165] Alexei Barrionuevo, *Italy Follows Trail of Secret South American Abductions*, N.Y. TIMES, Feb. 22, 2008 p. A12.

[166] *Id.*

[167] *Id.*

[168] G.A. Res. 61/177 (2006), *available at* http://daccessdds.un.org/doc/UNDOC/GEN/N06/505/05/PDF/N0650505.pdf?OpenElement.

Chapter 13
PRISONER TRANSFER TREATIES AND OTHER POST-CONVICTION PROBLEMS

SYNOPSIS

§ 13.01   Prisoner Transfer Treaties
§ 13.02   Recognition of Foreign Criminal Judgments

§ 13.01   PRISONER TRANSFER TREATIES

Prisoners may wish to serve a prison sentence in a country other than where they have been convicted. To accommodate these requests, countries have entered into agreements allowing prisoners to be transferred to another country for the purpose of serving their prison sentence.[1] Most often these requests are made so that prisoners can serve the time in their home country.[2] The basic rationale for such arrangements is succinctly stated in two paragraphs of the preamble to the resolution of 1985 United Nations Congress on the Prevention of Crime and the Treatment of Offenders adopting the United Nations Model Agreement on the Transfer of Foreign Prisoners:

> *Recognizing* the difficulties of foreigners detained in prison establishments abroad owing to such factors as differences in language, culture, customs and religion,

> *Considering* that the aim of social resettlement of offenders could best be achieved by giving foreign prisoners the opportunity to serve their sentence within their country of nationality or residence.[3]

The treaties that allow for prisoner transfer are bilateral, multilateral, and in some cases they are a part of an International Convention dealing also with other issues. In the United States there are federal treaties that allow for the transfer of prisoners both to and from this country. Additionally, state statutes often specifically provide for the transfer of prisoners to another country when it is pursuant to a treaty.[4] For example, an Arizona state statute[5] provides that

> If a treaty in effect between the United States and a foreign country provides for the transfer or exchange of convicted offenders to the country of which they are citizens or nationals, the governor may, on behalf of this state and subject to the terms of the treaty, authorize the director of the

---

[1] For a history of transferring prisoners within Europe and by France and her former African colonies, see JORDAN J. PAUST, M. CHERIF BASSIOUNI, MICHAEL SCHARF, JIMMY GURULÉ, LEILA SADAT, BRUCE ZAGARIS & SHARON A. WILLIAMS, INTERNATIONAL CRIMINAL LAW 564 (2d ed. 2000). On the history of prisoner transfer arrangements, *see also* ROGER S. CLARK, THE UNITED NATIONS CRIME PREVENTION AND CRIMINAL JUSTICE PROGRAM: FORMULATION OF STANDARDS AND EFFORTS AT THEIR IMPLEMENTATION 205–6 (1994).

[2] *See generally* M. Cherif Bassiouni & Grace M.W. Gallagher, *Transfer of Prisoners: Policies and Practices of the United States, in* 2 INTERNATIONAL CRIMINAL LAW 505, 505 n. 5 (M. Cherif Bassiouni ed., 2d ed. 1999).

[3] Model Agreement on the Transfer of Foreign Prisoners, *in* UNITED NATIONS OFFICE ON DRUGS AND CRIME, COMPENDIUM OF UNITED NATIONS STANDARDS AND NORMS IN CRIME PREVENTION AND CRIMINAL JUSTICE (2006).

[4] Individual State Prisoner Statutes, *available at* http://www.usdoj.gov/criminal/oeo/prisonert.htm.

[5] Az. Stat. § 41-105 (2004).

department of corrections to consent to the transfer or exchange of offenders and take any other action necessary to initiate the participation of this state in the treaty.

Irrespective of whether the offense committed by an individual in another country would be a state or federal crime in the United States, individuals who are transferred to the U.S. serve their sentence in the federal prison system.[6] U.S. statutes allow for the transfer of offenders on probation[7] or parole,[8] outlining the conditions for such a transfer and the placement of the individual should a transfer occur. Military personnel can also be eligible for a transfer.[9]

The U.S. "International Prisoner Transfer Program" began in 1976 and 1977 with this country negotiating the initial treaties with Mexico and Canada to allow for such transfers. Although the treaties are "negotiated principally by the United States Department of State," the actual transfer mechanism is through the Department of Justice.[10] The U.S. presently has 12 bilateral treaties or transfer agreements, with Bolivia, Canada, France, Hong Kong, Marshall Islands, Mexico, Micronesia, Palau, Panama, Peru, Thailand, and Turkey. It is also a party to two multilateral treaties[11] that allow for the transfer of prisoners.[12] In total, arrangements are in place between the United States and over seventy countries.

In the United States, a federal framework statute provides the conditions under which prisoner transfers will be allowed.[13] The United States only transfers prisoners "to a country of which the offender is a citizen or national." Likewise the United States only accepts citizens and nationals.[14] Transfer to or from the United States requires the prisoner's consent.[15] It also is necessary that the crime meet the double criminality rule, thus being a crime in both the sending and receiving country.[16] The Attorney General plays a crucial role in prisoner transfer matters,

---

[6] *See* Transfer of Prisoners, http://www.usdoj.gov/criminal/oeo/tranfer.htm.

[7] 18 U.S.C. § 4104. *See also* United Nations Model Treaty on the Transfer of Supervision of Offenders Conditionally Sentenced or Conditionally Released, *in* UNITED NATIONS OFFICE ON DRUGS AND CRIME, COMPENDIUM OF UNITED NATIONS STANDARDS AND NORMS IN CRIME PREVENTION AND CRIMINAL JUSTICE 197 (2006).

[8] 18 U.S.C. §§ 4106, 4106A.

[9] *See* 10 U.S.C. § 955 (2004).

[10] DOJ, Criminal Division, International Prisoner Transfer Program, *available at* http://www.usdoj.gov/criminal/oeo/index.htm.

[11] The U.S. is a party to the prisoner transfer treaties of the Council of Europe (COE) and the Organization of American States (OAS) (Inter-American Convention on Serving Criminal Sentences Abroad). *See* Prisoner Transfer Treaties, *available at* http://travel.state.gov/travel/transfer.html.

[12] *See* Lists of Participating Countries and States, Department of Justice, *available at* http://www.usdoj.gov/criminal/oeo/lists.htm; *see also* Prisoner Transfer Treaties, *available at* http://travel.state.gov/travel/transfer.html.

[13] 18 U.S.C. § 4100 et seq.

[14] 18 U.S.C. § 4100(b).

[15] *Id.* A formal consent verification hearing is held to determine that the offender consents and that the "consent is voluntary and given with full knowledge of the consequences." 18 U.S.C. §§ 4107, 4108. Prisoners are entitled to counsel at "proceedings to verify consent of an offender for transfer." 18 U.S.C. § 4109.

[16] *See* § 11.02[C], *supra.* Double criminality is specifically defined in the context of prisoner transfers. *See* 18 U.S.C. § 4101(a). *See also* William V. Dunlap, *Dual Criminality in Penal Transfer Treaties,* 29 VA. J. INT'L L. 813 (1989).

as he or she "is authorized to act on behalf of the United States as the authority referred to in a treaty."[17]

In order for him to be transferred, the offender's case needs to have reached a certain level of finality, as transfers are not granted if there is an appeal or a pending "collateral attack upon the conviction."[18] If, however, the country sending a prisoner to the United States, notifies the U.S. that the individual sent "has been granted a pardon, commutation, or amnesty, or that there has been an ameliorating modification or a revocation of the sentence," the statute requires the United States to honor this change in circumstances.[19]

A key decision concerning prisoner transfer treaties is *Rosado v. Civiletti*.[20] Petitioners, United States citizens, were transferred to the United States from Mexico, where they had been convicted and sentenced to serve nine years. The petitioners argued successfully in the district court that their consents to transfer to the United States were "unlawfully coerced by the brutal conditions of their confinement in Mexico." The Second Circuit, however, reversed this decision, despite recognition of the "shocking brutal treatment to which [the petitioners] fell prey."[21]

The court "reaffirm[ed] the authority of the federal courts to hear due process claims raised" "by citizens held prisoner within the territorial jurisdiction of the United States."[22] The court, however, noted that the Mexican-United States treaty foreclosed a prisoner seeking transfer to the United States, from contesting his or her conviction or sentence outside the Mexican court system. Therefore, the petitioners were bound to these terms by agreeing to being transferred from Mexico to the United States. The court in *Rosado* admitted that influencing its decision was "the interest of those Americans currently incarcerated in Mexico."[23] The court stated that "[w]hatever hope the Treaty extends of escaping the harsh realities of confinement abroad will be dashed for hundreds of Americans if we permit these three petitioners to rescind their agreement to limit their attacks upon their convictions to Mexico's courts."[24]

The constitutionality of prisoner transfer treaties that foreclose assertion of constitutional rights in the United States has been the subject of judicial review. The cases uphold the treaties.[25]

As seen in the decision of Rosado, there is a clear advantage to allowing an incarcerated individual the opportunity to serve a sentence in his or her home

---

[17] *See* 18 U.S.C. § 4102. The Department of Justice's website provides factors that are considered by the DOJ in deciding upon a transfer. For example, they consider "the strength of the offender's ties to each country," and "occasionally special humanitarian concerns — such as the terminal illness of a prisoner or a close family member." *See* How the Program Works, Department of Justice, *available at* http://www.usdoj.gov/criminal/oeo/program.htm; *see also* Guidelines for Evaluating Prisoner Applications for Transfer, *available at* http://www.usdoj.gov/criminal/oeo/guidlines.html.

[18] 18 U.S.C. § 4100(b).

[19] 18 U.S.C. § 4100(d).

[20] 621 F.2d 1179 (2d Cir. 1980).

[21] *Id.* at 1201.

[22] *Id.* at 1182.

[23] *Id.* at 1200.

[24] *Id.*

[25] *See, e.g.*, Pfeifer v. U.S. Bureau of Prisons, 615 F.2d 873 (9th Cir. 1980); Mitchell v. United States, 483 F. Supp. 291 (E.D. Wis. 1980).

country. Professor Herbert Wechsler, testifying before the Senate Foreign Relations Committee, presented several arguments in favor of finding the treaties constitutional, including that the individual retains the right to attack the conviction and sentence in the "courts of the transferring state."[26]

§ 13.02 RECOGNITION OF FOREIGN CRIMINAL JUDGMENTS

In a famous dictum, Marshall C.J. proclaimed that "[t]he courts of no country execute the penal laws of another."[27] Joseph Story, in the first great American work on Conflict of Laws, asserted that

[t]he common law considers crimes as altogether local, and cognizable and punishable exclusively in the country where they are committed. No other nation, therefore, has any right to punish them; nor is under any obligation to take notice of, or to enforce any judgment, rendered in such cases by the tribunals having authority to hold jurisdiction within its territory, where they are committed.[28]

Since that time, this absolute position has been significantly altered by treaty and statute. The United States has not gone as far as some European countries and a United Nations Model Treaty have gone in permitting the transfer of proceedings between different countries.[29] Nevertheless, it has gone much further than Marshall and Story might have expected in taking cognizance of foreign penal judgments.

Foreign convictions can, in modern law and practice, have an effect on United States individuals in a host of different ways.[30] For example, if a pre-sentence report of a person convicted for a crime includes a prior conviction from another country, the court might consider this foreign conviction in making its sentencing decision and increase the defendant's sentence as a result of the prior foreign conviction.[31] There also can be collateral consequences to having a foreign conviction. For example, the foreign conviction may be a bar to a person trying to

---

[26] *Penal Treaties with Mexico and Canada: Hearings Before the Senate Comm. on Foreign Relations*, 95th Cong. 90, 93–94 (1977) (testimony of Herbert Wechsler) (reprinted in part in EDWARD M. WISE, ELLEN S. PODGOR & ROGER S. CLARK, INTERNATIONAL CRIMINAL LAW: CASES AND MATERIALS 559–60 (2d ed. 2004).) *See also* JORDAN J. PAUST, M.CHERIF BASSIOUNI, MICHAEL SCHARF, JIMMY GURULÉ, LEILA SADAT, BRICE ZAGARIS & SHARON A. WILLIAMS, INTERNATIONAL CRIMINAL LAW 581 (2d ed. 2000) (discussing the pros and cons of prisoner transfer treaties).

[27] *The Antelope*, 23 U.S. 268 (1825). Marshall seems to be referring to a Spanish law prohibiting the slave trade; some of his colleagues would at least have "enforced" it to the extent of regarding "title" to the Africans in question as void. In short, there may be collateral effects of foreign criminal law.

[28] JOSEPH STORY, COMMENTARIES ON THE CONFLICT OF LAWS, FOREIGN AND DOMESTIC 516 (1834). Story does note that some foreign jurists took a different view. *Id.* at 517.

[29] *See* ROGER S. CLARK, THE UNITED NATIONS CRIME PREVENTION AND CRIMINAL JUSTICE PROGRAM: FORMULATION OF STANDARDS AND EFFORTS AT THEIR IMPLEMENTATION 219–22 (1994).

[30] *See generally* A. Kenneth Pye, *The Effect of Foreign Criminal Judgments Within the United States*, 32 U.M.K.C. L. REV. 114 (1964), *reprinted in* INTERNATIONAL CRIMINAL LAW 479 (Gerhard O. W. Mueller & Edward M. Wise eds., 1965).

[31] *See, e.g.*, United States v. Kole, 164 F.3d 164 (3d Cir. 1998); § 9.04, *supra*; *see also* Martha Kimes, Note, *The Effect of Foreign Criminal Convictions Under American Repeat Offender Statutes: A Case Against the Use of Foreign Crimes in Determining Habitual Criminal Status*, 35 COLUM. J. TRANSNAT'L L. 503, 506–10 (1997).

obtain a license, such as a professional license. Questions of whether disclosure of this conviction is necessary on an employment application may arise.[32]

A foreign conviction may also be a factor in considering whether a person has already been tried for the specific crime now under consideration. Although the dual sovereignty rule allows different jurisdictions to proceed on conduct premised from the same factual setting, internal guidelines may advocate against proceeding in two different forums for the same criminal activity.[33] In the federal system, the Petite Policy of the Department of Justice instructs prosecutors not to proceed on most federal cases where the state has already prosecuted the same criminal conduct.[34]

It is becoming more common for courts to face the question of whether a foreign conviction should be used by a United States court in a pending matter. For example, in the case of *United States v. Moskovits*,[35] a district court in Pennsylvania was faced with the issue of whether a prior felony drug conviction could be used as an enhancement at sentencing when the conviction was from a Mexican court where the defendant "did not have counsel at crucial phases of the proceeding."[36] Although the procedures were within the norms of Mexican standards of criminal justice, the defense argued that this was irrelevant since the conviction was being used as an enhancement in a United States court.[37] In contrast, the government argued "that so long as there was conformity with Mexican requirements and with norms of fundamental fairness, the Mexican conviction and sentence" could be used to enhance the sentence.[38]

The court in *Moskovits* stated that use of an "invalid prior conviction" "depends on what light the sentencing judge gained from the prior convictions."[39] In this case the judge failed to use his "discretion" in determining whether this conviction represented a "pattern of antisocial behavior."[40] Since the conviction was used without scrutiny of the underlying conduct, the court vacated the sentence.

There have been several cases where courts have wrestled with the issue of whether it is proper to use a foreign conviction in enhancing the sentence of a

---

[32] *See* EDWARD M. WISE, ELLEN S. PODGOR & ROGER S. CLARK, INTERNATIONAL CRIMINAL LAW: CASES AND MATERIALS 563 (2d ed. 2004) (citing A. Kenneth Pye, *The Effect of Foreign Criminal Judgments Within the United States*, 32 U.M.K.C. L. REV. 114 (1964), *reprinted in* INTERNATIONAL CRIMINAL LAW 479 (Gerhard O. W. Mueller & Edward M. Wise eds., 1965)).

[33] *See* JEROLD H. ISRAEL, ELLEN S. PODGOR, PAUL D. BORMAN & PETER J. HENNING, WHITE COLLAR CRIME: LAW AND PRACTICE 25 (2d ed. 2003). *See also* Laurie L. Levenson, *Ex Post Facto Law*, NAT'L L. J., March 17, 2008 at 15 (discussing change in California statutory double jeopardy provisions which had prevented re-trial after conviction or acquittal in other countries).

[34] *Id.* Almost all cases hold that the guidelines and policy are not enforceable by the accused in a court of law. *See generally* Ellen S. Podgor, *Department of Justice Guidelines: Balancing "Discretionary Justice,"* 13 CORNELL J. L. & PUB. POL'Y 167 (2004).

[35] 784 F. Supp. 183 (E.D. Pa. 1991). The defendant was resentenced as a result of this decision, however, and a new trial was eventually ordered on other grounds. *See* United States v. Moskovits, 844 F. Supp. 202 (E.D. Pa. 1993). After retrial his conviction was affirmed on appeal. This also had to be modified as there was an improper increase in sentence. *See* United States v. Moskovits, 86 F.3d 1303 (3d Cir. 1996), *cert. denied*, 519 U.S. 1120 (1997).

[36] *Id.* at 184.

[37] *Id.* at 189.

[38] *Id.* at 189–90.

[39] *Id.* at 192.

[40] *Id.*

defendant. In some instances the court will consider the foreign conviction, while others will not allow it to be used.[41] Some courts will focus on whether it deprives the accused of fundamental fairness.[42] Another issue of concern is whether a court can rely on the evidence supporting a questionable foreign conviction.[43] A growing body of case law provides some guidance in resolving these issues.[44]

In *Small v. United States*,[45] the Supreme Court was faced with the issue of whether to include convictions beyond the United States in interpreting an "unlawful gun possession" statute. Specifically, the Court needed to ascertain whether Congress had foreign convictions in mind in 18 U.S.C. § 922(g)(1), which makes it "unlawful for any person . . . who has been convicted in any court, of a crime punishable by imprisonment for a term exceeding one year . . . to . . . possess . . . any firearm." In this case a failure to include the criminal conviction outside the United States would result in a finding that the accused had not violated this "unlawful gun possession" statute.

The majority of the Court in *Small* started with a presumption against extraterritorial coverage. It then examined the totality of the legislation and its legislative history and concluded, in an opinion by Justice Breyer, that a prior Japanese conviction could not provide the necessary predicate for the possession offense. A forceful dissent by Justice Thomas, joined by Justices Scalia and Kennedy, argued that "any" had its natural meaning in the context of the statute and that there was nothing extraterritorial about restricting the defendant's conduct within the United States in light of what he had done before.

---

[41] *See generally* Alex Glashausser, *The Treatment of Foreign Country Convictions as Predicates for Sentence Enhancement Under Recidivist Statutes*, 44 DUKE L.J. 134, 238–39 (1994).

[42] *See* Martha Kimes, Note, *The Effect of Foreign Criminal Convictions Under American Repeat Offender Statutes: A Case Against the Use of Foreign Crimes in Determining Habitual Criminal Status*, 35 COLUM. J. TRANSNAT'L L. 525 (1997).

[43] *See* United States v. Delmarle, 99 F.3d 80 (2d Cir. 1996).

[44] *See generally* EDWARD M. WISE, ELLEN S. PODGOR & ROGER S. CLARK, INTERNATIONAL CRIMINAL LAW: CASES AND MATERIALS 571–74 (2d ed. 2004).

[45] 544 U.S. 385 (2005).

PART FOUR
THE PROSECUTION OF INTERNATIONAL CRIMES

Chapter 14
INTERNATIONAL CRIMES

§ 14.01   WHAT IS AN INTERNATIONAL CRIME?

What is considered an "international crime" is problematic as the concept is oftentimes blurred.[1] Historically it appeared to have at least two meanings: one which focused on violations of international law and the other which created international crimes through transnational means.[2] Clearly when an international body, such as an international tribunal imposes punishment on an individual, the act committed by that individual can be termed an international crime. Thus, the four crimes included in the International Criminal Court Statute are usually recognized as international crimes.[3] Less clear, however, is the extent to which agreements reached by countries to prosecute conduct makes the conduct an international crime.[4] Adding to this confusion is the concept of an "international concern" and whether crimes that fit this category ever fall within the realm of an international crime.[5]

Several concepts and practices assist in forming the body of international crimes. There is customary international law that prohibits certain conduct as violations *jus cogens*.[6] There are also crimes that emanate from bilateral and multilateral suppression treaties. International crimes sometimes involve discussion of "universal jurisdiction" or obligations *erga omnes*.[7] In some cases the discussion is framed

---

[1] *See generally* M. Cherif Bassiouni, *Universal Jurisdiction for International Crimes: Historical Perspectives and Contemporary Practice*, 42 Va. J. Int'l L. 81 (2001); Edward M. Wise, *International Crimes and Domestic Criminal Law*, 38 DePaul L. Rev. 923 (1989).

[2] *See* Sir John Fischer Williams, Chapters on Current International Law and the League of Nations 232, 244 (1929) (cited in Edward M. Wise, Ellen S. Podgor & Roger S. Clark, International Criminal Law: Cases and Materials 1 (2d ed. 2004)).

[3] These are the crime of genocide, crimes against humanity, war crimes, and the crime of aggression. The Rome Statute of the International Criminal Court, Art. 5, *available at* http://www.icc-cpi.int/home.html; *see also* § 17.02[B].

[4] *See* § 1.01, *supra*.

[5] *See* M. Cherif Bassiouni, *Introduction to Symposium on the Teaching of International Criminal Law*, 1 Touro J. Transnat'l L. 129 (1988).

[6] § 1.03[E], *supra*.

[7] § 1.03[C], *supra*.

in terms of "offenses against the law of nations," or "crimes against the peace and security of mankind." Irrespective of whether one broadly defines the concept to include all crimes that cross borders or narrowly as only those crimes punishable by an international tribunal, the substantive body of law pertaining to international crimes is increasing.

Looking at the crime of terrorism emphasizes the problems inherent in categorizing criminal conduct as either an international or non-international crime. In the case of *United States v. Yousef*,[8] the defendant was accused of several terrorist-related acts including conspiracy to bomb the World Trade Center. The Second Circuit, in examining a jurisdiction issue presented in the case, discussed what falls within the category of "universal jurisdiction."

> The historical restriction of universal jurisdiction to piracy, war crimes, and crimes against humanity demonstrates that universal jurisdiction arises under customary international law only where crimes (1) are universally condemned by the community of nations, and (2) by their nature occur either outside of a State or where there is no State capable of punishing, or competent to punish, the crime (as in a time of war).[9]

The court in finding that terrorism was not a crime of universal jurisdiction stated that:

> Unlike those offenses supporting universal jurisdiction under customary international law — that is, piracy, war crimes, and crimes against humanity — that now have fairly precise definitions and that have achieved universal condemnation, "terrorism" is a term as loosely deployed as it is powerfully charged. . . .[10]

Others, however, push for the inclusion of terrorism as an international crime.[11]

Professor M. Cherif Bassiouni, in his work, *Introduction to International Criminal Law*,[12] provides a blueprint for categorizing crimes as international crimes.[13] His study produces a list of "international crimes,"[14] "international delicts,"[15] and "international infractions."[16]

§ 14.02 RELATED CONCEPTS

Certain concepts are inherent to a discussion of international crimes. Most of these have previously been discussed in different contexts. For example, a discussion of international crimes cannot occur without recognition of two key terms: *jus cogens*[17] and obligations *erga omnes*. These terms emphasize that

---

[8] 327 F.3d 56 (2d Cir. 2003).

[9] *Id.* at 105.

[10] *Id.* at 106.

[11] *See, e.g.*, Vincent-Joël Proulx, *Rethinking the Jurisdiction of the International Criminal Court in the Post-September 11th Era: Should Acts of Terrorism Qualify as Crimes Against Humanity?*, 19 Am. U. Int'l L. Rev. 1009 (2004).

[12] M. Cherif Bassiouni, Introduction To International Criminal Law (2003).

[13] *Id.* at 114–20.

[14] *Id.* at 121.

[15] *Id.* at 122.

[16] *Id.* at 123–24.

[17] *See* § 1.03[E], *supra*.

international crimes are serious crimes and differ from the crimes one often finds prosecuted in a national system.

International crimes are sometimes seen as crimes with universal jurisdiction.[18] Universal jurisdiction is not without controversy, as some see it as a vehicle for combating human rights violations, while others express concern over the possible loss of state sovereignty.[19]

Equally controversial is the role that state responsibility should have in international criminal law. The International Criminal Court Statute limits its jurisdiction to individuals. Others, however, advocate for state "criminal" responsibility.[20]

A discussion of international crimes also requires recognition of a draft code that was prepared concerning "Crimes Against the Peace and Security of Mankind." After the Nuremberg Trial, the United Nations General Assembly instructed the International Law Commission (ILC), its subsidiary charged with codification and progressive development of international law, to engage in two codification exercises. One was to "formulate" the principles contained in the Nuremberg Charter and Judgment; the other was to work on a broader project to prepare a draft code of offenses against the peace and security of mankind. The second project proceeded on the basis that the Nuremberg crimes — war crimes, crimes against humanity and crimes against peace — were part of a more general category, the details of which would emerge from rational analysis.

The formulation of principles was completed in 1950.[21] In addition to asserting that the three Nuremberg crimes were punishable under international law, the codification distilled a number of general statements from the Charter and Judgment. These were: that a person who commits an act which constitutes a crime under international law is responsible therefor and liable to punishment; that the fact that internal law does not impose liability for an act which constitutes a crime under international law does not relieve the person who committed the act from responsibility under international law; that there is no head of State or Government official immunity; that the fact that a person acted pursuant to order of his Government or of a superior does not relieve him from responsibility under international law, provided a moral choice was in fact possible to him; a person charged with a crime under international law has the right to a fair trial on the facts and the law; and that complicity in a crime against peace, a war crime, or a crime against humanity is a crime under international law. None of this was especially controversial in the wake of the Nuremberg and Tokyo trials.

The wider work, however, became very controversial. The three Nuremberg crimes were soon joined by the crime of genocide, an offshoot of the persecution branch of crimes against humanity. Beyond that, work proceeded slowly. By 1991, the ILC provisionally adopted a version of the draft code which included articles on the crimes of aggression, threat of aggression, intervention, colonial domination, genocide, apartheid, systematic or mass violations of human rights, exceptionally serious war crimes, recruitment, financing and training of mercenaries, international terrorism, illicit drug trafficking, and willful and severe damage to the

---

[18]　*See* § 2.04[E], *supra.*

[19]　*See* Edward M. Wise, Ellen S. Podgor & Roger S. Clark, International Criminal Law: Cases and Materials 56 (2d ed. 2004).

[20]　*Id.* at 56–57.

[21]　Report of the International Law Commission, U.N. GAOR, 5th Sess., Supp. No. 12, at 11–14 (1950).

environment. This was more than the traffic would bear and governmental reactions were overwhelmingly unfavorable. A final draft appeared in 1996 that included only the three Nuremberg crimes, plus genocide and crimes against United Nations and associated personnel.[22] This narrower version had some influence on the set of crimes included two years later in the Rome Statute of the International Criminal Court, but the latter provisions were defined in much more detail than the 1996 draft Code.[23]

§ 14.03 SPECIFIC CRIMES

This section deals with the core international crimes *stricto sensu*, aggression, genocide, crimes against humanity and war crimes. Their core status is confirmed by their inclusion in the Rome Statute of the International Criminal Court. None of the other "international" crimes proposed for inclusion (notably terrorism and serious drug offenses) could command a consensus. It has to be noted at the outset, that aside from the special case of aggression, the other three crimes overlap to a significant degree. As is typically the case with overlapping offenses against the person in domestic law, they therefore generate ample alternative choices for a prosecutor.[24]

[A] Aggression

The most controversial crime in the International Criminal Court Statute is the crime of aggression. As the "crime against peace," it played a prominent role in the Nuremberg and Tokyo trials at the end of the Second World War.[25] It was defined very generally as "planning, preparation, initiation, or waging of a war of aggression, or a war in violation of international treaties, agreements or assurances, or participation in a common plan or conspiracy for the accomplishment of any of the foregoing."[26] It had been the subject of repeated efforts at definition since the 1920s.[27] The International Military Tribunal at Nuremberg insisted that "[t]o initiate a war of aggression, therefore, is not only an international crime; it is the supreme international crime differing from other war crimes in that it contains within itself the accumulated evil of the whole."[28]

In spite of this ringing endorsement of the crime in 1946, codifying the details of what it entailed continued to prove difficult. At the time of the adoption of the

---

[22] Report of the International Law Commission, U.N. GAOR, 51st Sess., Supp. No. 10, at 9, U.N. Doc. U.N. Doc. A/51/10 (1996) (Draft Code of Crimes against the Peace and Security of Mankind).

[23] *See* § 14.03[C] and [D] *infra*.

[24] For additional discussion *see* § 14.03[E], *infra*.

[25] *See* §§ 16.02 and 16.03, *infra*.

[26] Art. 6(a), Agreement for the Prosecution and Punishment of the Major War Criminals of the European Axis and Charter of the International Military Tribunal, August 8, 1945, 82 U.N.T.S. 279; Art. 5(a), Charter of the International Military Tribunal for the Far East, *available at* http://www.yale.edu/lawweb/avalon/imtfech.htm.

[27] *See* Roger S. Clark, *Nuremberg and the Crime against Peace*, 6 Wash. U. Global Stud. L. Rev. 527 (2007). Note Justice Robert Jackson's efforts to obtain more precision in the Nuremberg Charter, *id.*, at 529–32.

[28] Judgment of the International Military Tribunal for the Trial of German Major War Criminals, in 1 Trial of the Major War Criminals before the International Military Tribunal-Nuremberg 171, 223 (1947).

Rome Statute, a definition had still not been agreed upon.[29] At the domestic level, many States do not have a crime against peace in their criminal law. A 2007 study examined a sample of 90 national penal codes and found that 25 of them included an offense of aggression, but that most of the definitions were rudimentary and the details differed widely.[30] There appear to have been no actual prosecutions at the national level. Nevertheless, it was very important to many of the States participating in the negotiations to create the International Criminal Court that aggression be included in its jurisdiction. This was especially so for most of the smaller States and members of the Non-Aligned Movement, but also the case for some larger powers like Germany, Italy and Japan. Accordingly, a compromise was reached. The Rome Statute provides that, "the crime of aggression" is one of the four crimes "within the jurisdiction of the Court,"[31] but that:

> The Court shall exercise jurisdiction over the crime . . . once a provision is adopted in accordance with articles 121 and 123 defining the crime and setting out the conditions under which the Court shall exercise jurisdiction with respect to this crime. Such a provision shall be consistent with the relevant provisions of the Charter of the United Nations.[32]

A Special Working Group of the Assembly of States Parties of the Court has been striving to conclude a draft of a "provision" which it is hoped will be finalized at the first "Review Conference" on the Rome Statute early in 2010.[33] (The Assembly of States Parties, or "ASP," is the membership body that oversees the work of the Court.) Its task, it will be noticed, is twofold: "defining" the crime and "setting out the conditions" for the exercise of jurisdiction. "Defining" refers to substantive criminal law issues; "conditions" relates to the vexed question of the relationship between what the ICC might do in the case of an individual accused and whatever antecedent action needs to be taken in a political or other organ of the United Nations, in particular the Security Council, the General Assembly or the International Court of Justice. The work has proceeded on the basis of a drafting convention that distinguishes between an "act of aggression" and a "crime of aggression." The former is what a state does which engages its *state responsibility*. The latter is what the individual actor does on behalf of a state and which engages that person's *individual responsibility*. There can be no "crime of aggression" without an "act of aggression."

It should be noted that while the ICC has jurisdiction only over the conduct of "natural persons"[34] the Rome Statute also provides that "[n]othing in this Statute relating to individual criminal responsibility shall affect the responsibility of States

---

[29] *See* § 17.02[B], *infra.*

[30] Astrid Reisinger Coracini, *National legislation on individual responsibility for conduct amounting to aggression*, summarized in report of Conference on International Criminal Justice, Turin, 14–18 May 2007, Doc. ICC-ASP/6/INF.2 at 35. In cases arising out of the Second Gulf War, the British House of Lords agreed in 2006 that aggression is a crime under international law, but declined to incorporate it into British law as a common law crime — their Lordships regarded making it part of domestic law as a task for the legislature. R. v. Jones, [2006] U.K.H.L. 16.

[31] The Rome Statute of the International Criminal Court, Art. 5(1).

[32] *Id.* at Art. 5(2).

[33] See the most recent Report of the Special Working Group available at the time of writing, Report of the Special Working Group on the Crime of Aggression, Doc. ICC-ASP/6/20, Annex III ("December 2007 SWGCA Report") produced at the Sixth Session of the ASP, 30 November-14 December 2007.

[34] Rome Statute of the International Criminal Court, Art. 25(1).

under international law."[35] The State's responsibility is to be determined elsewhere, such as in the International Court of Justice, which has appropriate jurisdiction.[36] Moreover, to the extent that the State's act of aggression is one of the elements of a criminal offense, the ICC must, in principle, be able to deal with it for the purposes of individual criminal responsibility. Beyond a near consensus on the drafting approach of distinguishing between an "act of aggression" and the "crime of aggression," just about everything else in the work is hotly debated.

It is unclear, at the very outset, whether the provision on aggression will apply potentially to all parties to the Rome Statute or only to those who ratify it. This turns, in large part, on what is to be made of the phrase "in accordance with articles 121 and 123" in Article 5(2) of the Statute. Articles 121 and 123 deal with amendments. It is questionable how they can be applied specifically to the crime of aggression, given that it is already included within the jurisdiction, but that the Court can not yet "exercise" that jurisdiction. Article 121 contemplates amendments agreed upon at regular meetings of the Assembly of States Parties; Article 123 relates to Review Conferences to consider amendments. The procedure is essentially the same in both cases. Ultimately, the processes by which states become party to amendments are contained in Article 121, Paragraphs 3, 4 and 5. Paragraph 3 deals with how a text is agreed upon. It says that "[t]he adoption of an amendment at a meeting of the Assembly of States Parties or at a Review Conference on which consensus cannot be reached shall require a two-thirds majority of the States Parties."[37] Paragraph 4 says that "[e]xcept as provided in paragraph 5, an amendment shall enter into force for all States Parties one year after instruments of ratification or acceptance have been deposited with the Secretary-General of the United Nations by seven-eighths of them." Paragraph 5 adds that

> [a]ny amendment to articles 5, 6, 7 and 8 of this Statute shall enter into force for those States Parties which have accepted the amendment one year after the deposit of their instruments of ratification or acceptance. In respect of a State Party which has not accepted the amendment, the Court shall not exercise its jurisdiction regarding a crime covered by the amendment when committed by that State Party's nationals or on its territory.

It makes a big difference whether paragraph 4 or paragraph 5 applies, since under paragraph 4 no State is bound until the seven-eighths agree. At that point everyone

---

[35] *Id.* at Art. 25(4).

[36] Armed Activities on the Territory of the Congo (DR Congo v. Uganda), 2005 ICJ, Judgment of Dec.19, 2005 (Court "[f]inds that the Republic of Uganda, by engaging in military activities against the Democratic Republic of the Congo on the latter's territory, by occupying Ituri and by actively extending military, logistic, economic and financial support to irregular forces having operated on the territory of the DRC, violated the principle of non-use of force in international relations and the principle of non-intervention.") *See also* Partial Award, *Jus Ad Bellum*, Eritrea Ethiopia Claims Commission, Dec. 19, 2005 (Permanent Court of Arbitration), *available at* http://www.pca-cpa.org/upload/files/FINAL%20ET%20JAB.pdf.

[37] Because of the use of "adoption" in this paragraph and "adopted" in Art. 5(2), there is an argument based on the literal language that nothing more is required to complete the addition of aggression to the "exercise" of the Court's jurisdiction than agreement on a text at a meeting of the ASP or a Review Conference. Many States find this literal interpretation unworkable, even absurd, and insist that more must be required. Others note that the language was not negotiated and added at the last minute and argue there is no reason not to apply the plain meaning.

is bound.[38] If Paragraph 5 applies, then once the time frame is met, any State that agrees is bound, including the first to do so; but even if seven-eighths agree they cannot bind the others who hold out.

A provision on aggression is plainly not an amendment to Articles 6, 7 or 8. But the question is whether it is an amendment *to* Article 5? It can be argued strongly that, far from being an amendment to Article 5, it is simply a fulfilment of its terms, and thus the default seven-eighths rule applies. The policy arguments are then joined: is it better to go with the principle of including the crime and simply waiting patiently as the numbers rise (paragraph 5); or is it better to treat aggression on an even footing with the other crimes, namely as applicable to everyone — or no one (paragraph 4). These questions must be resolved by the time of the Review Conference.

There is also an issue regarding the final sentence of Article 5(2) of the Statute. It states: "Such a provision shall be consistent with the relevant provisions of the Charter of the United Nations." Some of the major powers (those with a veto in the Security Council) take the position that this means that there is no act of aggression unless the Security Council says so. On this argument, the Security Council's power to decide upon the existence of an act of aggression is exclusive. The Court's role, if this is the correct position, is to make the natural person connections that constitute the "crime of aggression." Others, not surprisingly, take the position that the Security Council cannot possibly be in the position of making a finding about a fundamental element of a crime. For them, the Council has power to determine the existence of an act of aggression for Charter purposes only[39] and there is no obstacle in the Charter to having the Court itself make the relevant determinations of all elements of the crime. Moreover, some argue that if the United Nations itself has some role, then the General Assembly[40] and the International Court of Justice,[41] which have in practice waded into these waters, also have a claim to participate that is parallel to that of the Security Council. The Council's power, described as "primary" in the Charter, can hardly be exclusive.[42] The Security Council, they add, has ample powers under Article 16 of the Rome Statute to put a halt to proceedings in the ICC when its interests are at stake.[43]

A subsidiary part to this argument is the nature of any determination that might be made by the Security Council or some other organ. Is such a determination conclusive as to the presence or absence of the "act of aggression" element of a particular crime? Or is the role of the United Nations organ (at most) that of giving a "green light" for the ICC to proceed? If the former were to be the case, it would be very difficult in terms of criminal law theory to build the remainder of the structure of the crime around this determination by an outside body. At the very least, it would be necessary to put a large weight on the mental element

---

[38] Subject to a right of a dissenting State to withdraw from the Statute under Art. 121(6).

[39] An example of this can be found in the purposes of Chapter VII of the Charter which deals with "action with respect to threats to the peace, breaches of the peace and acts of aggression."

[40] *See, e.g.*, Uniting for Peace Resolution, G.A. Res. 377A (V) (1950) and G.A. Res. 498 (V), Feb. 1, 1951 (finding that China and North Korea were engaging in aggression in Korea).

[41] *See, e.g.* Armed Activities on the Territory of the Congo (DR Congo v. Uganda), 2005 ICJ, Judgment of Dec.19, 2005.

[42] U.N. Charter, Art. 24(1) reads: "In order to ensure prompt and effective action by the United Nations, its Members confer on the Security Council primary responsibility for the maintenance of international peace and security. . . . "

[43] On Art. 16 of the Rome Statute, *see* § 17.02[B], *infra*.

requirement, and its obverse, the "defense" of mistake. Since there is no guarantee that the Security Council or other organ, would act in a totally principled way, it might be difficult to know in marginal cases what it would do. If an "act of aggression" is whatever the Security Council says it is, after the event, this creates some fundamental problems with the principle of legality. Either it would be necessary to give wide latitude to mistakes, or it would be necessary to include a "manifest" or "flagrant" modifier in the definition, so as to protect, at least in part, against criminal responsibility for the marginal cases.[44]

So far as defining the crime is concerned, it should be apparent from what has gone before that there are two aspects to this, what is meant by the element "act of aggression by a state," and how to describe the necessary conduct, circumstance and mental elements required of individual actors.[45] As to the act of aggression, it is widely accepted that substantial guidance has to be found in the General Assembly's 1974 Definition of Aggression.[46] That resolution contains both a *prima facie* presumption that the first use of certain kinds of force by a State amounts to aggression (Article 2) and a list of the kinds of force (Article 3). As contained in Article 3, these kinds of force are:

(a) The invasion or attack by the armed forces of a State of the territory of another State, or any military occupation, however temporary, resulting from such invasion or attack, or any annexation by the use of force of the territory of another State or part thereof;

(b) Bombardment by the armed forces of a State against the territory of another State or the use of any weapons by the armed forces of a State against the territory of another State;

(c) The blockade of the ports or coasts of a State by the armed forces of another State;

(d) An attack by the armed forces of a State on the land, sea or air forces, or marine and air fleets of another State;

(e) The use of armed forces of one State which are within the territory of another State with the agreement of the receiving State, in contravention of the conditions provided for in the agreement or any extension of their presence in such territory beyond the termination of the agreement;

(f) The action of a State in allowing its territory, which it has placed at the disposal of another State, to be used by that other State for perpetrating an act of aggression against a third State;

(g) The sending by or on behalf of a State of armed bands, irregulars or mercenaries, which carry out acts of armed force against another State of such gravity as to amount to the acts listed above, or its substantial involvement therein.

Resolution 3314 also says that the Security Council can conclude that other actions amount to aggression and, on the other hand, that even if the conditions in the definition are met, it may conclude that there was not in fact an aggression. This creates some problems for inserting Resolution 3314 into a definition of the crime. In the first place, it deals with state responsibility; in the second, it is open-ended. The first problem can be dealt with by using it to define only the "act of aggression."

---

[44] *See infra* note 48 (discussing the addition of a requirement that the breach be "manifest").

[45] *See* § 17.02[C] (examining the conceptual structure of the offenses in the Rome Statute).

[46] G.A. Res. 3314 (XXIX) (1974), U.N. GAOR, 29th Sess., Supp. No. 31, at 24, U.N. Doc. A/9631 (1975).

The second requires either making some general reference to it and leaving the Court to "work it out," or taking the provisions of some or all of Article 3, paragraphs (a) to (g) and incorporating them into a reasonably precise definition. Both of these, as well as other possibilities, are still open.[47]

There is the further question of whether *all* the examples of aggressive acts contained in Article 3 of the Definition should come within the criminal ambit of aggression and (perhaps *or*) whether some other "threshold" modifier should be established. There has been some support (and some adamant rejection) for modifying the term "act of aggression" by some phrase like "such as, in particular, a war of aggression or an act which has the object or result of establishing a military occupation of, or annexing, the territory of another State or part thereof." There is also support (perhaps increasing),[48] for using the phrase "which, by its character, gravity and scale, constitutes a manifest violation of the Charter of the United Nations." Both attempts at modification start with the premise that it is only the most grave of acts that should come within *criminal* jurisdiction, whatever might be said of state responsibility. Using a term like "manifest" injects an evaluative element (some sort of reasonable person test). "War of aggression"[49] and the like suggest that particular kinds of acts of force are inherently more objectionable that others. This proposition is not accepted by all. Some states, for example, would be especially offended if the references to bombardments and blockades in Article 3 of the 1974 Definition were not included within the ICC definition.

As to what the individual actor does, and his or her connection with the State, it is agreed on all sides that "aggression is a leadership crime." It is not a crime that can be committed by the foot-soldier or by the janitor in the Ministry of Foreign Affairs. But determining who fits the definition of leader can be difficult. The current effort to capture the leadership concept describes the term as: "persons being in a position effectively to exercise control over or to direct the political or military action of State."[50] Some in the Working Group worry that this formula is too narrow, in particular that it does not adequately encompass those who are not formally members of the governmental structure but nevertheless contribute strongly to aggressive war. In particular, there is the question of industrialists whose situation was considered at the second round of Nuremberg trials pursuant to Control Council Law No. 10.[51] "Shape or influence" has garnered some support

---

[47] For a possible text incorporating the relevant provisions of Arts 1 and 3 of the definition contained in G.A. Res. 3314 (XXIX) into a definition of "act of aggression," See *Non-Paper Submitted by the Chairman on Defining the State Act of Aggression*, in Report of the Intersessional Meeting of the Special Working Group on the Crime of Aggression held in Princeton, New Jersey, June 2007) ("2007 SWGCA Intersessional Report"), Doc. ICC-ASP/6/SWGCA/INF.1 at 21 (2007) (defining the State act of aggression and incorporating the relevant provisions of Arts 1 and 3 of G.A. Res. 3314 (XXIX) definition). *Cf.* the December 2007 SWGCA Report, *supra* note 33 at ¶¶ 14–23 (presenting a wide divergence of views on how to deal with G.A. Res. 3314 (XXIX)).

[48] *See* December 2007 SWGCA Report, *supra* note 33 at ¶ 25.

[49] Critics of the use of "war" here note the indeterminacy of the concept. It seems to involve a "certain level" of the clash of arms. The critics point out that the way the Nuremberg Charter was drafted, the invasion and conquest of, for example, Bohemia and Moravia by Germany was not a "war" even if it involved a massive military threat. On the other hand it was made criminal by the language of Control Council Law No. 10. The latter defined "crimes against peace" as: *"[i]nitiation of invasions of other countries and wars of aggression. . . . "* (emphasis added), *See* http://www.yale.edu/lawweb/avalon/imt/imt10.

[50] *See* 2007 SWGCA Intersessional Report, *supra* note 47, Annex at 9.

[51] *Id.* ¶ 9; *See also* Kevin Jon Heller, *Retreat from Nuremberg: The Leadership Requirement in the*

to replace "control over or to direct" in the language describing a leader. This is both because that was the phrase used historically at Nuremberg and because it ensures that the potential of prosecuting such persons comes clearly within the definition. (Some think it is already implicit.) The leadership language is, in terms of Article 30 of the Statute, a kind of "circumstance" element, as it describes the person's function. "Effectively" takes care of the figurehead monarch or president who exercises no control. What the person does (the conduct element) is described as follows: "the planning, preparation, initiation or execution of an act of aggression/ armed attack."[52] Obviously, this does not mean that an accused is solely responsible, but he or she must have made some, perhaps substantial, contribution to the act of aggression.

The crime of aggression has, ultimately, to be fitted within the structure of the Rome Statute, both as a matter of drafting technique and of substance. A significant feature of the Rome Statute, compared with earlier instruments like the Nuremberg and Tokyo Charters, is the detail of its "General Part."[53] There is little difficulty in fitting the crime of aggression within the basic framework of mental and material elements contained in Article 30 of the Statute[54] and of accommodating it to the mistake provisions of Article 32.[55] A difficulty that arose in respect of how to deal with Article 25(3) of the Statute's provisions on complicity has led to a re-structuring of the earlier drafts. The early drafts, going back into the work of the International Law Commission, assumed that the provision on aggression would be self-sufficient and contain within itself all the necessary "general part" material, including possible modes of complicity for a "leader."[56] Later drafts have distinguished between this "monist" approach and what came to be called the "differentiated approach." The "differentiated approach" proceeds with both a "special part" provision on the crime of aggression, which captures what a primary actor does, and "general part" provisions that deal with "secondary" actors.

The "differentiated approach," which has gained substantial acceptance, defines "the crime of aggression" as meaning "the planning, preparation, initiation or execution of an act of aggression/armed attack. . . . " An addition to Article 25 (a new paragraph 3 bis) states that: "With respect to the crime of aggression, the

---

Crime of Aggression, 18 EUROP. J. INT'L L. 477 (2007) (no German leaders were ultimately convicted, but the potential was there in the right factual setting); Allison Marston Danner, *The Nuremberg Industrialist Prosecutions and Aggressive War*, 46 VA. J. INT'L L. 651 (2005–2006).

[52] 2007 SWGCA Intersessional Report, *supra* note 47, Annex II at 17. "Act of aggression" seems to be winning the day over "armed attack" to describe the "state" element. *See* 2007 SWGCA Intersessional Report, *supra* note 47, ¶ 37.

[53] *See* § 14.03, *infra*.

[54] *See* § 15.02[C], *infra*.

[55] *Id.*

[56] On the final effort of the Commission in this respect, contained in its 1996 Draft Code of Crimes against the Peace and Security of Mankind, *see* Report of the International Law Commission on the work of its forty-eighth session, 6 May–26 July 1996, U.N. GAOR, 51st Sess., Supp. No. 10, at 20–21, U.N. Doc. A/51/10 (1996). The Commentary of Article 16 of the Draft Code ("crime of aggression") states:

> The perpetrators of an act of aggression are to be found only in the categories of individuals who have the necessary authority or power to be in a position potentially to play a decisive role in committing aggression. These are the individuals whom article 16 designates as "leaders" or "organizers", an expression that was taken from the Nürnberg Charter. These terms must be understood in the broad sense, i.e. as referring, in addition to the members of a Government, to persons occupying high-level posts in the military, the diplomatic corps, political parties and industry, as recognized by the Nürnberg Tribunal. . . .

provisions of the present article shall only apply to persons being in a position effectively to exercise control over or to direct the political or military action of State.[57] With the modifier (paragraph 3 bis), it seems likely that the various modes of complicity in Article 25 can be made to "fit" well with the leadership nature of the crime.

The ultimate status of the "crime of aggression" remains an open question as it remains to be seen exactly what will be agreed upon at the Review Conference and then what happens subsequently in terms of states ratifying whatever text is agreed upon. The high stakes involved for all concerned in the effort to complete the definition of aggression, thus allowing the ICC to "exercise" its jurisdiction, are neatly summarized in a recent article:

> The criminalization of aggression is a worthwhile endeavor if it reduces human suffering and mitigates harm. Proponents hope that a widely accepted minimum standard will function as a focal point to help coordinate actions — domestic, international, transnational — that will deter or prevent leaders from resorting to state/collective violence. But there are a number of risks. The standard may deter the wrong sort of violent actions, actions that reduce human suffering such as the unauthorized use of force to prevent genocide. A related risk inherent in any prohibition is the implicit permission contained therein. If the threshold is set too high, the crime of aggression may in fact legitimize objectionable acts of violence by not capturing them. Furthermore, mandating the ICC to prosecute aggression may undermine its effectiveness in domains of other crimes within its jurisdiction.[58]

[B] Genocide

The term "genocide" was coined in 1944 by the Polish scholar Raphael Lemkin to describe Nazi efforts to reconstruct the German social and economic structure, to Aryanize, and to destroy a sense of separate national identity in German occupied territories.[59] Genocide was not a specific crime listed in the Charter of the Nuremberg Tribunal. It was perhaps seen as encompassed within the "persecution" branch of crimes against humanity.[60] The United Nations General Assembly in its first session in 1946, however, declared unanimously that "genocide is a crime under international law" that is punishable "whether the crime is committed on religious, racial, political or any other grounds."[61]

The 1948 Convention on the Prevention and Punishment of Genocide, a convention that entered into force in 1951, was the first human rights treaty

---

[57] 2007 Report of SWGCA, Annex, at 9.

[58] Noah Weisbord, *Prosecuting Aggression*, 49 HARV. INT'L L. J. 161, 220 (2008).

[59] RAPHAEL LEMKIN, AXIS RULE IN OCCUPIED EUROPE (1944). For a depressing account of genocide across history, see BEN KIERNAN, BLOOD AND SOIL: A WORLD HISTORY OF GENOCIDE AND EXTERMINATION FROM SPARTA TO DARFUR (2007).

[60] *See* EDWARD M. WISE, ELLEN S. PODGOR & ROGER S. CLARK, INTERNATIONAL CRIMINAL LAW: CASES AND MATERIALS 811 (2d ed. 2004). The Nuremberg Charter, 82 U.N.T.S. 279, defined "crimes against humanity" in Art. 6 to include "persecutions on political, racial or religious grounds," the term "persecution" being broad enough to include killing. That language became the core of the conceptual basis for the Genocide Convention.

[61] G.A. Res. 96 (I), of Dec. 11, 1946, Resolutions and Decisions of the General Assembly during the second part of its First Session, 23 Oct.–15 Dec., 1946.

adopted under the auspices of the United Nations.[62] The parties to the Convention "confirm that genocide, whether committed in time of peace or in time of war, is a crime under international law which they undertake to prevent and to punish." Nevertheless, the Convention narrowed Lemkin's understanding of the concept, and that of the 1946 General Assembly resolution, by dropping the possibility that genocide could be committed against a political group. Instead, the Convention lists a number of "acts" that can amount to genocide, if they are "committed with intent to destroy, in whole or in part, a national, ethnical, racial or religious group, as such." This list of "protected" groups is closed for the purposes of the Genocide Convention; attacks on other groups might constitute different crimes, for example crimes against humanity. The acts are "(a) Killing members of the group; (b) Causing serious bodily harm to members of the group; (c) Deliberately inflicting on the group conditions of life calculated to brings about its physical destruction in whole or in part; (d) Imposing measures intended to prevent births within the group; and (e) Forcibly transferring children of the group to another group."[63]

Each of these "acts" entails it own conduct and implicit mental element, accompanied by the over-arching "particular" or "specific" intent to destroy. The Convention refers not only to the punishment of primary actors, but also to conspiracy to commit genocide, direct and public incitement to commit genocide, attempt to commit genocide and complicity in genocide.[64] Proscription of conspiracy (referring in the present context to a preparatory, or inchoate conspiracy) is almost unique in international criminal law instruments and perhaps reflects the gravity of the crime. There is little question, though, that it represented the triumph of an Anglo-Saxon concept that does not have an exact counterpart in most civil law systems.[65] Unusual also is the reference to direct and public incitement to commit genocide, another inchoate offense that can be committed even if no one takes up the call and actually commits any genocidal acts.

Genocide is defined in the International Criminal Court Statute in language taken almost verbatim from the 1948 Convention.[66] During the negotiation of the Rome Statute, some States sought to expand the definition and come closer to Lemkin's original conception that included political groups, but the effort was unsuccessful. There was a reluctance to tamper with what many regarded as a canonical statement in a widely ratified agreement.

One of the many difficult conceptual issues surrounding the crime of genocide is distinguishing mass murderers, even the individual mass murderer who kills on

---

[62] Convention on the Prevention and Punishment of the Crime of Genocide, G.A. Res. 260A (III), Dec. 9, 1948, *available at* http://www.unhchr.ch/html/menu3/b/ p_genoci.htm ("Genocide Convention").

[63] *Id.* at Art. II.

[64] *Id.* at Art. III.

[65] *See* WILLIAM A. SCHABAS, GENOCIDE IN INTERNATIONAL LAW 260–1 (2000) (discussing the preparatory work of the Convention); GEORGE W. MUGWANYA, THE CRIME OF GENOCIDE IN INTERNATIONAL LAW: APPRAISING THE CONTRIBUTION OF THE UN TRIBUNAL FOR RWANDA 163–5 (2007).

[66] The Rome Statute of the International Criminal Court, Art. 6; *see also* § 17.02[B], *infra*. The Rome definition does not, however, include (inchoate) conspiracy to commit genocide, which is included in the 1948 Convention, Art. III. Complicity liability and liability for attempts and incitement are covered by the provisions of Art. 25 of the Statute which, aside from the genocide-specific incitement provision, apply generally to all the Statute offenses. There seems to have been some confusion about inchoate conspiracy in the negotiations. Some participants thought that it was covered by the "common purpose" mode of complicity in Art. 25(3)(d), but that is a mode of complicity in a completed or attempted offense, not a way to deal with inchoate agreements unaccompanied by action.

racial or other grounds, from the *génocidaire* who is part of something larger. That "something larger" will typically be a Governmental policy, but there is no requirement in the definition of genocide akin to that in respect of torture[67] that requires that the accused be a governmental actor or at least acting in some official capacity. The "something larger" may be a group that is not part of the Government (although it may be aiming at overthrowing it). The drafters of the ICC Elements of Crimes came up with the following "circumstance" or "contextual circumstance" element to describe this: "The conduct took place in the context of a manifest pattern of similar conduct directed against that group or was conduct that could itself effect such destruction."[68] While this language does not come directly from the words of the Genocide Convention or the Rome Statute, it probably emerges fairly from the spirit of the definitions.

Convictions for genocide, though few in number, have been emerging from the *ad hoc* Tribunals. Particularly significant discussions may be found in the Rwanda Tribunal's *Akayesu* decision[69] and that of the Yugoslav Tribunal in *Krstic*.[70] There is also useful consideration of state responsibility for breaches of the Genocide Convention in the 2007 decision of the International Court of Justice in *Application of the Convention on the Prevention and Punishment of the Crime of Genocide*.[71]

A significant issue that has emerged in the case-law is what *mens rea* is required of an aider and abettor, as opposed to a principal in the commission of the crime. Must the aider and abettor both have knowledge of what the principal party intends and also share that intent, or is it enough that he or she furnish aid knowing of the other's genocidal intent? Interpreting its Statute, the Yugoslav Tribunal took the latter position in the case involving General Krstic, Commander of Drina Corps, the group of the Bosnia Serb Army responsible for the massacre of between 7,000 and 8,000 Muslim men in the United Nations "safe area" of Srebenica in July of 2005.[72] The Tribunal believed that this result was supported by French, German, Swiss, English, Canadian, and Australian law and by "some jurisdictions in the United States."[73] It is, of course, not the majority rule in the United States,[74] nor the rule espoused in the American Law Institute's Model Penal Code.[75] How this issue plays out under the Rome Statute of the International Criminal Court is no doubt a matter that will be argued at an early stage of the Court's life. Article 30 of the Rome statute insists that, "unless

---

[67] *See* § 15.02[B].

[68] ICC, Elements of Crimes, final paragraph of definitions of various ways in which genocide can be committed, *available at* http://www.icc-cpi.int/library/about/officialjournal/Element_of_Crimes_English.pdf.

[69] Prosecutor v. Akayesu, I.C.T.R., Case No. 96-4, Appeals Chamber Judgment of June 1, 2001.

[70] Prosecutor v. Krstic, I.C.T.Y., Case No. IT-98-33-A, Appeals Chamber Judgment of April 19, 2004. (The Judgment is especially interesting on the meaning of "in whole or in part" in the Genocide Convention and on the aiding an abetting issue about to be mentioned in the text.)

[71] Bosnia and Herzegovina v. Serbia and Montenegro, I.C.J. 2007, Judgment of Feb. 26, 2007.

[72] *Supra* note 70. General Krstic was convicted of aiding and abetting the genocide at Srebenica and sentenced (on this and other crimes) to 35 years in prison.

[73] *Id.* ¶ 141. *See also* Application of Genocide Convention, *supra* note 71, Declaration of Judge Keith, ¶¶ 1–7 (discussing the knowledge issue in the context of Serbia's responsibility for Srebenica)

[74] JOSHUA DRESSLER, UNDERSTANDING CRIMINAL LAW 474–5 (3d ed. 2001).

[75] Model Penal Code, Official Draft (1962), § 2.06(3) ("purpose of promoting or facilitating the commission of the offense" required).

otherwise provided," there is a requirement that material elements of an offense be "committed with intent and knowledge." Article 25(3)(c) on aiding and abetting requires that assistance be given "[f]or the purpose of facilitating the commission of such a crime." On the other hand, Article 25(3)(d) which deals with "common purpose" liability, suggests that a contribution made to a group acting with a common genocidal purpose "with knowledge of the intention of the group to commit the crime" may be enough. On the whole, it is easier to justify knowledge–based secondary liability in relation to war crimes and crimes against humanity than is the case of genocide with its very special intent requirement.

Article VI of the Convention provided that:

> Persons charged with genocide or any of the other acts enumerated in article III shall be tried by a competent tribunal of the State in the territory of which the act was committed, or by such international penal tribunal as may have jurisdiction with respect to those Contracting Parties which shall have accepted its jurisdiction.

No international tribunal had jurisdiction over the crime until the creation of the Tribunals for Former Yugoslavia and Rwanda and later the International Criminal Court. The ICC thus represents the ultimate fulfillment of the promise given, five decades previously, in Article VI of the Genocide Convention.

The United States did not immediately ratify this Convention, but eventually did so in 1988, subject to several reservations and understandings. In particular, the United States did not accept the jurisdiction of the I.C.J. envisaged in the Convention over disputes between states "relating to the interpretation, application or fulfillment" of its provisions.[76] Another reservation was that "nothing in the Convention requires or authorizes legislation or other action by the United States of America prohibited by the Constitution of the United States as interpreted by the United States." Both of these reservations drew objections from several other parties to the Convention (including the United Kingdom and The Netherlands).[77] The first drew objections on the basis that it was incompatible with the Convention, the second on the ground that it created uncertainty with respect to what obligations the United States was prepared to assume, and was subject to the general principle of treaty interpretation according to which a party may not invoke the provisions of its internal law as justification for failure to perform a treaty.[78]

The United States also expressed an interpretative "understanding" that, as used in the Convention, (1) the phrase intent to destroy a group "in whole or in part" means the specific intent to destroy it "in whole or substantial part"; and (2) the term "mental harm" means "permanent impairment of mental facilities through drugs, torture or similar techniques." The second understanding seems to be

---

[76] Genocide Convention, Art. IX (jurisdiction of International Court of Justice).

[77] The Netherlands went so far as to say that it did not regard the United States as a party to the Convention as a result of the reservation to Art. IX. (Netherlands has consistently taken that position with others who made the same reservation.) The Court, however, applied the reservation against Yugoslavia (which did not object to the United States reservation) in the Case concerning Legality of Use of Force (Yugoslavia v. U.S.) Order of June 2, 1999 dismissing proceedings, 1999 I.C.J. To the same effect is Armed Activities on the Territory of the Congo (New Application: 20002) (D.R. Congo v. Rwanda), Jurisdiction of the Court and Admissibility of the Application, Judgment of Feb.3, 2006, 2006 I.C.J.

[78] That principle is contained in Art. 27 of the Vienna Convention on the Law of Treaties.

functionally a reservation which may, in some instances, amount to a significant narrowing of the scope of the Convention. It did not, however, receive any objections from other parties.

Congress passed federal legislation, the Genocide Convention Implementation Act of 1987, to implement the provisions of the Convention, incorporating the understandings in the statutory definition.[79] On its face, the Genocide Convention requires the parties to exercise jurisdiction on the basis of territoriality.[80] It does not prohibit a wider exercise of jurisdiction. The 1987 legislation implemented the obligation to assert jurisdiction where the offense is committed in the United States but went further to create jurisdiction where the accused is a national of the United States.[81] In 2007, the jurisdictional bases were extended to include, as well, the circumstances where the alleged offender is an alien lawfully admitted for permanent residence in the United States, where the alleged offender is a stateless person whose habitual residence is in the United States, and where after the conduct required for the offense occurs, the alleged offender is brought into or found in the United States, even if the conduct occurred outside the United States.[82] This last basis is consistent with the received wisdom that universal jurisdiction is permissible for genocide under international customary law.[83]

[C] Crimes Against Humanity

"Crimes Against Humanity" is another one of the four crimes included in the International Criminal Court Statute.[84] Unlike the Article 6 definition of genocide, which is carried forward almost verbatim from the Genocide Convention, Article 7 of the Rome Statute contains significant new material. It represents the latest effort to codify an offense that has had a slightly shifting series of definitions under customary international law and in various non-treaty instruments. The Charter of the Nuremberg Tribunal crystallized use of the term, which had its roots in the nineteenth century where it was applied both to the slave trade and to King Leopold of Belgium's rapacious rule in the Congo.[85] The Nuremberg Charter defined crimes against humanity as:

> [N]amely, murder, extermination, enslavement, deportation or other inhu-
> man acts committed against any civilian population, whether before or
> during the war, or persecutions on political, racial, or religious grounds in
> execution of or in connection with any crime within the jurisdiction of the

---

[79] *See* 18 U.S.C. § 1091 et seq.

[80] *See* Genocide Convention, Art. VI, which, as noted above, also refers to the jurisdiction of "such international penal tribunal as may have jurisdiction with respect to those Contracting Parties which shall have accepted its jurisdiction."

[81] *See* 18 U.S.C. § 1091(d).

[82] Genocide Accountability Act of 2007, amending 18 U.S.C. § 1091(d).

[83] The Restatement (Third) of the Foreign Relations Law of the United States, § 404 (1987).

[84] The Rome Statute of the International Criminal Court, Art. 7; *see also* § 17.02[B], *infra*. The most thorough account of the Rome material is PHILIPPE CURRAT, LES CRIMES CONTRE L'HUMANITE DANS LE STATUT DELA COUR PENALE INTERNATIONALE (2006).

[85] *See* Roger S. Clark, *Crimes against Humanity and the Rome Statute of the International Criminal Court, in* INTERNATIONAL AND NATIONAL LAW IN RUSSIA AND EASTERN EUROPE: ESSAYS IN HONOR OF GEORGE GINSBURGS 139, 140–43 (Roger S. Clark, Ferdinand Feldbrugge & Stanislaw Pomorski eds. 2001).

tribunal, whether or not in violation of the domestic law of the country where perpetrated.[86]

As applied in Nuremberg, crimes against humanity encompassed essentially those aspects of Nazi rule that applied within Germany itself. Similar depredations that took place in occupied territories were considered, for the most part, under the war crimes rubric.[87]

There was considerable debate in the subsequent literature about whether crimes against humanity could stand on their own or whether it was necessary for them to be connected to war crimes or, perhaps more generally, to an aggressive war. Article 6(c) of the Nuremberg Charter had qualified the definition of crimes against humanity with the words "in execution of or in connection with any crime within the jurisdiction of the Tribunal." There was, from the start, debate about whether these words were part of the substantive law governing the crime or whether they were merely jurisdictional — as applied specifically to the Nuremberg Tribunal. Many scholars had thought that any such connection had been abandoned by the 1990s, if it ever existed.

The requirement, however, found its way back into the Statute of the Tribunal for Former Yugoslavia which spoke of the jurisdiction of the Tribunal over crimes against humanity "when committed in armed conflict."[88] Speaking to this phrase, the Appeals Chamber of the Tribunal commented in its first decision, in *Tadic*, that "the nexus between crimes against humanity and either crimes against peace or war crimes, required by the Nuremberg Charter, was peculiar to the jurisdiction of the Nuremberg Tribunal. Although the nexus requirement was carried over to the [1946 and 1950] General Assembly resolution[s] affirming the Nuremberg principles, there is no logical or legal basis for this requirement and it has been abandoned in subsequent State practice with respect to crimes against humanity."[89] The Statute of the Rwanda Tribunal contained another limitation that most commentators thought was unnecessary and which is not carried forward into the Rome Statute. It referred to crimes which were committed "as part of a widespread or systematic attack against any civilian population *on national, political, ethnic, racial or religious grounds.*"[90]

The Rome Statute definition begins by stating that it "means any of the following acts when committed as part of a widespread or systematic attack directed against any civilian population, with knowledge of the attack."[91] This is the "threshold" requirement which ensures that the acts in question go beyond ordinary crime and amount to what the Preamble to the Rome Statute calls "the most serious crimes of concern to the international community as a whole." A great deal of attention was given in drafting the Rome Statute to whether the attack had to be both widespread *and* systematic or whether either one would suffice. "Widespread" has objective

---

[86] Agreement for the Prosecution and Punishment of the Major War Criminals of the European Axis and Charter of the International Tribunal, August 8, 1945, Art. 6(c), 82 U.N.T.S. 279.

[87] Clark, *supra* note 85 at 150 n. 60.

[88] Statute of the Tribunal for Former Yugoslavia, Art. 5.

[89] Prosecutor v. Tadic, ICTY Appeals Chamber, Case No. IT-94-1-AR72, Decision on the Defense Motion for Interlocutory Appeal on Jurisdiction, Oct. 2, 1995, ¶ 140.

[90] Statute of the Tribunal for Rwanda, Art. 3 (emphasis added). The persecution variety of crimes against humanity entailed such a modifier, but there was no need for it to apply to all the crimes — the "attack on a civilian population" threshold provided sufficient means to ensure that only crimes with a dimension of concern to the international community were included.

[91] Rome Statute of the International Criminal Court, Art. 7(1) (chapeau).

connotations of size, a kind of volume threshold, rather than a statement about the subjective purposes of those in charge. The ordinary meaning of "systematic," on the other hand, seems more subjective and has connotations of a deliberate plan. There was a widespread jubilation among the NGOs and the "Like-Minded" States in Rome on the basis that the disjunctive "or" in the final text represented a great victory. (The "Like-Minded" was a coalition of the States most determined to see the Rome process succeed.) The disjunctive supposedly makes it easier for a prosecutor to prove than if both prongs were required. But the definition of "attack" in paragraph 2(a) places some restraints:

> "Attack directed against any civilian population" means a course of conduct involving the multiple commission of acts referred to in paragraph 1 against any civilian population, pursuant to or in furtherance of a State or organizational policy to commit such attack.

The word "multiple" catches most cases of "widespread" unless one can imagine numerous incidents which are nevertheless not widespread — a difficult intellectual feat, unless "widespread" means, perversely, "over a wide geographical area" rather than "large-scale." "Organizational policy" appears close to "systematic." In short, if an incident meets the definition of paragraph 2(a), that is, it is widespread and has a policy behind it, the "additional" elements of widespread *and* systematic seem *both* to have been met anyway! Put it the other way around: something close to both widespread *and* systematic appears to be required by the very definition of "attack." At all events, a significant threshold is required and, as the last words of the chapeau ("with knowledge of the attack") make clear, it must be proved that the individual actor knew he was part of something bigger than himself.

The array of conduct listed as potential constituents of crimes against humanity is extensive, namely murder; extermination; enslavement; deportation or forcible transfer of population; imprisonment or other severe deprivation of physical liberty in violation of fundamental rules of international law; torture; rape, sexual slavery, enforced prostitution, forced pregnancy, enforced sterilization, or any other form of sexual violence of comparable gravity; persecution against any identifiable group or collectivity on political, racial, national, ethnic, cultural, religious, gender,[92] or other grounds that are universally recognized as impermissible under international law, in connection with any act referred to in this paragraph or any crime within the jurisdiction of the Court;[93] enforced disappearance of persons; the crime of *apartheid*; other inhuman acts of a similar character intentionally causing great suffering, or serious injury to body or to mental of physical health.[94] The meanings of many of the terms in this definition are given in Article 7 of the Rome Statute.

For the most part, the drafters took a conservative approach to how far international customary law had developed the concept of crimes against humanity

---

[92] The controversial nature of listing "gender" as one of the proscribed grounds for the "persecution" offense resulted in the addition of a strange definition, based on prior usage at United Nations Conferences on Women: "For the purpose of this Statute, it is understood that the term 'gender' refers to the two sexes, male and female, within their context of society. The term 'gender' does not indicate any meaning different from the above." Rome Statute of the International Criminal Court, Art. 7(3).

[93] The reference to the persecution crimes being "in connection with any act referred to in this paragraph or any crime within the jurisdiction of the Court" is an echo of the threshold provision in the Nuremberg Charter. Now that the general threshold is an attack on a civilian population, it would appear to serve no useful purpose to have a further threshold here, except perhaps to counsel caution in giving a wide interpretation to "persecution."

[94] The Rome Statute of the International Criminal Court, Art. 7.

since 1945. The "new" South Africa insisted, however, that there be a place in the definition for the crime of *apartheid*, and re-established democracies in Latin America insisted on dealing with the matter of enforced disappearances. More controversial was being explicit about several of the sexual offenses. In particular, "forced pregnancy," carried out in Former Yugoslavia, Rwanda, and East Timor (among other places), created some difficulties with those opposed to abortion whatever the cause of the pregnancy.[95] But it won the day here, and also in the war crimes Article.

Unlike the crime of genocide, there was, at least until the conclusion of the Rome Statute, no specific international suppression convention defining crimes against humanity. Interestingly, two of the "newer" versions of it that were included in the Rome Statute, *apartheid*, and disappearances *are* also the subject of separate suppression conventions.[96]

The United States has never enacted legislation providing for the punishment of crimes against humanity. Most of the constituent acts, but not the overarching framework, amount to crimes under state or federal law, but only if committed on United States territory. A number of parties to the Rome Statute of the International Criminal Court that had, similarly, not made it part of their domestic law in the past, have concluded that the spirit of the complementarity regime in the Statute requires them to punish such crimes under domestic law, and indeed to exercise universal jurisdiction over them.[97] This is an issue that the United States will need to revisit should it decide in the future to become a party to the Rome Statute.

[D]   War Crimes

"War crimes" is the final category of offenses included in the International Criminal Court Statute.[98] The Statute includes an extensive list of conduct that can form the basis for a charge of this crime. Some of the conduct listed is the same or similar to activities upon which a crime against humanity can be based. For example, war crimes include "torture or inhuman treatment, including biological experiments."[99] Prior to the ICC, one found war crimes as a basis for prosecution in the Nuremberg and Tokyo Tribunals, and also in the International Criminal Tribunals for the former Yugoslavia and Rwanda. None of these instruments came even close to the detail with which the relevant war crimes are stated in the Rome Statute.

---

[95] "Forced pregnancy" is defined in Rome Statute, Art. 7(2)(f) as "the unlawful confinement of a woman forcibly made pregnant, with the intent of affecting the ethnic composition of any population or carrying out other grave violations of international law. This definition shall not in any way be interpreted as affecting national laws relating to pregnancy."

[96] International Convention for Suppression and Punishment of the Crime of *Apartheid* (1973), 1015 U.N.T.S. 243; International Convention for the Protection of all Persons from Enforced Disappearance, 2006, G.A. Res. 61/177, *available at* http://daccessdds.un.org/doc/UNDOC/GEN/N06/505/05/PDF/N0650505.pdf?OpenElement.

[97] *E.g.*, Germany, Helmut Satzger, *German Criminal Law and the Rome Statute — A Critical Analysis of the New German Code of Crimes against International Law*, 2 INT'L CRIM. L. REV. 261, 279–80 (2002); Samoa, International Criminal Court Bill, 2007, §§ 6 and 13; New Zealand, International Crimes and Criminal Court Act, 2000, §§ 8 and 10.

[98] The Rome Statute of the International Criminal Court, Art. 8.

[99] The Rome Statute of the International Criminal Court, Art. 8(2)(a)(ii).

"War" is not defined in the Rome Statute, but it seems clear that the intent of the drafters was to include within the concept, here, at least, the notions often referred to in modern usage as "international and non-international armed conflict." A very useful explanation of these is to be found in the *Tadic* decision of the International Criminal Tribunal for Former Yugoslavia:

> [A]n armed conflict exists whenever there is resort to armed force between States or protracted violence between governmental authorities and organized armed groups or between such groups within a State. International humanitarian law applies from the initiation of such armed conflicts and extends beyond the cessation of hostilities until a general conclusion of peace is reached; or, in the case of internal conflicts, a peaceful settlement is achieved.[100]

The laws of armed conflict are to be found in overlapping treaty and customary rules and principles. The main treaties include the Hague Conventions of 1907,[101] the Geneva Conventions of 1949,[102] the 1925 Geneva Protocol for the Prohibition of the Use in War of Asphyxiating, Poisonous or Other Gases, and of Bacteriological Methods of Warfare,[103] the 1977 Protocols to the Geneva Conventions,[104] and the 1993 Convention on the Prohibition of the Development, Production, Stockpiling and Use of Chemical Weapons and on their Destruction.[105] Each of these treaties is, at least in part, a suppression convention, requiring criminalization of certain forbidden activities during armed conflict. To the extent that the Hague and Geneva Conventions had, in their day, represented a substantial codification (and also a little progressive development) of existing law, they were rather like a domestic penal code, although perhaps not as ambitious. They suffered the same kind of "degradation" that some American scholars have described as happening to American State Criminal Codes.[106] Piecemeal amendments are made; additions to the corpus of criminal proscription are made in other pieces of legislation; no one is looking at conformity of the legislative output. Not surprisingly, some of the same problems have emerged at the international level. Drafting the Rome Statute provided something of an opportunity to codify and clarify, an opportunity that was not always taken.

---

[100] Prosecutor v. Tadic, I.C.T.Y., Case No. IT-94-1-AR72, Appeals Chamber Decision of Oct. 2, 1995, on Defense Motion for Interlocutory Appeal on Jurisdiction, ¶ 70.

[101] Notably Convention (No. IV) respecting the Laws and Customs of War on Land (with Annex of Regulations), concluded at The Hague, Oct. 18, 1907, found at http://www.icrc.org/ihl.nsf/FULL/195.

[102] Convention (No. I) for the Amelioration of the Condition of the Wounded and Sick in Armed Forces in the Field; Convention (No. II) for the Amelioration of the Condition of Wounded, Sick and Shipwrecked Members of the Armed Forces at Sea; Convention (No. III) relative to the Treatment of Prisoners of War; Convention (No. IV) relative to the Protection of Civilian Persons in Time of War, all done on Aug. 12, 1949, 6 U.S.T.S. 3114, http://www.icrc.org/ihl.nsf/CONVPRES?OpenView.

[103] Protocol for the Prohibition of the Use in War of Asphyxiating, Poisonous or other Gases and of Bacteriological Methods of Warfare, June 17, 1925, 94 L.N.T.S. 65.

[104] Protocol Additional (No. I) to the Geneva Conventions of August 12, 1949, and relating to the Protection of Victims of International Armed Conflicts; Protocol Additional (No. II) to the Geneva Conventions of August 12, 1949, and relating to the Protection of Victims of Non-International Armed Conflicts, *available at* http://www.icrc.org/ihl.nsf/CONVPRES?OpenView.

[105] 31 I.L.M. 800 (1993).

[106] Paul H. Robinson & Michael T. Cahill, *The Accelerating Degradation of American Criminal Codes*, 56 Hastings L.J. 633 (2004–5).

Article 8 is, nevertheless, a serious attempt to draw together and rationalize the material as much as a highly political process will allow. The "General Principles of Criminal Law" contained in the Rome Statute also represent the first time that an attempt has been made in such an international codification to add a general part. The relationship between the general part and the special part suffered a little in coherence because of some constraints in the process. It was often not possible in drafting the special part to modify language from old treaties that did not fit well with the general language. There were fundamental failures to communicate among the negotiators as to the assumptions they were making about the role of a general part (and in particular of the mental elements therein). Some, but not all, of these fault lines were between the civil and the common lawyers. Many of those problems were addressed post-Rome during the drafting of the so-called "Elements of Crimes."[107]

As a general point, it should be noted that, as in the case of crimes against humanity, most participants in the ICC negotiations took a conservative view on how far the law had developed beyond the treaties. Since the Rome Statute was to operate only for the future, it was surely open to the drafters to include anything on which agreement could be reached. For the most part, though, the drafters insisted that they were trying to capture the state of customary law. Yet what exactly that custom required was often hard to determine.[108] There was, in 1998, a dearth of jurisprudence from international tribunals, although there has been a great deal more in the decade since.[109] Domestic cases applying international law often in fact turn on some domestic point. Military prosecutions are typically under the local military law, rather than for breaches of the Geneva Conventions. What is included in the list was thus chosen pragmatically. It is in there if a consensus could be reached to keep it there; if there was no consensus, it got dropped, even if a majority wanted it. There were ultimately no votes whatsoever on matters of substance concerning the detail of the Statute's provisions.

It was important to the negotiators that not every war crime would come within the jurisdiction of the Court, only the "most serious." This is reflected in paragraph 1 of Article 8, the "war crimes" article of the Statute. It says that "[t]he Court shall have jurisdiction in respect of war crimes in particular when committed as part of a plan or policy or as part of a large-scale commission of such crimes." On the face of it, this appears to be a "jurisdictional" element of each crime and should perhaps be proved as such. But the "in particular" is awkward. Primarily, the language must

---

[107] See § 17.03[C], infra.

[108] During the drafting process, the International Committee of the Red Cross, guardian of the Geneva Conventions, made numerous suggestions about what it thought the customary law was, typically speaking through the delegations of New Zealand and Switzerland. It has since produced a comprehensive study. See JEAN-MARIE HENCKAERTS & LOUISE DOSWALD-BECK, CUSTOMARY INTERNATIONAL HUMANITARIAN LAW, 2 Vols (Vol. I, Rules, Vol. II, Pts 1 and 2, Practice) (2005). For a laudatory view of this effort, see Theodor Meron, Revival of Customary Humanitarian Law, 99 AM. J. INT'L L. 817 (2005). A less enthusiastic response is contained in Letter from John Bellinger III, Legal Adviser, U.S. Dept. of State, and William J. Haynes, General Counsel, U.S. Dept. of Defense to Dr. Jakob Kellenberger, President, International Committee of the Red Cross, regarding Customary International Law Study, Nov. 3, 2006, 46 I.L.M. 514 (2007). See also International Committee of the Red Cross: Response of Jean-Marie Henckaerts to Bellinger/Haynes Letter on Customary International Law Study, July 2007, 46 I.L.M. 959 (2007).

[109] Much of the jurisprudence is analyzed in WILLIAM A. SCHABAS, THE UN INTERNATIONAL TRIBUNALS: THE FORMER YUGOSLAVIA, RWANDA, AND SIERRA LEONE (2006).

speak to the Prosecutor, counseling caution in the use of limited resources. But perhaps the Court itself ought to dismiss the case where it concludes in its discretion that the threshold is not met.

So far as details are concerned, Article 8, paragraph 2, the definition of war crimes, begins in subparagraph (a) with the "grave breaches" of the 1949 Conventions, the penal consequences of which had been specifically delineated in the Conventions themselves. In the case of grave breaches, a list of which appears in each of the four Conventions, Parties to the Conventions have an obligation to search for and to bring those accused of committing such breaches, regardless of nationality, before their own courts. They may, if they prefer, hand such persons over for trial to another Party which has made out a *prima facie* case. There is, in short, a prosecute or extradite requirement, accompanied by an expectation of universal jurisdiction. By definition in the 1949 Conventions, the grave breaches provisions apply only in international armed conflict. The list in Article 8, paragraph 2(a), culled from the four Conventions, includes willful killings of those protected by the Conventions, torture or inhuman treatment, willfully depriving a prisoner of war or other protected person of the rights of fair and regular trial, and taking of hostages.

Subparagraph (b) deals with "other serious violations of the laws and customs applicable in international armed conflict, within the established framework of international law. . . . " It is a significant codification of material contained, for the most part, in the Fourth Hague Convention, Protocol I of 1977 and customary law. It includes intentionally directing attacks against the civilian population as such or against individual civilians not taking a direct part in hostilities; killing or wounding a combatant, who, having laid down his arms or having no longer means of defense, has surrendered at discretion; and committing outrages upon personal dignity, in particular humiliating and degrading treatment. Its most innovative provision is subparagraph (b)(xxii) on crimes of sexual violence. It proscribes "[c]ommitting rape, sexual slavery, enforced prostitution, forced pregnancy, as defined in Article 7, paragraph 2(f), enforced sterilization, or any other form of sexual violence also constituting a grave breach of the Geneva Conventions."[110]

Subparagraph (c) deals with armed conflict not of an international character and essentially contains the prohibitions of Common Article 3 of the 1949 Conventions. It provides:

> (c) In the case of an armed conflict not of an international character, serious violations of article 3 common to the four Geneva Conventions of 12 August 1949, namely, any of the following acts committed against persons taking no active part in the hostilities, including members of armed forces who have laid down their arms and those placed *hors de combat* by sickness, wounds, detention or any other cause:
>
> (i) violence to life and person, in particular murder of all kinds, mutilation, cruel treatment and torture;
>
> (ii) committing outrages upon personal dignity, in particular humiliating and degrading treatment;
>
> (iii) taking of hostages;
>
> (iv) the passing of sentences and the carrying out of executions without previous judgment pronounced by a regularly constituted

---

[110] *See* note 95, *supra* (providing a definition of forced pregnancy).

court, affording all judicial guarantees which are generally recognized as indispensable.

The main debate surrounding inclusion of these provisions in the Rome Statute was as to their "criminal" nature. Including the common provisions on non-international armed conflict was a significant development in the 1949 Conventions. Nevertheless, breaches of Common Article 3 are not described as "grave breaches" in the Conventions, although Parties to the Conventions are under a clear obligation to take measures to suppress such violations. Most participants in the Rome process ultimately had little difficulty in concluding that, whatever might be the case about whether they give rise to universal jurisdiction,[111] it was possible to subject them to the jurisdiction of an international tribunal.

Subparagraph (e) goes further with another set of prohibitions dealing with non-international armed conflict. These are mostly derived from the Hague Regulations, the Geneva Conventions and Protocol II. Much of the actual language comes, in fact, with appropriate modifications, from subparagraph (b) on international conflict. The subparagraph is a recognition of the extent to which the distinctions between the prohibitions contained in non-international and in national conflict are being collapsed in contemporary law. Of particular interest is the threshold provision for the application of subparagraph (e), namely subparagraph (f). It says that the subparagraph applies to armed conflicts not of an international character and thus does not apply to situations of internal disturbances and tensions, such as riots, isolated and sporadic acts of violence or other acts of a similar nature. It adds, affirmatively, that it applies "to armed conflicts that take place in the territory of a State when there is protracted armed conflict between governmental authorities and organized armed groups or between such groups."

The reference to "between such groups" is extremely important in modern conflicts. Once a certain level of intensity is reached, the provision may apply, even though the Government is not fielding a player in the conflict. The threshold clause in subparagraph (f) goes beyond existing definitions of scope in at least two respects. Article 1 of 1977 Protocol II, on which it is based, referred to armed conflicts "which take place in the territory of a High Contracting Party between its armed forces and dissident armed forces or other organized armed groups which, under responsible command, exercise such control over a part of its territory as to enable them to carry out sustained and concerted military operations and to implement this Protocol." Thus the 1977 formulation, does not apply to a conflict where there is no government involvement; and the dissidents must control part of the territory. These constraints are loosened in the Rome Statute, which is described by two key participants in the negotiations as "pos[ing] a much lower threshold than Protocol II."[112] This threshold is nonetheless perhaps a little higher than that delineating when Common Article 3 applies. Article 3 does not contain the requirement that the conflict be "protracted."

It is worth making a few comments about prohibited weapons and the Statute.[113] There appears to be a deep-seated feeling in the human psyche, reflected vaguely

---

[111] The right of States to exercise jurisdiction in such cases is espoused by the International Committee of the Red Cross, JEAN-MARIE HENCKAERTS & LOUISE DOSWALD-BECK, I CUSTOMARY INTERNATIONAL HUMANITARIAN LAW, RULES 604–6 (2005).

[112] Herman von Hebel & Darryl Robinson, *Crimes within the Jurisdiction of the Court, in* THE INTERNATIONAL CRIMINAL COURT: THE MAKING OF THE ROME STATUTE, ISSUES, NEGOTIATIONS, RESULTS 79, 121 (Roy S. Lee ed. 1999).

[113] *See generally,* Roger S. Clark, *The Rome Statute of the International Criminal Court and*

in policy and in international law, that some weapons are beyond the range of acceptability, even in a situation where killing and maiming is the order of the day. It is possible to think of a general category of such weapons, namely those which cause superfluous injury or unnecessary suffering.

Another category name entered into popular discourse with the invention of the atomic bomb, that of a Weapon of Mass Destruction. The very first resolution adopted by the United Nations General Assembly at its inaugural Session in 1946 created an Atomic Energy Commission.[114] It was to deal with the problem of atomic weapons and "other weapons of mass destruction." A related General Assembly Commission of the day, dealing with Conventional Armaments, spent some time working out the division of labor between the two Commissions. For this purpose, it said that "weapons of mass destruction should be defined to include atomic explosive weapons, radio active material weapons, lethal chemical and biological weapons, and any weapons developed in the future which have characteristics comparable in destructive effect to those of the atomic bomb or other weapons mentioned above."[115] "WMD" may not have become a legal term of art in international law beyond this mode of bureaucratic jurisdictional delineation, but it has considerable emotional and even explanatory force. Witness the efforts from 1991 on to rid Saddam Hussein of his (real and imagined) weapons. At its 1992 Summit meeting of Heads of State and Government, the Security Council even went as far as to pronounce that "[t]he proliferation of all weapons of mass destruction constitutes a threat to international peace and security."[116] United States law, in fact, makes criminal the use of a weapon of mass destruction against a national of the United States, or within the United States, or by a national outside the United States.[117] There is, however, no treaty basis for this crime.

Article 8(2)(b) of the Rome Statute regards as criminal, employing poison or poisoned weapons; employing asphyxiating, poisonous or other gases, and all analogous liquids, materials or devices; and employing bullets which expand or flatten easily in the human body, such as bullets with a hard envelope which does not entirely cover the core or is pierced with incisions.[118] The drafts had included, in various permutations, references to the use or threat of use of nuclear weapons and to using bacteriological (biological) agents or toxins, and using chemical weapons. The Non-Aligned Movement and the South Pacific countries, in particular, worked very strongly for the inclusion of such weapons. Many of those involved had worked on the Nuclear Weapons Advisory proceedings in the International Court of Justice.[119] There, a majority of the Court had held that " the threat or use of nuclear weapons would generally be contrary to the rules of international law

---

Weapons of a Nature to Cause Superfluous Injury or Unnecessary Suffering, or which are Inherently Indiscriminate, in INTERNATIONAL HUMANITARIAN LAW: CHALLENGES 259 (John Carey, William V. Dunlap & R. John Pritchard eds. 2004).

[114] G.A. Res. 1 (I), Resolutions adopted by the General Assembly during the first part of its First Session, 10 Jan.–14 Feb. 1946.

[115] [1947–48] U.N.Y.B. 477.

[116] *The Responsibility of the Security Council in the Maintenance of International Peace and Security*, Decision of the Security Council, Jan. 31, 1992, Resolutions and Decisions of the Security Council 1992, 65, 67, U.N. Doc. S/INF/48 (1992).

[117] 18 U.S.C. § 2332a. *See* § 7.01[B] *supra.*

[118] Rome Statute of the International Criminal Court, Art. 8(b)(xvii)–(xix).

[119] The Legality of the Threat or Use of Nuclear Weapons, Advisory Opinion of 8 July 1996, 1996 I.C.J.

applicable in armed conflict, and in particular the principles and rules of humanitarian law."[120] Those opposed to nuclear weapons saw the Rome negotiations as a chance to move the "generally" into the category of "never." They pushed for a *per se* rule of illegality, as espoused by three dissenting members of the World Court.

The inclusion of nuclear weapons among the ranks of the forbidden was, however, opposed by the permanent members of the Security Council and most of the NATO allies of Britain, France, and the United States. They were sufficiently aroused to regard it as a "deal-breaker" — a clause which would ensure that they could never become a party to the treaty. In a consensus negotiation, something seen as a deal breaker by the major powers could not survive and most of the proponents of banning nuclear weapons backed off. At the very last moment, however, when it was clear that nuclear weapons could not be proscribed, Egypt, in particular, insisted that the poor person's weapons of mass destruction could not be included either. Accordingly, the references to bacteriological and chemical weapons were deleted.[121] India tried, on the very last day of the Conference, to add a reference in the Statute to "employing weapons of mass destruction, i.e., nuclear, chemical and biological weapons." Its draft was the subject of a "no-action" motion which was adopted overwhelmingly.[122] So none of the weapons of mass destruction find a place in the Rome Statute.

In particular instances, of course, using weapons of mass destruction will run foul or such provisions of Article 8 as "[i]ntentionally directing attacks against the civilian population as such . . . "[123] or "intentionally launching an attack in the knowledge that such attack will cause incidental loss of life or injury to civilians or damage to civilian objects or widespread, long-term and severe damage to the natural environment which would be clearly excessive in relation to the concrete and direct overall military advantage anticipated."[124] But many participants would have preferred a *per se* rule on the illegality of such instruments of death and destruction. What they did get was a provision in Article 8(2)(b)(xx) which "proscribes"

> Employing weapons, projectiles and material and methods of warfare which are of a nature to cause superfluous injury of unnecessary suffering or which are inherently indiscriminate in violation of the international law of armed conflict, provided that such weapons, projectiles and material and methods of warfare are the subject of a comprehensive prohibition and are included in an annex to this Statute, by an amendment in accordance with the relevant provisions set forth in articles 121 and 123.

This simply postpones a solution for the future. Whether something has become "the subject of a comprehensive prohibition" will undoubtedly be a matter of great debate in concrete cases.

---

[120] *Id.*, ¶ 105(E).

[121] Herman von Hebel & Darryl Robinson, *Crimes within the Jurisdiction of the Court*, *in* THE INTERNATIONAL CRIMINAL COURT: THE MAKING OF THE ROME STATUTE, ISSUES, NEGOTIATION, RESULTS 79, 113–6 (Roy S. Lee ed. 1999).

[122] United Nations Diplomatic Conference of Plenipotentiaries on the Establishment of an International Criminal Court, Rome, 15 June–17 July 1998, Official Records, Vol. II, (Committee of the Whole) at 360–61, U.N. Doc. A/CONF.183/13 (2002).

[123] Rome Statute of the International Criminal Court, Art. 8(2)(b)(i).

[124] Rome Statute of the International Criminal Court, Art. 8(2)(b)(iv).

Moreover, a careful examination of Articles 121 and 123 suggests some serious difficulties to adding weapons via the amending process. It will be recalled from the discussion of aggression,[125] that, generally speaking, in order to come into force, amendments have to be accepted by individual States Parties.[126] Except as provided in paragraph 5 of that Article, they become effective for everybody once they have been accepted by seven-eighths of the parties. This very high threshold was, in itself designed to make amendment difficult. Paragraph 5 creates a different rule for amendments affecting the substance of the crimes as set out in Articles 5, 6, 7 and 8. In this case, if a party does not accept the amendment, the Court is not able to exercise jurisdiction regarding a crime covered by the amendment when committed by the state party's nationals or on its own territory. As in the case of aggression,[127] it is not clear what rule applies to placing items in the currently empty "annex." Is such an addition an "amendment to" Article 8, or is it something else, such as a fulfillment of the expectations of the drafters — a completion rather than an amendment? The issue is completely unsettled and there are no current proposals for additions before the Court.

There is another way in which debate on the question of weapons of mass destruction illuminates an aspect of "war crimes" that has already been mentioned, namely the (shrinking) difference between the rules applicable in international and in non-international armed conflict. Some participants approached this during the Rome Preparatory Committee from the point of view of nuclear weapons, but the issue is more general. Consider the 1925 Protocol[128] which prohibits the use of gas and bacteriological weapons "in war." "War" as used in this treaty in 1925 quite clearly meant war between States. Thus when Saddam Hussein used gas against Iran, it was easy enough to denounce him in terms of the Protocol, since both States are parties. But when he used it on his own people, it was more difficult. It cannot be the case, surely, that it was acceptable in the late twentieth century to use such proscribed substances domestically and there were appropriate criticisms made by numerous States and International Organizations when he gassed Kurdish opponents. In the appellate decision on jurisdiction in the *Tadic* Case, the International Tribunal for Former Yugoslavia discussed at some length how customary law had expanded the norms of the 1925 Protocol from international into non-international conflict, particularly in the context of events in Iraq.[129]

By the same token, if it is illegal to use other kinds of weapons of mass destruction internationally, it ought to be equally illegal to use them in non-international armed conflict. In one of the versions of the war crimes provision sent on from the Preparatory Committee to the Rome Conference, there was mention of a potential provision in the part on non-international armed conflict that would be

---

[125] § 14.03[A], *supra.*

[126] Aside from some provisions of the Statute of "an institutional nature" that can be amended by a two-thirds majority of the Assembly of States Parties under Art. 122 of the Rome Statute.

[127] § 14.03[A] *supra.*

[128] Protocol for the Prohibition of the Use in War of Asphyxiating, Poisonous or other Gases and of Bacteriological Methods of Warfare, June 17, 1925, 94 L.N.T.S. 65.

[129] Prosecutor v. Tadic, Case No. IT-94-1-AR72, Decision of October 2, 1995 on Defense Motion for Interlocutory Appeal on Jurisdiction, at ¶ 120-7. *See also id.*, ¶ 70 on the meaning of "armed conflict." A Dutch citizen, Frans van Anratt, was subsequently convicted in The Netherlands of complicity in war crimes for supplying components for chemical weapons used on the Kurds. He was acquitted of genocide as the prosecution could not prove the necessary *mens rea. Saddam's 'Dutch Link,'* available at http://news.bbc.co.uk/2/hi/middle_east/4358741.stm.

added "in the light of the discussions" of the sub-paragraph on weapons in international conflict.[130] This seemed to be correct in principle. This provision, however, simply disappeared from the draft text well before the end game that removed chemical and biological weapons along with nuclear ones from the purview of the Statute. Whatever one thinks of the legality of weapons of mass destruction, it must surely be the case under customary law at this point that whatever is forbidden in international armed conflict is almost certainly equally forbidden in internal conflict.

[E] Overlapping Crimes

There is significant overlap among genocide, crimes against humanity and war crimes (and, for that matter, among the various categories of war crimes).[131] Genocide and crimes against humanity always overlapped. Genocide as a matter of treaty drafting was born of the persecution part of the already heinous category of crimes against humanity; it was established as the most heinous of the heinous. It would appear that virtually any genocide could be prosecuted as a crime against humanity, but with a less demanding *mens rea*. A genocide will almost inevitably carry with it an "attack on a civilian population" sufficient to meet that element of crimes against humanity. The converse is not true; crimes against humanity include much conduct that is not encompassed by genocide.

Crimes against humanity, like genocide, do not require an armed conflict threshold, although there is something of the functional equivalent in the case of crimes against humanity with the attack requirement. The Genocide Convention itself makes explicit that genocide is a crime under international law "whether committed in time of peace or in time of war."[132] In the meantime, via Common Article 3 of the 1949 Geneva Conventions and the Second Protocol of 1977 to those Conventions, "war crimes" have increasingly thrust themselves into domestic, non-international conflict. With genocide being possible in time of war or peace, crimes against humanity having no required link to armed conflict, and war crimes expanding their reach into non-international armed conflict, all three offences appear to have been expanding since the 1940s. Some of this expansion has been onto one another's turf. A prosecutor deciding what to prosecute in a modern setting will have ample overlapping possibilities from each of the three categories in the Statute.[133] There are many difficult questions, substantive as well as procedural, that still have to be worked out concerning the overlap.[134]

---

[130] Report of the Preparatory Committee on the Establishment of an International Criminal Court, in THE STATUTE OF THE INTERNATIONAL CRIMINAL COURT: A DOCUMENTARY HISTORY 127 (M. Cherif Bassiouni comp. 1998).

[131] § 14.03 *supra*.

[132] Genocide Convention, Art. I.

[133] *See generally*, WILLIAM A. SCHABAS, THE U.N. INTERNATIONAL CRIMINAL TRIBUNALS: THE FORMER YUGOSLAVIA, RWANDA AND SIERRA LEONE 434–8 (2006) (discussing ways in which the Courts have tried to avoid unfairness to defendants at the sentencing stage as a result of multiple possible convictions for offenses with slightly different material elements).

[134] *See* Payam Akhavan, *Reconciling Crimes Against Humanity with the Laws of War*, 6 J. INT'L CRIM JUST. 21 (2008).

§ 14.04   THE GENERAL PART OF INTERNATIONAL CRIMINAL LAW

A system of criminal law does more than proscribe specific offenses (in its "special part"); it also contains general principles and rules, a "general part." A general part, whether contained in customary[135] or common law,[136] or in a codification like the Model Penal Code,[137] deals with issues cutting across specific crimes. These issues include: the structure in which crimes are conceptualized; what constitutes culpable conduct; what mental states are germane to criminal responsibility; when particular results can be attributed to a particular actor; responsibility for the conduct of others and for inchoate crimes; general justifications for otherwise wrongful conduct; excuses that entirely or partially exclude culpability; and the grading of offenses and sanctions according to different levels and degrees of culpability and harm.

Until the Rome Statute of the International Criminal Court, general part provisions in the constituent instruments of international tribunals (like special part provisions) tended to be rudimentary. The Charter of the Nuremberg Tribunal, for example, in addition to definitions of the crimes within the jurisdiction of the Tribunal, had some provisions on responsibility of accomplices and those engaged in a "common plan or conspiracy."[138] It also contained the fundamental proposition that "[t]he official position of defendants, whether as Heads of State or responsible officials in Government Departments, shall not be considered as freeing them from responsibility or mitigating punishment."[139] It added that "[t]he fact that the Defendant acted pursuant to an order of his Government or of a superior shall not free him from responsibility, but may be considered in mitigation of punishment if the Tribunal determines that justice so requires."[140]

The Statutes of the Tribunals for Former Yugoslavia and Rwanda contained stripped-down provisions on "individual criminal responsibility" which dealt with complicity, official position, and superior orders.[141] They also included a "command responsibility" theory of liability, namely that "[t]he fact that any of the acts referred to in . . . the present Statute was committed by a subordinate does not relieve his superior of criminal responsibility if he knew or had reason to know that

---

[135] The Nuremberg Principles, *supra* § 14.02, are best seen as a codification of customary law.

[136] For classic efforts to summarize the general principles of the common law, see GLANVILLE WILLIAMS, CRIMINAL LAW: THE GENERAL PART (1961) (English law); JEROME HALL, GENERAL PRINCIPLES OF CRIMINAL LAW (1960) (American law).

[137] AMERICAN LAW INSTITUTE, MODEL PENAL CODE, PROPOSED OFFICIAL DRAFT (1962). For an interesting recent effort at codification which includes a comprehensive general part, see MODEL CODES FOR POST-CONFLICT CRIMINAL JUSTICE (Vivienne O'Connor & Colette Rausch ed. 2007).

[138] Agreement for the Prosecution and Punishment of the Major War Criminals of the European Axis and Charter of the International Military Tribunal, London, August 8, 1945, Art. 6, 82 U.N.T.S. 279.

[139] *Id.* at Art. 7.

[140] *Id.* at Art. 8.

[141] Statute of the International Tribunal for the Prosecution of Persons Responsible for Serious Violations of International Humanitarian Law Committed in the Territory of the Former Yugoslavia, since 1991, adopted by S.C. Res. 827 (1993), Art.7, ¶¶ 1, 2, and 4; Statute of the International Tribunal for the Prosecution of Persons Responsible for Genocide and Other Serious Violations of International Humanitarian Law Committed in the Territory of Rwanda and Rwandan Citizens Responsible for Genocide and other Violations Committed in the Territory of Neighboring States, between 1 January 1994 and 31 December 1994, annexed to S.C. Res. 955 (1994), Art. 6, ¶¶ 1, 2, and 4.

the subordinate was about to commit such acts or had done so and the superior failed to take the necessary and reasonable measures to prevent such acts or to punish the perpetration thereof."[142] Command responsibility liability had not been significant in Nuremberg, but was the subject of discussion in Tokyo,[143] apparently on the basis of general principles of law — it was not mentioned in the Tokyo Charter.

The Yugoslavia and Rwanda Statutes contained one other "general part" provision that had not been articulated in earlier Charters, a *non bis in idem* or double jeopardy principle.[144] In an effort at clarification that made matters more complex, the Statutes of the two *ad hoc* Tribunals also added language specific to the Genocide Convention[145] about conspiracy to commit genocide, direct and public incitement to commit genocide, attempt to commit genocide and complicity in genocide.[146] "Complicity" overlapped the individual criminal responsibility provisions of the Statute, but there was no liability for conspiracy, attempts and public incitement in respect of the other offenses within the jurisdiction of the Tribunals.

Beyond such provisions, however, the general part was left to the international judges to try to extract what they could from the general principles applied across domestic legal systems and in previous decisions, including those of military tribunals. The challenges presented by such analysis are well demonstrated in the judgment of the Appeals Chamber of the International Criminal Tribunal for the Former Yugoslavia in *Prosecutor v. Erdemovic*.[147] Erdemovic pleaded guilty to a charge of committing "crimes against humanity" by participating, as a member of the Bosnia Serb army, in the massacre of Bosnian Muslims that followed the fall of the United Nations "safe area" of Srebenica in 1995. Questions were raised about the propriety of the guilty plea, given that the accused had a potential defense of duress. All five judges agreed that duress would excuse some crimes, but what of homicides? Ultimately, a 3-2 majority of the Appeals Chamber held that "duress does not afford a complete defense to a soldier charged with a crime against humanity and/or a war crime involving the killing of innocent human beings,"[148] although it could be relevant in mitigation of penalty. Finding that no clear rules emerged from previous decisions which could be characterized as based on international customary law, and that different positions are taken on the issue in the principal legal systems of the world, the majority thought it appropriate to look to policy arguments. It reasoned that:

> There must be legal limits as to the conduct of combatants and their commanders in armed conflict. In accordance with the spirit of international humanitarian law, we deny the availability of duress as a complete defence to combatants who have killed innocent persons. In so doing, we give notice in no uncertain terms that those who kill innocent persons will

---

[142] *Id.*, Yugoslavia Statute, Art. 7, ¶ 3; Rwanda Statute, Art. 6, ¶ 3.

[143] 2 THE TOKYO JUDGMENT 30 (B. Roling & C. Ruter eds. 1977).

[144] Yugoslavia Statute Art. 10, Rwanda Statute, Art. 9.

[145] *See* Genocide Convention, Art. III.

[146] Yugoslavia Statute, Art. 4(3); Rwanda Statute, Art. 2(3).

[147] I.C.T.Y., Case No. IT-96-22-A, Appeals Chamber Judgment, Oct. 7, 1997. *See* Aaron Fichtelberg, *Liberal Values in International Criminal Law: A Critique of Erdemovic*, 6 J. INT'L CRIM. JUST. 3 (2008).

[148] *Id.* at ¶ 19.

not be able to take advantage of duress as a defence and thus get away with impunity for their criminal acts in the taking of innocent lives. . . .[149]

The dissent in *Erdemovic* was not persuaded by the policy arguments and thought the majority relied too heavily on common law analysis to the exclusion of other legal systems. The dissent was not convinced that the common law exception to duress in the case of killing was sufficient to create a general principle to that effect.

It is noteworthy that the Rome Statute of the International Criminal Court, in a provision that combines both "duress by others" and "duress of circumstances"[150] defenses, is closer to the dissent's position in *Erdemovic*.[151] Its duress defense applies potentially to all offenses. The Rome Statute does not, however, spell out all the possible grounds for the exclusion of responsibility. The methodology adopted in *Erdemovic* will undoubtedly be examined closely at the ICC when the time comes to consider un-codified grounds for exclusion of responsibility.[152]

Indeed, the Rome Statute contains by far the most detailed general part ever found in an international instrument. The relevant provisions, found in Part III of the Rome Statute, will be discussed in the final chapter of this book.[153] The necessity to examine the fundamental structure of offenses, in terms of material (or physical) elements and mental elements, became acute during the efforts to draft the Elements of Crimes required by Article 9 of the Rome Statute and significant attention will be given to that in the same chapter.

---

[149] *Id.*, Joint Separate Opinion of Judge McDonald and Judge Vohrah, ¶ 80. *See also* Separate and Dissenting Opinion of Judge Li, ¶ 8.

[150] "Duress of circumstances" is known as "necessity" in many legal systems.

[151] Rome Statute of the International Criminal Court, Art. 31(1)(d) (person's "conduct" excluded from criminal responsibility where it "has been caused by duress resulting from a threat of imminent death or of continuing or imminent serious bodily harm against that person or another person, and the person acts necessarily and reasonably to avoid this threat, provided that the person does not intend to cause a greater harm than the one sought to be avoided. Such threat may either be: (i) Made by other persons; or (ii) Constituted by other circumstances beyond that person's control.")

[152] *See* § 17.02[C] *infra.*

[153] § 17.02 *infra.*

Chapter 15
INTERNATIONAL HUMAN RIGHTS AND CRIMINAL PROCEDURE

§ 15.01 GENERAL PRINCIPLES

International Covenants, Conventions and other instruments such as "Declarations" and "Principles" provide numerous examples recognizing human rights. The plethora of documentation demonstrates an international concern and desire to promote safety, security, and rights to individuals throughout the world. Many human rights in the civil and political category are of direct concern to those involved in the criminal process, whether at the national or the international level.[1]

Some of the crucial events that made human rights an international concern are World War II, the Nuremberg Trial, and the founding of the United Nations.[2] Article 68 of the U.N. Charter provided for the creation of a U.N. Commission on Human Rights to engage in the "promotion" of human rights.[3] From this Commission came the establishment of an "international bill of rights." First in December 1948, the Universal Declaration of Human Rights was adopted by the General Assembly.[4] Later the Covenant on Economic, Social and Cultural Rights[5] and Covenant on Civil and Political Rights[6] were passed by the General Assembly. Other human rights documents have also come from the United Nations through

---

[1] For thorough treatment of the material, see NIGEL RODLEY, THE TREATMENT OF PRISONERS UNDER INTERNATIONAL LAW (2nd ed 1999); STEFAN TRECHSEL, HUMAN RIGHTS IN CRIMINAL PROCEEDINGS (2005); AMNESTY INTERNATIONAL, FAIR TRIALS MANUAL (1998).

[2] *See generally* EDWARD M. WISE, ELLEN S. PODGOR & ROGER S. CLARK, INTERNATIONAL CRIMINAL LAW: CASES AND MATERIALS 575–81 (2d ed. 2004).

[3] Charter of the United Nations, *available at* http://www.un.org/aboutun/charter/.

[4] Universal Declaration of Human Rights, U.N. General Assembly Resolution 217A (III) (10 December 1948), *available at* http://www.un.org/Overview/rights.html.

[5] International Covenant on Economic, Social and Cultural Rights, U.N. General Assembly Resolution 2200A (XXI) (16 December 1966), *available at* http://www.ohchr.org/english/law/cescr.htm.

[6] International Covenant on Civil and Political Rights, U.N. General Assembly Resolution 2200A (XXI) (16 December 1966), *available at* http://www.ohchr.org/english/law/ccpr.htm.

the same route. For example, in 1965 there was the International Convention on the Elimination of All Forms of Racial Discrimination,[7] and in 1989 there was the Convention on the Rights of the Child.[8] There is also the Convention on Elimination of All Forms of Discrimination against Women.[9] Today the U.N. reports that "virtually every United Nations body and specialized agency is involved in some degree in the protection of human rights."[10] In spite of its extensive normative activity, the Commission on Human Rights was regarded as flawed and it was replaced in 2006 by a Human Rights Council composed of 47 Member States elected by secret ballot in the General Assembly. In its empowering resolution,[11] the Assembly decided that those States becoming a member of the Council would receive special scrutiny of their human rights record. Whether the Council will avoid the criticism leveled at the Commission that "[t]oo many countries sought membership to protect themselves against criticism, or to criticize others,"[12] remains to be seen.

The advancement of human rights is not exclusive to the United Nations. Other bodies have also accomplished significant inroads in this area of the law. For example, in 1950 the Council of Europe adopted the European Convention on Human Rights.[13] There is also the African Commission of Human and Peoples' Rights[14] and the Organization of American States has provisions in its Charter pertaining to human rights as well as a specific treaty-regime devoted to human rights.[15]

[A]   Universal Declaration of Human Rights

The Universal Declaration of Human Rights was adopted by the General Assembly on December 10, 1948, a date now celebrated as "Human Rights Day." It contains a Preamble followed by thirty Articles. While it was regarded as essentially a moral or political statement when it was originally adopted, some believe that significant provisions within this document should now be considered customary international law.[16] It is the "first international statement to use the

---

[7] International Convention on the Elimination of All Forms of Racial Discrimination, U.N. General Assembly Resolution 2106A (XX) (21 December 1965), *available at* http://www.unhchr.ch/html/menu3/b/d_icerd.htm.

[8] Convention on the Rights of the Child, U.N. General Assembly, Document A/RES/44/25 (12 December 1989), *available at* http://www.hrweb.org/legal/child.html.

[9] Convention on the Elimination of All Forms of Discrimination Against Women (18 December 1979), 1249 U.N.T.S. 13, *available at* http://www.hrweb.org/legal/cdw.html.

[10] Human Rights, U.N., *available at* http://www.un.org/rights/prerights.htm.

[11] G.A. Res. 60/251 of March 15, 2006, *available at* http://www2.ohchr.org/english/bodies/hrcouncil/docs/A.RES.60.251_En.pdf.

[12] U.S. representative John Bolton explaining his position before voting against the near-unanimous resolution (which also received negative votes from Israel, Marshall Islands, and Palau), *available at* http://www.un.org/News/Press/docs/2006/ga10449.doc.htm.

[13] *Available at* http://www.hri.org/docs/ECHR50.html. The Council of Europe has broader membership than the European Union and now has 47 Members.

[14] *See generally* EDWARD M. WISE, ELLEN S. PODGOR & ROGER S. CLARK, INTERNATIONAL CRIMINAL LAW: CASES AND MATERIALS 575–81 (2d ed. 2004).

[15] American Convention on Human Rights, O.A.S. T. S. No. 36, 1144 U.N.T.S. 123, entered into force July 18, 1978. The U.S. has not yet ratified this treaty which was sent to the Senate by President Carter.

[16] EDWARD M. WISE, ELLEN S. PODGOR & ROGER S. CLARK, INTERNATIONAL CRIMINAL LAW: CASES AND MATERIALS at 578 (2d ed. 2004).

term 'human rights,' and has been adopted by the Human Rights movement as a charter."[17] Within the Preamble, Member States pledge "in cooperation with the United Nations, the promotion of universal respect for and observance of human rights and fundamental freedoms."[18] Its rights encompass civil and political rights, as well as economic, social and cultural ones. Thinking on the latter rights was significantly influenced by Franklin Delano Roosevelt and his widow Eleanor Roosevelt, Chair of the Commission on Human Rights when the Universal Declaration was adopted.

Basic rights are expressed in Articles One through Three of the Declaration, such as a statement of non-discrimination,[19] an expression that "[e]veryone has the right to life, liberty and security of person,"[20] and that "[a]ll human beings are born free and equal in dignity and rights."[21] Article Four prohibits all forms of slavery,[22] Article Five prohibits torture or "cruel, inhuman or degrading treatment or punishment,"[23] and Article Six promotes Equality.[24]

The next few articles pertain to the justice process, with a provision concerning the right to recognition as a person before the law,[25] redress in national courts for wrongs committed,[26] "fair and public hearing by an independent and impartial tribunal,"[27] a presumption of innocence in criminal matters,[28] and a prohibition against proceeding ex post facto.[29]

Rights covered in the First Amendment to the United States Constitution are seen in this document. For example, one finds provisions on privacy and freedom of movement,[30] as well as a right to take part in government,[31] and freedom of "peaceful assembly and association."[32] Rights regarding freedoms with respect to nationality,[33] marriage,[34] ownership of property,[35] freedom of religion,[36] and

---

[17] A Summary of United Nations Agreements on Human Rights, *available at* http://www.hrweb.org/legal/undocs.html.

[18] Universal Declaration of Human Rights, U.N. General Assembly Resolution 217A (III) (10 December 1948), *available at* http://www.un.org/Overview/rights.html. This language echoes the fundamental obligation to promote human rights and fundamental freedoms accepted by Members in Art. 55 of the United Nations Charter.

[19] *Id.* at Art. 2.

[20] *Id.* at Art. 3.

[21] *Id.* at Art. 1.

[22] *Id.* at Art. 4.

[23] *Id.* at Art. 5.

[24] *Id.* at Art. 7.

[25] *Id.* at Art. 6.

[26] *Id.* at Art. 8.

[27] *Id.* at Art. 10.

[28] *Id.* at Art. 11(1).

[29] *Id.* at Art. 11(2).

[30] *Id.* at Art. 13(1).

[31] *Id.* at Art. 21.

[32] *Id.* at Art. 20.

[33] *Id.* at Art. 15.

[34] *Id.* at Art. 16.

[35] *Id.* at Art. 17.

freedom of opinion[37] are mentioned in this Declaration of Human Rights. One also finds provisions pertaining to reasonable work hours,[38] right to education,[39] and the right to "participate in the cultural life of the community."[40] Other rights are also expressed in this document.

[B]   International Covenant on Civil and Political Rights

When the time came to put the rights in the Universal Declaration into treaty form, it was decided to break the material into two Covenants, one on civil and political rights, the other on economic, social and cultural rights. Most countries have chosen to ratify both treaties, the United States being an exception, having ratified only the Civil and Political Covenant. (China, on the other hand, is one of the few to ratify the Economic, Social and Cultural Rights Covenant but not that on Civil and Political Rights.) By and large, the United States has been more inclined to ratify international criminal law treaties, especially on drugs and terrorism, than those on human rights.

The International Covenant on Civil and Political Rights (ICCPR), adopted by the United Nations General Assembly in 1966, came into force in 1976 after it had been ratified by the required thirty-five countries. It is a more detailed document than the Universal Declaration of Human Rights, and adds strength to some of the same rights mentioned in the Declaration of Human Rights, but also provides other expressions of human rights. It has 53 Articles and is the Covenant most relevant to criminal justice. By April 2008, there were 67 signatories and 160 parties to this covenant. The United States became a party to the ICCPR in 1992, but had five reservations, five understandings, and three declarations.[41] Thus, although the United States is a party to the agreement, it has not agreed to all the items presented in the ICCPR.[42] Non-governmental human rights organizations and some scholars were especially critical of the "Declaration" made by on ratification that the substantive provisions of the Covenant are "not self-executing."[43] This probably means that it is not possible to rely directly on Covenant provisions in state or federal courts. International lawyers argue that, nonetheless, the rights in the Covenant may be relied upon to inform interpretation of relevant constitutional, statutory and common law principles. They may also reflect customary international law.[44]

---

[36] *Id.* at Art. 18.

[37] *Id.* at Art. 19.

[38] *Id.* at Art. 24.

[39] Id. at Art. 26.

[40] *Id.* at Art. 27.

[41] International Covenant on Civil and Political Rights, Declarations and Reservations, *available at* http://www.ohchr.org/english/countries/ratification/4_1.htm.

[42] *See generally* William A. Schabas, *Invalid Reservations to the ICCPR: Is the United States Still a Party?*, 21 BROOKLYN J. INT'L L. 277 (1995); David P. Stewart, *United States Ratification of the Covenant on Civil and Political Rights: The Significance of the Reservations, Understandings and Declarations*, 42 DEPAUL L. REV. 1183 (1993).

[43] *See generally* Louis Henkin, *U.S. Ratification of Human Rights Conventions: The Ghost of Senator Bricker*, 89 AM. J. INT'L L. 341 (1995). There are also some complex federalism issues amongst the understandings to this and other conventions. *See* Duncan Hollis, *Executive Federalism: Forging New Federalist Constraints on the Treaty Power*, 79 S. CAL. L. REV. 1327 (2006).

[44] For litigants, the hope is that international rights might be broader than existing domestic ones.

There is an Optional Protocol to the Covenant that allows for the Human Rights Committee established by this Covenant to "to receive and consider, as provided in the present Protocol, communications from individuals claiming to be victims of violations of any of the rights set forth in the Covenant."[45] The Committee examines the communications and the submissions of both sides and then forwards "its views to the State Party concerned and to the individual."[46] The "views" are not "binding" the way a court judgment would be, but most States make a good faith effort to comply, amending their laws or administrative practices if necessary. A Second Protocol is aimed at the abolition of the death penalty.[47]

The Covenant provides for rights of both peoples and individuals. It starts with a Preamble that references both the Charter of the United Nations and the Universal Declaration of Rights. It states that "in accordance with the Universal Declaration of Human Rights, the ideal of free human beings enjoying civil and political freedom and freedom from fear and want can only be achieved if conditions are created whereby everyone may enjoy his civil and political rights, as well as his economic, social and cultural rights."[48]

The rights of peoples is in Part I of the Covenant. For example, one finds in Article One the "right to self determination."[49] Part II describes the obligations of State Parties to the Covenant, such as that "[e]ach State Party to the present Covenant undertakes to respect and to ensure to all individuals within its territory" rights in the Covenant. It also speaks against discrimination.[50] Article 3 of the Covenant provides that "[t]he States Parties to the present Covenant undertakes to ensure the equal right of men and women to the enjoyment of all civil and political rights set forth in the present Covenant."[51]

Part III provides for rights of individuals and prohibits certain conduct. For example it provides a "right to life" and places restrictions on the use of the death penalty, prohibiting its use against pregnant women and individuals under the age of eighteen.[52] Additionally, in countries that have not abolished the death penalty, this Covenant restricts its use to only the "most serious crimes in accordance with the law in force at the time of the commission of the crime and not contrary to the

---

This may not always be so. *See e.g.,* United States v. Duarte-Acero, 208 F.3d 1281 (11th Cir. 2000) (international double jeopardy standard limited, like United States Constitution, by "same sovereign" doctrine). *See also* § 1.03[F], *supra.*

[45] Optional Protocol to the International Covenant on Civil and Political Rights, *available at* http://www.hrweb.org/legal/cpr-prot.html. The United States is not one of the 110 parties to this instrument.

[46] *Id.* at Art. 5.

[47] Second Optional Protocol to the International Covenant on Civil and Political Rights, aiming at the elimination of the death penalty, 1989, *available at* http://www.ohchr.org/english/countries/ratification/12.htm.

[48] International Covenant on Civil and Political Rights, Preamble, *available at* http://www.ohchr.org/english/law/ccpr.htm.

[49] *Id.* at Art. 1.

[50] *Id.* at Art 2.

[51] *Id.* at Art. 3.

[52] The United States entered a reservation to the Convention, reserving the right to execute people for what they did as juveniles. This became moot after the Supreme Court's decision in Roper v. Simmons, 543 U.S. 551 (2005).

provisions of the present Covenant and to the Convention on the Prevention and Punishment of the Crime of Genocide."[53]

Other rights included in Part III include rights related to the judicial process, such as the presumption of innocence[54] and right to have a conviction reviewed by a higher tribunal.[55] A particularly significant set of rights, which are often used by official and unofficial human rights organizations to assess the fairness of criminal proceedings, are contained in Article 14, paragraph 3 of the Covenant:

3. In the determination of any criminal charge against him, everyone shall be entitled to the following minimum guarantees, in full equality:

(a) To be informed promptly and in detail in a language which he understands of the nature and cause of the charge against him;

(b) To have adequate time and facilities for the preparation of his defence and to communicate with counsel of his own choosing;

(c) To be tried without undue delay;

(d) To be tried in his presence, and to defend himself in person or through legal assistance of his own choosing; to be informed, if he does not have legal assistance, of this right; and to have legal assistance assigned to him, in any case where the interests of justice so require, and without payment by him in any such case if he does not have sufficient means to pay for it;

(e) To examine, or have examined, the witnesses against him and to obtain the attendance and examination of witnesses on his behalf under the same conditions as witnesses against him;

(f) To have the free assistance of an interpreter if he cannot understand or speak the language used in court;

(g) Not to be compelled to testify against himself or to confess guilt.

These provisions have also played a significant role in the creation of fair procedures for the various *Ad Hoc* Tribunals, Special Courts and the International Criminal Court, which will be discussed in Chapters 16 and 17. In some cases, they are spelled out almost verbatim in the relevant instruments; in others they are taken as given.

The Covenant also provides for rights similar to those found in the First Amendment to the United States Constitution, such as the right to freedom of expression,[56] and rights of assembly[57] and association.[58]

Part III also prohibits conduct such as slavery[59] and torture.[60] It forbids "[a]ny propaganda for war," and "[a]ny advocacy of national, racial or religious hatred that constitutes incitement to discrimination, hostility or violence."[61] This particular

---

[53] *Id.* at Art. 6.

[54] *Id.* at Art. 14(2).

[55] *Id.* at Art. 14(5).

[56] *Id.* at Art. 19(2).

[57] *Id.* at Art. 21.

[58] *Id.* at Art. 22.

[59] *Id.* at Art. 8.

[60] *Id.* at Art. 7.

[61] *Id.* at Art. 20.

Article caused the United States to enter a reservation so as not to "restrict the right of free speech and association protected by the Constitution and laws of the United States."[62]

Part IV of the Covenant establishes the United Nations Human Rights Committee (HRC). A body distinct from the old Human Rights Commission, the Committee monitors application of the Covenant. Part IV provides the structure and duties of this Committee. It also tells how the eighteen person committee[63] is selected.[64] The main function of the Committee is to examine reports that the States Parties are required to make explaining how they are giving effect to the Convention.[65] The dialogue involved between the Committee and State representatives has become a very important part of the effort to promote and protect human rights for many countries. Receiving complaints from those countries that have accepted the "communications" aspect of its jurisdiction, by becoming party to the First Optional Protocol, is another important area of the Committee's work. It has resulted in a significant body of case-law interpreting the Covenant.[66] Part V provides that nothing in the Covenant shall impair either existing powers of U.N. agencies with respect to human rights violations[67] or "the inherent right of all peoples to enjoy and utilize fully and freely their natural wealth and resources."[68] Part VI provides the final clauses such as the mechanics of ratification, entry into force, and amendment.[69]

§ 15.02 TORTURE

[A] Generally

Both international and United States law prohibit torture. At the forefront of the international discussion is "The Convention against Torture and Other Cruel, Inhuman or Degrading Treatment or Punishment"[70] adopted by the General Assembly in 1984. Other Conventions also prohibit torture.[71] In the United States, federal statutes specifically prohibit conduct that meets the definition of torture. Torture is a topic that has been a focus of recent media attention, most vocally in the context of activities at the Abu Ghraib prison and at Guantanamo Bay. Much of the discussion has related to United States legal memoranda regarding interrogation techniques, often called the "torture memos," that came out of

---

[62] International Covenant on Civil and Political Rights, Declarations and Reservations, *available at* http://www.ohchr.org/english/countries/ratification/4_1.htm.

[63] International Covenant on Civil and Political Rights, Art. 28, *available at* http://www.ohchr.org/english/law/ccpr.htm.

[64] *Id.* at Art. 28–32.

[65] *Id.* at Art. 40.

[66] *See* ALEX CONTE, SCOTT DAVIDSON & RICHARD BURCHILL, DEFINING CIVIL AND POLITICAL RIGHTS: THE JURISPRUDENCE OF THE UNITED NATIONS HUMAN RIGHTS COMMITTEE (2004).

[67] International Convention on Civil and Political Rights, Art. 46.

[68] *Id.* at Art. 47.

[69] Id. at Art. 48–53.

[70] Convention Against Torture, and other Cruel Inhuman or Degrading Treatment or Punishment, *available at* http://www.ohchr.org/english/law/cat.htm.

[71] Various provisions of the Geneva Conventions prohibit torture. *See, e.g.*, Summary of International and U.S. Law Prohibiting Torture and Other Ill-treatment of Persons in Custody, *available at* http://www.hrw.org/english/docs/2004/05/24/usint8614.htm.

various government agencies.[72] These events raised significant questions about United States' compliance with the Torture Convention and also with the prohibitions against torture in the Geneva Conventions. At least at the normative level, the military's ban on the techniques that ran foul of treaty obligations is now absolute. The military's Field Manual entitled HUMAN INTELLIGENCE COLLECTOR OPERATIONS provides as follows:

5.75 If used in conjunction with intelligence interrogations, prohibited actions include, but are not limited to —

- Forcing the detainee to be naked, perform sexual acts, or pose in a sexual manner.

- Placing hoods or sacks over the head of a detainee; using duct tape over the eyes.

- Applying beatings, electric shock, burns, or other forms of physical pain.

- "Waterboarding."

- Using military working dogs.

- Inducing hypothermia or heat injury.

- Conducting mock executions.

- Depriving detainee of necessary food, water, or medical care.[73]

The situation with the CIA is more ambiguous. The President vetoed legislation early in March 2008 which would have prohibited the CIA from doing what the military is now prohibited from doing.[74]

[B]   Convention Against Torture

The Convention Against Torture and Other Cruel, Inhuman or Degrading Treatment or Punishment, adopted in 1984, entered into force on June 26, 1987. The United States ratified the Convention in 1994 with two reservations, five understandings, two declarations, and one proviso.[75] It contains thirty-three articles of which the first sixteen are the essence of the prohibitions of torture. This is followed by articles pertaining to establishing a Committee against Torture, and

---

[72] See Bush Administration Documents on Interrogation, WASH. POST, June 23, 2004, available at http://www.washingtonpost.com/wp-dyn/articles/A62516-2004Jun22.html. See also, JOSHUA L. DRATEL & KAREN J. GOLDBERG, THE TORTURE PAPERS: THE ROAD TO ABU GHRAIB (2d ed. 2005); Memorandum dated March 14, 2003, from John Yoo, Office of Legal Counsel, to William J. Haynes II, Re: Military Interrogation of Alien Unlawful Combatants Held Outside the United States, available at http://gulcfac.typepad.com/georgetown_university_law/files/march.14.memo.part1.pdf.

[73] FM 2-22.3 of September 2006, on HUMAN INTELLIGENCE COLLECTOR OPERATIONS, at 5–21, giving effect to Detainee Treatment Act of 2005, § 1002(a) (which protects people under control of Department of Defense from being subject to methods of interrogation not approved in the Field Manual).

[74] See Bush Vetoes Bill Banning Waterboarding, CNN Rep., Mar. 8, 2008, available at www.cnn.com/2008/POLITICS/03/08/bush.torture.ap/ (quoting President to effect that the Bill "would take away one of the most valuable tools on the war on terror"). See also Interpretation of the Geneva Conventions Common Article 3 as Applied to a Program of Detention and Interrogation Operated by the Central Intelligence Agency available at http://www.whitehouse.gov/news/releases/2007/07/20070720-4.html (providing an executive order that is not as precise in its prohibitions).

[75] See EDWARD M. WISE, ELLEN S. PODGOR & ROGER S. CLARK, INTERNATIONAL CRIMINAL LAW: CASES AND MATERIALS 280 (2d ed. 2004); see also David P. Stewart, The Torture Convention and the Reception of International Criminal Law within the United States, 15 NOVA L. REV. 449 (1991).

the final part, Part III, has the usual provisions of ratification, signature, and amendment. There is one Optional Protocol to the Convention, which came into force in June 2006. It states as its objective, "to establish a system of regular visits undertaken by independent international and national bodies to places where people are deprived of their liberty, in order to prevent torture and other cruel, inhuman or degrading treatment or punishment."[76]

The Convention begins with mention of the U.N. Charter, and also notes that "article 5 of the Universal Declaration of Human Rights and article 7 of the International Covenant on Civil and Political Rights, both . . . provide that no one may be subjected to torture or to cruel, inhuman or degrading treatment or punishment."[77] Article One provides the definition of the term "torture" for purposes of the Convention. It states:

> torture means any act by which severe pain or suffering, whether physical or mental, is intentionally inflicted on a person for such purposes as obtaining from him or a third person information or a confession, punishing him for an act he or a third person has committed or is suspected of having committed, or intimidating or coercing him or a third person, or for any reason based on discrimination of any kind, when such pain or suffering is inflicted by or at the instigation of or with the consent or acquiescence of a public official or other person acting in an official capacity. It does not include pain or suffering arising only from, inherent in or incidental to lawful sanctions.[78]

After providing a definition, Article Two provides a clear prohibition against torture and prohibits exceptions to the strict rule against torture. It requires each State Party to "take effective legislative, administrative, judicial or other measures to prevent acts of torture in any territory under its jurisdiction."[79] Underscoring the absolute nature of the prohibition, the Convention provides that no exceptional circumstances, including "a state of war or a threat of war, internal political instability or any other public emergency, may be invoked as a justification of torture,"[80] nor can arguments of superior orders be used to justify torture.[81] The Convention provides obligations to State Parties to make torture illegal "under its criminal law."[82] To this end, a State Party is required to exercise jurisdiction over the offenses created by the treaty (a) when they are committed in any territory under its jurisdiction or on board a ship or aircraft registered in that State; (b) when the alleged offender is a national of that State; and (c) when the victim is a national of that State if that State considers it appropriate.[83] It is also obligated to establish its jurisdiction over the offenses in cases where the alleged offender is present in its

---

[76] Optional Protocol to Convention Against Torture, and other Cruel Inhuman or Degrading Treatment or Punishment, General Assembly Resolution A/RES/57/199 (Dec. 18, 2002), *available at* http://www.ohchr.org/english/law/cat-one.htm. The U.S. is not one of the 30-odd parties to this Protocol.

[77] Convention Against Torture, and other Cruel Inhuman or Degrading Treatment or Punishment, Introduction, *available at* http://www.ohchr.org/english/law/cat.htm.

[78] *Id.* at Art. 1.

[79] *Id.* at Art. 2(1).

[80] *Id.* at Art. 2(2).

[81] *Id.* at Art. 2(3).

[82] *Id.* at Art. 4.

[83] *Id.* at Art. 5(1).

territory and it does not extradite that person to a state exercising territorial or nationality jurisdiction.[84]

The Convention is emphatic that Parties "shall ensure that any statement which is established to have been made as a result of torture shall not be invoked as evidence in any proceedings, except against a person accused of torture as evidence that the statement was made."[85] Other specific obligations of the State Parties are outlined in the Convention. These include preventing in any territory under its jurisdiction other acts of cruel, inhuman, or degrading treatment or punishment which do not amount to torture as defined, when those acts are committed by or at the instigation of or with the consent or acquiescence of a public official or other person acting in an official capacity.[86]

The second part of the Convention, starting with Article 17, establishes a Committee against Torture.[87] The Articles immediately thereafter discuss the composition and activities of the Committee, and are followed by Part III which provides the final clauses such as the mechanics of ratification, entry into force, and amendment.

The Convention prohibits returning a person to a country if there are "substantial grounds for believing that he would be in danger of being subjected to torture."[88] In the case of *Julmiste v. Ashcroft*,[89] the petitioner brought a writ of habeas corpus challenging an order of removal issued by an immigration judge. Petitioner claimed that he should not be sent to Haiti because it would be a violation of Article Three of the Torture Convention. The court rejected his argument and upheld the immigration judge's decision, because the petitioner had "failed to produce sufficient evidence to suggest a likelihood that he, himself, would be subjected to torture."[90] Some cases in the United States brought under Article Three, however, have been successful, in spite of the burden of proof being on the applicant.[91] In the case of an extradition request where torture is feared, the Secretary of State, as opposed to the courts, has power to refuse extradition.[92]

[C]   United States Laws Against Torture

The federal statutes implementing the provisions of the Convention Against Torture and Other Cruel, Inhuman or Degrading Treatment or Punishment are found in title 18. 18 U.S.C. § 2340 is a definition statute, that includes a definition of torture. It states, " 'torture' means an act committed by a person acting under the color of law specifically intended to inflict severe physical or mental pain or suffering (other than pain or suffering incidental to lawful sanctions) upon another

---

[84] *Id.* at Art. 5(2). This is a classic "extradite or prosecute" obligation. *See* § 2.04[E], *supra*.

[85] *Id.* at Art. 15.

[86] *Id.* at Art. 16.

[87] *See* Committee Against Torture, Office of the United Nations High Commissioner for Human Rights, *available at* http://www.ohchr.org/english/bodies/cat/index.htm.

[88] Convention Against Torture, and other Cruel Inhuman or Degrading Treatment or Punishment, Art. 3, *available at* http://www.ohchr.org/english/law/cat.htm.

[89] 212 F. Supp. 2d 341 (D.N.J. 2002).

[90] *Id.* at 348.

[91] *See, e.g.*, Zheng v. Ashcroft, 332 F.3d 1186 (9th Cir. 2003).

[92] *See* 22 C.F.R. § 95 (2004).

person within his custody or physical control."[93] Other definitions are also provided, such as the definition of "severe mental pain and suffering," and the definition of "United States" which provides the scope of jurisdiction for this statute.[94]

The actual offense of torture in the United States legislation applies only to the commission, attempted commission or conspiracy to commit torture "outside the United States."[95] Jurisdiction is available if the alleged offender is a national of the United States, or if the alleged offender is present in the United States, irrespective of the nationality of the victim or alleged offender.[96] The United States did not exercise its option under the Convention to take jurisdiction on a passive personality basis. The Committee against Torture has faulted the United States for not legislating to criminalize torture as defined in the Convention when it is committed in the United States itself.[97] The United States takes the position that the offense is already adequately punished under existing federal and state law on offenses against the person. The offense carries of penalty of twenty years, but can be increased to death or life imprisonment "if death results to any person from conduct prohibited" under this subsection of the statute.[98]

The federal torture statute states explicitly that it is not to be interpreted as the exclusive basis for proceeding with a prosecution.[99] Thus, a state or federal prosecutor may have the ability to proceed with battery, homicide, or other charges should the conduct fit these or other crimes, although there will be jurisdiction to do so only in a limited number of cases since the United States does not exercise general jurisdiction over what its citizens do abroad. It is even more unlikely that there will be any domestic law basis to charge a foreign citizen with assaults abroad, other than the secondary or fallback universal jurisdiction for torture contained in the Convention and the statute. The legislation giving effect to the Convention also provides that this statute does not create "any substantive or procedural right enforceable by law by any party in any civil proceeding."[100]

[D] Sexual Violence as Torture

Sexual violence has been recognized in both international documents and courts as an international crime. In some instances rape has been identified as "a form of torture or inhuman treatment."[101] For example, "[s]ince 1986, reports of the Special Rapporteur on Torture of the U.N. Commission on Human Rights have defined the rape of female prisoners while in detention or under interrogation as an act of torture."[102]

---

[93] 18 U.S.C. § 2340(1).

[94] *Id.* at § 2340(2), (3).

[95] 18 U.S.C. § 2340A(a) and (c) (conspiracy provision added by the USA Patriot Act of 2001, § 811(g)).

[96] 18 U.S.C. § 2340A(b). See also § 2.04[B] and [E] *supra*, on bases of jurisdiction.

[97] Conclusions and Recommendations of the Committee against Torture, May 15, 2000, U.N. Doc. CAT/C/24/6 (2000).

[98] 18 U.S.C. § 2340A(a).

[99] 18 U.S.C. § 2340B.

[100] *Id.*

[101] EDWARD M. WISE, ELLEN S. PODGOR & ROGER S. CLARK, INTERNATIONAL CRIMINAL LAW: CASES AND MATERIALS 301 (2d ed. 2004).

[102] *Id.*

In the ad hoc Tribunal of Yugoslavia, decisions have found that in some circumstances, such as in times of war, rape and sexual violence can be international crimes.[103] For example, in the case of *Prosecutor v. Furundzija*,[104] a court in the International Criminal Tribunal for the former Yugoslavia stated that "[r]ape in time of war is specifically prohibited by treaty law: the Geneva Conventions of 1949, Additional Protocol I of 1977 and Additional Protocol II of 1977."[105] The court in the *Furundzija* case stated that "rape in fact constitutes torture when inflicted by or at the instigation of or with the consent or acquiescence of a public official or other persons acting in an official capacity."[106] Other decisions in international tribunals have taken the same position.[107]

§ 15.03   THE DEATH PENALTY

The use of the death penalty as a form of punishment has sparked considerable international debate. All of Europe is abolitionist, as are most of the States in the Americas, including Mexico and Canada. There is a Second Optional Protocol to the Covenant on Civil and Political Rights, aiming at the Abolition of the Death Penalty to which over 60 States are party. Some countries refuse to extradite an individual to the United States if the death penalty could possibly be received by the extradited individual.[108] There has also been a growing movement to have the imposition of the death penalty considered a violation of customary international law.[109] The United Nations General Assembly is on record favoring a moratorium on the use of the death penalty,[110] but there are some dissents from this position.[111] Both within and outside the United States there have been strong human rights challenges to the death penalty.[112] With respect to its imposition with juveniles, arguments that it is a violation of customary international law and *jus cogens* seem largely to have carried the day.[113] In *Roper v. Simmons*[114] the United States

---

[103] *See generally* Kelly D. Askin, *Sexual Violence in Decisions and Indictments of the Yugoslav and Rwandan Tribunals: Current Status*, 93 Am. J. Int'l L. 97 (1999).

[104] Case No. IT-95-17/1-T Judgement (International Criminal Tribunal for the former Yugoslavia, Dec. 10, 1988).

[105] It was also stated that "Other serious sexual assaults are expressly or implicitly prohibited in various provisions of the same treaties." *Id.* at ¶ 165.

[106] *Id.* at ¶ 176.

[107] *See* Prosecutor v. Delalic, Case No. IT-96-21-T, Judgment (International Criminal Tribunal for the former Yugoslavia, Nov. 16, 1998).

[108] *See* § 12.02[D], *supra*.

[109] *See, e.g.*, Human Rights and the Death Penalty, *available at* http://www.derechos.org/dp/; William A. Schabas, The Abolition of the Death Penalty in International Law (3d ed. 2002).

[110] G.A. Res. 62/149, Dec. 18, 2007, *available at* http://daccessdds.un.org/doc/UNDOC/GEN/N07/472/71/PDF/N0747271.pdf?OpenElement.

[111] See Note verbale dated Feb. 2, 2008, from 58 States insisting that they are "in persistent objection to any attempt to impose a moratorium on the use of the death penalty or its abolition in contravention to existing stipulations under international law." U.N. Doc. A/62/58 (Feb. 2, 2008).

[112] *See, e.g.*, U. of Minnesota Human Rights Library, Death Penalty and Human Rights Links, *available at* http://www1.umn.edu/humanrts/links/deathpenalty.html.

[113] *See, e.g.*, Summary of Customary International Law and *Jus Cogens* as pertains to Juvenile Offenders, International Justice Project, *available at* http://www.internationaljusticeproject.org/juvJusCogens.cfm. For a definition of the term *jus cogens* see § 1.03[E], *supra*. This report notes that the most recent executions of juveniles have been by China, the Democratic Republic of Congo, Iran, Nigeria, Pakistan, Saudi Arabia, and Yemen, the last of them, however (by Iran) in 2005.

Supreme Court, with the majority referring to international developments, held capital punishment for those under the age of 18 at the time of the crime to be unconstitutional. When it ratified the Covenant on Civil and Political Rights, the United States had entered a reservation insisting that it retained the right to execute people for what they did while juveniles. This was rendered moot by *Roper*.

Soering v. United Kingdom[115] is a case before the European Court of Human Rights involving the extradition of Jens Soering,[116] a German citizen, to the United States to face charges in Virginia relating to the alleged homicides of his girlfriend's parents.[117] The charges included capital murder for the deaths of both individuals. The United States requested extradition pursuant to the Extradition Treaty of 1972 between the United States and the United Kingdom.[118] Applicant Soering argued that extradition would "give rise to a breach by the United Kingdom of Article 3 of the [European] Convention [on Human Rights], which provides: 'No one shall be subjected to torture or to inhuman or degrading treatment or punishment.' "[119]

The European Court of Human Rights found that an extradition in this particular case would amount to a violation of Article 3.[120] The court looked at four particular circumstances of this case, namely, the "length of detention prior to execution," "conditions on death row," "the applicant's age and mental state," and the "possibility of extradition to the Federal Republic of Germany."[121] The Court noted that Soering would likely run the risk of the "death row phenomenon," but that "some element of delay between imposition and execution of the sentence and the experience of severe stress in conditions necessary for strict incarceration are inevitable." The finding of a violation of Article 3 here was because:

> in the Court's view, having regard to the very long period of time spent on death row in such extreme conditions, with the ever present and mounting anguish of awaiting execution of the death penalty, and to the personal circumstances of the applicant, especially his age and mental state at the time of the offence, the applicant's extradition to the United States would expose him to a real risk of treatment going beyond the threshold set by Article 3. A further consideration of relevance is that in the particular instance the legitimate purpose of extradition could be achieved by another means which would not involve suffering of such exceptional intensity or duration.[122]

---

[114] 543 U.S. 551 (2005).

[115] 161 Eur. Ct. H.R. (ser. A) (1989), also *available at* http://www.worldlii.org/eu/cases/ ECHR/1989/ 14.html.

[116] Soering is a German National. *Id.* at ¶ 11.

[117] The homicides occurred in Bedford, Virginia. *Id.* at ¶ 12.

[118] Extradition was also sought for Elizabeth Haysom, Soering's girlfriend and a Canadian national who surrendered for extradition to the United States and plead guilty "as an accessory to the murder of her parents." *Id.* at 18. Germany also sought extradition of Soering, evidently planning to try him on the basis of nationality jurisdiction. The United Kingdom chose to process the United States request and informed Germany that an extradition would be conditioned on assurances from the United States regarding "the question of death penalty." *Id.* at ¶ 19.

[119] *Id.* at ¶ 80.

[120] *Id.* at ¶ 111.

[121] *Id.* at ¶ 104–10.

[122] *Id.*

Soering was eventually extradited to the United States, stood trial for these homicides and was sentenced to life imprisonment.[123] The extradition was premised on assurances by the United States that they would not impose the death penalty.[124] Extraditions to the United States in other cases have also been premised upon the death penalty not being under consideration as a possible sentence.[125]

The new frontier in the United States for issues of penalties is life imprisonment without the possibility of parole. One aspect of this is the question of juvenile offenders. Human Rights Watch, a non-governmental human rights organization, reported in January 2008 that there were at least 2380 people (mostly males) imprisoned in the United States without the possibility of parole for crimes committed while under the age of 18. Of these, 227 were in California and 59 percent were first offenders. Only seven were known of in the rest of the world.[126] The Convention on the Rights of the Child,[127] to which all States except Somalia and the United States are parties, prohibits such punishment for those who committed the crime while under the age of 18.

While the matter has probably not gone as far in international law as in the case of juveniles, several countries have constitutional prohibitions on life without parole that extend to *all* persons, not only juveniles, and many of them regard this issue as one of international human rights.[128]

§ 15.04 THE VIENNA CONVENTION ON CONSULAR RELATIONS

Article 36(1)(b) of the 1963 Vienna Convention on Consular Relations provides certain rights to individuals arrested outside their home country. One of the rights, the notification requirements of the Vienna Convention on Consular Relations, has been a source of significant discussion in recent appellate decisions.[129] The Convention requires that arrested foreign nationals be informed of their right to notify their consular officers.

In the United States federal system, a provision in the Code of Federal Regulations specifically outlines the procedure for notifying consular officers upon

---

[123] Soering v. Deeds, 255 Va. 457, 499 S.E.2d 514 (1998) (denial of habeas corpus).

[124] See Richard Lillich, *The Soering Case*, 85 Am. J. Int'l L. 128 (1991).

[125] See Edward M. Wise, Ellen S. Podgor & Roger S. Clark, International Criminal Law: Cases and Materials 608–09 (2d ed. 2004) (discussing cases where extradition was granted after the countries received assurances from the United States that the death penalty would not be imposed).

[126] Human Rights Watch Report, *When I Die, They'll Send Me Home: Youth Sentenced to Life Without Parole in California*, available at www.hrw.org/reports/2008/us0108/index.htm.

[127] 1577 U.N.T.S. 3, Art. 37. See also G.A. Res. 61/146 (2006) on Rights of Child, ¶ 31 of which calls upon all States to abolish "the death penalty and life imprisonment without possibility of release for those under the age of 18 at the time of the commission of the offense."

[128] See Dirk Van Zyl Smit, Taking Life Imprisonment Seriously in National and International Law (2002).

[129] See, e.g., United States v. Jimenez-Nava, 243 F.3d 192, 200 (5th Cir. 2001) (holding that even if defendant had right to notification of consulate, suppression of statements was not an appropriate remedy); United States v. Page, 232 F.3d 536 (6th Cir. 2001) (claiming that defendant was not notified of his right to contact the Barbados consulate); United States v. Chaparro-Alcantara, 226 F.3d 616, 622 (7th Cir. 2000) (holding that suppression of a confession was not an available remedy for violation of Article 36 of the Vienna Convention).

the arrest of a foreign national.[130] The regulation notes that some treaties mandate this notification, while others require it "only upon the demand or request of the arrested foreign national."[131] The regulation explicitly requires law enforcement to notify arrested foreign nationals of their right to consular notification.[132]

Additionally, the U.S. State Department provides "Instructions for Federal, State, and Other Local Law Enforcement and Other Officials Regarding Foreign Nationals in the United States and the Rights of Consular Officials to Assist Them."[133]

Despite the existence of these measures, there are continual occurrences of non-compliance with the Vienna Convention on Consular Relations. Most courts in the United States have rejected defendants' argument claiming that they had not been properly notified under the Vienna Convention on Consular Rights and ruled that the treaty does not "create an exclusionary rule" that would require suppression of the evidence[134] or dismissal of the action.[135] Courts have also found that the treaty did not create rights that private parties can enforce.[136] Some decisions have focused on the harm to the defendant, finding that absent prejudice to the defendant, there is no basis for relief.[137] Defendants are unsuccessful in some cases because of procedural impediments such as those seen in the Supreme Court's decision in *Breard v. Greene*,[138] where the failure to raise the issue in state court precluded later relief. Many of these decisions have been met with scholarly criticism.[139]

Several recent cases have brought the issue to the forefront in the international arena. For example, in the *Breard* case the petitioner was a Paraguayan national who faced the death sentence. Paraguay brought an action against the United States in the International Court of Justice (ICJ) claiming that the accused had not been afforded his rights pursuant to the Convention. Despite the ICJ's Order that Breard not be executed while this matter was pending, he was executed.[140]

---

[130] *See* 28 C.F.R. § 50.5 (2002).

[131] *Id.*

[132] *Id.* at (a)(1).

[133] Consular Notification and Access, Office of Public Affairs of Policy Coordination for Consular Affairs, *available at* http://travel.state.gov/consul_notify.html (last visited October 16, 2002).

[134] *See, e.g.*, United States v. Page, 232 F.3d 536 (6th Cir. 2000); United States v. Lawal, 231 F.3d 1045 (7th Cir. 2000); United States v. Amano, 229 F.3d 801 (9th Cir. 2000); United States v. Chaparro-Alcantara, 226 F.3d 616 (7th Cir. 2000); United States v. Lombera-Camorlinga, 206 F.3d 882 (9th Cir. 2000) (en banc).

[135] *See, e.g.*, United States v. Awadallah, 202 F. Supp. 2d 17 (S.D.N.Y. 2002).

[136] *See, e.g.*, United States v. Jimenez-Nava, 243 F.3d 192 (5th Cir. 2001); United States v. DeLa Pava, 268 F.3d 157 (2d Cir. 2001); United States v. Emuegbunam, 268 F.3d 377 (6th Cir. 2001).

[137] *See, e.g.*, United States v. Rodrigues, 68 F. Supp. 2d 178, 183 (S.D.N.Y. 1999).

[138] 523 U.S. 371 (1998).

[139] *See, e.g.*, Mark J. Kadish, *Article 36 of the Vienna Convention on Consular Relations: A Search for the Right to Consul*, 18 Mich. J. Int'l L. 565 (1997); Jordan J. Paust, Breard *and Treaty-Based Rights Under the Consular Convention*, 92 Am. J. Int'l L. 691 (1998).

[140] Summary of the Order, Case Concerning the Vienna Convention on Consular Relations (Paraguay v. United States of America), *available at* http://www.ICJ-cij.org/ICJwww/idocket/ipaus/iPAUSsummaries/ipaussummary19980409.html. The United States later formally apologized to Paraguay and promised steps to ensure better compliance with the Convention in the future. *See also* EDWARD

A disregard of the Vienna Convention was also brought to the ICJ's attention in the case of two brothers who were German nationals, and who were set for execution in the State of Arizona. Despite a provisional order of the ICJ staying the execution of Walter LaGrand pending their review of the matter in the international tribunal, he was executed.[141] Unlike Paraguay that chose not to proceed following the execution of Breard, Germany went forward with the case before the ICJ. The Court found that the United States had "breached its obligations to the federal republic of Germany and to the LaGrand brothers under Article 36, paragraph 1."[142]

In some cases relief has been granted. For example, in the *Case Concerning Avena and Other Mexican Nationals (Mexico v. U.S.)*,[143] the ICJ ruled that the United States had violated the Vienna Convention on Consular Relations. Of particular significance in this case is the discussion of what remedy should be afforded the defendants who were deprived of their consular rights. The ICJ rejected the United States' argument that the clemency process was sufficient "review and reconsideration," although it did note "that appropriate clemency procedures can supplement judicial review and reconsideration."[144] The Court held that more would be needed to be a sufficient "review and reconsideration."

Within two months of the entry of the *Avena* decision, one of the Mexican nationals named in the ICJ proceeding, who had been set for execution, had his death sentence commuted to life imprisonment by the Governor of Oklahoma.[145]

In the case of *Valdez v. Oklahoma*,[146] the parties agreed that there had been a violation of rights under the Consular Convention. When consular officials were finally informed of Valdez's arrest, conviction, and death sentence, they began to assist him in his clemency process. As a result of their assistance, it was discovered that the defendant suffered "injuries as a youth which greatly contributed to and altered his behavior."[147] Although the new information caused the Oklahoma Board of Pardons and Parole to recommend a sentence of life without parole, clemency was not granted by the governor.[148] Despite the claim being available to the defendant for his prior post-conviction petition, the appellate court decided to remand the case for resentencing. The court found that it had "power to grant relief when an error complained of has resulted in a miscarriage of justice, or constitutes a substantial violation of a constitutional or statutory right."[149]

M. Wise, Ellen S. Podgor & Roger S. Clark, International Criminal Law: Cases and Materials 613 (2d ed. 2004).

[141] Karl LeGrand, the other brother, had already been executed. *See also* Howard S. Schiffman, *The LeGrand Decision: The Evolving Legal Landscape of the Vienna Convention on Consular Relations in U.S. Death Penalty Cases*, 42 Santa Clara L. Rev. 1099 (2002).

[142] *See* The LaGrand Case (Germany v. United States of America) (Judgment of June 27, 2001), *available at* http://www.ICJ-cij.org/ICJwww/idocket/igus/igusframe.htm.

[143] Case Concerning Avena and Other Mexican Nationals (Mexico v. U.S.) (Judgment of March 31, 2004), *available at* http://www.ICJ-cij.org/ICJwww/idocket/imus/imusframe.htm.

[144] *Id.* at ¶ 143.

[145] *See* Edward M. Wise, Ellen S. Podgor & Roger S. Clark, International Criminal Law: Cases and Materials 623 (2d ed. 2004).

[146] 46 P.3d 703 (Ct. App. 2002).

[147] *Id.* at 706.

[148] *Id.*

[149] *Id.* at 710. Until the *Breard* case surfaced, defense counsel seem to have been stunningly ignorant

The issue of how to comply with the I.C.J.'s ruling in *Avena* found its way to the Supreme Court where in *Medellin v. Texas*,[150] the United States Supreme Court examined the question of whether the President had authority to order a state court to re-examine a case when the accused had not been told of his right to consult with the Mexican consulate. Despite the International Court of Justice ruling that Medellin's case, along with fifty other Mexicans on death row, should be granted hearings to determine if the deprivation of the right to consult with a consulate affected the case, the Supreme Court held that an international court decision was not binding on state courts. Chief Justice Roberts, writing the majority opinion, stated that "the *Avena* judgment is not domestic law." The Court stated:

> [W]hile the ICJ's judgment in *Avena* creates an international law obligation on the part of the United States, it does not of its own force constitute binding federal law that pre-empts state restrictions on the filing of successive habeas petitions. As we noted in *Sanchez-Llamas*,[151] a contrary conclusion would be extraordinary, given that basic rights guaranteed by our own Constitution do not have the effect of displacing state procedural rules Nothing in the text, background, negotiating and drafting history, or practice among signatory nations suggests that the President or Senate intended the improbable result of giving the judgments of an international tribunal a higher status than that enjoyed by 'many of our most fundamental constitutional protections.'

A three-person dissent took issue with this holding. Justice Breyer, writing for this dissent, presented the position that because the president had decided that it was important to enforce the International Court of Justice position, and Congress had not spoken to the contrary, the action should be considered binding.

§ 15.05   UNITED NATIONS STANDARDS AND NORMS

In addition to the treaty standards and other instruments such as the Universal Declaration of Human Rights that have emerged mostly from the "human rights" part of the United Nations, located in Geneva, there is an important body of normative material that has come out of the Crime Prevention and Criminal Justice part of the operation, located in Vienna.[152] This body of "soft-law" material, which is mostly in recommendation form, is usually referred to as United Nations Standards and Norms.[153]

Many of these standards were adopted at the five-yearly Congresses on criminal justice held under United Nations auspices. For example, the First Congress in 1955 agreed to the text of the Standard Minimum Rules for the Treatment of

---

of the possibilities of consular assistance in finding evidence, interpreters and witnesses.

[150] 552 U.S.(2008) *available at* http://www.supremecourtus.gov/opinions/07pdf/06-984.pdf.

[151] In *Sanchez-Llamas* v. *Oregon*, the Court held that despite a ruling of the International Court of Justice, the Vienna Convention on Consular Relations did not preclude the application of state default rules. *See* Sanchez-Llamas v. Oregon, 548 U. S. 331 (2006).

[152] The Geneva secretariat is the Office of High Commissioner for Human Rights (UNHCHR), while the Vienna part is the U.N. Office of Drugs and Crime (UNDOC). The political part in Geneva is now the Human Rights Council, the Vienna part is the Commission on Crime Prevention and Control.

[153] *See* United Nations Office on Drugs and Crime, Compendium of United Nations Standards and Norms in Crime Prevention and Criminal Justice (2006) (collecting these materials), discussed in Roger S. Clark, The United Nations Crime Prevention and Criminal Justice Program: Formulation of Standards and Efforts at Their Implementation (1994).

Prisoners,[154] which modernized principles that had earlier been approved by the League of Nations. The Fifth Congress in 1975 produced the text of what became the General Assembly's Declaration on the Protection of All Persons from Being Subjected to Torture and other Cruel, Inhuman or Degrading Treatment or Punishment.[155] The 1985 Congress drafted the General Assembly's Declaration of Basic Principles of Justice for Victims of Crime and Abuse of Power.[156] In addition to insisting that victims were entitled to decent treatment in the criminal process, the Declaration spelled out obligations in respect of reparation and restitution. Later Congresses and the Commission on Crime Prevention and Criminal Justice have addressed the treatment of juveniles in the criminal justice system and, in recent years, the program has been addressing issues of reparative justice.

Many of the principles in these instruments, and even some of their exact language, have migrated into other parts of the United Nations system and into the work of tribunals and the ICC. The 1975 Declaration on Torture was the basis for the drafting of the 1984 Convention against Torture.[157] Some of the fundamental principles concerning victims in the 1985 Declaration on Victims can be found in treaties such as the United Nations Convention against Corruption,[158] the Statute of the Special Tribunal for Lebanon,[159] and the Rome Statute of the International Criminal Court.[160] These instruments make binding, within their aegis, the hortatory words of the Declaration. Human rights supervisory bodies, such as the Human Rights Committee, often use the detail of instruments like the Standard Minimum Rules for the Treatment of Prisoners to give concrete content to more general provisions in treaties like the International Covenant on Civil and Political Rights.[161]

---

[154] E.S.C. Res. 663 (XXIV)C, U.N. ESCOR, 24th Sess., Supp. (No. 1) at 11, U.N. Doc. E/3048 (1957) (as amended in 1977).

[155] G.A. Res. 3452 (XXX), U.N. GAOR, 30th Sess., Supp., No. 34, at 91, U.N. Doc. A/10034 (1976).

[156] G.A. Res. 40/34, U.N. GAOR, 40th Sess., Supp. No. 53, at 213, U.N. Doc A/40/53 (1986).

[157] § 15.02[B], *supra*.

[158] § 3.02, *supra*. Note, in particular Arts 32–35 of the United Nations Convention against Corruption, *available at* http://untreaty.un.org/English/notpubl/Corruption E.pdf.

[159] S.C. Res. 1757, discussed in § 16.08 *infra*.

[160] Rome Statute of the International Criminal Court, U.N. Doc. A/CONF.183/9 (1998), especially Art. 68, discussed in § 17.02[F], *infra*.

[161] ROGER S. CLARK, THE UNITED NATIONS CRIME PREVENTION AND CRIMINAL JUSTICE PROGRAM: FORMULATION OF STANDARDS AND EFFORTS AT THEIR IMPLEMENTATION 273–6 (1994).

Chapter 16
INTERNATIONAL TRIBUNALS

§ 16.01   GENERALLY

Throughout the years, international tribunals have allowed for the prosecution of conduct that requires international condemnation. Prior to the 1998 Rome Statute creating an International Criminal Court, there was no permanent international tribunal, so it was necessary to form special tribunals when countries wished to proceed with international criminal trials.

The two initial tribunals were the Nuremberg Tribunal, established to hear cases of war crimes emanating from Germany,[1] and the Toyko Tribunal, the tribunal for the Far East.[2] The work of both of these tribunals was done in the 1940s. It was not until 1993 that another international tribunal was created, the International Criminal Tribunal for the Former Yugoslavia (ICTY).[3] In 1994 the International Criminal Tribunal for Rwanda (ICTR) was created.[4] Both of these tribunals, formed by the Security Council under its powers for the maintenance of international peace and security, are funded out of the United Nations budget.

In some instances, special courts are created to handle crimes of an international magnitude. For example, the Special Court for Sierra Leone, established in 2002, results from a letter sent by President Alhaji Ahmad Tejan Kabbah of Sierra Leone to the United Nations. This letter served as the basis for an agreement "between the Government of Sierra Leone and the United Nations," with a purpose to try " 'those who bear greatest responsibility' for war crimes and crimes against humanity committed in Sierra Leone" after November 30, 1996.[5]

---

[1] *See* § 16.02, *infra.*

[2] *See* § 16.03, *infra.*

[3] *See* § 16.04, *infra.*

[4] *See* § 16.05, *infra.*

[5] Basic Facts, Special Court for Sierra Leone, *available at* http://www.sc-sl.org/basicfactspamphlet09.pdf.

Tribunals have not been without criticism. The International Criminal Tribunal for the Former Yugoslavia has been criticized for the slowness of the process and for its expense. Its annual budget of around $100,000,000 is greater than the budgets of a number of poorer member States of the United Nations and the combined cost of it and the ICTR represents a significant portion of the regular United Nations budget. Criticism has been levied against the International Criminal Tribunal of Rwanda for its "narrow" mandate. Numerous other criticisms have been expressed against using international tribunals, such as the propriety of having "a court whose mandate seems to override national sovereignty."[6] For many, that is exactly the point; if the organs of the State are unable to prevent international crimes, or are themselves deeply involved in the crimes, then the argument goes that sovereignty must give way. The remoteness of the physical location of the ICTY and the ICTR from the scene of the crimes with which they deal has lead to the criticism that they lack relevance to re-establishing peace and justice where the crimes occurred. Both tribunals have engaged in considerable efforts at "outreach" in order to offset this problem.

Some countries reject having a tribunal created by the Security Council. For example, until now East Timor (Timor-Leste) has rejected having a United Nations tribunal "to deal with Indonesia's failure to punish any military or police personnel over the carnage unleashed in the period surrounding the territory's 1999 vote for independence."[7] This position was taken despite the requests of various human rights groups.[8] But it remains uncertain as to whether a court will in fact eventually be established.[9] As will be seen,[10] another course was taken there but that may not be the end of the story.

Other countries seek alternatives to creating an international tribunal. For example, South Africa proceeded with a truth and reconciliation commission. The commission was established to "[i]nvestigate[ ] apartheid-era atrocities."[11] "Supporters of the commission believe that its structure encourages disclosure of the crimes and allows the public to assign blame to responsible individuals."[12] Sierra Leone has proceeded on the basis that *both* kinds of mechanism could be useful for transitional justice.[13]

§ 16.02 NUREMBERG TRIBUNAL

An agreement formed by the governments of the "United Kingdom of Great Britain and Northern Ireland, the Government of the United States of America, the Provisional Government of the French Republic, and the Government of the Union of Soviet Socialist Republics," served as the foundation for the formation of the first

---

[6] Criticism of Tribunals, War Crimes Tribunals, *available at* http://www.facts.com/icof/critic.htm.

[7] *East Timor Says No to UN Tribunal*, GLOBAL POLICY FORUM, *available at* http://www.globalpolicy.org/intljustice/tribunals/timor/2004/0809no.htm.

[8] *Id.*

[9] *See* M. Taufiqurrahman, *International Tribunal Could Try Rights Abusers: Jones*, THE JAKARTA POST/JAKARTA, Nov. 8, 2004, *available at* http://www.jsmp.minihub.org/News/04_11/08nov04_jp_internationaltribunal_eng.htm.

[10] § 16.09, *infra.*

[11] Truth and Reconciliation Commission, South Africa, Home Page, *available at* http://www.doj.gov.za/trc/.

[12] *Id.*

[13] § 16.06, *infra.*

international tribunal that would oversee the prosecutions of war crimes.[14] Nineteen other allied countries "expressed their adherence to the Agreement," including Australia, New Zealand, Greece, Denmark, India, and Poland.[15]

A Charter provided detailed functions of the court, stating that "[t]he Tribunal was invested with power to try and punish persons who had committed crimes against peace, war crimes, and crimes against humanity as defined in the Charter."[16] The Indictment lodged against the defendants accused them of "crimes against peace by the planning, preparation, initiation and waging of wars of aggression, which were also wars in violation of international treaties, agreements and assurances; with war crimes; and with crimes against humanity." Additionally, the charges included "participating in the formulation or execution of a common plan or conspiracy to commit all these crimes."[17]

Included in the arguments of the defense, especially with respect to the count for crimes against peace, were claims that there should be no punishment as there was no "pre-existing law."[18] In rejecting this position, the Tribunal stated, "[o]ccupying the positions they did in the government of Germany, the defendants, or at least some of them must have known of the treaties signed by Germany, outlawing recourse to war for the settlement of international disputes; they must have known that they were acting in defiance of all international law when in complete deliberation they carried out the designs of invasions and aggression."[19]

In assessing the illegality of the Nazi aggressions, the Tribunal relied heavily on the provisions of the Kellogg-Briand Pact, the General Treaty for the Renunciation of War.[20] The parties to that treaty (including Germany) had unequivocally renounced war as an instrument of policy. By its terms, it spoke to state responsibility. Yet the Tribunal had no hesitation in concluding that there was individual criminal responsibility for its breach. In a famous aphorism, it asserted that: "[c]rimes against international law are committed by men, not by abstract entities, and only by punishing individuals who commit such crimes can the provisions of international law be enforced."[21] In reality, in appropriate cases both the "abstract entity" that we call a "State" and the individual may be responsible for breaches of international law. There has been, however, no agreement to characterize the State's responsibility as "criminal." Indeed, the significant conceptual breakthrough in the Nuremberg analysis was the understanding that responsibility

---

[14] Judgment of the International Military Tribunal for the Trial of German Major War Criminals, *available at* http://www.yale.edu/lawweb/avalon/imt/proc/judcont.htm; *see also* THE NUREMBERG TRIAL AND INTERNATIONAL LAW (G. Ginsburgs & V.N. Kudriavtsev, eds., 1990); M. CHERIF BASSIOUNI, CRIMES AGAINST HUMANITY IN INTERNATIONAL LAW (2d ed. 1999); ROBERT K. WOETZEL, THE NUREMBERG TRIALS IN INTERNATIONAL LAW (2d ed. 1962).

[15] Judgment of the International Military Tribunal for the Trial of German Major War Criminals, 41 AM. J. INT'L L. 172, 172, also *available at* http://www.yale.edu/lawweb/avalon/imt/proc/judcont.htm.

[16] *Id.*

[17] *Id.* The Tribunal ultimately held that the (inchoate or preparatory) conspiracy count was good only in respect of the crime against peace. It was not a crime under the Charter or customary law to conspire to commit war crime or crime against peace. Those who were part of a group committing the crime could nonetheless be held liable on a complicity theory even if they were not the "principals." *Id.* at 221–24.

[18] This is the doctrine of "*nullum crimen sine lege, nulla poena sine lege*," that precludes *ex post facto* punishment as a violation of law. *Id.* at 217.

[19] *Id. See also* Herbert Wechsler, *The Issues of the Nuremberg Trial*, 62 POL. SCI. Q. 11 (1947).

[20] Aug. 27, 1928, 94 L.N.T.S. 57.

[21] 41 AM. J. INT'L L. at 221.

of the State did not preclude responsibility of the individual. This intellectual move is at the back of all the subsequent exercises in punishing international crimes outside the domestic judicial apparatus. The move was most dramatic at Nuremberg in respect to crimes against peace and crimes against humanity as they had never previously been the distinct subject of a criminal prosecution.

It is worth emphasizing that the Nuremberg analysis proceeds on the basis that the crimes in question existed under international law at all relevant times. The sources of the law[22] regarded as existing at the outbreak of war can be seen in several places. Essentially, the crime against peace emerged from the Kellogg-Briand Pact and thus may be seen as, at least in part, treaty-based. The treaty argument was bolstered by numerous discussions at the League of Nations and elsewhere that might be regarded as state practice contributing to customary law. The war crimes charges relied especially on the Fourth Hague Convention of 1907 and the Geneva Convention of 1929. Applying the Hague Convention was awkward because of its "general participation" clause which provided: "The provisions contained in the Regulations [respecting the Laws and Customs of War on Land] referred to in Article 1 as well as in the present Convention do not apply except between contracting powers, and then only if all the belligerents are parties to the Convention."[23] Several of the belligerents were not parties. The Tribunal, therefore, relied on customary law, as follows:

> The rules of land warfare expressed in the Convention undoubtedly represented an advance over existing international law at the time of their adoption. But the Convention expressly stated that it was an attempt "to revise the general laws and customs of war," which it thus recognized to be existing, but by 1939 these rules laid down in the Convention were recognized by all civilized nations, and were regarded as being declaratory of the laws and customs of war which are referred to in Article 6 (b) of the Charter.[24]

While the Tribunal was never as explicit about the source of crimes against humanity as it is in respect of the other two crimes, it must be the case that this crime rested firmly on general principles of law.[25]

What was being created after the event, then, was a tribunal to try individual cases for violations of international laws believed to have existed at the time the accused acted. The source of the power of the Allies to do this is delineated in these famous paragraphs:

> The making of the Charter was an exercise of the sovereign legislative power by the countries to which the German Reich unconditionally surrendered; and the undoubted right of these countries to legislate for the occupied territories has been recognized by the civilized world. The Charter is not an arbitrary exercise of power on the part of the victorious nations, but in the view of the Tribunal . . . it is the expression of international law existing at the time of its creation; and to that extent is itself a contribution to international law.

---

[22] *See* § 1.02, *supra* (discussing sources).

[23] Art. 2, Convention (No. IV) respecting the Laws and Customs of War on land (with Annex of Regulations), U.S.T.S. 539.

[24] 41 Am. J. Int'l L. at 248–9.

[25] Perhaps the clearest support for this comes from a comment during the drafting by Herbert Wechsler, cited in Roger S. Clark, *Crimes against Humanity at Nuremberg* in The Nuremberg Trial and International Law 177, 193 n. 65 (G. Ginsburgs & V.N. Kudriavtsev eds., 1990).

The Signatory Powers created this Tribunal, defined the law it was to administer, and made regulations for the proper conduct of the Trial. In doing so, they have done together what any one of them might have done singly; for it is not to be doubted that any nation has the right thus to set up special courts to administer law. With regard to the constitution of the court, all that the defendants are entitled to ask is to receive a fair trial on the facts and law.[26]

Twenty-two individuals were tried in proceedings conducted in four languages.[27] The judgment was delivered on September 30 and October 1, 1946. Ten of the twelve people sentenced to death were hanged, with one sentenced in absentia and one committing suicide. Three individuals received life sentences, four received sentences of ten to twenty years, and three were acquitted.[28] Additionally, certain groups were found to be criminal organizations, while others were found not to be criminal organizations.[29]

The judgment of the tribunal, in discussing the war crimes and crimes against humanity described the evidence as:

. . . overwhelming, in its volume and its detail. It is impossible for this Judgment adequately to review it, or to record the mass of documentary and oral evidence that has been presented. The truth remains that war crimes were committed on a vast scale, never before seen in the history of war.[30]

The judgment sets forth the evidence of "Murder and Ill-Treatment of Civilian Population," "Slave Labour Policy," and "Persecution of the Jews." The atrocities outlined in this document include the "gathering of Jews from all German occupied Europe in concentration camps," and extermination of Jews.[31] Some of these crimes were regarded as war crimes and some were regarded as crimes against humanity, since there was considerable overlap in the definitions of the two offenses. Essentially, though, what Germans did to Germans was punished under the rubric of crimes against humanity; what was done in the occupied territories was regarded as war crimes.[32]

While the International Military Tribunal at Nuremberg focused on the prosecution of high-level individuals, various allies and other countries proceeded with prosecutions against individual defendants who were participants and actors in

---

[26] 41 AM. J. INT'L L. at 216–7.

[27] English, Russian, French, and German.

[28] *See* http://motle.wiesenthal.com/test/x32/xr3207/html.

[29] "The Leadership Corps, the Gestapo, the SS and SD were declared (with the qualifications set out in the Judgment) to be criminal organizations. The SA, Reich Cabinet, and General Staff and High Command were acquitted." EDWARD M. WISE, ELLEN S. PODGOR & ROGER S. CLARK, INTERNATIONAL CRIMINAL LAW: CASES AND MATERIALS 638 (2d ed. 2004). The Soviet member of the tribunal dissented on the acquittal of three individuals, the sentence given to one person, and the failure of the tribunal to "declare criminal the following organisations: the Reichscabinet, General Staff and OKW." *See* Dissent Opinion, Judgment, *available at* http://www.yale.edu/lawweb/avalon/imt/proc/juddiss.htm.

[30] 41 AM J. INT'L L. at 224.

[31] The Judgment states, "Adolph Eichmann, who had been put in charge of this programme by Hitler, has estimated that the policy pursued resulted in the killing of 6,000,000 Jews, of which 4,000,000 were killed in the extermination institutions." *Id.* at 245.

[32] See analysis of Nuremberg Judgment in Roger S. Clark, *Crimes against Humanity at Nuremberg*, in THE NUREMBERG TRIAL AND INTERNATIONAL LAW, 177, 194–8 (G. Ginsburgs & V.N. Kudriatvsev eds., 1990).

these war crimes.[33] For example, Israel tried Adolph Eichmann, a World War II Nazi war criminal.[34] Germany itself ultimately held many trials.

The Judgment of the Tribunal served an important role in the drafting of later international documents, such as the "Genocide Convention, adopted by the United Nations on December 9, 1948," and the "the Human Rights Declaration of December 10, 1948."[35] The Nuremberg Principles issued by the International Law Commission in 1950 provided that individuals could be held liable for crimes in international law, irrespective of whether the conduct was a crime under internal law.[36] Heads of state could be held criminally culpable.[37] Additionally, individuals claiming to follow orders, "provided a moral choice was in fact possible to him," would not be relieved of criminal responsibility.[38] Individuals charged with crimes against peace, war crimes, and crimes against humanity[39] would be entitled to a "fair trial on the facts and law."[40] "Complicity in the commission of a crime against peace, a war crime, or crime against humanity" would also be a "crime under international law."[41]

§ 16.03 INTERNATIONAL MILITARY TRIBUNAL FOR THE FAR EAST

The tribunal established to handle war crimes in the Far East was the International Military Tribunal for the Far East (IMTFE), often referred to as the "Toyko Tribunal" or "Toyko War Crimes Tribunal." The Charter, originated under the command of General MacArthur, covered "crimes against peace," "conventional war crimes," and "crimes against humanity."[42] The trials were conducted in both

---

[33] Allied Control Council Law No. 10 also provided for the prosecution of German war criminals by the four major occupying countries. They and others, such as Canada and Italy, also carried out numerous trials through military commissions. EDWARD M. WISE, ELLEN S. PODGOR & ROGER S. CLARK, INTERNATIONAL CRIMINAL LAW: CASES AND MATERIALS 644 (2d ed. 2004); *see also* War Crimes Tribunals, *available at* http://www.facts.com/icof/nazi.htm.

[34] See Attorney General v. Eichmann, 36 I.L.R. 18 (Dist. Ct. Jerusalem 1961), aff'd, 36 I.L.R. 277 (Sup. Ct. Israel 1962); *see also* HANNAH ARENDT, EICHMANN IN JERUSALEM: A REPORT ON THE BANALITY OF EVIL (1964). *See also* § 12.06[B], *supra.*

[35] Museum of Tolerance Multimedia Learning Center, *available at* http://motle.wiesenthal.com/text/x32/xr3207.html.

[36] Principle II, Report of the International Law Commission, 5 U.N. GAOR, Supp. No. 12 (A/1316), at 11-14 (1950) (cited in EDWARD M. WISE, ELLEN S. PODGOR & ROGER S. CLARK, INTERNATIONAL CRIMINAL LAW: CASES AND MATERIALS 640 (2d ed. 2004)).

[37] *Id.* at Principle III.

[38] *Id.* at Principle IV.

[39] *Id.* at Principle VI.

[40] *Id.* at Principle V.

[41] *Id.* at Principle VII.

[42] *See* Charter of the International Military Tribunal for the Far East, Art. 5, *available at* http://www.yale.edu/lawweb/avalon/imtfech.htm; *see also* Roger S. Clark, *Nuremberg and Toyko in Contempory Perspective, in* THE LAW OF WAR CRIMES (T.L.H. McCormack & G.J. Simpson eds., 1997); R. John Pritchard, *The International Military Tribunal for the Far East and the Allied National War Crimes Trials in Asia, in* 3 INTERNATIONAL CRIMINAL LAW 109, 127–31 (M. Cherif Bassiouni ed., 1999); THE TOKYO WAR CRIMES TRIAL: THE COMPLETE TRANSCRIPTS OF THE PROCEEDINGS OF THE INTERNATIONAL MILITARY TRIBUNAL FOR THE FAR EAST (R. John Pritchard ed., with Sonia Maganua Zaide, 22 vols., 1981).

English and the language of the accused,[43] had rules of procedure[44] and the Charter assured the accused a fair trial.[45]

Eleven countries composed the tribunal, and there were eleven judges drawn from the Allies who had fought Japan in the Far East.[46] It was a slow process, starting on May 3, 1946 and ending April 16, 1948. The judgment, issued in November of 1948, found all twenty-five defendants guilty and sentenced seven to death.[47] This time, there was considerable dissent among the judges. Justice Pal of India thought the whole proceedings were *ex post facto* and totally illegitimate. General MacArthur refused to publish Pal's lengthy dissent and he published it himself some years later. Justices Bernard of France and Roling of the Netherlands also dissented on several points. The death penalty not being acceptable to the judges from Australia and the USSR, at least one of the decisions to execute had the support of only six judges.

The Tokyo Trial was significant conceptually in analyzing the criminal responsibility of military and civilian leaders for crimes committed by their subordinates. This issue later assumed some significance in the negotiations for the International Criminal Court.[48] The Tribunal came down firmly for a "reasonable official" standard:

[Members of the Government and other officials] are not responsible if a proper system and its continuous efficient functioning be provided for and conventional war crimes be committed unless:

(1) They had knowledge that such crimes were being committed, and having such knowledge, they failed to take such steps as were within their power to prevent the commission of such crimes in the future, or

(2) They are at fault in having failed to acquire such knowledge.[49]

Other individuals were prosecuted through the national military courts of many of the Allies, including Australia and The Netherlands. Some of the cases preceded the Tokyo trial. For example, in *Application of Yamashita*,[50] the Supreme Court permitted the "Commanding General of the Fourteenth Army Group of the Imperial Japanese Army" to be tried by an American military commission for charges of "violation of the law of war."[51]

---

[43] Japanese and English were the two languages used.

[44] *See* Rules of Procedure of the International Military Tribunal for the Far East, April 25, 1946, *available at* http://www.yale.edu/lawweb/avalon/imtferul.htm.

[45] Charter of the International Military Tribunal for the Far East, Art. 9, *available at* http://www.yale.edu/lawweb/avalon/imtfech.htm.

[46] *See* EDWARD M. WISE, ELLEN S. PODGOR & ROGER S. CLARK, INTERNATIONAL CRIMINAL LAW: CASES AND MATERIALS 642 (2d ed. 2004).

[47] *Id.* at 643.

[48] *See* § 17.02[C] *infra*.

[49] 2 THE TOKYO JUDGMENT 30 (B. Roling & C. Ruter eds., 1977).

[50] 327 U.S. 1 (1946).

[51] *Id.* at 25. This case, which occasioned sharp dissents from Justices Murphy and Rutledge, is an important contribution to the doctrine of command responsibility, a matter that, however, received more careful analysis by the IMTFE.

§ 16.04 AD HOC TRIBUNAL FOR THE FORMER YUGOSLAVIA

The International Criminal Tribunal for the Former Yugoslavia (ICTY) was created on May 25, 1993, when the United Nations Security Council adopted Resolution 827. It was the first tribunal established since Nuremberg and the International Military Tribunal for the Far East (Toyko Trial). It focused initially on "atrocities in the early years of the Bosnian civil war."[52] Its jurisdiction is, however, ongoing until the Security Council terminates it, and there were later indictments in respect to events in Kosovo between January 1 and June 20, 1999.[53] In fact, the Prosecutor also faced the question whether NATO forces had been guilty of war crimes in their bombing aimed at protecting the Kosovo Albanians.[54] He declined to prosecute NATO military on the merits, while accepting that there was potential jurisdiction. The ICTY, located in The Netherlands, at The Hague, has a mission "to bring to justice persons allegedly responsible for serious violations of international humanitarian law, to render justice to the victims, to deter further crimes, and to contribute to the restoration of peace by promoting reconciliation in the former Yugoslavia."[55] "Humanitarian law" was once a term that applied solely to the laws of armed conflict. As used by the Security Council in the Statutes of the ICTY and the Tribunal for Rwanda (ICTR), the term now encompasses, as well as the laws of armed conflict, genocide and crimes against humanity.

The jurisdiction of the Tribunal is concurrent with that of the courts of Former Yugoslavia. The Tribunal, however, can "formally" insist on asserting its primacy.[56] In this respect it is in a stronger position over national courts than the "complementarity" regime that applies to the International Criminal Court.[57]

Prosecutors, who are independent of the Security Council, bring indictments based upon their own information or information provided to them by outside sources such as governments and international organizations. It is necessary, however, for a prosecutor to receive judicial confirmation prior to bringing the indictment.[58] There is a Trial Chamber that hears the case, judges the facts and law, and issues sentences. An Appeals Chamber, shared with the Tribunal for Rwanda, takes up the appellate matters. Not all of the judges are permanent members of the court, but those who are have the added responsibility to "draft and adopt the legal instruments regulating the functioning of the ICTY, such as the

---

[52] War Crimes Tribunal, *available at* http://www.facts.com/icof/tribun.htm.

[53] *See* Prosecutor v. Milosevic et al, Second Amended Indictment, Case No. IT-99-37-PT.

[54] Final Report to the Prosecutor by the Committee Established to Review the NATO Bombing Campaign Against the Federal Republic of Yugoslavia, *available at* www.un.org.icty/pressreal/nato061300.htm. *See* Paolo Benvenuti, *The ICTY Prosecutor and the Review of the NATO Bombing Campaign against the Federal Republic of Yugoslavia*, 12 Europ. J. Int'l L. 503 (2001) (providing a critical review of this document).

[55] The ITCY at a Glance, General Information, *available at* http://www.un.org/icty/glance-e/index.htm.

[56] Statute of the International Tribunal, Art. 9 (2).

[57] § 17.02[B], *infra*.

[58] *See* Fact Sheet on ICTY Proceedings, *available at* http://www.un.org/icty/cases-e/factsheets/generalinfo-e.htm.

Rules of Procedure and Evidence."[59] Finally, there is a Registry that performs the function of the "administration and judicial support services of the Tribunal."[60]

Neither the Tribunal nor its parent, the United Nations, could be expected to have its own prisons to house people undergoing long sentences. Prisoners waiting trial and appeal are housed in space provided by The Netherlands. Agreements have been reached with a number of States to take convicted prisoners and place them within their own prison systems.[61] In addition, a few countries have made their "witness relocation" programs available for witnesses who would be in grave danger if they returned home after giving testimony in The Hague. Indeed, significant attention has been made to attending to the needs of witness and victims in an effort to ensure that they do not suffer from "secondary victimization." The experience with the ICTY led to even more concentration on this issue in Rome Statute and in the practice of the ICC.[62]

The ICTY had its first indictment in 1994, and its first trial ended in 1997. Apprehending the accused was a slow business in the early years, but it gradually picked up. Many others have been indicted, are awaiting trial, have been convicted, or have been transferred to serve a sentence.[63] Those indicted include Slobodan Milosevic, who served as President of the Federal Republic of Yugoslavia, Radovan Karadzic, political leader of the Bosnia Serbs and Ratko Mladic, Chief of Staff of the Bosnia Serb military.[64] A big disappointment for many was the death of Milosevic before his lengthy trial could be completed. In a report to the Security Council on Human Rights Day, December 10, 2007, the President of the Tribunal referred to what he regarded as the Tribunal's "unparalleled efficiency":

> Out of the 161 accused indicted by the International Tribunal, trial and appeal proceedings against 111 accused have been completed. Of the 50 accused whose cases remain to be completed, four remain at large, eight accused have pending appeals, 27 have commenced trial and 11 are currently in the pre-trial stage. Two contempt proceedings have also been initiated. The dramatic increase shown in these figures, particularly in the last years, clearly surpasses any reasonable expectation.[65]

Karadzic and Mladic have been fugitives since they were indicted in 2005 and their capture and trial remains the Tribunal's most significant unfinished business. They face charges of genocide, crimes against humanity and war crimes. Most of the defendants have been Serbian, but there have been Bosnian and Croatian accused also. A news report in March 2008 records the opening of the trial of Croatian General, Ante Govina, and two of his colleagues concerning their actions during the "three day blitz that drove the Serbs out of Croatia."[66] The report adds

---

[59] *Id.*

[60] *Id.*

[61] As of March 2008, 14 States had so agreed. *See* http://www.un.org/icty/legaldoc-e/index.htm.

[62] *See* § 17.02[F].

[63] War Crimes Tribunal, *available at* http://www.facts.com/icof/tribun.htm.

[64] Key Figures of ICTY Cases, http://www.un.org/icty/cases-e/factsheets/procfact-e.htm.

[65] Statement by Judge Fausto Pocar, President, International Criminal Tribunal for the Former Yugoslavia to the Security Council 10 December 2007, *available at* http://www.un.org/icty/pressreal/2007/pr1203e-pres.htm.

[66] THE GUARDIAN, March 12, 2008, at 20.

that "[t]he former president [of Croatia], Franjo Tudjman, his defence minister, Gojko Susak, and two other senior officers would have been in the dock too had they not died."[67]

The ITCY's jurisdiction covers crimes "committed on the territory of the former Yugoslavia since 1991."[68] Four crimes are subject to prosecution. These are grave breaches of the 1949 Geneva Conventions, violations of the laws or customs of war, genocide, and crimes against humanity.[69] Individuals, as opposed to organizations or legal bodies, are subject to prosecution by the Court. In the early case of *Prosecutor v. Tadic*,[70] the accused was charged with "grave breaches" of the Geneva Conventions and "violations of the laws and customs of war," for alleged crimes of "murder, torture, and sexual violence committed against Muslims and Croats in northwestern Bosnia during the summer of 1992."[71] The court's jurisdiction was questioned in an appeal that claimed that the ICTY was not established lawfully, that its claim of primacy over "competent domestic courts" was improper, and that it "lack[ed] subject-matter jurisdiction."[72] In a lengthy opinion, the appeals chamber met each of these arguments and demonstrated the Court's jurisdiction. Tadic faced trial on thirty-one counts and was convicted of eleven counts.[73] After appeals he received a maximum sentence of twenty years and was transferred to Germany to serve this sentence.[74]

The ICTY credits itself with "five core achievements." First is "spearheading the shift from impunity to accountability." For example, it notes that prosecutions of individuals provides "their removal from office permanently if found guilty." Second the ICTY notes that it has accomplished "establishing the facts." By this the Court notes that the trials have provided transparency to what occurred in Yugoslavia and disputed accounts of events are being resolved. Third is "bringing justice to thousands of victims and giving them a voice." The fourth achievement generally states "the accomplishments in international law" and then specifies accomplishments such as how the tribunal in its ten year existence has set significant precedents that will be useful in the future. Finally, the fifth achievement is its "strengthening the rule of law." In this regard, one achievement of the Court is that "ICTY Judges and staff have extensively shared their expertise with those involved in the development of other international courts, such as the ICC and the Special Court for Sierra Leone."[75]

Prompted, in part, by prosecution fatigue in the Security Council, the Tribunal is looking forward to a "completion strategy" aimed at having all the trials

---

[67] *Id.*

[68] Statute of the International Tribunal, Art. 1, approved by S.C. Res. 827 (1993).

[69] *Id.*

[70] ICTY, Case No. IT-94-1-AR72 Appeals Chamber, Decision on the Defense Motion for Interlocutory Appeal on Jurisdiction (Oct. 2, 1995).

[71] EDWARD M. WISE, ELLEN S. PODGOR & ROGER S. CLARK, INTERNATIONAL CRIMINAL LAW: CASES AND MATERIALS 678 (2d ed. 2004).

[72] *Id.*

[73] Prosecutor v. Tadic, Opinion and Judgment, Case No. IT-94-1-T (May 7, 1997).

[74] *See* EDWARD M. WISE, ELLEN S. PODGOR & ROGER S. CLARK, INTERNATIONAL CRIMINAL LAW: CASES AND MATERIALS 678 (2d ed. 2004).

[75] Bringing Justice to the Former Yugoslavia, the Tribunal's Five Core Achievements, *available at* http://www.un.org/icty/cases-e/factsheets/achieve-e.htm.

completed by the end of 2009 and the appeals by 2011.[76] The President of the Tribunal has reiterated that a significant part of the completion strategy has been to share know-how with domestic courts. Rule 11*bis* of the Court's Rules permits the referral of cases to competent national jurisdictions. President Pocar noted that "[t]en accused have been transferred to the Special War Crimes Chamber of Bosnia and Herzegovina, two accused have been transferred to the authorities of Croatia and one accused has been transferred to Serbia."[77]

§ 16.05   AD HOC TRIBUNAL FOR RWANDA

The International Criminal Tribunal for Rwanda (ICTR) was created on November 8, 1994 when the United Nations Security Council adopted Resolution 955. Located in Arusha, United Republic of Tanzania, the tribunal "was established for the prosecution of persons responsible for genocide and other serious violations of international humanitarian law committed in the territory of Rwanda between" January 1, 1994 and December 31, 1994.[78] It will be noted that, unlike the Tribunal for Yugoslavia, whose temporal jurisdiction has been continuing, the Rwanda Tribunal was afforded competence only over the horrendous events that occurred during this single year. Like the ICTY,[79] the ICTR can assert its primacy over domestic tribunals with which it has concurrent jurisdiction.[80]

The jurisdiction of the court comprises the crimes of genocide, crimes against humanity and violations of Article 3 common to the Geneva Conventions and of Additional Protocol II thereto, as "committed by Rwandans in the territory of Rwanda and in the territory of neighboring States, as well as non-Rwandan citizens for crimes committed in Rwanda."[81] As with the ICTY, the ICTR is structured with a trial chambers, appeals chamber, office of the prosecutor and a registry.

Under the "authority of the Registrar" is a "Witnesses and Victims Support Section," that serves both prosecution and defense witnesses. It is "responsible for protecting the privacy and ensuring the security and safety of all witnesses called by both the Defence and the Prosecution."[82] Also under the authority of the Registry is the "Defence Counsel and Detention Management Section." The "Defence Counsel" aspect is to make certain that there is appropriate indigent

---

[76] Statement by Judge Fausto Pocar, President, International Criminal Tribunal for the Former Yugoslavia to the Security Council 10 December 2007, *available at* http://www.un.org/icty/pressreal/2007/pr1203e-pres.htm.

[77] *Id.* The Special War Crimes Chambers in Bosnia and Herzegovina, part of the State court system, have been "internationalized" with both international judges and prosecutors. The internationals are being phased out. *See generally, International Spotlight: War Crimes Chamber of Bosnia and Herzegovina,* Int'l Jud. Monitor, *available at* http://www.judicialmonitor.org/archive0707/spotlight.html.

[78] International Criminal Tribunal for Rwanda, General Information, *available at* http://www.ictr.org/ENGLISH/geninfo/index.htm. "In the three months between April 7 and July 17, 1994, over a half million and perhaps closer to a million Rwandans were killed by their neighbors. Most of the killers were members of the majority Hutu ethnic group; most of the victims were minority Tutsi." Edward M. Wise, Ellen S. Podgor & Roger S. Clark, International Criminal Law: Cases and Materials 702 (2d ed. 2004).

[79] *See* § 16.04, *supra.*

[80] Statute of the International Criminal Tribunal for Rwanda, Art. 8 (2).

[81] International Criminal Tribunal for Rwanda, General Information, *available at* http://www.ictr.org/ENGLISH/geninfo/index.htm.

[82] *Id.*

defense counsel for those accused of crimes. All of the defendants before both *Ad Hoc* Tribunals have been granted legal aid, although there are suspicions that some have looted assets hidden somewhere. The Detention Management Section provides a "United Nations Detention Facility (UNDF) with 56 purpose built cells within the Arusha prison complex."[83]

When the Nuremberg Trial took place, it was taken for granted that capital punishment would be a sentencing option. This question was not so open and shut at Tokyo.[84] By the time of the creation of the ICTY, a sea change had taken place on the issue, especially among European States. The United Kingdom and France made it clear in the Security Council that the death penalty was an unacceptable option. The debate was a hotter one when the ICTR was being established. Rwanda, which had asked the Security Council to act, lost its enthusiasm when it realized that the major violators might well be tried at the Tribunal and subject to imprisonment, while lesser actors could be subject to the death penalty under domestic law. The logic that Rwanda should solve the problem by becoming abolitionist did not immediately carry the day and there were some domestic executions before Rwanda finally abolished the death penalty in 2007. There is clearly an emerging norm of customary international law forbidding the death penalty.[85] Undecided perhaps is whether this is a norm that applies universally in all cases, or only in all but the most egregious ones.[86]

The first indictment came on November 28, 1995, and this case has been followed by the prosecution of other cases. Cases have been resolved with both trials and appeals. Perhaps the most noted prosecution is that of "Jean Kambanda, the Prime Minister of the Rwandan Government during the genocide, who was the first head of Government to be indicted and subsequently convicted for genocide."[87] Kambanda's guilty plea and sentence to life imprisonment were followed by the conviction of several prominent members of the governmental and business communities for genocide and crimes against humanity, including the Ministers of Finance and Transport. Numerous local government officials and some journalists, youth leaders, priests and pastors were also convicted.[88]

The case of *Prosecutor v. Akayesu*[89] was the first international prosecution for the crime of genocide. The indictment charged a "total of 15 counts covering genocide, crimes against humanity and violations of Article 3 Common to the 1949 Geneva Conventions and Additional Protocol II of 1977."[90] Many issues were raised regarding this indictment, including arguments against the jurisdiction of the

---

[83] *Id; see also* International Criminal Tribunal for Rwanda, Detention of Suspects and Imprisonment of Convicted Persons, The Detention Facility, *available at* http://www.ictr.org/ENGLISH/factsheets/7.htm.

[84] *See* § 16.03, *supra.*

[85] *See generally* § 15.03, *supra.*

[86] *See generally* Jens David Ohlin, *Applying the Death Penalty to Crimes of Genocide*, 99 Am. J. Int'l L. 747 (2005).

[87] International Criminal Tribunal for Rwanda, General Information, *available at* http://www.ictr.org/ENGLISH/geninfo/index.htm.

[88] There is a discussion of the Tribunal's jurisprudence and a useful table of trials in George William Mugwanya, The Crime of Genocide in International Law: Appraising the Contribution of the U.N. Tribunal for Rwanda (2007).

[89] International Criminal Tribunal for Rwanda, Case No. ICTR-96-4-T, Trial Chamber I, Judgement (Sept. 2, 1998).

[90] *Id.* at 1.4.

Court. For example, the court was faced with the issue of whether there was a violation of double jeopardy or the *non bis in idem*[91] principle, as the Indictment charged several crimes for the same set of facts.[92] The Court looked to cases from the ICTY to resolve this issue and held:

> that it is acceptable to convict the accused of two offences in relation to the same set of facts in the following circumstances: (1) where the offences have different elements; or (2) where the provisions creating the offences protect different interests; or (3) where it is necessary to record a conviction for both offences in order fully to describe what the accused did. However, the Chamber finds that it is not justifiable to convict an accused of two offences in relation to the same set of facts where (a) one offence is a lesser included offence of the other, for example, murder and grievous bodily harm, robbery and theft, or rape and indecent assault; or (b) where one offence charges accomplice liability and the other offence charges liability as a principal, e.g. genocide and complicity in genocide.[93]

The court also examined the Tribunal's power to prosecute individuals for the crime of genocide, as Akayesu was charged with genocide, complicity in genocide, and incitement to commit genocide.[94] Akayesu was found guilty of two counts of genocide and incitement to commit genocide, but was found not guilty of complicity to commit genocide, "on the ground that the same person cannot be both a principal and an accomplice to the same offense."[95] Additionally he was found guilty of seven counts of crimes against humanity and in 1998 he received a sentence of life imprisonment.[96]

Like the Tribunal for Former Yugoslavia, the Rwanda Tribunal has negotiated agreements for convicted persons to serve their sentences in various places other than the seat of the Tribunal.[97] A number of those convicted have been serving their sentences in Mali. Early in 2008, an agreement was reached with Rwanda itself so that prison terms could be served in Rwanda. Noting that similar agreements had already been entered into with Mali, Benin, Swaziland, France, Italy, and Sweden, the Registrar of the ICTR said that "Rwanda had made significant progress in ensuring that it meets the necessary standard of prisons to accommodate ICTR convicts."[98]

Also like the ICTY, the ICTR has adopted a completion strategy.[99] It hopes to complete its trial work by the end of 2008. With the abolition of the death penalty in Rwanda and the adoption there of new laws guaranteeing a fair trial, some cases may be referred to the Rwandan courts. Other efforts have been made to transfer

---

[91] *See* § 1.03[F].

[92] International Criminal Tribunal for Rwanda, Case No. ICTR-96-4-T, Trial Chamber I, Judgment (Sept. 2, 1998) at 6.1

[93] *Id.* 6.1, ¶ 468.

[94] *Id.* 6.3.1, ¶ 493.

[95] Edward M. Wise, Ellen S. Podgor & Roger S. Clark, International Criminal Law: Cases and Materials 701 (2d ed. 2004).

[96] *Id.*

[97] *See* http://69.94.11.53/ENGLISH/agreements/index.htm.

[98] War Crimes Prosecution Watch, Vol. 3, Issue 15 (March 17, 2008), at 52.

[99] *See* ICTR website, *available at* http://69.94.11.53/default.htm.

some cases to other African or European countries where the courts may presumably be able to operate on the basis of universal jurisdiction.[100]

The sheer size of the Rwandan genocide forced attention to an important aspect of international justice: there is no way that international courts can handle a large volume of defendants. They are not engines for a giant jail delivery; at best, they can deal with (some of) those "most responsible." Following the genocide, there were about 130,000 people in custody in Rwanda, and hundreds of thousands of others had contributed to the slaughter. Most of the lawyers had been killed or had fled. In these circumstances, choices had to be made. A decision was made to have domestic court trials for the "most serious." By 2005 William Schabas was able to report that 10,000 had been tried in what must have been fairly rough and ready procedures, with some international assistance.[101] For the rest, justice was left to a resurrected form of traditional justice called *gacaca*. Schabas comments that although *gacaca* "defers significantly to traditional models, it is really nothing more than a very decentralized system of justice administered by non-professionals at the local level."[102] History will no doubt have a verdict on how successful this experiment has been. Its main claim to success will surely be that its local roots give it more legitimacy than the distant trials in Arusha,[103] and it has moved far more cases along.[104]

§ 16.06 SPECIAL COURT FOR SIERRA LEONE

The Sierra Leone Special Court (SCSL) is perhaps the most successful example of what are usually referred to as "hybrid" courts.[105] While the Court was created pursuant to an agreement between Sierra Leone and the United Nations, its expenses have not been charged to the United Nations budget. Instead, it has relied on voluntary contributions from various States — not always a happy experience as the check was not always in the mail. Its judges are a mixture of Sierra Leone judges and judges appointed by the Secretary-General of the United Nations. The latter form a majority of both the Trial and Appeals Chambers. As is typical of the hybrids, the Special Court has jurisdiction over both international crimes and "ordinary" crimes under national law.[106] There is jurisdiction over crimes against humanity; violations of Article 3 common to the Geneva Conventions and of Additional Protocol II; over a short closed list of what are described as "other

---

[100] For a number of different perspectives on the ICTR, see Special Issue on Genocide in Rwanda, 3 (4) J. Int'l Crim. Just. (September 2005).

[101] William A. Schabas, *Genocide Trials and* Gacaca *Courts*, 3 J. Int'l Crim. Just. 879, 888 (2005).

[102] *Id.* at 895.

[103] *See* Ashley Clark, A Bitter Pill: Comparison of Transitional Justice Apparatuses in Rwanda and Sierra Leone 96 (unpublished Honors Thesis, Middlebury College, 2007).

[104] It had dealt with 58,000 of those in custody by 2006. *Id.* at 104.

[105] *See generally* New Approaches in International Criminal Justice: Kosovo, East Timor, Sierra Leone and Cambodia (Kai Ambos & Mohamed Othman eds., 2003); Internationalized Criminal Courts: Sierra Leone, East Timor, Kosovo, and Cambodia (Cesare R. Romano, André Nollkaemper & Jann K. Kleffner eds., 2004).

[106] The idea was not entirely new. At one point in the negotiations on the Nuremberg Charter, it was contemplated that the Tribunal would have jurisdiction over crimes defined in the law of the various countries where the depredations occurred. *See* Roger S. Clark, *Crimes against Humanity at Nuremberg, in* The Nuremberg Trial and International Law 177, 182 (G. Ginsburgs & V.N. Kudriavtsev eds., 1990).

serious violations of international humanitarian law;" and over a group of crimes under Sierra Leone law. The "serious violations" are:

a.   Intentionally directing attacks against the civilian population as such or against individual civilians not taking direct part in hostilities;

b.   Intentionally directing attacks against personnel, installations, material, units or vehicles involved in a humanitarian assistance or peacekeeping mission in accordance with the Charter of the United Nations, as long as they are entitled to the protection given to civilians or civilian objects under the international law of armed conflict;

c.   Conscripting or enlisting children under the age of 15 years into armed forces or groups or using them to participate actively in hostilities.[107]

The Sierra Leonean crimes are:

a.   Offences relating to the abuse of girls under the Prevention of Cruelty to Children Act, 1926 (Cap. 31):

i.   Abusing a girl under 13 years of age, contrary to section 6;

ii.   Abusing a girl between 13 and 14 years of age, contrary to section 7;

iii.   Abduction of a girl for immoral purposes, contrary to section 12.

b.   Offences relating to the wanton destruction of property under the Malicious Damage Act, 1861:

i.   Setting fire to dwelling — houses, any person being therein, contrary to section 2;

ii.   Setting fire to public buildings, contrary to sections 5 and 6;

iii.   Setting fire to other buildings, contrary to section 6.

In furtherance of its mandate to try "those who bear greatest responsibility,"[108] the prosecution issued 13 indictments, which were confirmed by a justice of the Special Court. Eleven of those indicted were apprehended and transferred to the Court's custody. Two of them, Foday Sankoh and Hinga Norman, died of natural causes in detention; one was killed in Liberia before arrest; and one has not been apprehended. Nine persons thus came to trial.[109] Each of the trials took place in Sierra Leone, except for that of the former Liberian President, Charles Taylor, whose trial was moved, for reasons of security, to premises rented from the International Criminal Court in The Hague. It was hoped that holding the trials in the land where the atrocities occurred would ensure local "ownership" of the process in ways that many commentators have felt was not the case for the Rwanda Tribunal (held in Arusha in neighboring Tanzania) and the Yugoslav Tribunal, which sits at The Hague.

The Special Court was the first international court to charge and try persons for the recruitment of child soldiers as a violation of the laws of armed conflict. In *Prosecutor v. Hinga*, the Appeals Chamber ruled by a majority that the recruit-

---

[107] Art. 4, Statute of the Special Court for Sierra Leone, *available at* http://www.sc-sl.org/ Documents/scsl-statute.html.

[108] § 16.01, *supra.*

[109] Report of Prosecutor, Stephen Rapp, to Security Council June 8, 2007, U.N. Doc. S/PV.5690 at 4 (2007).

ment of child soldiers had crystallized as a crime under customary international law prior to November 1996, the period covered by the Special Court's mandate.[110]

The other side of the child soldier issue, whether to prosecute the children themselves for the awful acts in which they engaged, came to the fore when the Statute of the Special Court was being negotiated. The Rome Statute of the International Criminal Court[111] has a "jurisdictional" solution to the issue. There is no jurisdiction over what a person did below the age of 18. This could be interpreted as an understanding that young persons should not come before international tribunals, or as a pragmatic decision in the particular instance. Some argued strongly that it had little implication for what should be done in Sierra Leone, given the hybrid status of what was contemplated.[112] The result was that the Statute provided that the Special Court has no jurisdiction over any person who was under the age of 15 at the time of the alleged commission of the crime. In the disposition of a case against a juvenile offender between the ages of 15 and 18, the Special Court was instructed to order any of the following: care guidance and supervision orders, community service orders, counseling, foster care, correctional, educational and vocational training programs, approved schools and, as appropriate, any programs of disarmament, demobilization and reintegration or programs of child protection agencies.[113] Ultimately, the Prosecutor decided not to use his resources on child soldiers and to concentrate on older persons.

The decision of the Appeals Chamber holding that former President Taylor is not entitled to immunity, in what the Chamber held to be an international court, is a major contribution to the developing case-law on this significant issue.[114] Indeed, the prosecution's theory against Taylor should be a warning to authoritarian leaders who become engaged in strife in neighboring countries. He is charged with various counts of war crimes (notably by terrorizing the civilian population), murder as a crime against humanity or alternatively as a violation of Common Article 3 or Protocol II, sexual violence, sexual slavery and physical violence, enlisting and use of child soldiers under the age of fifteen, abductions, forced labor and looting. In respect of his individual responsibility, the prosecution argues that the crimes committed were ones which the accused "planned, instigated, ordered, committed or in whose planning, preparation or execution, the ACCUSED otherwise aided and abetted, or which crimes were involved within a common plan, design or purpose in which the ACCUSED participated, or were a reasonably foreseeable consequence of such a common plan, design or purpose." The prosecution also has a command responsibility theory.[115] The United Kingdom has solved the difficult problem of

---

[110] Prosecutor v. Hinga, Case No. SCSL-2003-14-AR72(E), Decision on Preliminary Motion based on Lack of Jurisdiction (Child Recruitment), May 21, 2004. Justice Geoffrey Robertson wrote a forceful dissent arguing that he was "in no doubt that the crime of non-forcible enlistment did not enter international criminal law until the Rome Treaty in July 1998."

[111] Rome Statute of the International Criminal Court, Art. 26.

[112] *See* Ilene Cohen, *The Protection of Children and the Quest for Truth and Justice in Sierra Leone*, 55 (1) J. INT'L AFF 1, 5–7 (2001).

[113] Statute of the Special Court for Sierra Leone, Art. 7.

[114] *See* Prosecutor v. Taylor, Special Court for Sierra Leone, Appeals Chamber, Decision of May 31, 2004, Case No. SCSL-2003-01-I.

[115] Special Court for Sierra Leone, Office of the Prosecutor, Second Amended Indictment, May 29, 2007, Case No. SWCSL-03-01-PT, Prosecutor v. Charles Taylor.

what to do with Taylor if he is convicted. It has agreed with the Special Court that, if convicted, he will serve his sentence in a British prison at British expense.[116]

The Special Court has been complemented in its efforts at transitional justice by a Truth and Reconciliation Commission that acted in parallel but completed its task much more quickly.[117] In creating the Commission, the relevant Sierra Leone legislation stated that the function of the Commission was to create an impartial historical record of violations and abuses of human rights and international humanitarian law related to the armed conflict in Sierra Leone, from the beginning of the conflict in 1991 to the signing of the Lomé Peace Agreement in July 1999; to address impunity, to respond to the needs of victims, to promote healing and reconciliation and to prevent a repetition of the violations and abuses suffered.[118] A "Memorandum of Objects and Reasons" attached to the Bill suggested, eloquently, that "the Peace Agreement envisaged the proceedings of the Commission as a catharsis for constructive interchange between the victims and perpetrators of human rights violations and abuses and from this catharsis the Commission is to compile 'a clear picture of the past.' " It might be added, that these are the same fundamental objectives that are stated in support of holding trials. A Truth and Reconciliation Commission can always allow far more people to "tell their story" than is necessarily the case with a trial process.

§ 16.07   EXTRAORDINARY CHAMBERS IN THE COURTS OF CAMBODIA

During the period 1975 to 1979, the Khmer Rouge regime in Cambodia was responsible for the deaths of somewhere between one and three million people, about a fifth of the total population. Various negotiations to bring some of those responsible to justice failed until 2003.[119] That year, the current Cambodian authorities and the United Nations reached agreement on trials for surviving senior leaders of the time and those who were most responsible for the crimes and serious violations of Cambodian penal law, international humanitarian law and custom, and international conventions recognized by Cambodia that were committed during the period of April 17, 1975 to January 6, 1979.[120] The mechanism that was established is known as the Extraordinary Chambers in the Courts of Cambodia for the Prosecution of Crimes Committed During the Period of Democratic Kampuchea. It

---

[116] Agreement between the Government of the United Kingdom of Great Britain and Northern Ireland and the Special Court for Sierra Leone on the Enforcement of Sentences of the Special Court for Sierra Leone, July 10, 2007, *available at* http://www.official-documents.gov.uk/document/cm72/7208/7208.pdf.

[117] *See* THE FINAL REPORT OF THE TRUTH AND RECONCILIATION COMMISSION OF SIERRA LEONE (2004), *available at* http://www.trcsierraleone.org/drwebsite/publish/index.shtml, William A. Schabas, *Internationalized Courts and their Relationship with Alternative Accountability Mechanisms: The Case of Sierra Leone*, in INTERNATIONALIZED CRIMINAL COURTS: SIERRA LEONE, EAST TIMOR, KOSOVO AND CAMBODIA 157 (Cesare P. Romano, André Nollkaemper & Jann K. Kleffner eds. (2004)).

[118] The Truth and Reconciliation Commission Act 2000 (Sierra Leone), § 6.

[119] On the national and international difficulties in bringing the guilty to account, notwithstanding the horrific nature of the crimes, see STEVEN R. RATNER & JASON S. ABRAMS, ACCOUNTABILITY FOR HUMAN RIGHTS ATROCITIES IN INTERNATIONAL LAW: BEYOND THE NUREMBERG LEGACY 227–89 (1997).

[120] Agreement between the United Nations and the Royal Government of Cambodia concerning the Prosecution under Cambodian Law of Crimes Committed during the Period of Democratic Kampuchea, June 6, 2003, *available at* http://www.cambodia.gov.kh/krt/pdfs/Agreement%20between %20UN%20and%20RGC.pdf.

is another example of a "hybrid" court, although in this instance, the majority of the judges at both levels are appointed by the Cambodian Government.[121] It is financed by voluntary contributions from interested Governments, mainly Japan, France, Great Britain, Germany and Australia. Cambodia itself is expected to contribute. The Chambers were suffering from a cash-flow crisis early in 2008.[122] Five surviving, but aging, members of the Khmer Rouge leadership were in the custody of the Chambers awaiting trial at the time, with the first trial-phase expected in July 2008 against Duch, the former chief of the prison camp Tuol Sleng (or "S-21"), the best known of the "killing fields," where close to 20,000 people were killed.[123] Unlike the ICTY, the ICTR and the SCSL, there is provision in the Rules of the Chamber for participation of victims.[124] These are influenced in part by Cambodia's experience of the French *partie civile* system, introduced in the colonial period, and in part by the Rome Statute of the International Criminal Court.[125]

As in the case of the Sierra Leone Special Court, there is jurisdiction over major Cambodian offenses against the person. The inevitable genocide counts perhaps underscore the limitations of the treaty definition of that crime. Genocide is not just a crime of mass killing; it must be targeted at specific groups. There is little question that minority groups (such as the Muslim Chams and those of Vietnamese origin) in Cambodia were targeted, as were Buddhist monks, but the vast bulk of the actions in the killing fields were by ethnic Khmers against other ethnic Khmers. It is thus much easier to characterize the crimes as crimes against humanity and war crimes rather than as genocide. This is uncomfortable for some who view genocide more as an epithet for massive human rights violations than as a narrowly defined criminal offense.

§ 16.08 SPECIAL TRIBUNAL FOR LEBANON (HARIRI TRIBUNAL)

On May 30, 2007, the United Nations Security Council adopted a resolution approving an Agreement between the United Nations and the Lebanese Republic on the establishment of a Special Tribunal for Lebanon.[126] Attached to the Agreement was the Statute of the Special Tribunal. The subject-matter and the time frame of the events over which the Tribunal has jurisdiction are described thus:

> . . . to prosecute persons responsible for the attack of 14 February 2005 resulting in the death of Former Lebanese Prime Minister Rafiq Hariri and in the death or injury of other persons. If the tribunal finds that other attacks occurred in Lebanon between 1 October 2004 and 12 December 2005, or any later date decided by the Parties and with the consent of the Security Council, are connected in accordance with the principles of criminal justice and are of a nature and gravity similar to the attack of 14

---

[121] *See generally* Symposium, *Cambodian Extraordinary Chambers — Justice at Long Last*, 4 J. CRIM. JUST. 283 (2006).

[122] WAR CRIMES PROSECUTION WATCH, Vol. 3, Issue 15 (March 17, 2008), at 4.

[123] *Id.* at 3.

[124] *See* Guido Acquaviva, *New Paths in International Criminal Justice? The Internal Rules of the Cambodian Extraordinary Chambers*, 6 J. INT'L CRIM. JUST. 129, 140–1 (2008).

[125] *See* § 17.02[F], *infra*.

[126] S.C. Res. 1757 (2007). *See generally* Symposium on Special Tribunal, 5 J. INT'L CRIM. JUST. 1061–1174 (2007).

February 2005, it shall also have jurisdiction over persons responsible for such attacks. This connection includes but is not limited to a combination of the following elements: criminal intent (motive), the purpose behind the attacks, the nature of the victims targeted, the pattern of the attacks (modus operandi) and the perpetrators.[127]

This is rather a convoluted factual standard for jurisdiction beyond the Hariri assassination (and the 21 others killed with him in a massive explosion). While the Tribunal is a hybrid, with a majority of international members on the panels, the substantive law is, unlike that applying in Sierra Leone and Cambodia, entirely domestic:

> The provisions of the Lebanese Criminal Code relating to the prosecution and punishment of acts of terrorism, crime and offences against life and personal integrity, illicit associations and failure to report crimes and offences, including the rules regarding the material elements of a crime, criminal participation and conspiracy; Articles 6 and 7 of the Lebanese law of 11 January 1958 on "Increasing the penalties for sedition, civil war and interfaith struggle."[128]

In terms of jurisdictional theory, Lebanon has apparently agreed to delegate some of its territorial (and perhaps effects) jurisdiction to the Tribunal.

The Statute of the Tribunal[129] has broad language in it about the participation of representatives of victims, apparently taken from the Rome Statute of the International Criminal Court.[130] Like the Nuremberg Tribunal, but unlike other recent tribunals, the Lebanon tribunal has power to try *in absentia* where the accused has "expressly and in writing waived his or her right to be present" or "[h]as not been handed over to the Tribunal by the State authorities concerned."[131]

The Registrar of the Tribunal was appointed in March 2008[132] and selection of the judges was pending at that time. Since it is likely that persons high in the Syrian Government were involved in the Hariri assassination and probably other acts of violence, gaining Syrian cooperation is bound to be a major challenge to the Tribunal.[133] Funding for the Tribunal is to come 49 percent from Lebanon and 51 percent from voluntary contributions. The seat of the Tribunal, by agreement with the Dutch authorities, is in The Netherlands.

---

[127] Agreement between the United Nations and the Lebanese Republic on the establishment of a Special Tribunal for Lebanon, Art. 1 (1).

[128] Statute of the Special Tribunal for Lebanon, Art. 2. *See also* § 16.05, *supra* (discussing international tribunals applying domestic law).

[129] Art. 17, Statute of the Special Tribunal for Lebanon.

[130] *See* § 17.02[F], *infra* (ICC) and § 16.07, *supra* (Extraordinary Chamber in Cambodia).

[131] Art. 22, Statute of the Special Tribunal for Lebanon.

[132] *Ban Ki-moon names top official for Lebanon tribunal*, UN News Centre, March 11, 2008, *available at* http://www.un.org/apps/news/story.asp?NewsID=25925&Cr=Leban&Cr1= (announcing appointment of Robin Vincent, one of cadre of officials associated with several *ad hoc* and hybrid tribunals).

[133] Bert Swart, *Cooperation Challenges for the Special Tribunal for Lebanon*, 5 J. INT'L CRIM. JUST. 1153 (2007).

§ 16.09   KOSOVO AND EAST TIMOR

This section records the existence of two rather different hybrids from those just discussed. These ones were created by Special Representatives of the Secretary-General, operating pursuant to authority delegated by the Security Council under its Chapter VII powers under the Charter. In both instances, the United Nations had moved into a power vacuum and the Security Council gave the Secretary-General essentially plenary legislative and executive power over the territory in question. There was some cross-fertilization of the thinking and the personnel responsible for the creation of the two sets of courts.

The United Nations Mission in Kosovo (UNMIK) was created by the Security Council[134] following the end of the NATO military campaign in June 1999. The following year, the Special Representative of the Secretary-General issued a Regulation[135] that permitted the appointment of international judges and prosecutors within the local system. The hope was that, in addition to clearing the dockets, this would foster impartiality and develop competence among the local functionaries. In this instance, the substantive law was that applying generally in Kosovo — there was no listing of international crimes. To the extent that international crimes were to be charged, this would be indirectly under the provisions of the relevant penal code.

There is considerable debate about the success or failure of this endeavor,[136] but it is hard to disagree with the cautious conclusion of two participant-observers:[137]

> First, if international administrators, army, and police will be needed in post-conflict situations, so will international judges and prosecutors and they should be involved at the very beginning of any international administration. This must be accompanied by the presence of independent legal system monitors who should be in place from the inception of law enforcement activity.

A thoughtful observer suggests that this kind of activity is really a different paradigm from cases like the ICTY and ICTR. He calls it the "concept of justice under transitional administration." It is characterized by "transitions in which international authorities exercise normative powers in the context of a process of judicial reconstruction, either exclusively or in conjunction with domestic authorities."[138]

The Seventh of December became a day of infamy for the second time in 1975. On that date, Indonesia invaded the long-time Portuguese colony of East Timor that was undergoing a messy process of decolonization following the Carnation

---

[134] S.C. Res. 1244 (1999).

[135] UNMIK Regulation 2000/6.

[136] Compare John Cerone & Clive Baldwin, *Explaining and Evaluating the UNMIK Court System*, *in* INTERNATIONALIZED CRIMINAL COURTS: SIERRA LEONE, EAST TIMOR, KOSOVO, AND CAMBODIA 41 (Cesare P.R. Romano, André Nollkaemper & Jann K. Kleffner eds., 2004) (mostly negative), with Jean-Christian Cady & Nicholas Booth, *Internationalized Courts in Kosovo: An UNMIK Perspective, id.* at 59 (mostly positive).

[137] Cerone & Baldwin, *id.* at 56.

[138] Carsten Stahn, *Justice under Transitional Administration: Contours and Critique of a Paradigm*, 27 HOUSTON J. INT'L L. 311, 313 (2005). It was experience such as that in Kosovo and East Timor that led to the development of the material in MODEL CODES FOR POST-CONFLICT CRIMINAL JUSTICE, Vol. I, MODEL CRIMINAL CODE (Vivenne O'Connor & Colette Rausch eds., 2007).

Revolution in Portugal. In the ensuing warfare and dislocation, perhaps 200,000 people, about a third of the population, perished from the fighting, starvation and disease. Indonesia purported to incorporate East Timor as its 26th province but the United Nations refused to accept this. Armed resistance continued until 1999 when Indonesia agreed to a "popular consultation" in East Timor on whether to accept an offer of limited autonomy. When some 78 percent of the voters rejected the Indonesian plan, effectively opting for independence, Indonesian troops and their local militia allies went on a rampage that caused enormous property damage, hundreds of deaths and another round of massive dislocation of the population. A United Nations-authorized force led by Australia arrived to restore order and the United Nations Security Council created the United Nations Transitional Administration for East Timor (UNTAET).[139] In this instance, the Special Representative of the Secretary-General decided to create internationalized courts, called "Special Panels," comprising two international judges and one local judge. They were given jurisdiction both over some crimes under domestic law and over genocide, war crimes and crimes against humanity, defined essentially as in the Rome Statute of the International Criminal Court.[140] The jurisdiction, *ratione tempore*, however, did not run back to 1975, but dealt only with the events of 1999.

Most of the commentary on the performance of the Special Panels and the internationalized Serious Crimes Unit (SCU) that organized the prosecutions has been critical.[141] A report prepared for the International Center for Transitional Justice summarizes the problems as follows:

> By the conclusion of its work in May 2005 the SCU had indicted 391 persons and the serious crimes process had resulted in 84 convictions and three acquittals. However, the work of the SCU and special panels has received strenuous criticism. Throughout most of the SCU's work a coherent prosecutorial strategy was lacking. The special panels lacked basic facilities such as translation and transcription. Its jurisprudence was weak and in some cases deeply flawed. Adequate defense representation was lacking for much of the special panels' process. Outreach to the community, including victims and witnesses, was weak. Finally, the vast majority of those indicted, including all of the most-senior suspects were in Indonesia. Thus, while a number of relatively low-level perpetrators were tried in Timor-Leste, those most responsible remained outside the special panels' jurisdiction.[142]

Around the time that these trials were getting under way, Indonesia sought to stave off calls for an international tribunal by establishing an *Ad Hoc* Human Rights Court. As the NGO ETAN (which works to support the East Timorese) notes:

> This process has been denounced widely as a sham, including by the U.S. State Department. A total of 18 people were indicted for failing to prevent

---

[139] S.C. Res. 1272 (1999).

[140] UNTAET Regulation 2000/15.

[141] *See, e.g.*, DAVID COHEN, INDIFFERENCE AND ACCOUNTABILITY: THE UNITED NATIONS AND THE POLITICS OF INTERNATIONAL JUSTICE IN EAST TIMOR (2006); LESSONS LEARNED: EAST TIMOR (David Cohen & Suzannah Linton eds., 2008). *See also* Report to the Secretary-General of the Commission of Experts to Review the Prosecution of Serious Violations of Human Rights in Timor-Leste (then East Timor) in 1999, annexed to U.N. Doc. S/2005/458 (offering a strongly critical "official" report).

[142] MEGAN HIRST, TOO MUCH FRIENDSHIP, TOO LITTLE TRUTH: MONITORING REPORT ON THE COMMISSION OF TRUTH AND FRIENDSHIP IN INDONESIA AND TIMOR-LESTE (2008).

crimes against humanity in East Timor, rather than for their actions committing such crimes. Twelve were acquitted on the first trial, and five had their convictions overturned by Indonesia's Appeals Court, which completed its rulings in 2004. Only the conviction of East Timorese militia commander Eurico Guterres stands as of now. The Appeals Court upheld his conviction but reduced the sentence by five years.[143]

East Timor also had a Commission for Reception, Truth, and Reconciliation which, despite having very limited resources, produced a blockbuster 2500 page report in October 2005. It was probably the most successful part of this tale of woe and contains a very useful historical record for the whole period back to 1975.[144] East Timor is currently engaged in a joint Indonesia-Timor Leste Commission of Truth and Friendship, which many NGOs see as "not a credible mechanism to seek justice or even truth regarding events in Timor-Leste in 1999, let alone from 1975 to 1999."[145] Some yearn for the Security Council to take definitive action to create an *ad hoc* tribunal to deal with the situation.[146]

§ 16.10   SOME CREATIVE "INTERNATIONAL" AND "HYBRID" INITIATIVES

In some instances there have been creative applications to deal with international issues. Two recent examples can be seen in Scotland and Iraq.[147]

[A]   Lockerbie

On December 21, 1987, the explosion of a bomb on board Pan Am Flight 103 killed 259 passengers and crew and 11 residents of Lockerbie, Scotland, where the plane crashed. Criminal charges were brought in the United States and in Scotland against two Libyan nationals accused of causing the explosion. The United Nations Security Council imposed sanctions on Libya for not handing the suspects over. Libya meanwhile instituted proceedings against the United States and the United Kingdom in the International Court of Justice, arguing that its obligations under the Montreal Convention were met by its willingness to prosecute the defendants if the evidence were supplied to the Libyan authorities. It argued that the United States and United Kingdom were the ones in breach of the Convention by trying to

---

[143] ETAN, Justice Processes and Commissions for Timor-Leste: An Overview (2007) *available at* http://etan.org/news/2007/03justsumm.htm. For comments by a trial observer, *see* Suzannah Linton, *Unravelling the First Three Trials at Indonesia's Ad Hoc Court for Human Rights Violations in East Timor*, 17 Leiden J. Int'l L. 303 (2004).

[144] *See* http://www.cavr-timorleste.org/.

[145] ETAN, Justice Processes and Commissions for Timor-Leste: An Overview (2007) *available at* http://etan.org/news/2007/03justsumm.htm.

[146] *See, e.g.*, Report to the Secretary-General of the Commission of Experts to Review the Prosecution of Serious Violations of Human Rights in Timor-Leste (then East Timor) in 1999, annexed to U.N. Doc. S/2005/458 at 120. (The Commission also examined the possibility that some arrangement could be made with the ICC to act for the Security Council, but doubted that the Rome Statute could be interpreted to cover events in 1999, well before its entry into force in 2002.)

[147] For the record, it is worth noting that the United Nations has for some years been negotiating with the authorities in Burundi to create both a special tribunal and a truth and reconciliation commission to deal with ethnic killings going as far back as independence from Belgium in 1962. The negotiations continue. *See Burundi Must Seize Present Opportunity for Peace, Justice, Development, available at* http://www.un.org/News/Press/docs/2007/pbc13.doc.htm (report by UN High Commissioner for Human Rights).

coerce Libya into surrendering suspects it was entitled to try itself. As a civil law country, Libya does not normally extradite its own citizens, but it was prepared to try them on an extraterritorial basis. The Court avoided the issue whether it could find the Security Council had acted *ultra vires* in insisting that the suspects be handed over, by declining to order "provisional measures" (the equivalent of an interim injunction), but by finding that it had jurisdiction to reach the merits.[148]

An agreement was ultimately reached to try the two defendants for murder under Scottish law[149] at a specially created venue in The Netherlands.[150] Since Scottish courts sit normally in Scotland and The Netherlands could not normally be expected to allow them to sit on its territory,[151] both countries had to enact appropriate legislation to make this possible. The case in the I.C.J. was discontinued by mutual consent in 2003.

The Court (composed of three Scottish judges) convicted one of the accused and acquitted the other and the conviction was upheld on appeal.[152] The defendant is now serving a sentence of life imprisonment in a Scottish prison, with a requirement that he serve at least twenty years. Whether the conviction was justified is a matter of some dispute. David Andrews who, as Legal Adviser to the United States Department of State, played a leading role in the negotiations that resulted in the trial in The Netherlands, was content with the proceedings, while conceding that this was a model that was perhaps unique. He commented that:

> There are some important lessons, however, that we ought to take from the experience. Perhaps most notable is that the third country trial is not a model that we ought to consider lightly, if ever. The process of setting up such a specialized tribunal is cumbersome and enormously time consuming. Given the political and practical situation we faced with Libya, this solution was appropriate, and it worked. But it is hard to imagine a situation in the future that would lend itself to a similar solution — I hope not, anyway, for the sake of my successors![153]

On the other hand, Edinburgh Law Professor Robert Black argues that the evidence for conviction was inadequate, as was the representation of the defense both at trial and on appeal. He concludes that "a shameful miscarriage of justice has been perpetrated and that the Scottish criminal justice system has been gravely sullied."[154]

---

[148] Questions of Interpretation and Application of the 1971 Montreal Convention Arising from the Aerial Incident at Lockerbie, 1992 I.C.J. 3, 114 and 1998 I.C.J. 9, 115.

[149] Murder is defined in Scotland by common law: "unlawful homicide with malice aforethought." There is no real discussion of law in the case; it turned on factual analysis. The "international" crimes here involve breaches of the Montreal Convention and perhaps "terrorism".

[150] This agreement and the other primary source materials are usefully collected in JOHN P. GRANT, THE LOCKERBIE TRIAL: A DOCUMENTARY HISTORY (2004).

[151] This is one of the core propositions of The Lotus, § 1.02[B], *supra.*

[152] Megrahi v. Her Majesty's Advocate, [2002] J.C. 99 (Scotland, Appeal Court, High Court of Justiciary), reproduced in JOHN P. GRANT, THE LOCKERBIE TRIAL: A DOCUMENTARY HISTORY 299 (2004).

[153] David R. Andrews, *A Thorn on the Tulip — A Scottish Trial in The Netherlands: The Story Behind the Lockerbie Trial*, 36 CASE W. RES. J. INT'L L. 307, 318 (2004).

[154] Robert Black, *Lockerbie: A Satisfactory Process But a Flawed Result*, 36 CASE W. RES. J. INT'L L. 443 (2004).

[B] Iraq

The Iraqi Special Tribunal that tried Saddam Hussein [155] has been described as "an odd creature. . . . an Iraqi-led mechanism designed and supported by foreigners. It is based on international law but relies heavily on Iraqi tradition and procedures."[156] Its Statute was originally adopted by the Coalition Provisional Authority in 2003[157] and "domesticated" in 2005.[158] Under the Statute, the Tribunal has jurisdiction over any Iraqi national or resident accused of the crimes listed in the Statute between July 17, 1968 and May 1, 2003, in Iraq and elsewhere, including crimes committed in connection with Iraq's wars against Iran and Kuwait. The crimes include genocide, crimes against humanity and war crimes (essentially as defined in the Rome Statute of the International Criminal Court). It also includes three crimes under Iraqi law: manipulations of the judiciary; wastage of national resources and squandering of public assets and funds; and "[t]he abuse of position and the pursuit of policies that may lead to the threat of war or the use of the armed forces of Iraq against an Arab country, in accordance with Article 1 of Law Number 7 of 1958, as amended."[159] Iraq is thus one of the fairly small band of countries with a domestic proscription of aggressive war,[160] yet it is a selective one. Invading Kuwait, an Arab State, was criminal under domestic law; invading Iran, Islamic but not Arab, was not a crime. Potentially the *war crimes* committed in Iran, like those in Kuwait, could have been charged to the former president. But his execution for crimes committed against his own people rendered this moot.

The provision for capital punishment and the fairness of the procedures when measured against obligations such as the International Covenant on Civil and Political Rights, to which Iraq is a party, resulted in much debate in the literature. The sentencing proceedings for Hussein's co-defendant, and former Vice-President, Taha Yassin Ramadan, drew a remarkable *amicus curiae* brief from the United Nations High Commissioner for Human Rights (and former ICTY Prosecutor) Louise Arbour.[161] She relied particularly on the Covenant. Conceding that capital punishment, *per se*, was not a breach of the Covenant, she argued that, under all the circumstances, killing him would be a human rights violation. He too was hanged.

---

[155] There is an enormous amount of useful information and opinion on the Hussein trial (and other Iraqi trials) on the Case Western Reserve Law School's "Groatian Moment" Blog, *available at* http://law.case.edu/saddamtrial/. *See also* Symposium, *Saddam Hussien on Trial: What Went Awry?* 5 J. INT'L CRIM. JUST. 257–300 (2007).

[156] Miranda Sissons, *And Now from the Green Zone . . . Reflections on the Iraq Tribunal's Dujail Trial*, 20 ETHICS & INT'L AFF. 505, 505 (2006).

[157] Coalition Provisional Authority Order 48, "Delegation of Authority Regarding an Iraqi Special Tribunal", *available at* http://www.cpa-iraq.org/regulations/20031210_CPAORD_48_IST_and_Appendix_A.pdf..

[158] International Center for Transitional Justice Briefing Paper, at 2, n. 1 (October 2005), *available at* http://www.ictj.org/images/content/1/2/123.pdf.

[159] Statute of the Iraqi Special Tribunal, Art. 14.

[160] *See* § 14.03[A], *supra*.

[161] http://law.case.edu/saddamtrial/documents/arbour_amicus_curiae_brief_en.pdf.

Chapter 17
ROME STATUTE OF THE INTERNATIONAL CRIMINAL COURT

§ 17.01　GENERALLY

The first permanent international criminal court emanates from the adoption of the 1998 Rome Statute (Statute) that came into force on July 1, 2002.[1] Several preparatory meetings were held prior to its passage at a Diplomatic Conference by an unrecorded vote of 120 to 7, with 21 abstentions.[2] The United States was one of the seven participants voting against adoption of the International Criminal Court (ICC). During the time it was open for signature (until the end of 2000), 139 States signed the Statute and, by late March 2008, 106 had ratified or acceded to it.[3] The United States signed the treaty during the final days of the term of President

---

[1] Web site of the International Criminal Court, *available at* http://www.icc-cpi.int/home.html; *See also* the website through passage of the International Criminal Court, *available at* http://www.un.org/law/icc/. Most of the relevant instruments are also collected in SECRETARIAT, ASSEMBLY OF STATES PARTIES, SELECTED BASIC DOCUMENTS RELATED TO THE INTERNATIONAL CRIMINAL COURT (2005).

[2] *See generally* M. CHERIF BASSIOUNI, THE STATUTE OF INTERNATIONAL CRIMINAL COURT: A DOCUMENTARY HISTORY (1998); THE INTERNATIONAL CRIMINAL COURT: THE MAKING OF THE ROME STATUTE, ISSUES, NEGOTIATIONS, RESULTS (Roy Lee ed., 1999); COMMENTARY ON THE ROME STATUTE OF THE INTERNATIONAL CRIMINAL COURT: OBSERVERS' NOTES, ARTICLE BY ARTICLE, (Otto Triffterer ed., 2d ed. 2008); LEILA SADAT, THE INTERNATIONAL CRIMINAL COURT AND THE TRANSFORMATION OF INTERNATIONAL LAW: JUSTICE FOR THE NEW MILLENIUM (2002).

[3] *See* International Criminal Court website, *available at* http://www.icc-cpi.int/statesparties.html.

Clinton,[4] but the Bush Administration later stated that it would not proceed with ratification.[5]

The Statute opens with a Preamble that provides the rationale for a permanent International Criminal Court (Court). Its first paragraph aims for the poetic. It proclaims that the Parties are "[c]onscious that all peoples are united by common bonds, their cultures pieced together in a shared heritage, and concerned that this delicate mosaic may be shattered at any time."[6] The dramatic image is one of a world that is potentially out of joint as a result of supreme evil, and in need of restorative justice to put it right. The Preamble then recognizes the atrocities of the past, the need for universal jurisdiction to proceed as a united front "to put an end to impunity for the perpetrators of these crimes and thus to contribute to the prevention of such crimes," and the need to reinforce the "Purposes and Principles of the Charter of the United Nations." The "independent permanent International Criminal Court" is established to have jurisdiction over "the most serious crimes of concern to the international community as a whole." It operates, however, as "complementary to national criminal jurisdictions."[7]

Following the Preamble, the Statute is divided into thirteen parts as follows: Part One — Establishment of the Court; Part Two — Jurisdiction, Admissibility and Applicable Law; Part Three — General Principles of Criminal Law; Part Four — Composition and Administration of the Court; Part Five — Investigation and Prosecution; Part Six — The Trial; Part Seven — Penalties; Part Eight — Appeal and Revision; Part Nine — International Cooperation and Judicial Assistance; Part Ten — Enforcement; Part Eleven — Assembly of States Parties; Part Twelve — Financing; Part Thirteen — Final Clauses.

§ 17.02   THE STATUTE

[A]   Part One — Establishment of the Court

This permanent Court, established to handle the "most serious crimes of international concern," allows for complementary jurisdiction[8] in both the Court and in "national criminal jurisdictions."[9] Normally the reference to national jurisdictions means a reference to a State on the territory of which a crime may have been committed or a State which exercises jurisdiction on the basis of the nationality of the alleged perpetrator.[10] The Court operates in alliance with the United Nations, with whom it has a relationship agreement[11] but it is a separate international organization. The seat of the Court is located in "The Hague in the

---

[4] Statement of the President, Signature of the International Criminal Court Treaty, December 31, 2000, *available at* http://clinton4.nara.gov/textonly/library/hot_releases/December_31_2000.html.

[5] *U.S. Renounces World Court Treaty*, BBC News, May 6, 2002, *available at* http://news.bbc.co.uk/1/hi/world/americas/1970312.stm (often referred to as the "un-signing").

[6] Opening paragraph of Preamble, Rome Statute of the International Criminal Court.

[7] The Rome Statute of the International Criminal Court, Preamble.

[8] *See* § 17.02[B], *infra* (discussing how this principle is made operational).

[9] The Rome Statute of the International Criminal Court, Art. 1.

[10] There is a possibility that complementarity may include the work of courts operating on the basis of universal jurisdiction also. *See* § 17.02[B], *infra* (discussing Art. 17).

[11] Negotiated Relationship Agreement between the International Criminal Court and the United Nations, *available at* http://www.icc-cpi.int/library/asp/ICC-ASP-3-Res1_English.pdf.

Netherlands."[12] The Court may sit elsewhere when it is desirable to do so.[13] The Court has "international legal personality" and may operate "within the territory of any State Party and, by special agreement, on the territory of any other State."[14]

[B] Part Two — Jurisdiction, Admissibility and Applicable Law

Part Two is a crucial section of the Court statute in that it sets forth the contours of the jurisdiction of the Court and the law that will be applied within the Court's jurisdiction. Four crimes are set forth as the "most serious crimes of concern to the international community" and "within the jurisdiction" of the Court.[15] These are "genocide," "crimes against humanity," "war crimes," and the "crime of aggression." As these have already been discussed in detail in Chapter 14, it is only necessary to offer a brief summary here.

At the time of the adoption of the Statute, the "crime of aggression" was not defined, and as such "exercise" of jurisdiction for this crime was predicated on the completion of a definition of aggression.[16] Definitions or examples are provided for the other three crimes: "genocide," "crimes against humanity," and "war crimes."

Five forms of conduct are used to encompass "genocide." These include "killing of members of the group," "causing serious bodily or mental harm to members of the group," and "forcibly transferring children of the group to another group." Genocide requires that the act be "committed with intent to destroy, in whole or in part, a national, ethnical, racial or religious group, as such."[17]

"Crimes against humanity" includes eleven different types of conduct when the act is "committed as part of a widespread or systematic attack directed against any civilian population, with knowledge of the attack." The eleven different types of acts include "murder," "extermination," "torture," "the crime of apartheid," and "enforced disappearance of persons."[18] Each of these acts is defined in the Rome Statute. For example, it states that " 'torture' means the intentional infliction of severe pain or suffering, whether physical or mental, upon a person in the custody or under the control of the accused; except that torture shall not include pain or suffering arising only from, inherent in or incidental to, lawful sanctions."[19]

The Court also has jurisdiction over "war crimes" but "in particular when committed as part of a plan or policy or as part of a large-scale commission of such crimes." It includes "grave breaches of the Geneva Conventions of 12 August 1949," "other serious violations of the laws and customs applicable in international armed conflict, within the established framework of international law," "in the case of an armed conflict not of an international character, serious violations of Article 3

---

[12] Rome Statute of the International Criminal Court, Art. 2.

[13] *Id.* at Art. 3.

[14] *Id.* at Art. 4. In The Hague and elsewhere, the Court and those associated with it are entitled to various privileges and immunities. *See id.* at Art. 48, and Agreement on the Privileges and Immunities of the International Criminal Court, adopted by the Assembly of States Parties on Sept. 9, 2002.

[15] Rome Statute of the International Criminal Court, Art. 5.

[16] *Id.* at Art. 5(2).

[17] *Id.* at Art. 6.

[18] *Id.* at Art. 7(1).

[19] *Id.* at Art. 7(2)(e).

common to the four Geneva Conventions of 12 August 1949,"[20] and "other serious violations of the laws and customs applicable in armed conflicts not of an international character."[21]

Article 9 of the Statute represented entirely new territory in international practice. Adopted at the insistence of the United States, it states that "Elements of Crimes shall assist the Court in the interpretation and application of articles 6, 7 and 8." Article 9 requires that these "Elements" be adopted "by a two-thirds majority of the members of the Assembly of State Parties." There can be amendments to the Elements as proposed by "any State Party," "the judges acting by an absolute majority," or the "the Prosecutor" of the Court. The same two-thirds majority is required for adoption of these amendments.[22] The judges have ultimate control over the validity of any particular Element, since the Article provides that "[t]he Elements of Crimes and amendments thereto shall be consistent with this Statute."

The concept of Elements of Offenses refers to the necessary and sufficient mental and physical (or "material") items that the prosecution must prove in order to win its case. Some common law participants in the process thought that the United States must have been thinking about Model Jury Instructions. Although there is no jury in the ICC, the Elements as finally agreed upon look somewhat similar to jury instructions. Others thought that the United States had in mind the definition of elements in the Model Penal Code.[23] But this was not exactly the case. What was on their mind was the way in which United States Military Manuals break down crimes into their constituent pieces in order to show what needs to be proved.[24] A complicating feature (and for which the theory of the Model Penal Code helped to show the way) was Article 30 of the Statute which contemplates that a "material element" must, "unless otherwise provided,"[25] be accompanied by "intent and knowledge." "Material elements" must be what in American usage are usually called "physical elements." "Material elements," by implication from the language of Article 30, can be divided into "conduct," "consequences" and "circumstances" which have similar meanings to their counterparts in the Model Penal Code.[26] Each material element needs a corresponding mental element and "intent and knowledge" is the default rule. By and large, the negotiators of the Statute were opposed to imposing responsibility for crime of the magnitude of those in the Statute on the basis of culpability elements short of intention or knowledge, that is to say, negligence and even recklessness is not sufficient for liability.[27] There are occasional exceptions to this in the Statute. For example, in

---

[20] It is not meant by these terms to include "internal disturbances and tensions, such as riots, isolated and sporadic acts of violence or other acts of a similar nature." *Id.* at Art. 8(d).

[21] *Id.* at Art. 8.

[22] *Id.* at Art. 9.

[23] Model Penal Code, § 1.02 (1962).

[24] The instructions for Military Commissions issued in 2007 are a direct descendant of the ICC Elements, containing much similar language. *See* UNITED STATES DEPARTMENT OF DEFENSE, MANUAL FOR MILITARY COMMISSIONS (2007).

[25] "Unless otherwise provided" is discussed further in the analysis of Art. 30, § 17.02[C], *infra.*

[26] Model Penal Code, § 1.13(9) (definition of "element of an offense"). The MPC has another category of "causation," which seems to be subsumed in the Rome Statute's "conduct" (or perhaps in that of "consequence").

[27] *Cf.* the MPC's default of recklessness, Model Penal Code § 2.02(3) (1962). On "recklessness" see also Art. 30, § 17.02[C], *infra.* Gerhard Werle & Florian Jessberger, *"Unless Otherwise Provided':*

the case of responsibility of military commanders for the conduct of their subordinates, negligence may be enough. In the similar case of the responsibility of non-military superiors, some sort of recklessness is required.[28]

Armed with some understanding that, by and large, the material elements (and sometimes the mental elements) could be gleaned from Articles 6, 7 and 8, and the mental elements could usually be gleaned from using Article 30 a default rule, it was possible to negotiate the Elements. This task was performed by the Preparatory Commission for the Court (PrepCom), which met between the time of the Rome Conference and the coming into force of the treaty in 2002. In fact, the PrepCom completed drafting the Elements in 2000 and the Assembly of States Parties adopted its draft without change when it first met late in 2002.[29]

Notable among the basic structural assumptions of the Elements is thus the default rule that "[w]here no reference is made in the Elements of crimes to a mental element for any particular conduct, consequence or circumstance listed, it is understood that the relevant mental element, i.e., intent, knowledge or both, set out in article 30 applies."[30] As far as material elements are concerned, the general introduction to the Elements reads as follows:

> The elements of crimes are generally structured in accordance with the following principles:
>
> — As the elements of crimes focus on the conduct, consequences and circumstances associated with each crime, they are generally listed in that order;
>
> — When required, a particular mental element is listed after the affected conduct, consequence or circumstance;
>
> — Contextual circumstances are listed last.[31]

Article 10 of the Statute provides that nothing in the part of the Statute defining the crimes of genocide, crimes against humanity and war crimes "shall be interpreted as limiting or prejudicing in any way existing or developing rules of international law for purposes other than the Statute."[32] Article 10 was extremely important to a number of States that were concerned that not everything in the

---

Article 30 of the ICC Statute and the Mental Element of Crimes Under International Criminal Law, 3 J. INT'L CRIM. JUST. 35 (2005), offers a different view of the preparatory work and interpret Art. 30 differently from that suggested above.

[28] See discussion of Art. 28 of the Statute, § 17.02[C], *infra. See also* discussion of Art. 33 on superior orders, *id.* ("manifestly unlawful" a type of negligence test). There is occasional use of negligence liability in the Elements when that seemed a sensible compromise. For example, in the case of the war crime of using, conscripting or enlisting children, it is enough in the Elements that "the perpetrator knew *or should have known* that such person or persons were under the age of 15 years." (Elements to Art. 8(2)(b)(xxvi)). (Emphasis added).

[29] Elements of Crimes, *available at* http://www.icc-cpi.int/library/about/officialjournal/ Element_of_Crimes_English.pdf. *See generally* THE INTERNATIONAL CRIMINAL COURT: ELEMENTS OF CRIMES AND RULES OF PROCEDURE AND EVIDENCE (Roy Lee et al. ed. 2001); Roger S. Clark, *The Mental Element in International Criminal Law: The Rome Statute of the International Criminal Court and the Elements of Offences,* 12 CRIM. L. F. 291 (2001).

[30] Elements of Crimes, General Introduction, ¶ 2.

[31] *Id.* at ¶ 7. "Contextual circumstances" refers to "a manifest pattern or similar conduct" in the case of genocide, "a systematic or widespread attack directed against a civilian population" in the case of crimes against humanity, and an "armed conflict" (international or non-international) in the case of war crimes.

[32] Rome Statute of the International Criminal Court, Art. 10.

Statute went as far as contemporary customary law, the list of war crimes for example. While it can certainly be argued that the Statute crystallizes the definitions of what is actually in there, they were concerned that the existence of the Statute might serve to freeze or stunt the development of law elsewhere. Examples might be the law relating to anti-personnel mines[33] or nuclear weapons.[34]

The Court only has jurisdiction for crimes committed after its entry into force,[35] that is to say, after July 1, 2002. This seems to be an absolute bar on the Court's competence over events occurring prior to that date.[36] In the case of a State that becomes a Party after the entry into force, "the Court may exercise its jurisdiction only with respect to crimes committed after the entry into force of this Statute for that State, unless that State has made a declaration under article 12, paragraph 3" of the Statute.[37] Article 12, paragraph 3 makes it possible for States to accept the jurisdiction of the Court on essentially an *ad hoc* basis for a particular crime or situation, so this apparently allows a State becoming a Party later to back-date the events over which there is jurisdiction to July 2002.

States who become a party to the Statute accept the jurisdiction of the Court with respect to the crimes outlined in the Statute.[38] Although States are parties to the Statute, only individuals are subject to be prosecuted under the Statute. States Parties may refer crimes to the Prosecutor to consider for possible prosecution.[39] The Security Council, acting under Chapter VII of the United Nations Charter, may also refer to the Prosecutor a situation in which one or more crimes within the jurisdiction of the Court appears to have been committed.[40] The Prosecutor may also initiate investigation *proprio motu*, without a referral from a State Party or the Security Council.[41] This trio of ways in which the Court may be seized is usually called the "trigger mechanism." Supporting the inclusion of the *proprio motu* power in the Statute was a crucial issue at Rome for the "Like-Minded Group," the group of States most committed to the success of the negotiations. They were not convinced that either State or Security Council referrals would be adequate to bring many situations to the Prosecutor. They noted the paucity of state against state

---

[33] At the time of the Rome negotiations, the ink was barely dry on the Convention on the Prohibition of the Use, Stockpiling, Production and Transfer of Anti-personnel Mines and on their Destruction, opened for signature December 3, 1997. 36 I.L.M. 1507 (1998). With over 150 parties by March 2008, its prohibitions are arguably now part of customary law, even if they were not at the time.

[34] *See* § 14.03[D], *supra*.

[35] Rome Statute of the International Criminal Court, Art. 11(1).

[36] *See* Report to the Secretary-General of the Commisssion of Experts to Review the Prosecution of Serious Violations of Human Rights in Timor-Leste (then East Timor) in 1999, annexed to U.N. Doc. S/2005/458, noted in § 16.09 *supra*.

[37] *Id.* at Arts. 11(2), 12(3).

[38] *Id.* at Art. 12(1) (subject to right to opt out of jurisdiction over war crimes for a seven year period under Art. 124 of the Statute).

[39] *Id.* at Art. 14. The assumption was that States would make referrals of other States. An unexpected feature of the early workings of the Court has been the phenomenon of "self-referrals," by the Democratic Republic of the Congo, Uganda and the Central African Republic. Each has alleged that it is unable to bring rebels to justice and needs the intervention of the ICC. The Prosecutor has insisted that this opens the Government to scrutiny also.

[40] *Id.* at Art. 13(b).

[41] *Id.* at Art. 15(1). The material on which he or she proceeds in this way is very likely to come from non-governmental human rights organizations.

complaints that have been made under human rights treaties, as countries hesitate to denounce the depredations of others for fear of drawing attention to their own shortcomings.

Understanding the complexities of the trigger mechanism helps with understanding the "jurisdictional" provisions of the Statute. In the case of a referral by a State Party, or the Prosecutor's exercise of *proprio motu* power, there is jurisdiction only if either, or both, the State on the territory of which the conduct in question occurred, or the State of which the accused is a national, are Parties to the Statute.[42] In the case of a Security Council referral, there is jurisdiction even if the State where the events are alleged to have occurred, or the State whose nationals are alleged to have done the deeds, are not Parties. In such cases, the Security Council is essentially exercising the same powers with respect to the maintenance of peace and security that it exercised in setting up the Tribunals for Rwanda and Former Yugoslavia. The Security Council made its first referral, concerning Darfur, Sudan, in a situation where Sudan is not a State Party.[43]

The Prosecutor has initial discretion to proceed with investigations that appear to meet the criteria of the Statute or upon information that he or she receives through referrals. When the Prosecutor determines "that there is a reasonable basis to proceed with an investigation, he or she shall submit to the Pre-Trial Chamber a request for authorization of an investigation." The Pre-Trial Chamber than examines the request and if it finds that "there is a reasonable basis to proceed with an investigation" and that the acts fall within the jurisdiction of the Court, it "shall authorize the commencement of the investigation." A denial of a request by the Pre-Trial Chamber does not preclude a later request when the Prosecutor acquires new facts or evidence.[44] The investigation cannot, however, be commenced or proceeded with when the Security Council passes a resolution requesting deferral of the matter.[45]

Article 17 of the Statute deals with "issues of admissibility." It is the article that gives operational effect to the principle of "complementarity" which is emphasized in the Preamble and Article 1 of the Statute. Cases are "inadmissible" when a State "which has jurisdiction" is investigating the matter, "unless the State is unwilling or unable genuinely to carry out the investigation or prosecution," the case has already been "investigated by a State" and has decided not to proceed, "unless the decision resulted from the unwillingness or inability of the States genuinely to prosecute," the person has already been prosecuted for this conduct, or "[t]he case is not of sufficient gravity to justify further action by the Court."[46] The meaning of a State "which has jurisdiction" is a matter of debate. The simplest situation is where the territorial State or the State of which the accused is a national is examining the matter. What is not so clear is how complementarity operates in respect of a State which is exercising jurisdiction based on a universal theory, a not unlikely possibility given the expansion in recent years of claims to such jurisdiction.[47] This

---

[42] *Id.* at Art. 12(2). Note also the ability of the State of territoriality or nationality to make a declaration pursuant to Art. 12(3) by which it accepts the jurisdiction "with respect to the crime in question."

[43] S.C. Res. 1593 (2005) (referring situation in Darfur since July 1, 2002 to Prosecutor).

[44] *Id.* at Art. 15.

[45] Deferrals of investigation or prosecution are for 12 months, but may be renewed by the Security Council. *Id.* at Art. 16. On the Council's dubious use of this power, see § 10.02[C], *supra*.

[46] *Id.* at Art. 17.

[47] *See generally* § 2.04[E] *supra*.

is an issue the Court will probably need to face early in its life, although given its limited resources the Court may often be content to let a State with an adequate legal system proceed, even on the basis of universal jurisdiction.

There are three categories of situation that can give rise to a finding of "unwillingness." The first is that "[t]he proceedings are being undertaken or the national decision was made for the purposes of shielding the person concerned from criminal responsibility for crimes within the jurisdiction of the Court."[48] The second is that "[t]here has been an unjustified delay in the proceedings which in the circumstances is inconsistent with an intent to bring the person concerned to justice."[49] The third is that "[t]he proceedings were not or are not being conducted independently or impartially, and they were or are being conducted in a manner which in the circumstances, is inconsistent with an intent to bring the person concerned to justice."[50]

In the determination of whether a State is "unable" in a particular case, "the Court shall consider whether, due to a total or substantial collapse or unavailability of its national judicial system, the State is unable to obtain the accused or the necessary evidence and testimony or otherwise unable to carry out its proceedings."[51] There is some flexibility provided to the Prosecutor to notify parties who may have referred a matter to the Prosecutor and "those States which, taking into account the information available, would normally exercise jurisdiction over the crimes concerned."[52] At this point, "a State may inform the Court that it is investigating or has investigated its nationals or others within its jurisdiction" with respect to crimes under the Statute.[53] Thereupon, the State concerned can effectively put the ICC proceedings on hold for six months and perhaps longer, subject to review by the Court, while it investigates.[54] In order to be sure that they can take advantage of the principle of complementarity, and to bolster the claim that they are able and willing, many States have seen fit to adopt legislation making it clear that the Rome offenses are part of their domestic law.[55]

There is a procedure outlined in the Statute to challenge both the jurisdiction of the Court and the admissibility of a case in accordance with Article 17.[56] Such challenges may be made by an accused or a person for whom a warrant of arrest or summons has been issued, by a State which has jurisdiction (on the ground it is

---

[48] Rome Statute of the International Criminal Court, Art. 17(2)(a).

[49] *Id.* at Art. 17(2)(b).

[50] *Id.* at Art. 17(2)(c). Kevin Jon Heller notes that complementarity is no help to the defense in the reverse situation where the domestic system is all-too-willing to convict: "article 17 permits the Court to find a State 'unwilling or unable' only if its legal proceedings are designed to make a defendant *more difficult* to convict. If its legal proceedings make the defendant *easier* to convict, the article requires the Court to defer to the State no matter how unfair those proceedings may be." Kevin Jon Heller, *The Shadow Side of Complementarity: The Effect of Article 17 on National Due Process*, 17 CRIM. L. F. 255 (2006) (emphasis in original).

[51] Rome Statute of the International Criminal Court, Art. 17(3).

[52] *Id.* at Art. 18(1).

[53] *Id.* at Art. 18(2).

[54] *Id.* at Art. 18(2)–(7).

[55] *See generally* INTERNATIONAL CENTRE FOR CRIMINAL LAW REFORM AND CRIMINAL JUSTICE POLICY, INTERNATIONAL CRIMINAL COURT: MANUAL FOR THE RATIFICATION AND IMPLEMENTATION OF THE ROME STATUTE (3rd ed. 2008).

[56] Rome Statute of the International Criminal Court, Art. 19.

investigating or prosecuting) and by a State from which acceptance of jurisdiction is required under Article 12 (that is the state of territoriality or nationality).[57]

"*Ne bis in idem*"[58] is closely related to issues of admissibility. It precludes prosecution when the individual has already been tried by the Court. It also precludes other courts from prosecuting those who were tried by the International Criminal Court. Finally, it precludes prosecution by the Court if the person was tried by a State, unless the State is proceeding solely to avoid the Court's jurisdiction or it was "not conducted independently or impartially in accordance with the norms of due process recognized by international law and w[as] conducted in a manner which, in circumstances, was inconsistent with an intent to bring the person concerned to justice."[59]

Part Two concludes by providing the applicable law that will be used in the International Criminal Court. First is of course the "Statute, Elements of Crimes, and its Rules of Procedure and Evidence." Second, "applicable treaties and the principles and rules of international law, including the established principles of the international law of armed conflict" may be used. Finally, if necessary, the law from "national laws of legal systems of the world including, as appropriate, the national laws of States that would normally exercise jurisdiction over the crime" may be used as long as these principles do not conflict with "international law and internationally recognized norms and standards." The Court is not precluded from using the precedent that develops in the Court. All interpretations must not discriminate improperly and must be consistent with international human rights.[60]

[C] Part Three — General Principles of Criminal Law

The Rome Statute contains the most comprehensive "general part" ever found in an international agreement. It is likely to have significant implications for the way in which arguments are structured in the Court.

In addition to requiring that the conduct for which a prosecution is brought must constitute, at the time it takes place, a crime within the jurisdiction of the Court, the Statute imposes a Rule of Lenity in interpreting its language. Any ambiguity is to "be interpreted in favour of the person being investigated, prosecuted, or convicted."[61] This principle is used in the criminal system in the United States.

A person who is convicted can only be punished pursuant to this Statute.[62] Like the United States system that precludes ex post facto prosecutions, the Statute also precludes the prosecution "for conduct prior to the entry into force of the Statute."[63] From these provisions one sees that conduct must be punishable by the Statute at the time of the act in order to hold the person criminally liable. When

---

[57] *Id.* at Art. 19(2).

[58] *See* § 1.03[F].

[59] Rome Statute of the International Criminal Court, Art. 20.

[60] *Id.* at Art. 21.

[61] *Id.* at Art. 22 (*Nullum crimen sine lege*). *See* Machteld Boot, Nullem Crimen Sine Lege and the Subject Matter Jurisdiction of the International Criminal Court: Genocide, Crimes against Humanity, War Crimes (2002).

[62] *Id.* at Art. 23 (*Nulla poena sine lege*).

[63] *Id.* at Art. 24(1).

the law changes, it will not apply retroactively to someone who is charged with a crime. The law most favorable to the person is the one that should be used.[64]

The Statute provides for the prosecution and punishment of individuals, as opposed to countries or organizations.[65] This does not preclude countries from being liable outside the Statute for violations of international law.[66] Criminal liability can be achieved through aiding and abetting,[67] solicitation,[68] attempt,[69] joint criminal liability,[70] or by contributing "to the commission or attempted commission of such a crime by a group of persons acting with a common purpose."[71] The contribution must be intentional and also have the "aim of furthering the criminal activity or criminal purpose of the group" or "be made in the knowledge of the intention of the group to commit the crime."[72] This type of liability is closely related to the "conspiracy" theory for linking individuals to specific crimes committed by a group, found in *Pinkerton v. United States*,[73] and in some states in the United States. Other common law countries use conspiracy only as a basis of inchoate liability and do not use it in this way. It is foreign to civil law systems. The *ad hoc* tribunals have developed a comparable theory known as "joint criminal enterprise."[74] It is by no means clear how the ICC will apply this doctrine, although it has a prominent role in the Prosecutor's theory in respect of the situation in Darfur. The definitions provided for many of these terms dealing with individual responsibility follow the Model Penal Code in the United States. For example, attempt requires a "substantial step" but allows a defense of "abandonment" when that abandonment is voluntary and complete.[75]

Infancy is a "jurisdictional" defense under the Statute, as the Statute only applies to the actions of individuals over the age of 18.[76] There is no statute of limitations to bar a prosecution that is not brought in a timely manner.[77]

There is also no defense of head of state immunity.[78] Thus, leaders of countries can be held criminally liable for actions that violate this Statute. By implication, this means that a Party to the Statute must be prepared to surrender such persons to the Court if so requested. For a number of countries, this has entailed changing

---

[64] *Id.* at Art. 24(2).

[65] *Id.* at Art. 25(1).

[66] *Id.* at Art. 25(4).

[67] *Id.* at Art. 25(3)(c).

[68] *Id.* at Art. 25(3)(b). With respect to the crime of genocide, one who "directly and publicly" incites others to commit this offense can also be held criminally liable. This is an inchoate offense, specific to the crime of genocide; it is not necessary that a completed offense, or even an attempt, take place.

[69] *Id.* at Art. 25(3)(f).

[70] *Id.* at Art. 25(3)(a). It is not necessary that all parties be criminally responsible for the crime. *Id.*

[71] *Id.* at Art. 25(3)(d).

[72] *Id.* This language may provide the basis for saying that it needs to be foreseeable.

[73] 328 U.S. 640 (1946)

[74] *See* William A. Schabas, The U.N. International Tribunals: The former Yugoslvia, Rwanda and Sierra Leone 309–14 (2006); Gerhard Werle, Principles of International Criminal Law 120–3 (2005).

[75] *Id.* at Art. 25(3)(f).

[76] *Id.* at Art. 26. *See also* § 16.06, *supra*.

[77] *Id.* at Art. 29.

[78] *Id.* at Art. 27.

the relevant constitutional or statutory provisions that would normally confer immunity.

There is also criminal liability for commanders and other superiors who fail in their duty of leadership. In the case of a military commander or person acting as a military commander there is responsibility if that person knew or should have known "that the forces were committing or about to commit such crimes" and the leader "failed to take all necessary and reasonable measures or to submit the matter to the competent authorities for investigation and prosecution."[79] In the case of superior and subordinate relationships outside the military hierarchy, superiors can be held liable for the criminal activity of subordinates when they knew, or consciously disregarded information which clearly indicated, that subordinates were committing or about to commit such crimes, the activity was within their "responsibility and control," and they failed to "take all necessary and reasonable measures within" their "power to prevent or repress" the criminal activity or report the matter to appropriate "authorities for investigation or prosecution."[80] The distinction between military leaders and other superior and subordinate relationships is that the former may be held responsible on what is essentially a negligence standard, whereas civilian leaders are responsible only if a type of subjective recklessness is shown.[81] Both of these standards are exceptions to the general default rule contained in Article 30 of the Statute and the Elements, namely that intent and knowledge are required.[82]

In addition to superiors having liability for acts under the statute, subordinates also can be found criminally liable for acts they commit when they were following the orders of their superior. If, however, the accused "was under a legal obligation to obey orders" of the Government or the superior in question, "the individual was unaware that this order was unlawful," and "the order was not manifestly unlawful," that person may be relieved of criminal responsibility. Crimes of genocide and crimes against humanity are considered "manifestly unlawful" so a defense of following orders will not be acceptable for these crimes.[83]

A key element for a crime brought in the ICC is that the material elements committed by the accused were with intent and knowledge.[84] Both knowledge and intent are defined in the Statute.[85] Earlier in the drafting process prior to Rome, there was an effort to define what is meant by the physical element or *actus reus*.[86] This effort foundered largely on efforts to define omissions and causation and was

---

[79] *Id.* at Art. 28(a).

[80] *Id.* at Art. 28(b).

[81] *Cf.* the Tokyo Trial where the same standard (negligence) was applied to military and non-military leaders, § 16.03 *supra*.

[82] *See* § 17.02[B] *supra*.

[83] Rome Statute of the International Criminal Court, Art. 33. The extent to which superior orders should be a defense is controversial and there have been numerous efforts to draft the "correct" standard. Not all involved in the process were happy with this version. *See generally*, Otto Triffterer, *Article 33*, *in* COMMENTARY ON THE ROME STATUTE OF THE INTERNATIONAL CRIMINAL COURT: OBSERVERS' NOTES, ARTICLE BY ARTICLE (Otto Triffterer ed., 2d ed. 2008).

[84] *Id.* at Art. 30(1).

[85] *Id.* at Art. 30(2), (3).

[86] *See* Roger S. Clark, *The Mental Element in International Criminal Law: The Rome Statute of the International Criminal Court and the Elements of Offences* 12 CRIM. L. F. 291, 303–04 (2001).

abandoned in Rome.[87] Article 30 of the Statute makes it clear that the structure of what came to be called the "material" elements of the offense is to be analyzed in terms of conduct, consequences and circumstances.[88]

Defenses ("grounds for the exclusion of responsibility")[89] that negate the crime include insanity,[90] intoxication,[91] self defense,[92] and duress.[93] Explicit definitions are provided in the Statute to designate when conduct meets one of these defenses. The Statute notes that these defenses are not the exclusive defenses, and that the accused may present other defenses that can be shown to be accepted in law.[94] The Court is the ultimate arbiter of when a defense may be used.[95]

Article 32 of the Statute deals specifically with the "defense" of mistake. It provides that "[a] mistake of fact shall be a ground for excluding criminal responsibility only if it negates the mental element required by the crime."[96] This was relatively uncontroversial and seems to be the rule in most legal systems. The only question debated was whether the rule needed even to be stated, since it flows from (or is the mirror image of) the basic requirement of intent or knowledge.[97] As to mistake of law, the Article adds:

> A mistake of law as to whether a particular type of conduct is a crime within the jurisdiction of he Court shall not be a ground for excluding criminal responsibility. A mistake of law, may, however, be a ground for excluding criminal responsibility if it negates the mental element required by such a crime, or as provided for in Article 33.[98]

Mistake of law is a difficult subject in any legal system and this probably hits the right note. In domestic law, for example, it is no defense to say "I did not know it is illegal to steal." On the other hand, it may be a defense to argue that "I thought the object was mine, not the property of another." Here the mistake may include a

---

[87] *Id.*

[88] *See also* discussion of Elements, § 17.02[B], *supra.*

[89] The use of the terms "justification" and "excuse" became very controversial across different legal systems and a neutral term had to be found to avoid difficulty.

[90] *Id.* at Art. 31(1)(a).

[91] *Id.* at Art. 31(1)(b).

[92] *Id.* at Art. 31(1)(c).

[93] *Id.* at Art. 31(1)(d). See also discussion of the *Erdemovic* case in the ICTY, § 14.03, *supra.*

[94] *Id.* at Art. 31(3). The structure of any defense arguments along these lines will, of necessity, depend on "applicable law" in Art. 21, but the kind of analysis in which the ICTY engaged in Erdemovic will no doubt offer some guidance as to technique.

[95] *Id.* at Art. 31(2).

[96] *Id.* at Art. 32(1).

[97] The same debate took place during the drafting of the Model Penal Code, with the same result — the inclusion of a specific provision on mistake. *See* AMERICAN LAW INSTITUTE, MODEL PENAL CODE AND COMMENTARIES, Comment to § 2.04, at 269–71 (1985).

[98] Rome Statute of the International Criminal Court, Art. 32(2). Art. 33, discussed above, deals with superior orders. It will be noted here that, at least in respect of war crimes, a mistake in following an illegal order that is not "manifestly unlawful" may be exculpatory. "Manifestly" is some kind of negligence standard. The core mistakes under Art. 32 need only be honest; there is no requirement that they be non-negligent. *See* Roger S. Clark, *The Mental Element in International Criminal Law: The Rome Statute of the International Criminal Court and the Elements of Offences*, 12 CRIM. L. F. 291, 308–9. But see a different view expressed by Professor Triffterer in respect of mistakes of law, discussed *id.* at 311–12.

legal component (or a mixed component of fact and law) and it may negate the crime. Such cases are typically mistakes about what the Rome Statute calls a "circumstance" element. War crimes, in particular, are rife with circumstance elements, such as whether there was an "armed conflict" or whether a particular person or place is "protected." Such questions are typically not pure questions of fact — they have a legal element and they may well be what the Article has in mind as a defense. It is no defense to say "I did not know it was illegal to commit war crimes." On the other hand, it may be a defense to say "I thought that Church was a legitimate target under the circumstances as I understood them."

[D] Part Four — Composition and Administration of the Court

There are four "organs" of the Court, described as such in the Statute: (a) The Presidency; (b) An Appeals Division, Trial Division, and Pre-Trial Division; (c) The Office of the Prosecutor; and (d) The Registry.[99] There are eighteen judges of the Court, although there is an option that allows this number to be increased.[100] The Statute provides the necessary qualifications to serve as judge[101] and the method to be used in selecting judges for this Court[102] including how to fill judicial vacancies.[103]

The judges, who are required to be "independent in the performance of their functions,"[104] divide themselves into the three divisions (appellate, trial, and pre-trial) with the Statute providing the number and qualifications of each of these divisions.[105] A judge who cannot be impartial in a case may be excused.[106]

The Office of the Prosecutor is separate from the Court, and is headed by the Prosecutor who serves as the administrator over deputies and the staff.[107] The Prosecutor and deputies, who serve full time, must be of different nationalities. Like judges they have to be of "high moral character, be highly competent," and have experience. They also have to be "fluent in at least one of the working

---

[99] *Id.* at Art. 34. The "Court" as a legal person acts through its "organs" which are more than just the judges. The Assembly of States Parties, the governing body of the Court, is arguably also an "organ" of the Court, as is the Trust Fund for Victims and its Secretariat, although the Statute does not expressly say so.

[100] *Id.* at Art. 36.

[101] *Id.* For example the judges must be qualified to be a member of the highest judicial offices in their jurisdiction; they need to be fluent in one of the working languages used by the Court; and have "established competence in relevant areas of" the law. This may be either criminal law or international humanitarian and human rights law. *Id.* at Art. 36(3). The working languages are English and French, although judgments are published in the official languages of the Court which are: "Arabic, Chinese, English, French, Russian, and Spanish." *Id.* at Art. 50.

[102] *Id.* at Art. 36(4–8). Separate provisions discuss how to fill the Presidency. *Id.* at Art. 38.

[103] *Id.* at Art. 37.

[104] *Id.* at Art. 40.

[105] *Id.* at Art. 39.

[106] *Id.* at Art. 41.

[107] Since the adoption of the Statute, the Prosecutor has issued a Paper on Some Policy Issues Before the Office of the Prosecutor, *available at* http://www.icc-cpi.int/otp/otp_policy.html. The paper discusses his basic prosecutorial strategy in a world of limited resources. *See* Ray Murphy, *Gravity Issues and the International Criminal Court*, 17 Crim. L. F. 281 (2006).

languages of the Court."[108] The method of election of the Prosecutor is outlined in the Statute as well as how to resolve issues of disqualifying the Prosecutor or deputies.[109]

The Registry handles the administrative aspects of the Court and is headed by the Registrar who answers to the Presidency of the Court. Again "high moral character" and fluency "in at least one of the working languages of the Court" are qualifications.[110] It is the responsibility of the Registrar to "set up a Victims and Witnesses Unit within the Registry" to offer protection to witnesses and victims and to assist with appropriate counseling.[111]

The Statute provides for the circumstances and removal from office of prosecutors and registrars.[112] It also notes that in less serious matters, disciplinary measures may be used.[113]

Other aspects of Court operation are also covered in Part Four. For example, it includes the method of determining salary[114] and the fact that the "Court shall enjoy in the territory of each State Party such privileges and immunities as are necessary for the fulfillment of its purposes."[115] It also provides that a "two-thirds majority of the members of the Assembly of States Parties" is necessary for adoption of the "Rules of Procedure and Evidence," and the method for amending these rules. The rules remain subservient to the Statute when a conflict arises.[116] Additionally, the Statute provides for the judges to "adopt, by an absolute majority, the Regulations of the Court necessary for its routine functioning."[117]

[E]   Part Five — Investigation and Prosecution

Part Five concerns the pretrial aspects of the Court, namely, the investigation and prosecution phase. It offers the contours of the prosecutor's role in deciding whether to proceed with an investigation and the "duties and powers of the Prosecutor with respect to Investigations."[118] One of the important considerations for the Prosecutor is whether, "[t]aking into account the gravity of the crime and the interests of victims, there are nonetheless substantial reasons to believe that an investigation would not serve the interests of justice." This consideration may be especially important in cases where the State concerned has granted an amnesty for crimes within the jurisdiction of the Court, especially following a truth and reconciliation process. The essential approach of the Statute is that there is no

---

[108] Rome Statute of the International Criminal Court, Art. 42. *See supra* note 101.

[109] *Id.*

[110] *Id.* at Art. 43. *See supra* note 101.

[111] *Id.* at 43.

[112] *Id.* at Art. 46.

[113] *Id.* at Art. 47.

[114] *Id.* at Art. 49.

[115] *Id.* at Art. 48. The details are spelled out in the Agreement on the Privileges and Immunities of the International Criminal Court, adopted by the Assembly of States Parties on Sept. 9, 2002.

[116] *Id.* at Art. 51.

[117] *Id.* at Art. 52. The Regulations, which deal with a number of procedural issues as well as matters relating to counsel and legal assistance (including representation of victims), detention standards, enforcement, and disciplinary matters, are *available at* http://www.icc-cpi.int/library/about/officialjournal/Regulations_of_the_Court_170604-EN.pdf.

[118] *Id.* at Art. 53–54.

impunity and the cases where an amnesty has been granted may well meet the admissibility criteria in the Statute. Nonetheless there could be situations where the exercise of prosecutorial discretion might be appropriate.[119] Another significant obligation of the Prosecutor is to "investigate incriminating and exonerating circumstances equally."[120]

Part Five also provides the "rights of persons during an investigation."[121] One finds rights of counsel, the right to remain silent, and the right "to be informed, prior to being questioned, that there are grounds to believe that he or she has committed a crime within the jurisdiction of the Court."[122]

A Pre-Trial Chamber exists to assist the Prosecutor in certain investigative roles. It acts to "ensure the efficiency and integrity of the proceedings and, in particular, to protect the rights of the defence." For example, the Pre-Trial Chamber may have a record made of the proceedings or appoint an expert to assist in the matter.[123] When the Prosecutor's failure to seek the assistance of the Pre-Trial Chamber is "unjustified," the Pre-Trial Chamber may "act on its own initiative," although the Prosecutor has the right to appeal this decision.[124] When requested by the Prosecutor, the Pre-Trial Chamber can "issue such orders and warrants as may be required for the purposes of an investigation."[125]

The Prosecutor also goes to the Pre-Trial Chamber for a "warrant of arrest or a summons to appear."[126] In order to issue a warrant for arrest, the Pre-Trial Chamber needs to be satisfied that "there are reasonable grounds to believe that the person has committed a crime within the jurisdiction of the Court," and "[t]he arrest of the person appears necessary." To be necessary it must be to "ensure the person's appearance at trial," to assure no obstruction or endangerment of the "investigation or court proceedings," or to make sure the criminal conduct will cease by that person.[127] The Prosecutor's application for a warrant must meet certain technical requirements, such as containing a concise statement of facts about the crime. There are also technical aspects to the warrant of arrest, which also requires a concise statement of facts about the crimes. The Prosecutor can amend this document through the Pre-Trial Chamber. [128]

A Prosecutor can also choose to proceed by filing an application asking the Pre-Trial Chamber to issue a summons. The summons needs to contain information such as the "specified date on which the person is to appear" and as with the warrant a "concise statement of the facts which are alleged to constitute the crime."[129]

---

[119] *See* Bruce Broomhall, International Justice and the International Criminal Court: Between Sovereignty and the Rule of Law 100–2 (2003).

[120] Rome Statute of the International Criminal Court, Art. 54(1)(a).

[121] *Id.* at Art. 55.

[122] *Id.* These rights find their origin in the International Covenant on Civil and Political Rights. *See* § 15.01[B], *supra*.

[123] Rome Statute of the International Criminal Court, Art. 56.

[124] *Id.*

[125] *Id.* at Art. 57.

[126] *Id.* at Art. 58.

[127] *Id.*

[128] *Id.*

[129] *Id.*

States that are party to the Statute need to "immediately take steps to arrest the person" when they receive a request for the arrest of an individual within their State.[130] There are provisions for interim release of the individual after notification and receipt of a recommendation from the Pre-Trial Chamber.[131] Upon arrival to the Pre-Trial Chamber, the Chamber needs to inform the accused of his or her rights.[132] Release of the accused may be granted, or the Pre-Trial Chamber needs to "periodically review its ruling on the release or detention of the person."[133]

The Statute provides for an initial or pre-trial type of hearing prior to trial. This is to confirm the charges. The accused is provided a copy of the charging document and needs to be informed of the evidence that the Prosecutor intends to use at the hearing. At this hearing, the accused has the right to "object to the charges; challenge the evidence presented by the Prosecutor; and present evidence."[134] Based upon the evidence presented, The Pre-Trial Chamber can confirm the charges and "commit the person to a Trial Chamber," reject the charges, or adjourn the hearing so that the Prosecutor can provide further evidence or amend the charge to more appropriately fit the evidence presented.

A Prosecutor can resubmit a charge despite a Pre-Trial Chamber having declined the charge, if he or she obtains additional evidence. Irrespective of this option, the Prosecutor does have the ability to amend charges before the start of trial if given permission by the Pre-Trial Chamber. Additionally, a Prosecutor can dismiss charges after the commencement of trial if he or she obtains the permission of the Trial Chamber.[135]

[F] Part Six — The Trial

The trial process is a unique amalgam of common law and civil law systems. Trials are to be held in The Hague,[136] with the accused present unless he or she disrupts the trial.[137] The accused should only be removed under exceptional circumstances and in that event technology should be used so that he or she can observe the trial.[138] Unless necessary to protect victims and witnesses or confidential information, the trial is to be held publicly.[139] A record is made of the trial proceedings.[140]

Throughout the Statute, respect for the rights of the accused and also "due regard for the protection of victims and witnesses" is emphasized.[141] The Statute

---

[130] *Id.* at Art. 59.

[131] *Id.*

[132] *Id.* at Art. 60.

[133] *Id.*

[134] *Id.* at Art. 61.

[135] *Id.*

[136] *Id.* at Art. 62. The Statute does provide that the Court can decide to hold it elsewhere, but the criteria are not specified in the document. Some national legislation giving effect to the Statute specifically permits the Court to sit in the relevant territory.

[137] *Id.* at Art. 63.

[138] *Id.*

[139] *Id.* at Art. 64(7).

[140] *Id.* at Art. 64(10).

[141] *Id.* at Art. 64(2); *see also* Art. 68.

and Rules of Procedure and Evidence control the trial conduct.[142] Specific procedures for the case, such as the "language or languages to be used at trial" are determined by the Trial Chamber conferring with the parties prior to the start of the trial. The parties also confer to discuss disclosure of discovery materials ("documents or information not previously disclosed") in order to prepare for trial.[143] Issues of joinder and severance of charges are also determined pre-trial.[144]

The trial starts by the Trial Chamber reading the accused the charges against him or her and making certain that the accused "understands the nature of the charges."[145] The accused has the option of entering an admission of guilt,[146] and if the accused takes this option, the Trial Chamber then determines whether that admission is satisfactory to serve as a conviction. In this regard, the Trial Chamber looks at whether the accused "understands the nature and consequences of the admission of guilt," that it is a voluntary admission after consulting with counsel, and that the facts of the case support the admission of guilt.[147]

Plea bargaining, as seen in the United States, is not a component of the International Criminal Court process. Although the Prosecutor and defense can modify charges, or agree on an admission of guilt or penalty, it is not binding on the Trial Chamber.[148] The ultimate decision on these issues is made by the Trial Chamber, subject to rights of appeal. Even guilty pleas are controversial in some legal systems and the reference to "admission of guilt" was a more congenial way to avoid both this concept and the concept of plea bargaining.

The Statute has a presumption of innocence standard, with the burden on the Prosecution to prove the accused guilty beyond a reasonable doubt.[149] The accused is afforded a list of rights comparable to those afforded defendants in the United States. These include the right "to be tried without undue delay," right to present a defense, right to compulsory process and the right to remain silent without it being held against him or her.[150] A provision that differs from rights afforded defendants in the United States, is the right "to make an unsworn oral or written statement in his or her defence."[151] What may prove to be a very significant guarantee for the defense is "[n]ot to have imposed on him or her any reversal of the burden of proof or any onus of rebuttal."[152] This is strong language which must mean that the accused can not be required to carry the burden of persuasion on defenses like insanity or self defense.[153] Whether the accused may, nevertheless,

---

[142] *Id.*

[143] *Id.* at Art. 64(3)(c).

[144] *Id.* at Art. 64(5).

[145] *Id.* at Art. 64(8)(a).

[146] *Id.*

[147] *Id.* at Art. 65(1).

[148] *Id.* at Art. 65(5). On developing international practice, see NANCY AMOURY COMBS, GUILTY PLEAS IN INTERNATIONAL CRIMINAL LAW: CONSTRUCTING A RESTORATIVE JUSTICE APPROACH (2007).

[149] *Id.* at Art. 66.

[150] *Id.* at Art. 67(1).

[151] *Id.* at Art. 67(1)(h). This is normal practice in civil law jurisdictions. In older English practice, before the accused was competent to give evidence, he or she was permitted to make an "unsworn statement from the dock." This practice continued in England and some Commonwealth countries for a time after the accused was allowed to testify.

[152] *Id.* at Art. 67(1)(i).

[153] Situations like those in Patterson v. New York, 432 U.S. 197 (burden of extreme emotional

be required to carry some evidentiary burden of going forward on an issue is unknown territory in international criminal law.

As previously noted, the Statute emphasizes the protection of victims and witnesses.[154] This includes having *in camera* hearings,[155] and obtaining advice on protection and security measures from the Victims and Witnesses unit.[156] The Prosecutor can adjust the method of submitting evidence, such as using a summary account, when the "disclosure of evidence or information" could "lead to the grave endangerment of the security of a witness or his or her family." There is also a strong emphasis in the Statute to protect national security, with detailed language on how best to accomplish this protection in accordance with the framework of the Statute.[157] The Statute, however, also stresses the need not to prejudice "the rights of the accused and a fair and impartial trial."[158]

A particularly significant procedural aspect of taking the situation of victims into account is contained in language taken almost verbatim from the 1985 General Assembly Declaration of Basic Principles of Justice for Victims of Crime and Abuse of Power:[159]

> Where the personal interests of the victims are affected, the Court shall permit their views and concerns to be presented and considered at stages of the proceedings determined to be appropriate by the Court and in a manner which is not prejudicial to or inconsistent with the rights of the accused and a fair and impartial trial. Such views and concerns may be presented by the legal representatives of the victims where the Court considers it appropriate, in accordance with the Rules of Procedure and Evidence.[160]

The Rules of Procedure and Evidence in fact permit the participation (and representation) of victims from a very early stage of the proceedings, subject to the Court's determination of what is "appropriate."[161] Several early decisions of Pre-Trial and Appeals Chambers of the Court have been devoted to working out some of the practicalities of this representation.[162]

Obtaining truthful testimony is considered an important aspect of the Statute. There is a requirement that a witness provide an initial statement of truthfulness prior to giving testimony, and a requirement of having live testimony, except in highly unusual circumstances.[163] The Court's Rules of Procedure and Evidence

---

disturbance carried by accused), and Martin v. Ohio, 480 U.S. 228 (1987) (defendant carries burden of proving self defense) would seem to come out the other way under the Statute, as they would under Model Penal Code § 1.12 (1962).

[154] Rome Statute of the International Criminal Court, Art. 64(2), 68.

[155] *Id.* at Art. 68(2).

[156] *Id.* at Art. 68(4).

[157] *Id.* at Art. 72.

[158] *Id.* at Art. 68(5).

[159] *See* § 15.05, *supra.*

[160] Rome Statute of the International Criminal Court, Art. 68(3).

[161] *See* RR. 89–93 of the Rules of Procedure and Evidence.

[162] *See* various proceedings in Prosecutor v. Thomas Lubanga Dyilo, *available at* http://www.icc-cpi.int/cases/RDC/c0106/c0106_docAppeal.html. *See generally* Marc Henzelin, Veijo Heisakanen & Guénaël Mettraux, *Reparations to Victims before the International Criminal Court: Lessons from International Mass Claims Processes*, 17 Crim. L. F. 317 (2006).

[163] *Id.* at Art. 69(1)–(2).

serve as the rules that are to be followed in advancing all of these measures aimed at protecting the fairness of the trial. The Statute accepts several evidentiary standards such as "privileges on confidentiality,"[164] taking judicial notice of "facts of common knowledge,"[165] and excluding evidence that is "obtained by means of a violation of this Statute or internationally recognized human rights" in circumstances where "[t]he violation casts substantial doubt on the reliability of the evidence."[166] The Statute accounts for confidential information that may come from third parties, by and large protecting the situation of the originator of the material.[167]

The Statute considers offenses that may arise in pre-trial or trial proceedings that can diminish the administration of justice. For example, giving false testimony[168] or bribing an official of the court[169] is some of the conduct that can result in a penalty of up to five years imprisonment.[170] Additionally, parties to the Court are instructed to provide jurisdiction in their national laws for offenses against the Court that occur in their home countries.[171] Finally, contemptuous conduct before the Court can result in imprisonment.[172]

Part Six of the Statute, in setting forth the rules governing a trial, describes the requirements of a Court decision. For example, the judges are bound in rendering a decision to the evidence presented at trial.[173] A written decision is to be provided by the Trial Chamber, and when there is no unanimity in the decision, it "shall contain the views of the majority and the minority."[174] The Statute also provides that "[t]he Court shall establish principles relating to reparations to, or in respect of, victims, including restitution, compensation and rehabilitation."[175] The Court may make an order directly against a convicted person specifying appropriate reparations to, or in respect of, victims.[176] Or it can order that the award be made through the Trust Fund for Victims which is contemplated in Part Seven of the Statute.[177] Finally, with regard to sentencing, the Statute provides for public pronouncement of the sentence,[178] a sentence determined by the Trial Chamber as

---

[164] *Id.* at Art. 69(5).

[165] *Id.* at Art. 69(6).

[166] *Id.* at Art. 69(7).

[167] *Id.* at Art. 73. R. 73 of the Court's Rules of Procedure and Evidence also has detailed provisions on privileged communications and information coming from medical doctors, psychiatrists, psychologists, clergy and the International Committee of the Red Cross.

[168] *Id.* at Art. 70(1)(b).

[169] *Id.* at Art. 70(1)(f).

[170] *Id.* at Art. 70(3).

[171] *Id.* at Art. 70(4)(a).

[172] *Id.* at Art. 71.

[173] *Id.* at Art. 74(2).

[174] *Id.* at Art. 74(5).

[175] *Id.* at Art. 75(1). It is not clear whether the Court is supposed to do this by acting in some kind of "legislative" mode or whether the development should take place case by case.

[176] *Id.* at Art. 75(2).

[177] *Id. See also* § 17.02[G] *infra.*

[178] *Id.* at Art. 76(4).

appropriate based upon "the evidence presented and submissions made during the trial."[179]

[G]   Part Seven — Penalties

Further detail regarding penalties is described in Part Seven of the Statute. Here one finds that the death penalty is not included as an available penalty and that the maximum that can be imposed under the Statute is life imprisonment, which may only be used "when justified by the extreme gravity of the crime and the individual circumstances of the convicted person."[180] Otherwise a term of imprisonment is limited to a maximum of thirty years.[181] These penalties do not preclude a State from imposing a penalty prescribed by its national laws in its domestic proceedings.[182]

In determining an appropriate sentence, the Court looks at the "gravity of the crime and the individual circumstances of the convicted person."[183] In yet another demonstration of the concern the drafters had for victims, the Statute provides that a Trust Fund "be established by decision of the Assembly of State Parties for the benefit of the victims of crimes within the jurisdiction of the Court, and of the families of such victims."[184] The Assembly has in fact set up such a Fund which can receive money not only from fines or reparation orders made by the Court, but also from voluntary contributions made by Governments, international organizations, individuals, corporations and other entities.[185] The Fund has its own (distinguished) Board of Directors and Secretariat. It is expected that it will be possible to disburse some emergency funds provided by donors to assist victims, even before prosecutions have been completed.

[H]   Part Eight — Appeal and Revision

The next part of the Statute, as one might suspect, pertains to appeals and modifications of a sentence. Both the prosecution and defense can appeal based upon a "procedural error," "error of fact," or "error of law."[186] Additionally the defense may appeal on "any other ground that affects the fairness or reliability of the proceedings or decision."[187] The sentence rendered by the Court is subject to review and appeal by either party.[188] Other decisions, usually pre-trial matters, can also be subject to interlocutory appeal. For example, "a decision with respect to jurisdiction or admissibility" may be appealed.[189]

---

[179] *Id.* at Art. 76(1).

[180] *Id.* at Art. 77(1)(b).

[181] *Id.* at Art. 77(1)(a).

[182] *Id.* at Art. 80.

[183] *Id.* at Art. 78.

[184] *Id.* at Art. 79(1).

[185] Regulations of the Trust Fund for Victims, Doc. ICC-ASP/1/Res. 6 (2002), *available at* http://www.icc-cpi.int/library/about/officialjournal/ICC-ASP-4-32-Res.3_English.pdf.

[186] Rome Statute of the International Criminal Court, Art. 81(1).

[187] *Id.* at Art. 81(1)(b).

[188] *Id.* at Art. 81(2).

[189] *Id.* at Art. 82.

Normally a convicted individual remains in custody pending the appeal and an acquitted individual is released. Specified circumstances, however, allow the Trial Chamber to modify this rule.[190]

The Appeals Chambers has several options if it finds "that the proceedings appealed from were unfair in a way that affected the reliability of the decision or sentence," or there was an error, such as a factual error. It can "reverse or amend the decision or sentence," or "order a new trial before a different Trial Chamber."[191]

An application for revision of the conviction or sentence may be made by the convicted individual or, after death, by certain members of his or her family. The basis for this revision needs to be premised on new evidence that could not be obtained previously, a showing that false evidence was used at trial, or "an act of serious misconduct or serious breach of duty" being made by a judge.[192] If there is a necessity to revise the conviction or sentence for one of these reasons, the Appeals Chamber can "reconvene the original Trial Camber, constitute a new trial Chamber, or retain jurisdiction over the matter" for the purpose of revising the judgment.[193] The Statute provides in certain circumstances for compensation to individuals who have been wrongly accused.[194]

[I]   Part Nine — International Cooperation and Judicial Assistance

Cooperation among parties to the Statute is an important aspect of making the Court successful.[195] The Court procedures for requests of cooperation are outlined in the Statute,[196] which also requires States who are a party to the Statute to adopt procedures to ensure cooperation with the Court.[197] Even those States that are in theory "monist" (and treaties become part of domestic law) will find it necessary to adopt implementing legislation to ensure they are able to comply fully with the Court's requests.[198]

Specific articles within the Statute outline the method of surrender of persons to the Court,[199] the contents and execution of a request for arrest and surrender,[200] assistance in investigations,[201] "cooperation with respect to waiver of immunity and consent to surrender,"[202] and how to resolve competing requests between the

---

[190] *Id.* at Art. 81(3).

[191] *Id.* at Art. 83.

[192] *Id.* at Art. 84(1).

[193] *Id.* at Art. 84(2).

[194] *Id.* at Art. 85.

[195] *Id.* at Art. 86.

[196] *Id.* at Art. 87.

[197] *Id.* at Art. 88.

[198] *See generally* INTERNATIONAL CENTRE FOR CRIMINAL LAW REFORM AND CRIMINAL JUSTICE POLICY, INTERNATIONAL CRIMINAL COURT: MANUAL FOR THE RATIFICATION AND IMPLEMENTATION OF THE ROME STATUTE (3rd ed. 2008).

[199] Rome Statute of the International Criminal Court, Art. 89.

[200] *Id.* at Arts. 91, 93, 96, 99.

[201] *Id.* at Art. 93.

[202] *Id.* at Art. 98.

Court and other States.[203] In some cases a "provisional arrest" may be warranted, and the Statute provides how to accomplish such a request in urgent cases.[204] The term "surrender" was chosen to describe the process of handing persons over to the Court in an effort to avoid the baggage that can come with the term "extradition." In particular, by avoiding the word "extradition," some countries can sidestep constitutional or statutory problems with handing over nationals. "Surrender" also avoids the rigors of the *prima facie* case requirement in some legal systems.

When an individual is surrendered pursuant to this Statute, absent consent of the surrendering country, the rule of speciality[205] applies.[206] In some cases there may be disputes or problems with a request, whatever that request might be, and the State Party receiving the request can consult with the Court "to resolve the matter."[207] In addition to discussing how to achieve cooperation in pre-trial and trial matters, Part Nine discusses who shall bear the costs of complying with requests.[208]

[J]   Part Ten — Enforcement

Sentences issued to defendants by the Court are served in a State determined by the Court from a list of States that have agreed "to accept sentenced persons."[209] The Court looks at several factors in determining the location of where the accused will serve his or her sentence, such as the "views of the sentenced person" and the "nationality of the sentenced person."[210] The Court retains the ability to transfer a prisoner to a different location.[211]

Irrespective of where the defendant serves the sentence, the States are bound to enforce it unless there has been a pre-approved agreement with the Court attaching conditions.[212] Prison conditions are controlled by the State, but the Statute requires adherence to "widely accepted international treaty standards governing treatment of prisoners."[213] The Statute outlines options for transfer of the inmate after he or she has completed the sentence.[214]

---

[203] *Id.* at Art. 90.

[204] *Id.* at Art. 92.

[205] *See* § 12.02[B].

[206] Rome Statute of the International Criminal Court, Art. 101.

[207] *Id.* at Art. 97.

[208] *Id.* at Art. 100.

[209] *Id.* at Art. 103. Two such agreements are *available at* the Court's website, one with the United Kingdom, http://www.icc-cpi.int/library/about/officialjournal/ICC-Pres-04-01-07-ENG.pdf, and one with Austria, http://www.icc-cpi.int/library/about/officialjournal/ICC-Pres-00-01-05-ENG.pdf.

[210] *Id.* at Art. 103(3).

[211] *Id.* at Art. 104.

[212] *Id.* at Arts. 103(1)(b), 105. A State that has a constitutional prohibition on life imprisonment, for example, would wish to impose an appropriate condition.

[213] *Id.* at Art. 106.

[214] *Id.* at Art. 107.

[K]   Part Eleven — Assembly of States Parties

Part Eleven, a section that is limited to a single Article of the Statute, sets forth the structure of the "Assembly of States Parties" (ASP), the governing body of the Court.[215] It provides that each State has one representative in the Assembly and non-state parties who signed the Statute or the Final Act of the Rome Conference[216] have the right to be observers.[217] The Rules of Procedure of the Assembly of States Parties[218] open up attendance at its meetings even further by permitting representatives of Intergovernmental Organizations, Nongovernmental Organizations,[219] and States that are not members or observers to participate without vote. State Parties have one vote on matters that come before the Assembly,[220] although the right to vote in some circumstances may be removed when there is a nonpayment of financial obligations to the Court.[221]

The Assembly has numerous functions, including, electing the judges,[222] "management oversight to the Presidency, the Prosecutor and the registrar regarding the administration of the Court."[223] A Bureau, to "assist the Assembly in the discharge of its responsibilities," serves as the representative body of the Assembly.[224] The composition of that Bureau is outlined in the Statute.[225]

[L]   Part Twelve — Financing

Operating a Court of this nature requires funding. The source of the funds is from the "assessed contributions made by States Parties," funds from the United Nations if approved by the General Assembly, "in particular in relation to the expenses incurred due to referrals by the Security Council,"[226] and voluntary contributions.[227] The Statute provides for the "assessment of contributions"

---

[215] *Id.* at Art. 112.

[216] It is customary at Diplomatic Conferences to draft a document called the "Final Act" which records who was there and briefly summarizes what took place. The United States signed the Rome Final Act and thus is entitled to participate in the work of the ASP, without vote. Unlike other non-parties such as Russia, China and Iran, the United States has not been attending in recent years.

[217] *Id.* at Art 112(1).

[218] RR. 92–94 of the Rules of Procedure of the Assembly of States Parties, in SECRETARIAT, ASP, SELECTED BASIC DOCUMENTS RELATED TO THE INTERNATIONAL CRIMINAL COURT 288 (2005).

[219] The process leading to Rome and beyond was a dramatic example of the participation of Nongovernmental Organizations ("civil society") in modern multilateral diplomacy. *See* MARLIES GLASIUS, THE INTERNATIONAL CRIMINAL COURT: A GLOBAL CIVIL SOCIETY ACHIEVEMENT (2006); William Pace & Mark Thieroff, *Participation of Non-Governmental Organizations*, in THE INTERNATIONAL CRIMINAL COURT: THE MAKING OF THE ROME STATUTE, ISSUES, NEGOTIATIONS, RESULTS 391 (Roy Lee ed. 1999).

[220] Rome Statute of the International Criminal Court, Art. 112(7).

[221] *Id.* at Art. 112(8).

[222] *Id.* at Art. 36(6) (election by secret ballot).

[223] *Id.* at Art. 112(2)(b).

[224] *Id.* at Art. 112(3).

[225] *Id.*

[226] *Id.* at Art. 115. The Security Council's first referral of a situation, that in respect of Darfur, S.C. Res. 1593 (2005), contained a paragraph stating that none of the costs would be born by the United Nations. This was apparently the price for a United States abstention on the resolution, thus allowing it to pass.

[227] *Id.* at Art. 116.

correlated to a significant degree with the amounts countries pay to the United Nations, but modified to take account of the fact that the largest contributor to the United Nations is not a party to the Rome Statute.[228] An independent auditor reviews "the records, books and accounts of the Court, including its annual financial statements."[229]

[M] Part Thirteen — Final Clauses

The final part focuses on acceptance and adoption of the Statute. It covers the method for settlement of disputes,[230] a provision that parties may not make reservations to the Statute,[231] and the procedure for making amendments to the statute.[232] Amendments that are not of an institutional nature,[233] can only be made after the Statute has been in force for seven years.[234] Additionally, after seven years the Statute is subject to review by the Review Conference convened by the Secretary-General of the United Nations.[235] Amending the treaty is, aside from special cases such as amendments of a technical nature,[236] a two-stage process. First an amendment has to be "adopted" and then it has to be "ratified" or "accepted." As to the first stage, the Statute says that "[t]he adoption of an amendment as at meeting of the Assembly of States Parties or at a Review Conference on which consensus cannot be reached shall require a two-thirds majority of States Parties."[237] Then comes the difficult part. The Statute goes on to say in paragraph 4 of Article 121 that "[e]xcept as provided in paragraph 5, an amendment shall enter into force for all states Parties one year after instruments of ratification or acceptance have been deposited with the Secretary-General of the United Nations by seven-eighths of them." Notice that when this applies, the typical amendment, the new material does not apply to anyone until the seven-eighths level is reached. Then it applies to everyone, those, agreeing, those objecting[238] and those guilty of inertia alike. In principle, an international organization needs some majority (or super-majority) rule to deal with recalcitrance and inertia,[239] but it will surely be difficult to attain a seven-eighths majority, so this provision comes close to making amendment impossible. This was

---

[228] *Id.* at Art 117. In the absence of the United States, Japan is the largest single contributor. The combined contribution of members of the European Union is, however, even larger.

[229] *Id.* at Art. 118.

[230] *Id.* at Art. 119.

[231] *Id.* at Art. 120.

[232] *Id.* at Art. 121.

[233] Amendments with regard to the institutional nature of the ICC are not subject to the seven year waiting period required of substantive amendments to the Statute. *Id.* at Art. 122(1) (a short, closed, list of such amendments, none of which have yet been made). Such amendments do not require any approval procedures beyond those of the ASP or a Review Conference. They "enter into force for all States Parties six months after their adoption. . . . " *Id.* at Art. 122(2).

[234] *Id.* at Art. 121(1).

[235] *Id.* at Art. 123. *See* § 17.04, *infra.*

[236] Art. 122 *supra.* There *may* be some other cases, namely adding aggression to the Statute and adding prohibited weapons to the "annex" where only approval by the Assembly is necessary, but this is much disputed. *See* §§ 14.03[A] and [D], *supra.*

[237] Rome Statute of the International Criminal Court, Art. 121(3).

[238] Objectors, however, have a right of immediate withdrawal, Art. 121(6).

[239] Art. 108 of the United Nations Charter provides, for example, that amendments come into effect

certainly the intention of those who insisted on such a high threshold, worried as they were about changes that might work to their detriment. Paragraph 5 then provides that:

> Any amendment to articles 5, 6, 7, and 8 of this Statute shall enter into force for those States Parties which have accepted the amendment one year after the deposit of their instruments of ratification or acceptance. In respect of a State Party which has not accepted the amendment, the Court shall not exercise its jurisdiction regarding a crime covered by the amendment when committed by that State Party's national or on its territory.[240]

There is one provision of the Statute that runs counter to the general prohibition on reservations.[241] The Statute does allow for a State to withhold acceptance for seven years from the entry into force of the Statute, as a transitional period, of jurisdiction for war crimes "when a crime is alleged to have been committed by its nationals or on its territory."[242]

The Statute remained open for signature from July 17, 1998 until December 31, 2000, but then required "ratification, acceptance or approval by signatory States."[243] The Statute is open to "accession" by any State that did not sign.[244] According to the Statute, sixty ratifications, acceptances, approvals or accessions,[245] were required for its entry into force.[246]

The Statute describes the method by which a country can withdraw from the ICC. Withdrawal requires written notice and takes "effect one year after the date of receipt of the notification, unless the notification specifies a later date."[247] Withdrawal does not negate pre-existing financial obligations and obligations to provide cooperation in investigations and proceedings.[248]

§ 17.03 ADOPTING THE ROME STATUTE

With sixty ratifications or accessions occurring by April 11, 2002, the Statute came into force on July 1, 2002. The number of ratifications and accessions has increased since then, and as of March 2008,106 countries were States Parties to the Rome Statute of the International Criminal Court.[249] The Preparatory Commission

---

for all Parties once they have been ratified by two thirds of the Members, including the five permanent members of the Security Council.

[240] Rome Statute of the International Criminal Court, Art. 121(5). *See* § 14.03[A] (aggression) and § 14.03[D] (war crimes) for a discussion of the difficulties in applying paragraphs 4 and 5 of Art. 121.

[241] Art. 120, *supra.*

[242] *Id.* at Art. 124. Only France and Colombia availed themselves of this opportunity. Their seven years will soon be up.

[243] *Id.* at Art 125.

[244] *Id.* at Art. 125(3). "Accession" is the technical term in United Nations usage to describe the process by which a State that has not signed a multilateral treaty may become party to it. Treaties, like the Rome Statute, are often "open" to signature for a limited period, but the right to join has no time limits.

[245] For reasons shrouded in mystery, some States prefer the terms "accept" or "approve" to "ratify" and "accede." The important thing is that a State clearly expresses its intent to be bound.

[246] *Id.* at Art. 126.

[247] *Id.* at Art. 127.

[248] *Id.* at Art. 127(2).

[249] International Criminal Court website, *available at* http://www.icc-cpi.int/statesparties.html.

for the Court was formed to continue the development of the Court. It prepared the Rules of Procedure and Evidence which were adopted by the Assembly of State Parties on September 31, 2002.[250] It also finalized the Elements of Crimes, which defines the terms in Articles 6, 7, and 8 of the Statute, that being the crimes of genocide, crimes against humanity, and war crimes.[251] Other "housekeeping" matters, necessary to get the Court up and running, were also handled by the Preparatory Commission.[252]

The United States is not a party to the Court. The basic concern that has been expressed has been with respect to military personnel and whether they might be subject to increased scrutiny if the United States participated in the Court.[253] Other concerns that have been voiced include arguments such as fears about U.S. sovereignty and concerns that the Statute might not afford procedural rights mandated by the Bill of Rights.[254] The validity of these arguments has been controversial.[255] Even with the accession of Japan to the Statute in 2007, some of the major powers are still outside, including three of the Permanent Members of the Security Council, China, the Russian Federation, and the United States. Given United States leadership in the proceedings in Nuremberg and Tokyo and its strong support for the *ad hoc* Tribunals, there are certain ironies here. In the memorable words of Justice Jackson in his opening address in Nuremberg:

> We must never forget that the record on which we judge these defendants today is the record on which history will judge us tomorrow. To pass these defendants a poisoned chalice is to put it to our own lips as well. We must summon such detachment and intellectual integrity to our task that this Trial will commend itself to posterity as fulfilling humanity's aspirations to do justice.[256]

Nevertheless, the United States has adopted several measures to protect servicemembers from the reach of the Statute. The American Servicemembers Protection Act of 2002 prohibits assistance to countries who are a party to the International Criminal Court Statute unless certain precautions are taken. One way of having the United States participate in a peacekeeping effort within a country is for that country to enter into an agreement with the United States in accordance with Article 98 of the ICC Statute. The agreement needs to prevent "the

---

[250] Rules of Procedure and Evidence, ICC-ASP/1/3, *available at* http://www.icccpi.int/library/officialjournal/Rules_of_Proc_and_Evid_070704-EN.pdf.

[251] Elements of Crimes, ICC-ASP/1/3/, *available at* http://www.icc-cpi.int/library/officialjournal/Elements_of_Crimes_120704EN.pdf.

[252] *See* Preparatory Commission for the Establishment of an ICC, *available at* http://www.un.org/law/icc/prepcomm/commissn.htm.

[253] *See* EDWARD WISE, ELLEN S. PODGOR & ROGER S. CLARK, INTERNATIONAL CRIMINAL LAW: CASES AND MATERIALS 789–90 (2d ed. 2004).

[254] *Id.* at 791.

[255] *Id.* For a strong argument in favor of United States participation, see Ron Sievert, *A New Perspective on the International Criminal Court: Why the Right Should Embrace the ICC and How America Can Use It*, 68 U. PITT. L. REV. 77 (2006). *See also* CONFERENCE REPORT, THE RESPONSIBILITY TO PROTECT AND THE INTERNATIONAL CRIMINAL COURT: AMERICA'S NEW PRIORITIES, Northwestern University School of Law, March 2008 (advocating, inter alia, United States "re-engagement" with ICC and development of an International Marshal Service), *available at* http://www.law.northwestern.edu/humanrights/R2PICC_report.pdf.

[256] Robert Jackson, Opening Statement before the International Military Tribunal, *available at* http://www.robertjackson.org/Man/theman2-7-8-1/.

International Criminal Court from proceeding against members of the Armed Forces of the United States present in that country."[257] Some, however, claim that these agreements are not in accord with the Rome Statute.[258] By 2008, the United States was not as aggressively pursuing such agreements. Commentators suggested that it was moving from a policy of "firm opposition" to one closer to "pragmatic exploitation" as suggested by its abstention on the Security Council resolution referring the situation in Darfur, Sudan to the Prosecutor.[259]

§ 17.04   THE FIRST REVIEW CONFERENCE

In a complex negotiation like the Rome Statute, it is inevitable that some issues on which it is not possible to get consensus will be left for another day, and that some errors will need to be corrected. Hence the provisions in Article 123 of the Statute dealing with review of the Statute. One obligatory Review Conference is stipulated, seven years after the entry into force of the Statute.[260] Thereafter, a Review Conference can be called upon approval of an absolute majority of States Parties.[261] Actually, the Statute says that the Secretary-General of the United Nations is to "convene" the first (and perhaps the only)[262] Conference seven years after entry into force of the Statute. The current plan is for him to circulate the invitations late in 2009, seven years after July 1, 2002, and for the Conference to be fitted into the international conference calendar early in 2010.

So far as the substance of the event is concerned, Article 123 says that the review is "to consider any amendments to this Statute."[263] It adds that "[s]uch review may include, but is not limited to, the list of crimes contained in article 5."[264] This is all very permissive and does not require that anything in particular be considered. There is only one provision in the Statute that is mandatory as far as the Review Conference is concerned, namely Article 124. Article 124, as has been noted,[265] permits States to opt out of jurisdiction over war crimes for a seven-year period. Article 124 itself states that "[t]he provisions of this article shall be reviewed at the Review Conference convened in accordance with article 123, paragraph 1." All this mandates is a discussion. The discussion may result in leaving the article as it is, in deleting it, or in some other proposal. France and Colombia being the only two States to avail themselves of it, the Parties could conclude that it is simply not worth worrying about and do nothing.

---

[257] 22 U.S.C. § 7424(c)(2) (2004).

[258] *See* EDWARD M. WISE, ELLEN S. PODGOR & ROGER S. CLARK, INTERNATIONAL CRIMINAL LAW: CASES AND MATERIALS 402–03 (2d ed. 2004). *See also* § 10.02[C] *supra*.

[259] *See* José A. Alvarez, *The Evolving U.S.-ICC Relationship*, 24 NEWSLETTER, AM. SOC. INT'L L. 1 (Jan./March 2008).

[260] Rome Statute of the International Criminal Court, Art. 123(1).

[261] *Id.* at Art. 123(2).

[262] Art. 109 of the United Nations Charter contemplates reviews to be "held at a date and place fixed" by the General Assembly and the Security Council, but none have taken place. The 1968 Nuclear Non-Proliferation Treaty (NPT), a partial model for the ICC provision, requires regular reviews every five years. The ICC provision is something of an amalgam of the UN and NPT provisions.

[263] *Id.* at Art. 123(1).

[264] *Id.*

[265] *See* § 13.02[M], *supra*.

It would appear, however, that the bulk of the Review will be devoted to whatever emerges from the Special Working Group on the Crime of Aggression.[266] Resolution F of the Final Act of the Rome Conference contemplated that proposals for a provision on aggression would be submitted to "a" Review Conference, not necessarily the first one.[267] Given the amount of effort devoted to the Special Working Group and the expectations raised, it would be a serious lack of good faith were the issue of aggression not to be the main focus. Suggestions have been made for considering adding provisions on drugs and terrorism[268] and weapons of mass destruction and on dealing with questions of defense counsel in the Statute itself,[269] but there were no firm proposals on the table early in 2008.[270]

Undoubtedly the participants will use the opportunity for some mutual congratulation, and perhaps even some serious stocktaking. The Review Conference will no doubt be an opportunity to see how far the Court has advanced the cause of international justice in its first seven years or so. It was expected that by mid-2008 the first trial would be under way, that of Thomas Lubanga Dyilo from the Democratic Republic of Congo for the recruitment and use of child soldiers. Two more accused from that nation were under arrest on similar charges. Arrest warrants had been issued in respect of crimes against humanity and war crimes in Uganda and Darfur, but the necessary cooperation to execute those warrants had not been forthcoming. The Security Council had been underwhelming in supporting the Prosecutor's efforts for Darfur. There is much to be done, but the Review Conference seems like the Rome Conference when it was in prospect only — not even the owners of crystal balls can predict with any certainty what it is likely to produce.

---

[266] *See* § 14.03[A], *supra.*

[267] Final Act of the Diplomatic Conference International Criminal Court, U.N. Doc. A/CONF/183/10. (1998).

[268] These were left over for the future in Resolution E, annexed to the Final Act of the Diplomatic Conference, U.N. Doc. A/CONF. 183/10 (1998), but the time may not yet be ripe.

[269] The crucial matter of defense is currently dealt with only in the Rules of Procedure and Evidence, RR. 20–22 and Chapter 4 of the Regulations of the Court. Some think that it would be better if the matter had a more solid basis in the Statute itself.

[270] For a fairly comprehensive discussion of the possibilities that have been raised, see Roger S. Clark, *Possible Amendments for the First ICC Review Conference in 2009*, 4 N.Z. Y.B. INT'L L 103 (2007).

TABLE OF CASES

[References are to page numbers.]

[References are to page numbers.]

[References are to page numbers.]

[References are to page numbers.]

[References are to page numbers.]

INDEX

[References are to page numbers.]

[References are to page numbers.]

[References are to page numbers.]

[References are to page numbers.]

[References are to page numbers.]